D1327835

ON THE OTHER SIDE(S) OF
150

ON THE OTHER SIDE(S) OF

150

Untold Stories and Critical Approaches to History, Literature, and Identity in Canada

LINDA M. MORRA *&* SARAH HENZI, EDITORS

WILFRID LAURIER
UNIVERSITY PRESS

Wilfrid Laurier University Press acknowledges the support of the Canada Council for the Arts for our publishing program. We acknowledge the financial support of the Government of Canada through the Canada Book Fund for our publishing activities. This work was supported by the Research Support Fund.

LIBRARY AND ARCHIVES CANADA CATALOGUING IN PUBLICATION

Title: On the other side(s) of 150 : untold stories and critical approaches to history, literature, and identity in Canada / edited by Linda M. Morra and Sarah Henzi.

Other titles: On the other side(s) of one fifty | On the other side(s) of one hundred and fifty

Names: Morra, Linda M., [date] editor. | Henzi, Sarah, 1977- editor.

Description: Includes bibliographical references.

Identifiers: Canadiana (print) 20200384155 | Canadiana (ebook) 20200386255 | ISBN 9781771125130 (hardcover) | ISBN 9781771125154 (EPUB) | ISBN 9781771125161 (PDF)

Subjects: LCSH: Canadian literature—History and criticism. | LCSH: Minorities in literature. | LCSH: Minorities in art. | LCSH: Indigenous peoples in literature. | LCSH: Indigenous peoples in art. | LCSH: National characteristics, Canadian, in art. | LCSH: National characteristics, Canadian, in literature. | LCSH: Canada—In literature. | LCSH: Canada—In art. | LCSH: Canada—Centennial celebrations, etc.

Classification: LCC PS8103.M56 O5 2021 | DDC C810.9/352900971—dc23

Cover design by Michel Vrana. Text design by Sandra Friesen.

© 2021 Wilfrid Laurier University Press
Waterloo, Ontario, Canada
www.wlupress.wlu.ca

This book is printed on FSC recycled paper and is certified Ecologo. It is made from 100% post-consumer fibre, processed chlorine free, and manufactured using biogas energy.

Printed in Canada

Table of Contents

SECTION TWO
Unbecoming Narratives

SECTION THREE
Memories from Below and Beyond the Border

Acknowledgments

The discussions that informed the chapters in this volume were first initiated at a conference in Ireland at the University of College Dublin in 2017. Dr. Linda M. Morra, who was the Craig Dobbin Chair for that year (2016–2017), conceived of the conference, *Untold Stories of the Past 150 Years*, which drew close to 100 scholars from around the globe. *Untold Stories* would not have occurred without the support and funding provided by the Craig Dobbin Chair, the UCD College of Arts and Humanities; the UCD Centre for Canadian Studies and its Director, Dr. Paul Halferty; the UCD Humanities Institute; Bishop's University; the Canadian Embassy in Ireland; and the Social Sciences and Humanities Research Council (SSHRC). We are also especially thankful to SSHRC, which provided financing for the publication of this book in its current form.

We are extremely grateful to the Principal of the School of Arts and Humanities at UCD, Dr. Sarah Prescott, a brilliant leader in the field, for her support in making the conference happen. We would also like to thank all those who participated in the conference: Rebecca Stephenson, Aubrey Hanson (Métis), Jeff Fedoruk, Renée Monchalin (Métis, Algonquin, Huron), Kristi Allain, Rebecca Draisey-Collishaw, Jamie Jelinski, Lisa Monchalin (Algonquin, Métis, Huron), Lisa Boivin (Dene), Shannon Webb-Campbell (Mi'kmaq), Eamonn Jordan, Agnieszka Rzepa, Alina Deja-Grygierczyk, John Maher, Carrie Dawson, David DeGrow, Wei Li, Hannah McGregor, Eric Lehman, Michael Laurentius, Chandrima Chakraborty, Laurel Ryan, Analays Alvarez Hernandez, Alan Filewod, Bart Vautour, Jennifer Wellington, Julie Ann Rodgers, Faye Hammill, Moira Day, Lucy Collins, Emily Murphy, Alice Ming Wai Jim, Eleanor Ty, Sandra Hobbs, Joseph LaBine, Paul Babiak,

Marc André Fortin, Karine Bertrand, Maria Campbell (Cree/Métis), Sylvia Maracle (Mohawk), Shelley Hulan, Gillian Roberts, Erin Wall, Tanis MacDonald, Emma Morgan-Thorp, Colin Samson, Richard Moran, Michael Brophy, Raymond Blake, Stephanie Dotto, Emily Scherzinger, Nora Foster Stovel, Catherine McCarthy, Pilar Somacarrera, Kaarina Mikalson, Kate Smyth, Julie Morrissy, John T. Davis, Kathleen McCracken, and Sue Rainsford. It almost goes without saying that we are also immensely grateful to those who were willing to continue these discussions beyond the conference for the purpose of the current volume, and whose names appear in the table of contents: Kailin Wright, Kit Dobson, Mary Ann Steggles, Erin Ramlo, Martha Langford, Brian Foss, Laura Moss, Jennifer Andrews, Benjamin Authers, Libe García Zarranz, Margery Fee, Krisztina Kodó, Gregory Betts, Alix Shield, Linda Warley, Erin Wunker, Kim Anderson (Metis), Rene Meshake (Anishinaabe), Shani Mootoo, and Deanna Reder (Cree/Métis). This book was deepened by the breadth and quality of the ideas explored herein.

The editors would also like to thank Dr. Kate Smyth (Trinity University, Ireland), for her assistance at the very early stages of the project; Marie-Eve Bradette (Université de Montréal) for carefully assembling the Works Cited; and Loch Baillie (Bishop's University) for speedily helping to locate seminal articles related to commemoration. We are grateful to Dr. Louis-Georges Harvey, who read and gave advice about an early version of the manuscript; Dr. Deanna Reder (Cree-Métis) for giving feedback about its overall shape; members of WLUP, especially the graphic designer whose ingenuity with our suggestions for the cover image was a delight; and the thorough peer reviewers of the volume, whose responses helped to structure and strengthen the volume.

When an editorial collaboration works—as it did in this instance—the key persons involved in the project often feel a sense of gratitude toward each other: we depended on each other, consulted each other, trusted and respected each other. It was a model of dependability, generosity, efficiency, and cooperation, and it made the project so much the richer for it. We are deeply thankful for this gift.

On the Other Side(s) of 150

Linda M. Morra and Sarah Henzi

The "Canada 150" celebrations staged across the nation in 2017 rolled out a discursive red carpet for the British North America Act, which established Confederation in 1867. As reported in *The Globe and Mail* and other national papers, the federal government poured millions of dollars into honouring its own anniversary: "Canada Day," author Charlotte Gray noted, "especially, will be a moment to reflect a little longer than usual on our country's achievements ... Break out the sparklers, people of Canada. This is your year." Several newspapers likened the celebrations scheduled throughout the country that year as analogous to what transpired in Expo 67, the one-hundred-year mark, a time when the country's population had

> little more than 20 million, where Indigenous people were largely ignored and in which most citizens were of British or French origin, spoke one of the two official languages and were predominantly churchgoers. Most English-speaking Canadians were blithely unaware of the gathering momentum of the Quebec sovereignty movement. General de Gaulle's "Vivre le Quebec libre!" speech from the Montreal City Hall balcony in July that year came as a profound shock. (Editorial)

In 2017, however, even newspapers that reported on the Canada 150 commemorative festivities and the official narrative with which it is associated were, at times, a little less enthusiastic, even ironic, when not downright critical—especially in relation to the nature and price tag of some of these celebratory displays, most notably the $200,000 giant yellow rubber duck that was brought to Toronto's waterfront.[1] These reports further observed that, if the population of the country had almost doubled, its composition had radically changed in its nature and its self-consciousness—indeed, so much so, that acts of commemoration involved re-evaluating, rather than celebrating official narratives and monuments and, where possible, effecting material transformations.

By the following year, those same critiques informed political decisions, such as the removal of the John A. MacDonald statue from the steps of City Hall in Victoria, British Columbia, because of his involvement in the treatment of Indigenous peoples in Canada (Woo). Across the country, in Regina and Montreal as other specific instances, statues of John A. MacDonald were repeatedly vandalized—twice in the former instance, six times in Montreal at the time of this volume's publication—and claimed by activists who characterized themselves as "anti-colonial" and "anti-racist" (Peritz, "Montreal's"). As Gray observed, "thousands of messages of protest and discontent were tweeted with hashtags such as #Resistance150 and #UNsettleCanada150," as Indigenous protests at last found a more "sympathetic audience within the non-Indigenous population." Even so, many in this country still celebrated Canada's 150th anniversary of Confederation without the kind of self-consciousness, detachment, or understanding of how many patriotic narratives exclude, repress, or even oppress others who live in this country—who lived in this country before it was recognized by some as "Canada." And, as of this past year, during a global pandemic and the vocal anti-racism demonstrations that are an extension of Black Lives Matter, it is becoming increasingly understandable why Canada Day has evolved into Cancel Canada Day protests, and why Idle No More organizers have asserted that "[w]e will not celebrate stolen Indigenous land and stolen Indigenous lives." At this historic juncture when many—the general public, scholars, universities—are recognizing the ways that Indigenous peoples have been damaged by colonization and the ways that their histories and stories have been suppressed, there is genuine trepidation about the way forward.

Commemoration, as the events of Canada 150 and recent incarnations of Canada Day show, is not a disinterested practice of remembering the past, but rather a powerful evocation of how identity and citizenship are called into being by their affiliated rituals—rituals that facilitate how participants may "feel authentic about autobiographical narratives of their purportedly shared past" (H. Saito 630).[2] What we remember, how we choose to remember and represent particular historical events and figures, who is given ontological weight (or not) in the acts of such remembering, and for whom these memories are being constituted, these are all determined and shaped by the needs of the present moment and irrevocably connected to frameworks of power. In this way, commemorative narratives reify common national tropes and images, (re)constitute identities, and (re)inscribe beliefs that are sometimes assumed to be irrefutable (H. Saito 630)[3]; they both "model" and "mold" citizenship, as Ekaterina V. Haskins would argue, and are therefore invoked by political, cultural, and economic agents—and not only to "inspire civic consensus" (11). Social cohesion is thus an endeavour often marked by inequitable power relations; yet, it is promoted as a general good and perceived as a natural, rather than naturalized, process. Even if what is commemorated is ultimately a fiction produced by some (and variable) degrees of consensus of the constituent members of a nation, what is selected as a *representational fiction* has a bearing on *fact*—on the material reality of those who must live with and abide by that fiction.[4] Even so, consensus is often challenged, and commemorative processes are often localized, if not divisive, because all actors—institutional, governmental, corporate, popular—have competing stakes in the process of enshrining a national identity and in the politics of its memory or history. Challenges to official forms of commemoration in Canada, with "stakes [that] involve possession and control of the past," as Kammen observes, may yet endeavour to include "oppositional histories" that become engaged in "question[ing] existing arrangements of power" (186; Strong-Boag 66).

Commemoration, then, has been particularly troubling in Canada for reasons related, in part, to its settler-colonial histories and origins, as the most recent sesquicentennial celebrations laid bare. Matthew Hayday traces its origins to Dominion Day celebrations, which were to serve as the foundation for what is now recognized as Canada Day, and the manner in which traditions have been invented to foster a sense of national solidarity. A decade after the Second World War, the federal government became interested in deliberately using Dominion Day as a tool for nation-building and identity construction. Instituted by John Diefenbaker, this holiday provided the opportunity for the federal government to experiment with a wide variety of different approaches to commemoration, nation-building, and identity formation, as July 1 came to occupy an important role in Ottawa's symbolic shaping of Canadian identity. As Hayday further notes, the celebrations were thus meant to emphasize the "formal, tradition-oriented aspects of the day that linked Canada to its British past and were very much reflective of the Diefenbaker government's attempts to shore up Canada's relations with Britain and the commonwealth" (296). By the 1960s, under Prime Minister Lester Pearson, a bilingual and bicultural focus was added; by the 1970s, a more communal, local-based approach was integrated; by the 1980s, new major national symbols, such as the flag and the renaming of the day as "Canada Day," were introduced to promote a particular vision of national identity; and by 1992, the year of Canada's 125th anniversary, both "tradition and public policy" worked to solidify the celebration of Canada Day. The latter "stressed a Canadian identity that was centred on diversity, individual rights, and achievement, and it was attracting significant public support" (Hayday 294). Changes to federal funding patterns by the late twentieth century in Canada also obliged artists and cultural producers to "frame works in terms that met the nationalist, often military, mandates of heritage project selection committees," while often bypassing Indigenous histories that detracted from such mandates (Vosters 16).

That said, at the same time, several countercultures developed out of "the climate of 1960s and 1970s liberatory politics and counter-culture," when English Canadians began to abandon their "British-centric identity models and adopted one rooted in bilingualism and multiculturalism" (Sugars and Ty 8; Hayday 293).[5] These acts of memorialization and recuperation proliferated by the 1990s to produce counter-memories (Sugars and Ty 8)—that is, "memor[ies] from below," as Sugars and Ty observe, which sought to critique, disrupt, or supplement articulations of national commemoration, and showcase and explain the inconsistencies in their representation (8). Likewise, as Helene Vosters suggests in *Unbecoming Nationalism: From Commemoration to Redress in Canada*, emerging counter-memorial performances "work to *un*become popular narratives of benevolent Canadian nationalism and advance the work of social memory beyond the official mandates of elegiac or celebratory national commemoration, toward a praxis of redress" (7).[6] She further adds that Canadian settler nationalism only functions when its "unbecoming acts" are regarded as "normalized (and ethical)," the legitimacy of which is unquestioned and operates "through a myriad of institutionalized mechanisms of white privilege" (8, 10). Counter-memories, then, serve to produce counter-histories that do not correspond with existing narratives, and showcase how and why hegemonic narratives might be called into question, or ultimately fail. And, indeed, while some narrative performances of Canada 150 were deeply invested in enforcing those more contemporary forms of colonial governmentality, as well as the specific manifestations of cultural and social memory, others were thoroughly involved in critiquing it—and this volume seeks to engage in the latter practice.

However, it is only logical that, as Veronica Strong-Boag remarks, "[w]hen it comes to defending past privilege ... professionals' allegiance to dominant cultural authorities and to efforts to enshrine race, gender, class and sexual hierarchies [should not be] entirely trusted" (48). Of this lack of trust, one must recognize that the ongoing context of settler colonialism does little to alleviate the anxieties of those whose lived experiences are the very material of the counter-memories of which we speak here. As noted by Cherokee scholar Daniel Heath Justice, "[g]iven the fact that most of settler North America has consistently been either willfully or circumstantially deaf to the words and perspectives of Indigenous peoples throughout colonial history, it is hardly surprising that the issue of voice is both profoundly personal as well as political in Indigenous writing and oratory today" ("Significant Spaces" 116). So, how do we go about addressing these profound senses of distrust and deafness, when we ourselves are complicit in those very positions of privilege and power dynamics, where we live and work? As settler scholars and editors of this volume, we are acutely aware of the ethical demands of settler criticism; much like several contributors to this volume as well, our work often takes place outside of the communities of writing with which we are engaging. This work must be done carefully, mindfully, and responsibly.

To this end, we find inspiration in, among others, settler scholar Renate Eigenbrod, who, in *Travelling Knowledges*, writes about being "a facilitator for the discussion of literatures that … should be read widely" (8), albeit from "a positionality of non-authority" (143); in settler scholar Sam McKegney, who highlights the need for our engagement with these literatures to be "undertaken from a position of commitment to the well-being of the author and the communities out of and for which she or he writes" (*Writer-Reader Reciprocity* 44); and, ultimately, in Cherokee scholar Daniel Heath Justice who, in *Why Indigenous Literatures Matter*, emphasizes that "we need to return truth to these discussions. We need to think of relationships as ongoing commitments, not one-time-only resolutions. If we're going to figure out how to live together, we need to accept that we're actually going to be doing so—and the terms of that relationship can't only be those that benefit settler society" (159). With *On the Other Side(s) of 150*, our hope is to honour our long-term commitment—and not blindly participate in a punctual hoopla—to being better allies, better guests, in these lands and territories claimed by Canada.

Critical Commemorative Practices in Canada

On the Other Side(s) of 150 situates itself within a critical trajectory related to commemoration scholarship produced by, among others, Hito Saito, Michael Kammen, Smaro Kamboureli, Christl Verduyn, Sophie McCall, Veronica Strong-Boag, Cynthia Sugars, Helene Vosters, and Ekaterina V. Haskins. Vosters, for instance, defines commemoration as encompassing a broad range of enactments of social memory, which are by no means neutral in their expression, and which "distract or blind settler Canadians from reflecting on the ongoing privileges of white settler nationalism, the ongoing violence of settler colonialism at home and of Canadian militarism abroad"—to which she adds that counter-memorial performances, in turn, often seek to pursue and foreground redress in their very enactments (11). Haskins, similarly, asserts that what makes memorial practices so unique in North America in this era is the "desire and ability of nonelite actors to coproduce narratives of public memory"; such actors do not experience these narratives passively, "as spectators or interactive extras," but rather participate directly and self-consciously in ways that foster "inclusion, diversity, and access" (4). Haskins further defines citizenship as a "relationship among strangers that is modeled by a discourse of public culture and embodied through performance"; commemorations are, therefore, from her perspective, "representations of civic identity and sites of stranger interaction" (2). These interactions are not, however, necessarily equal in terms of capital—economic, cultural, and otherwise—and call upon various degrees of commitment and a wide range of political affiliations, even if, as Robert Cupido asserts, "hegemony is a matter of negotiation rather than straightforward coercion" (65). It is thus limiting to see commemorative practice as simply a struggle between "elite narratives of civic virtue underwritten by [existing] political and economic powers" and "expressions of marginalized identities" (2): there is, clearly, a spectrum of engagement, protest, and comprehension of what commemoration is, how it might devolve, and whose interests it represents. As Ben Authers in this volume shows, commemorative acts, including those related to reconciliation, also transform over time in response to the shifting needs and structures of a given society.[7]

Haskins also notes that critics often neglect to differentiate properly between the *production* and the *reception* of commemorative rituals, and also between *popular* (or, as John Bodnar terms it, "vernacular") and *democratic* forms of commemoration. Key narratives are produced, appropriated, and reapppropriated over time—as those about Louis Riel, for instance, as Gregory Betts, Margery Fee, and Krisztina Kodó explore in their chapters—as new contexts develop, temporally and ideologically, with their own sets of demands. Popular forms, moreover, have been regarded suspiciously by scholars because they are sometimes seen to "promote a simplistic, decontextualized, and often self-congratulatory relationship with the past" (5); democratic forms are, conversely, characterized as expanding the participation of "'ordinary' people in producing—and not just consuming—public memory," which thus also permits greater self-awareness in relation to one's agency in the development of historical narratives (5). However, as Haskins argues, these delineations are, again, limiting. Popular conceptualizations of expression emanate from subjects "whose identities are continuously formed and reformed through a complex process of enculturation and rhetorical negotiation" (6). Haskins further notes,

> this notion of popular memory, with its related connotations of unvarnished authenticity, genuine connection to lived experience, and, perhaps more crucially, marginalized political status, animates much of the scholarship that valorizes memory's "subaltern" status and works to recover the voices of marginalized "others."
>
> Maintaining the line between "official" and "vernacular" expressions becomes difficult, however, if we take into account the success of some grassroots projects, and the impact of their success on institutions of memory …
>
> Popular participation in memory work does not render it instantly more democratic, nor does the stamp of approval from government or mainstream media necessarily diminish the political charge of grassroots efforts. (6–7)

In other words, commemorative acts are far more complex in the way that they are produced, appropriated, and applied, and how they transport communal potential. Additionally, this process is far more complex in an age of social media, in which the clash of popular views often transpires and, specifically for Canada, definitions of "what exactly Canadian culture is, or should be," have been contested and marked by conflict, struggle, and resistance since its inception (Hayday and Blake 14).

Commemoration, ultimately, is most often featured in narratives that celebrate the nation's virtues, and that are easily consumed and circulated, not only for members of a politicized body, but also for tourists or visitors to the nation, for whom "histories would be suppressed and subsumed by the anodyne certainties that tourism/history deployed" (Morgan, "Making Heroes" 8).[8] Citizenship is, in this sense, performed and, in its performances, offers particular models of inclusion (and exclusion), as it compels its potential members to participate in these available models to gain legitimacy; what is clear in this latter assertion is that commemoration is not simply about the "invention" of such narratives, but also about their reception (Haskins 14). Participation and consensus is required in the making of meaning. So, Haskins notes, "The *representation of models* of citizenship [has] the rhetorical power to conjure compelling images of civic identity and invite audiences to inhabit them, or at least to consider them as legitimate claims on the collective imaginary" (12). The most recognizable forms of commemoration are thus relayed through narratives, whether mainstream, institutional, formal and informal. These are the stories that we tell and share, and that extend beyond the literary disciplinary matrix to visual art, theatre, photography, and others.

This volume thus follows and extends Haskins' ideological characterization of the production of commemorative narratives. The contributors to *On the Other Side(s) of 150*, as a whole, observe that, even though symbols of patriotic pride may be ubiquitous, and certainly distinct from the historical record, participatory publics in commemorative acts are less homogeneous or monolithic than these symbols might otherwise suggest, and the binary between popular and democratic forms is not as clear. Both elite and non-elite actors participate in the production and reception of narratives of public memory, and the latter are subject to evolving in relation to this participation within any given temporal framework. The result is the contestation of such narratives within the very framework of the nation referred to as "Canada," even as there may yet be considerable dissatisfaction expressed by actors, elite and non-elite alike, with the narratives or the figures highlighted as exemplary of its accomplishment and history.[9] This may in part account for why, in Canada, as Veronica Strong-Boag explores, commemoration has been a "contested business," especially since it has been mediated by, for example, the Historic Sites and Monuments Board of Canada, which was launched in 1919 in response to the "heightened patriotism" after the First World War, and which has been increasingly reshaped and balanced by "voices on the margins" (61, 47).[10] The logic for commemoration, the "role of the state in producing particular forms of history and conceptions of heritage," is made evident here: to express patriotism, or to capture the ethos and multiple sources of national pride; to mourn losses, civilian and military; to recollect events from multiple perspectives; and to develop new bonds of community (Morgan 2010, 1, 4). Who is involved in its production extends well beyond governmental institutions, academics, and the general public. Indeed, the "flagrant and tasteless commercialization and commodification" of commemorative symbols of the nation—the various marketing strategies at work—demonstrate that even large-scale corporations have an economic interest at stake (Kammen 199).

Provisional Perspectives: On the Other Side of and the Other Sides to Canadian Commemorative Narratives

Participation in a "national" framework is considerably fraught when the very parameters exacted by the nation are being contested and when the terms of engagement may differ considerably from one period to the next, from one community to another. A range of institutional and socio-political forms of legitimation are implicated in citizenship and determine who becomes visible as the very "citizen" who, in turn, undertakes acts of commemoration. As Haskins notes, "[m]emory practices constitute a major cultural technology of citizenship: memorials, commemorations, and other rituals of retrospection mediate citizenship both by envisioning models of civic identity and by engaging experiences through which people come to embrace or reject these models" (9). Indeed, to commemorate certain narrative forms and symbols within current recognizable national discourse is a reminder that its alleged "members" are inconsistently willing participants, tangentially or marginally represented or intersecting, and that these members are often contained within the very same colonial frameworks that have engendered considerable harm.

In this sense, then, the book has been titled *On the Other Side(s) of 150*— to suggest the *multiple facets of and different perspectives* that have profilerated *around* commemoration, its narratives, symbols, and figures, and then *beyond* it: what happens once a commemorative moment has passed? Like a Cubist painting, this modality offers a critical strategy by which also to approach the volume as *dismantling, reassembling, and re-enacting existing commemorative tropes; as offering multiple, conditional, and contingent viewpoints that unfold over time; and as generating a broader (although far from being comprehensive) range of counter-memorial performances.* The chapters in this volume are thus provisional, interconnected, and adaptive: they offer critical assemblages by which to approach commemorative narratives or showcase lacunae therein; by which to return to and intervene in ongoing readings of the past from the present moment; and by which not necessarily to resolve, but rather to understand the troubled and troubling narratives of the present moment. The chapters in this volume propose that these preoccupations are not a means of turning away from present concerns, but rather a means of grappling with how the past informs or is shaped to inform them, and how such concerns are defined by immediate social contexts and networks.

Discursive and symbolic identities are modified over time, from one period to the next, with a tendency to revisit the past to make it more coherent for immediate needs or relevant to the landscape of the present moment. The relevance of these symbolic identities is often framed by nation-states, which attempt to co-opt elements of the past in order to establish a sense of continuity or stability that may otherwise provide a challenge to present conditions. Books such as Benedict Anderson's *National Imagined Communities* (1983) and John Gillis' *Commemorations: The Politics of National Identity* (1994), for example, examine the process by which national cultural memory is forged.[11] What is clear in these processes is how these symbolic identities shift in response to particular communities that were formerly unengaged, unrepresented, omitted, or forgotten. In this way, *On the Other Side(s) of 150*, as a whole, draws productive attention to the complexities and multi-faceted nature of commemoration in Canada, especially as a function of settler-colonial relations, and the disjunction that often exists between commemorative narratives and symbols that tend to reify settler-colonial and other hegemonic narratives, as well as the facticity of historical events that clearly disturb such narratives. A return to the past, to representations of that past, thus invites a reconsideration of the acts we choose to highlight and privilege—narratives and symbols that we have received and continue to receive—and, ultimately, allows for a necessary process of recognition, redress, and restitution.

Silencing Voices

If a reconsideration of the collective past entails a re-evaluation of how that past has been represented in, and what it means (and how much it means) for the present moment, and which events and figures are highlighted from the historical record, it then becomes evident why commemoration in Canada has expanded, since the 1990s, to include Indigenous communities, ethnocultural communities, and women "as proper targets for national commemoration" (Strong-Boag 63). Indeed, Indigenous peoples were notably and largely absent from commemorative practices until recently,[12] in part because the North was constructed as an amorphous void that was a stand-in for Canadian potential, in primarily economic terms.[13] As David Neufeld notes, Indigenous peoples were either "rendered invisible or incorporated as components of the national vision," and the North "as an area without a past, an area whose only significance was as part of Canada's distinct and independent identity" (24, 26). Moreover, commemorative practices largely focused on the South. And even though Indigenous peoples were "included" in such practices, those commemorative narratives often elided the fact that "Canadian citizenship is not a gift or even a reparative gesture to be bestowed upon Aboriginal peoples by the state; instead *Canadian citizenship is the product of Aboriginal peoples' conditional permission*, through historical treaty processes"

(Henderson, 115–16, emphasis added). And yet, when Indigenous peoples were represented in commemorative events, they were often relegated to a "distant past," so as to diffuse Indigenous material claims that have assumed greater significance in the legal, political, and social realms in recent history (Caldwell and Leroux 454). In response, as Vosters notes, "the long history of Indigenous assemblages engaged in practices of resistance to Canadian settler colonialism" has shifted in recent years to become "prolific, highly visible movements of political insurgence and cultural insurgence" (18).

The processes undergirding the production of collective subjectivity have required, as Lynn Caldwell and Darryl Leroux argue, that "narratives and displays actively suppress daily political and social realities, in particular of racialized and Indigenous peoples" (452). The critiquing of commemorative narratives has thus recently elicited apologies from the government for its conduct toward various racialized and ethnic groups, including Japanese Canadians and Italian Canadians, who received an apology and redress from the government in, respectively, 1988 and 2005 for their internment of members of their community during the Second World War; and Chinese Canadians, who in 2006, "after years of pressure from the Chinese Canadian National Council, the federal government went a step further to issue a formal apology for the Chinese Head Tax and immigration exclusion" (Strong-Boag 51). In 2008, the government at last apologized to Indigenous peoples for its role in the residential school system. Thus, in an attempt to reconsider the many ways in which commemorative narratives have systematically celebrated some voices while obscuring others, this volume takes on this historic reframing of such events and persons, with the objective of asking readers to question what it is that is/was being celebrated, and, in many instances, what is not—that is, what remains untold or obscured. For instance, commemoration has yet to address narratives of Quebec properly, and why engagements between the two solitudes remain scarce or fraught with tension, even within this volume. Additionally, configurations of Quebec in popular media across the nation still point to manifestations of racism, which clearly do exist, while ignoring the reiteration of such racism in other parts of Canada. Moreover, several diasporas in Canada are also under- or completely unrepresented in this volume, and in many scholarly circles, including Asian-Canadian, Italian-Canadian, Polish-Canadian, Indo-Canadian, and Ukrainian-Canadian communities. In spite of both institutional and academic attempts at inclusiveness, Black Canadian literatures and history are persistently only marginally addressed—here and elsewhere, including at the conference out of which this volume arises; yet, as Cecilia Morgan notes about African

Canadians and commemoration, "the publication of fugitive slave narratives, the formation of Black historical societies in the 1970s and 1980s, and efforts to locate and memorialize the Underground Railroad in southern Ontario, for example, all suggest African-Canadians' persistence in crafting historical narratives" (*Commemorating* 5–6). These historical narratives have yet received only cursory attention, as they also do here.

That said, this volume does not aim for comprehensiveness in addressing those omissions; rather, it calls for both a continued rethinking of the narratives that are already in circulation in Canada and a greater representation of at least some of those stories that have remained untold. As such, the volume contributes to various commemorative lineages and to a seminal body of literary criticism that has invited further reflection about existing Canadian narratives and art forms, including *Commemorating Canada: History, Heritage, and Memory, 1850s–1990s* (Morgan), *Trans.Can.Lit: Resituating the Study of Canadian Literature* (Kamboureli and Miki), *Canadian Literature and Cultural Memory* (Sugars and Ty), *Remembering Air India: The Art of Public Mourning* (Chakraborty, Dean, and Failler), *Cultural Grammars of Nation, Diaspora, and Indigeneity* (McCall, Kim, and Baum), *Refuse: CanLit in Ruins* (McGregor, Rak, and Wunker), and *Critical Collaborations* (Kamboureli and Verduyn). Although this volume, unlike its critical predecessors, is interdisciplinary in focus, we recognize the pivotal importance of these scholarly works for their demand for greater accountability in terms of what writers and stories are recognized and valorized, and what other voices, communities, individuals, and texts are disregarded in the process. In so doing, this volume adds to, complicates, and redresses more dominant (and sometimes self-congratulatory) narratives.

The Contributions

The objective of this volume is thus not to offer a celebratory moment but rather to take stock—to reflect, mull over, and challenge what official narratives have been celebrated and privileged, to complicate those narratives, to address how others have been impeded by hegemonic representations, and to add many that have gone unnoticed and remain unheard. This volume asks its readers to think about what stories have still not been recognized by, or *what comes beyond*, these celebrations, amid the increasing calls for reconciliation, consultation, accountability, and justice. One need only look at the numerous movements and/or pushbacks that took over social media (#UBCaccountable, #appropriationprize, #dumpsterfire, #MeToo, #Resistance150) that very same year (or soon before/after) to assess how this conversation is being had across the country within our institutional walls and well beyond them. In this way, it has become necessary to engage in an ongoing process of "unsettling" (Regan), to retrace the different spaces and histories we come from, and to account for the multiple allegiances and resistances we answer to (and why). As Anishinaabe scholar Niigaanwewidam James Sinclair notes,

> Canada was never founded by two nations but hundreds, even thousands, with French and English communities bringing food to an already bustling and full feast … The riches of Canada lie not in imaginations of gold and spices—and the policies and stories we create from this vision—but in strong, healthy, and equal relationships with people, the land, and the world around us. That's the Kanata we deserve to tell stories about.

It is ultimately our hope that readers will find knowledge and wisdom in the at-long-last-told stories included here. For this reason—and as distinct from our literary critical predecessors—we practically reframe the chapters by strategically locating Indigenous voices at the beginning and end of the volume, to address a glaring omission related to Indigenous epistemologies, communities, and identities in books about commemoration in Canada. Even when commemorative scholarship *does* acknowledge the need for greater accountability, the resulting volumes, to date, have at times not included and certainly not foreground Indigenous voices, representation, and stories in this way.

If stories are "who we are," as Thomas King argues, the stories chosen to commemorate and represent national identity require careful consideration. When they remain uninterrogated, their coercive power remains invisible, and their complacency unchallenged. Although this volume encompasses various aesthetic forms, literature particularly may be used to critique "public debates." As Smaro Kamboureli posits speaking directly to and about this particular discipline, it "is never fully harmonized" with such debates, and thus registers "the limits of cultural knowledge and politics" (vii). So, she observes,

> If the state posits Canada as an imagined community, CanLit is both firmly entangled with this national imaginary and capable of resisting it. The body literary does not always have a symmetrical relationship to the body politic; the literary is inflected and infected by the political in oblique and manifest ways, at the same time that it asserts its unassimilability. (vii)

Literature in Canada is, on the one hand, engaged "with the double ethos of filiation and complicity," while it is also appropriated as a tool to contest narratives, complicate them, and allow for a multiplicity of voices and concerns (Kamboureli and Verduyn 1). Diasporic literature offers one such articulation, while it is also complicit in the hegemonic structures that grant it its status. As Kamboureli and Verduyn note, those structures have "accommodated and instrumentalized" diasporas in its development as a nation-state (Kamboureli and Verduyn 8).[14] Likewise, Kamboureli and Christl Verduyn's study, *Critical Collaborations*, demonstrates how "epistemic breaks" in, at least, the field of literary studies are a response to approaching that body of literature as if it were a singular construct, and that such a response is necessary in relation to "intensified attention to Indigenous, diasporic, and ecological concerns" (9). Similarly, Sophie McCall, Christine Kim, and Melina Baum address the "tensions within and between concepts of indigeneity and diaspora" and the "ways those tensions transform concepts of nation" (9). It is, ultimately, the appearance of these kinds of fissures in that construct that show the multiplicity of voices and communities— Black-Canadian, Asian-Canadian, Québécois, French-Canadian, and ethnic minorities—that occasions the need to reconsider whose stories we are telling, who is represented by these stories, and what other stories need telling. Kinship, in this sense, Kamboureli and Verduyn argue, functions in terms of diversity rather than exclusion.

The scholars in this volume approach Canada 150 as a different kind of opportunity: it offers a pivotal moment whereby they could re-evaluate the dominant narratives that helped to shape Canadian national identity; reconsider those narratives that, until recently, were suppressed or given considerably less attention in public forums and debates; and re-envision the kinds of inclusive narratives that we might disseminate in their place. Many of the nation's dominant stories, master narratives, and foundational myths offer a particular vantage point about the country's origins and development which, in turn, diminish, marginalize, or altogether silence other narratives—even as the latter have been equally crucial to how Canada has come to assume its current shape, politically, sociologically, and otherwise. This volume of interdisciplinary contributions thus provides a forum for the exploration of these untold stories, as well as to nuance and complicate the existing record: it gives space for the further consideration of narratives that have only begun to attract national attention in the past couple of decades, and that have yet to receive comprehensive, critical attention.

Earlier versions of several chapters that appear in *On the Other Side(s) of 150* were first presented at "Untold Stories of the Past 150 Years"; the idea found its origins with and was orchestrated by Dr. Linda M. Morra as the Craig Dobbin Chair of Canadian Studies (2016–2017). She circulated a call for papers internationally, and then staged the conference at the University College Dublin in April 2017. An assemblage of "existing stories, recuperation of lost stories, and the proposal of new methods for the study and comprehension of deliberately excluded stories," the conference was designed to open up a bilingual dialogue across disciplines about elements of national identities in Canada that remain untold or only partially told—and to consider why—as scholars reimagine and challenge existing narratives. One of the submissions to the conference, that by Chandrima Chakraborty, for example, examined Canada's failure to recognize the Air India tragedy in public discourse, and how paradigms of belonging intersect with racialized politics that produce and shape what is memorialized—or not memorialized at all. While no chapter regrettably represents that essential work within this volume, her contribution to the conference has since appeared in *Remembering Air India: The Art of Public Mourning* (Chakraborty, Dean, and Failler). As a whole, however, the conference did give space for further consideration of a multiplicity of narratives, especially those related to Indigenous matters, sex and gender, race and immigration, and Québécois and Canadian identity.

The volume is divided into four sections, each with its own particular set of concerns that addresses issues that have persisted or areas of neglect in Canada. The first section, titled "Contemporary Counter Memories and Narratives," focuses on critiquing the contemporary political, celebratory, and self-congratulatory rhetoric deployed by the government to occlude practices—related to Indigenous claims, to pipelines, to the environment, among others—that are less concerned with constructing a coherent body politic than with financial gain for a select few. Stories have been told, as Dr. Deanna Reder (Cree-Métis) demonstrates in the opening chapter, that challenge this political agenda, but a key intervention must also be the act of listening and understanding why these practices are largely harmful and have future, detrimental effects. In her contribution, "Recuperating Indigenous Narratives: Making Legible the Documenting of Injustices," Reder considers how the study and teaching of Indigenous texts continue to require risky moves out of institutionalized and hierarchical disciplinary ways of knowing. Specifically, she tracks, on the one hand, the various ways that neglected and newly recovered Indigenous texts document injustices and yet, on the other hand, how they remain non-legible to mainstream audiences. This, in turn, means that growing the Indigenous literary canon is not simply an archival search, whereby Indigenous texts need to be recovered, read, and told; rather, new ways of reading and thinking need to replace standard approaches. Reder frames her analytical questioning with stories of personal importance, drawing attention to the necessity of "thinking about what is considered credible and why"—and notes that these do not always need to be recorded or authenticated. She further argues that "[w]e need to believe Indigenous writers—that is, we need to accord Indigenous authors and their narratives the same credibility we accord non-Indigenous writers and writing." Reder then turns to two examples of recovered texts by *The People and the Text*, a research collective that attends to the neglected literary archives of Indigenous authors; the works of these two authors, Edward Ahenakew and Vera Manuel, were not published because, at the time, there was no readership, no infrastructure or curriculum, no "appropriate venues to get the story out or the social status to add legitimacy to our words to make them credible, to make them believable." She concludes with one last story about the necessity of believing—even if, at times, it seems impossible to do so. Reder ultimately reminds us that recovery "will always be an insufficient project if it isn't accompanied by the development of methodological and institutional infrastructures, from our literary histories to our digital archives" (McGregor n.p.).

In the next groundbreaking (and haunting) chapter, Reder collaborates with Alix Shield to expose, almost for the first time since its publication in 1973, the excised passage from Métis author Maria Campbell's memoir *Halfbreed*.[15] Not only does the excised passage speak to the repression of memories and narratives, as well as the real censorship of Indigenous voices within the publishing industry in the 1970s, but it also uncovers more broadly the lack of justice in and public attention to cases of sexual assault on Indigenous women—both then and now, as the *Final Report of the National Inquiry into Missing and Murdered Indigenous Women and Girls*, released in June 2019, reveals.

In his contribution, Ben Authers pursues the harms inflicted by internment camps, specifically those related to the Japanese in Canada, but also focuses on means of redress, and how government responses to past wrongs often inform legal processes and public apologies. The complete disavowal of past policies that instituted unjust conditions and even violated human rights, however, creates a discontinuity between a past moment and a present situation that remains informed by a past injustice. Authers argues that appropriate redress needs to draw attention to these counter-memories, to account for how the implications of past wrongs continue to unfurl in a present moment—that is, past harms have legacies and outcomes that cannot be anticipated and, as such, reparation must be a process that is reconceptualized as those outcomes materialize. He concludes that untold stories—and literature, more generally—are one means of offering redress by "supplementing, but also interrogating, the more 'official' forms of redress." These stories cannot "supplant law's institutional entrenchment" but offer a "representational complexity of harm" that law may not accomplish.

Laura Moss is uniquely positioned in terms of her examination of discursive platitudes and representations about the environment that were circulated during the Canada 150 celebrations. She compares these with the "critical tenor of many community groups, activists, and artists," and draws upon the work of three Canadian writers, Robert Kroetsch, Rita Wong, and Annabel Soutar, who adopt various strategies in their literary work to subvert such platitudes. Their literary production, she argues, offers a counter-narrative, a critical context by which readers can identify the political agendas that inform banal responses to environmental issues and highlight the actual complexity and multiplicity of perspectives. These writers thus facilitate the articulation of untold stories about the urgency, appeals, and critiques related to environmental change and the detrimental effects of the corporation of agriculture.

The second section of the volume, "Unbecoming Narratives," borrows its terminology from Vosters to draw attention to shifts in analyses of contemporary discourses about race, sexual orientation, and gender: these narratives must "unbecome" or undo those that have limited or denied wider representation and understanding about the multiplicity and complexities of identity. Trinidadian-Canadian-Irish author Shani Mootoo casts a general look at the contemporary political climate and the real challenges for—and sometimes outright oppression of—immigrants to this country. Fantasies about the identities of these immigrants have fuelled various tropes and narrative lines, which a dominant culture attributes and deems appropriate to their lives—untold stories, conversely, lie beyond these expectations, which otherwise deny immigrants the possibility of recognizing Canada on their own terms. Mootoo differentiates between those who position themselves as outsiders voluntarily, and those who desire to belong, but whose imposed sense of otherness merely reinscribes their undesirable or unbecoming status as outsiders. New narratives may evolve, but only, as Mootoo argues, by "stray[ing] from the safety of a [literary] niche that permits a single note [or] voice" and by "unlearning" the trademarks of the outsider. Forfeiting that role in the very land in which one lives, however, is no easy endeavour. Forging a meaningful connection with the place in which one lives, she notes, offers that opportunity to develop new narratives, rather than some half-hearted rendering of another context from which one has been removed. The latter is generated to pander to "insiders," or to those who have insisted on boundaries that have determined the identities of insiders and outsiders, and what they may or may not write about.

In this same section, Kit Dobson's chapter looks at the past persecution of LGBTQ2S people in Canada. Dobson considers the "persistent inequalities of Canada's shifting gender politics." He specifically examines the collaborative project *Gender Failure*, by trans writers and performers Ivan E. Coyote and Rae Spoon, to show how the narrative of gender inclusion in Canada denies and fails "particular, non-conforming bodies, and that it does so with increasing force in a neoliberal economy that seeks to define and delimit the ways in which some bodies are deemed more human than others." The available, gendered scripts regulate and determine behaviour in such a way that "unbecoming" bodies are situated outside of that logic, and rendered illegible as subjects.

Libe García Zarranz also investigates how dominant narratives—especially those related to "sustainability"—have disallowed particular expressions or ways of being. She examines how these may be interrogated to make known both the limits to sustainability and those who are rendered invisible by such limits. Indeed, she observes how the discursive abundance of "sustainability" does not correlate to an ethics of sustainability, which would demand practices and measures that would dismantle the very structures in place that impede it. Using the work of Cassils, a Montreal-born, LA-based trans-masculine visual artist and bodybuilder, and Emma Donoghue, an Irish-Canadian queer writer and literary historian, García Zarranz looks at acts of bodily transformation to put "ethics at the centre of enquiry to interrogate received conceptualizations of the body politic" and to consider how such acts produce counter-narratives—untold stories that draw attention to and work past received discourses—that mobilize "an ethics of sustainability" and that instructively model more ethical ways of seeing.

Erin Wunker examines how contemporary poetry addresses recently told feminist perspectives that are linked to issues of social justice. She investigates how to tell a story that is immediate, and often troubling, and how the "poetics and praxis of friendship" may offer a medium by which to explore, share, and tell. Calling upon the poetry of Vivek Shraya, specifically *even this page is white*, Wunker showcases how the codes of "white civility," as defined by Daniel Coleman, determine and recognize certain modes of conduct and interaction. Shraya's lyric poems work to represent realities that are located beyond those governed by white civility.

Kailin Wright shares this perspective, as she also assumes a longer view of Canadian history in her chapter—a longer history that is, ultimately, "unbecoming" of claims to national self-aggrandizement: using contemporary writer George Elliott Clarke and his play *Beatrice Chancy*, she examines Black slavery in Canada and particularly the dramatization of "racial reproductive futurism." "Reproduction, race, and futurity," she argues, "are mutually constitutive." If queer resistance to heteronormativity reveals how queerness is illegible, narratives of reproduction heighten these biases and those related to questions of race. She thus contextualizes Beatrice Chancy in the context of the Supreme Court of Canada's *R. v. Morgentaler* case in 1988, when the play was first performed, to highlight how the mechanisms of the current system allow for the lack of recognition of Black families.

Erin Ramlo invites readers to rethink a Canadian literary narrative in relation to the critical role played by The Writers' Union of Canada, an organization developed to support Canadian writers. Her own research has uncovered the document "Authors and Archives," which the Union produced in 1979 to prepare its members to develop their own archival materials for posterity. In so doing, she argues, its membership was equipped to "stake out archival space and authority" and demonstrated how the Union was investing in "the archival futurity of their membership." Such an investment, on the one hand, allows for an extraordinary range of potential "untold stories" that remain in the archives to this day; on the other hand, the organization's national agenda was limited, since it "operated in the service of a decidedly white image of the Canadian nation." Nonetheless, she argues, the document discloses how a significant number of writers were educated about how to "navi[gate] the Canadian literary archival landscape."

The third section, "Memories from Below and Beyond the Border," encompasses chapters related to the visual and practising arts, as specific manifestations of "untold stories." Mary Ann Steggles offers, in her piece, an account of the revival of craft, particularly the flourishing of ceramics in Canada, as a result of the American refugees of the Vietnam War—their positive influence, she notes, has not been properly acknowledged, in part the result of a bias that determines that ceramics have "no place within contemporary art." As Jennifer Andrews elsewhere in this volume explains, this pattern of the violation of rights in relation to internment camps and the means by which these kinds of stories have been either omitted, repressed, or misrepresented is continued in relation to the Vietnam War resisters who found their way to and settled in Canada. Their omission from national narratives is striking, especially when their contributions to the Canadian cultural and socio-political arenas have been so extensive. Canadian narratives often position the country as "liberal, hospital, and humanitarian" to Vietnam War resisters, for having offered them a place in the period, but fail to recognize that they also materially contributed to the country. Instead, some Canadians expressed resentment at the time about the fact that many such Americans took up academic positions in several universities across the country, even though there were no qualified Canadians to take their place.

Martha Langford's chapter issues a more provocative challenge to notions of history by suggesting that, in the case of Canadian photography, no comprehensive narrative has been written—and therefore, we cannot even offer a counter-history or counter-memory. Calling upon the photography of Larry Towell, an award-winning Canadian photojournalist and documentarian who would occupy a place in the history of photography of Canada—if one existed—Langford develops a case study related to the photographic representation of the Mennonites, an Anabaptist Christian movement that founded colonies in Canada and elsewhere. Using the photographs of this community—a series of complex and ethical knots that she adroitly disentangles—she explores the "distinction between told and untold stories, between official and counter-histories, essentially asking 'which is which?' and what can be gained from their entanglement in an inclusive history."

Brian Foss and Jacques Des Rochers, for their part, recognize that there *is* such a history for Canadian art, and offer a counter-narrative that explores the gendering of art production in Canada through their historicizing of the Beaver Hall Group. Founded in the spring of 1920, the Beaver Hall Group enjoyed a three-year lifespan, but historical documentation and attention began to diminish at the time of its dissolution in 1923 until the mid-1960s. The lack of records, Foss and Des Rochers observe, means that much remains "frustratingly unknown." However, since gender has been increasingly pivotal to understanding the Group's dynamics and membership, to emergent narratives about aesthetics, interest has been growing: as this chapter demonstrates, "evolving discourses about gender have positioned and repositioned the Beaver Hall Group within the canon of Canadian art."

Jennifer Andrews' chapter is predicated on the historical details of a literary novel and highlights how Canada has been complicit in some questionable—even outright racist—practices. This chapter is a study of the discursive emphasis on Canadian exceptionalism as a means of differentiating our brand of nationalism from that of the United States. Andrews ultimately problematizes such beliefs, and even contradicts the persistence of Canadian exceptionalism by focusing on the historical events related to the Amherst internment camp, as represented by the American author P.S. Duffy. Developed during the First World War, the camp was located at the old Malleable Iron Foundry, beside railway tracks that transported POWs to local work assignments. The camp housed as many as 853 prisoners, until it closed in 1919. Given this history, Andrews observes, it is too facile to remark upon, as is frequently done in popular rhetoric, Canadian inclusivity and tolerance as superior features of our identity, especially in comparison to the United States.

The fourth and final section, "Rhetorical Renegotiations," provides a sense of mindful circularity by closing with Indigenous critiques and texts. All these considerations are not, as celebratory moments tend to highlight, punctual and finite; rather, they are continuous and call upon us to address them continuously, if we are to hope for a better, healthier future. The first contribution re-evaluates and offers a fresh perspective about the determined—if not over-determined—figure of Louis Riel. The chapters, written by settler scholars Krisztina Kodó, Gregory Betts, and Margery Fee, collectively return to Riel's contested status as, at turns, icon and traitor—the multi-dimensional, multi-faceted nature of his status is indicative of how one figure or one symbol may be appropriated in various ways and for various purposes. Betts argues that Riel has become renowned in Canadian history "for the way that the competition over national symbolism overwhelmed his life," so much so that he "lost control of his own story." He thus takes up the argument that Riel's function is to serve as "an *interruption* of nationalist narratives, as himself, in his martyrdom, as a kind *supra legem* intervention existing outside of the free-play of the structure of Canada, especially colonial Canada." The Canadian government was invested in making the nation "internally coherent," even if the means to achieve such coherence were ultimately violent. Riel was thus regarded as disruptive, as engendering confusion and instability, and his removal was seen as necessary. As Betts observes, the result is that the unsolvable aspects of Riel's life allow for writing, rewriting, and reinterpretation. In his chapter, he examines the work of Newlove and bp Nichol, each of whom takes up this figure to debunk the absurdity of the mythological accretions that have formed around him, while critiquing the myopic white hegemony that impedes proper recognition of this historical figure.

In her chapter, Kodó demonstrates how Riel has indeed been recuperated by others but in terms that are well beyond national—begging the question of his status within national commemorative narratives. In this instance, the dramatist John Coulter appropriates Riel for his own political agenda. Riel is a cipher, Kodó argues, upon whom others can impose new meaning—even within international contexts. These contexts, on the one hand, may suggest how he may be co-opted for other political agendas, but, on the other hand, they may also give rise to new, nuanced perspectives and shed light on the historical accounts that have proliferated around Riel. These contexts make visible new contours of his character, of staid narratives, and render visible the kinds of biases that were perhaps not so evident in an earlier period. Reading Riel as a tragic figure, as Coulter does, suggests that he is at once admirable for his heroic aspirations and profoundly flawed. As Kodó observes, even in such international contexts, he remains an "enigmatic global figure," whose individual nature has been "lost in the course of historical events: instead, a legendary [persona] emerges." Ultimately, she argues, he remains "an untold story." Margery Fee would disagree with the elements of his history that are seemingly obscure, as she offers the logic for the persistent fascination with this figure. She maintains that Riel is not an "untold story," in some ways, because he has occupied substantial critical and literary attention. Instead, Fee posits that, while he may be in many ways like the Irish figure Thomas D'Arcy McGee, Riel has sustained such notice because of his more highly contested, popular—and unresolved—status.

In this same section, Linda Warley returns to the 1970s and offers an analysis of three memoirs written by Indigenous authors (or co-written—that is, heavy editorialized) on their residential school experiences. This is framed as a discussion of "before" *Secret Path*, Gord Downie's project on the life and tragic death of Chanie Wenjack. Indeed, she notes, "[m]emoirs from this period offer nuanced, sometimes ambivalent, accounts of residential school experiences that do not necessarily provoke the anger, sadness, and outrage that more recent texts such as *Secret Path* tend to provoke." Additionally, Warley draws attention to how these texts have not received sufficient critical attention, in part the result of their being mostly unavailable. Whereas Downie's graphic novel certainly did put an instant spotlight on one residential school story (although the Wenjack story has been told by others before)[16], it is crucial that we not forget about those testimonies that came before, and that deserve as much, if not more, attention.

In February 2018, and within weeks of each other, two important cases that captured the attention (and hearts) of many delivered a blow to those who were hoping for justice: the two men who were standing trial for second-degree murder—Gerald Stanley, who shot 22-year-old Colten

Boushie in the head in a "freak accident" (Friesen), and Raymond Cormier, who was accused of killing and disposing of the body of 15-year-old Tina Fontaine—were found not guilty by, in the first instance, an "all-white" jury and, in the second instance, a "mostly white" jury (Palmater). These are not untold stories; they were highly publicized, and led to several vigils, marches, panels, calls for action, and other interventions. While they may not have been untold, they are, like many others, not truly heard or heeded. Rather, and to recall the words of Daniel Heath Justice above, such stories account for the "deafness" of settler North America (116). With this history in mind, our volume closes with a chapter that has been strategically placed outside of the last section: "Still Here," by Kim Anderson and Rene Meshake, who, writing about Boushie, note that "[m]any of us are wondering if this story will ever change." That said, the title of their piece signals resilience, much like the title of Reder and Shield, who borrow from Campbell, "I write this for all of you." Whereas such contributions address devastating loss, they also both highlight that, despite silence, censorship, violence, and non-guilty verdicts, in the words of Rene Meshake, "We are still here!"—and, in being here, will be heard, heeded, and commemorated.

NOTES

1 "Giant Rubber Duck Arrives in Toronto for Canada 150 After Controversy." *The Globe and Mail*, 30 June 2017, https://www.theglobeandmail.com/news/toronto/giant-rubber-duck-arrives-in-toronto-after-controversy/article35526362/.

2 As Barry Schwartz observes, if "chronicling allows for the marking and preservation of the historically real," commemoration, "the evaluative aspect of chronicling, celebrates and safeguards the ideal" (377).

3 As Linda K. Fuller notes, "national days encourage ... image making." See also David McCrone and Gayle McPherson's *National Days*.

4 While this book does not champion an absolutist theoretical stance, which would embrace the nature of the events or historical figures themselves as of crucial importance, neither does it hold fast to a relativistic point of view, which would locate "the significance of events in the standpoint of the observer" (Schwartz 376).

5 See also Eva Mackey, *The House of Difference*.

6 Vosters relies here on Benedict Anderson's understanding of how nationalism produced imagined communities that were—and still are—integral to (neo)colonial expansion.

7 Likewise, as Saito argues, "incremental change may influence the overall trajectory of commemorative rituals gradually over time or transform them dramatically or in

conjunction with contingent events. Commemorative rituals thus exhibit a seemingly contradictory combination of continuities and discontinuities because of their fundamentally temporal nature" (634).

8 See Morgan, who notes in her view of David Lowenthal's *In the Province of History* that "tourism/history discouraged its audience from engaging with the past in a multifaceted and dynamic fashion; instead, it 'encouraged the passive reception of images ... [and] forcefully imposed an authoritative reading (backed by state resources) that made any such dialogue difficult if not impossible'" (7).

9 As Matthew Hayday and Raymond B. Blake observe, "inventing traditions" is more common when "there has been a rapid transformation of society that challenges or destroys old social patterns or traditions" (11).

10 See also David Neufeld's "The Commemoration of Northern Aboriginal Peoples by the Canadian Government" and Yves Yvon J. Pelletier's "The Politics of Selection."

11 Sugars and Ty also add David Lowenthal's *The Past Is a Foreign Country* (1985), Patrick Wright's *On Living in an Old Country* (1985), and Louis Parkinson Zamora's *The Usable Past: The Imagination of History in Recent Fiction of the Americas* (1997) as other critical examples.

12 These omissions travel in different directions. The city of Montreal, which was coincidentally also celebrating its 375th anniversary in 2017, did not, as noted by Nakuset, co-chair of the Montreal Urban Aboriginal Community Strategy Network, consult with Indigenous artists or communities at first (Turnbull). A few months later, on February 14, then-mayor Denis Coderre "announced the new flag of Canada's second largest city would include some kind of nod to Indigenous peoples, and, at the same time, acknowledged Montreal was on Kanien'kehá:ka (Mohawk) land" (Bonspiel).

13 See for example W.L. Morton's "The North in Canadian Historiography."

14 See also Sophie McCall, Christine Kim, and Melina Baum, who argue that "diaspora and nation are interdependent and mutually constituting, just as indigeneity and nation are reciprocally contingent and responsive" (9).

15 "'I write this for all of you': Recovering the Unpublished RCMP 'Incident' in Maria Campbell's *Halfbreed* (1973)" by Deanna Reder and Alix Shield was first published online by *Canadian Literature* on May 29, 2018 (now in print in volume 238).

16 See, for example, Lee Maracle's short story "Charlie" and Willie Dunn's song "Charlie Wenjack."

SECTION ONE

Contemporary Counter Memories and Narratives

Recuperating Indigenous Narratives: Making Legible the Documenting of Injustices

Deanna Reder (Cree-Métis)

The main goal of the research project *The People and the Text: Indigenous Writing in Canada up to 1992*[1] has been to bring attention to stories by Indigenous authors in Canada that have been untold or, more often, stories that have been told but not heard. Even when the author clearly articulates injustices perpetuated by the Canadian state against Indigenous peoples, these critiques remained illegible to dominant society[2]—told, but not heard. Our research, then, is not simply a recovery mission. To recuperate Indigenous stories, to be able really to hear these stories, we have to eliminate the barriers around the reading and understanding of them. It is not simply a matter of reminding people to listen. Instead, what is needed is the effort to reframe what readers understand Indigenous expression to be and to look to Indigenous epistemologies for guides to understanding.

There are several moves we need to make even to begin. First, we need to find a word that will prevent us from seeing the oral and the literary as opposites—and, in fact, we need a word that encompasses both. Some Indigenous critics propose *story*, which has within it a special obligation to remove from the word *story* the associations of children's entertainment (as in storytime) or telling fibs (as in "that was some story!"). For the purposes of this chapter, I will use *story* and *narrative* alternately, to remind the reader to abandon orature and literature as opposites and that, instead, stories/narratives encompass both.

The second move we need to make is to replace the notion that literacy is a complex technology belonging to so-called advanced civilization, so that settler Canada may not continue to ignore or underestimate Indigenous authors. The third move is to see all these varieties of narrative as equally valid: in so doing, we will see all these varieties of narrative as equally Indigenous. This is a strategy to avoid categorizing any unconventional narrative as not *really* Indigenous. Finally, we need to believe Indigenous writers—that is, we need to accord Indigenous authors and their narratives the same credibility as we accord non-Indigenous writers and writing.

LET ME GIVE YOU AN EXAMPLE USING A STORY THAT IS REALLY IMPORTANT TO ME. It is a family story told to me by my mother and my aunties about my grandmother, my Kohkum, who lived in northern Saskatchewan. All throughout my childhood, I was told how powerful my grandmother was, how authoritative. Mom would tell me about how Kohkum ran a trapline, how she worked as a midwife, about how she, along with her mother, my Çapan, made medicines. She was well enough known for this knowledge that people would come to her for help. Women would come to ask her to deliver their babies. And, one day, during my mother's childhood, a young Cree man named Absolum Halkett came to Kohkum with a problem. He wanted to move away to go to school. He wanted to study to become an Anglican minister. But he was going blind. He came to Kohkum because he knew she made medicines and might be able to help him.

A point in the story that was always emphasized was that Kohkum wasn't sure what to do right away. While Kohkum had lots of remedies for a variety of ailments, this wasn't something she had dealt with before. She asked Abbie to give her some time to think. That night, Kohkum had a dream that a bear was being choked by the boughs of a willow tree. When she awoke she went looking for those leaves, collected them, and from them made a poultice. When Abbie returned, she told him that every night he would need to apply this paste to his eyes, and every morning he would need to wake up and walk to the lake and wash if off. He was to do this for three days.

When Mom told me the story, she always ended it with the same anti-climactic comments: "It worked. But he never did become a minister." This was not, to Mom's ears, a disappointment. What mattered in her telling of the story was that Kohkum was strong and reliable. She had cured Abbie.

Over the years, as I have thought about, told, and retold the story, I have learned a lot more about Abbie, who was born in 1928 and would have left for university about twenty years later. While he did train to become a minister, he never found permanent work as such. He was a schoolteacher for a time and then returned home, where from 1954 to 1965 he served as a band councillor for the Lac La Ronge Indian Band, as well as a prospector.

On the July long weekend in 2002, I was visiting with family in La Ronge. I told the story about Kohkum to my cousin Eric and my Uncle Vic, and was surprised to hear that Eric did not know what to me was a famous family story. Could it be, we wondered, that because he and his brothers and sisters went to residential school, he never got the chance to hear it? Was it because his mom had passed away when her kids were still young that she never had the chance to share this with him? I looked to Uncle Vic, and he confirmed that he knew the story. But he admitted that he knew a slightly different version. "I never heard about the dream," he told me. I was dumbfounded.

On my way back home, I stopped in Saskatoon for a short visit with my Auntie Irene. I asked her right away about the story, and if I had all the details right. Did Kohkum have the dream about the bear? "Of course," Auntie Irene shrugged. "How else would Kohkum have known what medicine to make?"

Her husband, my Uncle Frank, had heard this healing story before and told me, "You know, there was a lot of things we knew. My own mother cured me of diabetes." I listened politely, although I felt no need to believe or disbelieve this, except for the fact that I suspected, that if it were true, it could help many people … maybe even that, if it were true, it would be common knowledge. But I didn't say any of this. I listened politely. "It was blueberries," Uncle Frank insisted. "She told me to eat blueberries, and, you know, it fixed me right up."

A few years later, in the summer of 2004, I was flipping through a newspaper in a café, the August 24th edition of the *National Post*. On page A7, I came across an article entitled, "The Little Blue Pill: Researchers Are Convinced of the Health Benefits of the Common, Delicious Blueberry." The story cites the work of University of Ottawa biologist John Arnason, who is "investigating the health effects of blueberries … that were used by native people for hundreds of thousands of years. In particular, he's tracking down the anti-diabetes potential in blueberries" (Spears A7). I remember feeling chastened that I hadn't believed my Uncle Frank.

A little while later my PhD supervisor gave me a copy of *Orders of the Dreamed: George Nelson on Cree and Northern Ojibwa Religion and Myth*. Although this work was originally written in 1823, it was re-released in 1988 with an afterword by Stan Cuthand, whom I knew to be a Cree teacher and long-time friend of Uncle Frank. For some reason, I had never read the afterword before and was surprised to learn that, in the days when Cuthand had been a young Anglican minister, he had gone up and lived in La Ronge for a while and had come into contact for the first time with the bad medicine that Maria Campbell talks about in *Halfbreed*. Campbell had been warned by her Cheechum and Dad to "never ever fool around with anyone who uses medicine. If someone used medicine on you, you had to find a more powerful medicine man or woman to either remove or return the spell" (43).

Cuthand discusses Nelson's old stories of people who were bewitched by medicine men, and Cuthand tells stories that he saw himself. However, what really caught my attention was his proviso that he, too, knew people who practised *good* medicine, medicine that could heal: "There were medicine people in La Ronge who were well known for their ability to heal the sick. Mrs. David Patterson and Mr. Jerrimiah McKenzie both have a wide reputation for their healing powers" (194–95). My grandmother, called Kohkum by us, the Old Lady by my grandfather, Mamma by her children, Victoria by the government, and Oh-soss by her best friend, was also Mrs. Patterson.

I was excited to find this reference to Kohkum and called one of my best friends, who was working at a local community archive. She was just as excited as I and shared with me the methods she used as an oral historian. I needed to call my family, she advised, and interview everyone as soon as possible, to get their stories about Kohkum on record. She even offered me the use of the equipment she used when collecting histories.

I hung up the phone a little concerned. What would I say? "Hey Uncle Frank ..." "Hey Uncle Vic ..." "Hey Auntie Irene ..." Even though all my life I have been told over and over and over that Kohkum was a healer, only at the moment that I have seen this in a book it must be true? That in order for what you have told me all my life to be authenticated and preserved, you have to tell me on a tape recorder, so that I can transcribe it and file it away?

I never made those phone calls. But it did start me thinking about what is considered credible and why.[3]

LET ME TELL YOU ABOUT A NARRATIVE THAT THE PEOPLE AND THE TEXT HAS HELPED RECUPERATE: One of the projects that my research team has been the most excited about is the transcription of what is currently known to be the oldest novel written by an Indigenous person in Canada: *Black Hawk*, written by Cree scholar and Anglican cleric Edward Ahenakew, circa 1918. Ahenakew's great-niece Heather Hodgson is working with Cree historian Dr. Winona Wheeler to release it.[4]

The sixth chapter, titled "The Council Meeting," describes men of the reserve coming together to complain about the injustices of the Indian Agents (also called Commissioners) who refuse to give them permits to sell their cattle or their hay. While it is clear that young Black Hawk, the title character, is literate and indeed bookish, the men in this conversation are from a previous generation and haven't learned how to read or write in English, while they might speak it a little. Brass Buffalo begins to speak in Cree:

> Then up spoke Brass Buffalo, councilor of the Band. He was a fiery man. He was an old man.
>
> "I was at the First Treaty and heard every single word that was put into the ears of the people. With honied and conciliatory speech, the representatives of the Queen spoke. They placed the book of God on the table to show they were speaking truth. They pointed to that Sun, it's there yet, they pointed to Saskatchewan river it flows yet, the treaty was to stand as long as those existed. Their speech was good and their hearts were friendly. We accepted that which they said, we accepted the Spirit of their promises. Our lands were to be reserved. That was the word they used—'reserved.' It was to be ours still as it had been ours from ages past. Did they tell us that we were to be like herded swine tied down hand and foot with our reserves as pastures? Did they say then that we would have to shed our manhood and be forever treated like little children and be at the mercy of any stray fancy that happens to come into the minds of some one man who bears the name of commissioner and who, under the idea of policy, issues decrees that must be applied on all fours to all reserves and all Indians in them without taking into considerations the differences of conditions ... [AND BRASS BUFFALO CONCLUDES:] Let us write [our letter of complaint] but Heaven knows there may not be much attained by such procedure." (30–31)

Ahenakew reveals in Brass Buffalo's short speech a character who, while unable to read and write in English, is well able to discuss, remember, and analyze the Treaty process. In fact, Brass Buffalo is particularly concerned with the role of words, from "the honied speech of the Queen's representatives" to the "book of God" and the treaty language of the sun and the river, all to emphasize the solemnity of the contract and to contrast this with the Crown's interpretation of "reserve." Brass Buffalo insists that the land is "ours still as it had been ours from ages past" even as any (White) person given the name of commissioner can issue decrees with no regard to the effects upon Indian people, and his situation in particular. The Chief and councilors decide to list their complaints in a letter to the Superintendent of Indian Affairs in Ottawa, and seek out the reserve clergyman to pen the letter for them:

> That afternoon they drove over to the mission and made their wishes known to the kindly faced minister. He welcomed them in and asked them to sit down. It

was plain that he was a good and earnest man, but it was plain also that he was of the conciliatory kind.

As soon as the Chief began to speak his face clouded over with anxiety and troubles. At last he held up his hand. "Just one minute" he said "I am your clergyman my duty is to tell you of the Good News, this matter is outside of my duties."

The Chief was taken aback. He had expected such an answer, but all the same he could not help showing his disappointment.

"You have been with us for years," said he, "you know what we say is true, do you think it is justice, do you think we are getting fair treatment?"

"No—you are not," said the minister, "but you must trust in God and bear it as best you can."

"Then," said the Chief, ignoring the last part, "is it not the teaching of Christ that God is just and loves justice? Is it not the duty of those who are able to do what they can to right wrong?"

"Yes, it is, but it is not for me, your Saviour suffered injustice for your sake, can ye not be like Him?"

"My father in God, I could still answer you, but I see that you have made up your mind as to your attitude with respect to this. Can you not write for us and you need not appear in it. After all you will only be the medium of communication. You need not subscribe to what is written."

"I will tell you Chief, I got into their bad books because I wrote for Indians once before. I am a humble servant of God and would not dabble in worldly things. They will say I am interfering in their work, they will produce reports and things to disprove what I say and I will be blamed." (31–32)

Rather than juxtapose the Chief and Councillors as illiterate and the cleric as literate, Ahenakew instead portrays the Indigenous men as assertive and courageous, while the clergyman is passive and weak. The Chief is seeking a "medium of communication"; the clergyman is trying to stay out of the government's "bad books." The issue is resolved when a young American comes into the Mission and upon hearing the problem, offers to write the letter, if the Priest would translate:

The clergyman agreed to do this much though there was some doubt in his mind as yet. He however interpreted very ably and the young man had it all written out in a very clear manner. It assumed a respectful tone, asking the department to apply the various aspects of its policy regarding the permit system in a more discriminative way. It pointed out the parts which proved to be very harmful to the work of the Indians. It respectfully asked that something be done to apply the rule in a way that would be beneficial and truly helpful to those Indians who were known to be industrious and careful.

The letter was signed by the Chief and Councilors. It was then registered and posted. The next day it went off on its way to Ottawa, the only way that the Indian voice had a chance of being heard. (32)

Whether Ahenakew had the confidence in the written supplications to the Superintendent[5] that the characters he creates proclaim, it is clear that those characters believe in the power of writing, that written communication has a status and an authority that oral communication does not—that their letter of complaint is "the only way that the Indian voice had a chance of being heard" by the powers that be. Again, like the conversation with the clergyman, their lack of ability to read and write in English is not what makes them powerless. It is the fact that they are, in the words of Brass Buffalo, "like herded swine tied down hand and foot with our reserves as pastures" (30).

In fact, the reader should not assume that the Chief and Councillors are illiterate because it is already established in the second chapter, "The Indian Home," that Black Hawk's father can read the Bible, written in Cree syllabics. It is highly possible that all the characters in the council meeting are literate—just not in English.

I caution you not to assume that this knowledge of Cree syllabics is solely the result of contact. Winona Stevenson, now Wheeler, in her 2000 article "Calling Badger and the Symbols of the Spirit Language: The Cree Origins of the Syllabic System," argues that the origin of the Cree syllabary has been miscredited. While Wesleyan Methodist Reverend James Evans has been credited with its creation, she disputes it. Stevenson writes:

> This great Canadian myth has endured for over 160 years virtually unchallenged. Few question colonialist/conqueror renditions of the past and even fewer bothered asking Cree people directly about the origins of their writing system. A handful of anthropologists are aware that an Indigenous version exists in Cree oral histories but most, like David Mendelbaum, choose to disregard it in favour of the James Evans story. (20)

I think there is sufficient evidence to argue that Ahenakew valued literacy; even though his ambitions to become a published fiction writer were never realized, he was a master of narrative in both Cree and English, a learned Cree polymath, and Christian who was bilingual and literate in both Cree and English. Yet readers should not attribute his learnedness to assimilation. First, the ability of a culture to adapt to new circumstances is a sign of resilience and strength. Indeed, Ahenakew portrays his Cree characters as resilient and strong even as the deck is stacked against them. And second, writing on rocks—a form of learnedness—long preceded contact. As Stevenson notes, "age-old petroglyphs abound in Cree territory, especially in the Canadian Shield area around Stanley Mission" (24). Ahenakew's understanding of the world as a man of letters is supported by his training as a Cree intellectual.

This reminds me that it was often said among family that Kohkum could read and write in syllabics and some relatives remember that she kept her recipes for her medicines in a notebook. We were told that she went away to school for a few months but got called home when her father was killed. Apparently, he was under the bridge in Prince Albert playing cards with policemen and he was winning. They got angry with him and killed him, and no one was ever charged.

In 2013, I and my husband were visiting family in La Ronge and had the chance to join some cousins on a trip to Stanley Mission, a remote village an hour's drive away over a gravel road and then a boat ride, where you can tour the oldest standing building in Saskatchewan, the Holy Trinity Anglican Church, built between 1854 and 1860. En route to the church and then to Nestowiak Falls, my cousin's friend who took us out on the lake stopped at one of the petroglyphs etched into the rock and showed us how to see the Thunderbird and the image of the man with two hands lifted up as if to warn us that as we proceeded, we were about to hit the rapids.

LET ME TELL YOU ABOUT ANOTHER NARRATIVE THAT THE PEOPLE AND THE TEXT HAS HELPED RECUPERATE: the collected plays, stories, and poetry of writer Vera Manuel, the daughter of Ktunaxa cultural leader Marceline Paul and Secwepemc leader George Manuel, author of *The Fourth World: an Indian Reality* (1974) with Michael Posluns.

During Vera Manuel's life, she only saw a bit of work in print. One was a short story, "The Abyss," published in 1993; another version of this story in the form of a play, *Strength of Indian Women*, was first performed in 1992 and later published in 1998. She also had a smattering of poems published up until her passing in 2010. Working together with Algonquin scholar Michelle Coupal, Métis poet Joanne Arnott, and Vera's sister, educator Emalene Manuel, we have assembled Vera's collected works.

Much of the impetus for this collection is a combination of efforts inspired by Manuel. While in graduate school, Michelle Coupal began teaching *Strength of Indian Women,* and her students, Manuel's readership, urged Michelle to bring this work back into print.[6] As Coupal and I began working together on this, we had the opportunity to speak with Métis poet Joanne Arnott, who had befriended Vera in her last few years of life and worked with her to select poems for publication. Excited by this, we decided to join efforts. We contacted the editors of the First Voices, First Texts series of the University of Manitoba Press, precisely because this series is meant to support the republication of works by people like Vera Manuel, who historically did not receive the kind of publication support they deserve, and the Press was encouraging.

As we worked together and were looking for other unpublished plays, we discovered that Emalene Manuel had protected her sister's archive (including the previously unpublished short stories). In the summer of 2016, Joanne visited Emalene at her home near Cranbrook and collected files from Vera's old computer and took photos of any materials that seemed relevant. From this, we found rough notes and chapter outlines for an incomplete novel, as well as three polished, amazing short stories that were produced for 1987 creative writing classes, with notes in the margin and comments throughout by both Vera and an unnamed teacher. We then worked with Iñupiaq research assistant Rachel Taylor, who transcribed the hard copies as we sorted through comments and integrated only those changes approved by the author herself. Our hope is that Vera Manuel will be recognized as a writer who was ahead of her time, who made profound contributions to our understandings of Indigenous trauma and healing. We hope that she will finally find the wide readership that she hoped and worked for, who can learn from her teachings long after she has gone.

Much of Manuel's work as an artist is founded on an intimate knowledge of the suffering brought on by colonial institutions. However, the success of her art and her healing vision is more than simply being a witness to trauma. First, she was able to conduct therapeutic work with her mother and at least one sister who grounded her intergenerationally and allowed her the insight to be able to see the damage done to her parents and community, which was then inflicted upon her, opening the door for her to accept and forgive the abuses she suffered. Next, she was able to articulate her experiences of abuse using the model of Indigenous storytelling in the venue of the theatre; while standard features of theatre performance are secular in context, she was able to incorporate spiritual exercises like drumming and singing alongside other acts of public storytelling. In a 2004 interview with Tahltan artist Peter Morin for *Redwire,* she discusses the opportunity to be creative in therapy and describes her first play, *Song of the Circle,* which included a lot of her personal story:

There was so much shame about the things that happened in my life that I didn't want it to come out; and I remember the first play and seeing all my secrets on the stage and thinking, "I wonder if these people know that this is all about me? … It was really well received … I remember attending this conference in Kamloops; it was the 20th anniversary of the UBCIC conference, and my father was still alive then, and they were going to honour him at this conference. They asked me to bring this play and they didn't really know what it was about so, I managed to bring this play. And they brought him out and put him in the first row. I was really nervous about that … During the break I went to go talk to my dad, just to see what his reaction was. He told me, "My only regret was that your mother wasn't alive to see this. She would be so proud of you." And I thought he really understood, part of him really understood. (Interview)

This personal experience of being able to share her story successfully with her family and community helped her understand the opportunities for healing using art, so that she was able to help future creative partners articulate the unspeakable, that which terrorized them.

One benefit of this method is her implicit ability to believe the stories of other survivors and hence her ability to document abuses that were not legible to dominant society. Indeed, some of these abuses are still hard for mainstream Canadians to process. For example, toward the end of *Strength of Indian Women*, a character tells the others gathered at this reunion that after her years at residential school she had met someone who had worked at the local flour mill; this former worker told her that he was instructed to doctor the flour intended for the residential school by including a cup of a mysterious white substance—the friend remembered getting fired when he asked what the substance was. In the play, the women around the table theorize its effects on them, as they remember how the food at the school made them sick.

It was not until 2013 that historian Ian Mosby revealed findings that support the suspicions of Manuel's characters. Mosby reported that government-approved researchers conducted nutrition experiments on selected residential school inmates in the 1940s and 1950s. For example, Mosby discusses an experiment begun in the 1940s by Lionel Pett, in which students at an unidentified residential school were fed a special flour that could not be legally sold in Canada because it broke laws against food additives. Mosby summarizes Pett's 1952 report that recounted "a set of unfortunate results. Rather than an improvement in nutritional status, the students at the experimental school saw their blood haemoglobin levels decline" ("Administering" 164).

In a 2014 blog, Mosby reflects on the media attention that his research garnered, first from survivors, whose experience was validated by his research, and second from a shocked Canadian public:

> [T]he confirmation of what had long been known by these survivors—that they were part of some kind of scientific experiment—had unleashed a flood of additional questions yet to be answered. It is, in many ways, a depressing commentary on contemporary Canadian society that such stories were not taken seriously by the government or the media until they were published in an academic journal by a white, male, settler historian.

Yet over two decades earlier than Mosby, Manuel took the stories about adulteration of flour at residential schools seriously. In the preface to her one published play she comments: "I didn't make up the stories told in *Strength of Indian Women*. They came from pictures my mother painted for me with her words, words that helped me see her as a little girl for the first time" (xx).

It is these same family stories that inspired Manuel to write the three new stories in 1987 that are only now published: "The Grey Building," about a daughter driving her mother past the residential school that the mother attended, as the mother remembers how her own grandmother had tried to hide her in the mountains to keep her from being taken away; "Theresa," about a strong, powerful girl in residential school who openly defied the nuns who tried to undermine the girls' sense of worth, only to be killed and the story untold by a conspiracy of silence; and "The Letter," about a girl living in small-town British Columbia in the 1960s, who is one of the first First Nations students to attend public school and has to navigate the racial logics that underpin her life and community.

In all these stories, Manuel understands the function of state and church deception and the residential schools' curriculum of shame, violence, and worthlessness. She also understood the ceremonial actions of witnessing that exist in Ktunaxa and Secwepemc ceremony that can be replicated in secular theatrical performances, and the subsequent healing power of performance and of respect.

Conclusion

I am reminded of a quotation by Edward Ahenakew written in 1925—he writes it as a preamble to a manuscript, *Old Keyam*, that describes his perspective of Canadian society as a member of a generation that was fluent in both Cree and English, with Western education and with family members who remember life before the Indian Act. Ahenakew wrote, "The time has come in the life of my race when that which has been like a sealed book to the masses of our Canadian compatriots—namely the view that the Indians have of certain matters affecting their lives—should be known" (9). Of course, Ahenakew never found a publisher for this manuscript during his lifetime. It wasn't until 1973 that portions of it were edited by Ruth M. Buck and published together with another manuscript to form *Voices of the Plains Cree*. Even though in 1925 Ahenakew was ready to tell, no press was ready to publish him. No publisher was ready to hear what he had to say. And when his words were finally published, they were changed by the process of time from contemporary political critique to historical artifact.

There are multiple, complex reasons why Ahenakew and Manuel and a series of other narratives have not been heard. Often, these narratives were composed, sent to publishers only to be rejected, or sitting among personal papers, forgotten. Part of this is because there wasn't a wider reading public that wanted to hear our stories; there wasn't a larger infrastructure like public school curriculum that created a demand for our work; there wasn't the social power to access the appropriate venues to get the story out or the social status to add legitimacy to our words to make them credible, to make them believable. Or the epistemology—the worldview—to understand what was being told.

One Final Story

On Thanksgiving 2005, my husband and I flew to Edmonton for my cousin Lindsay's wedding. Standing there, I saw Uncle Vic, and I told him that Auntie Irene, who had passed on the previous January, had confirmed that Kohkum had dreamed of a bear, the part of the story he had never been told. "What I wonder," I told him, "was why you didn't know this part of the story. Why weren't you told?"

He replied, "What you don't understand is that we were told that the Indian stuff was no good and that the White man's things were better. I remember laughing at some medicine that Mom made and my sister Bella got angry with me and told me that I had to believe. That she would say this, that really surprised me.

"But you know," he continued, "there were lots of things that happened that you wouldn't believe. Once Dave was canoeing out on the lake and they figured he made someone angry by going too close to their campsite, so that when he came home one of his hands was limp. I remember the old ladies, my mom, her mom and an old friend got together to figure out how to heal him. I remember them talking about it for quite a bit and then they started to work on him and they healed him.

"There was medicine like that that you had to be careful with," he told me. "You know Abbie Halkett; he went to school, he was educated. An old man from Stanley Mission came to him, just like you would do in the old days, and told Abbie that he wanted him to marry his daughter. Abbie was going to be a minister; he didn't know what to say, but he didn't want to marry her this way. That upset the old man, who cursed him and told Abbie he was going to become blind."

NOTES

1 Thanks to the Social Sciences and Humanities Research Council (SSHRC) for funding *The People and the Text* from 2015 to 2020. I was the Principal Investigator and my co-applicants were Margery Fee and Cherokee writer and Canada Research Chair Daniel Heath Justice. See thepeopleandthetext.ca for more details.

2 Specific recognition needs to go to Dr. Margery Fee, whose work has been influential on my own; we co-presented at a 2016 conference at Concordia University, where we identified five barriers to the collection of Indigenous literatures in Canada:

- First, there is the persistent, uncritical belief in a binary opposition that defines non-Indigenous culture as literate and Indigenous culture as oral.
- Second, Indigenous texts written in English are devalued and often languish in public or personal archives, forgotten or unpublished.
- Third, the library cataloguing systems marginalize texts by Indigenous authors. In our work to recognize, valorize, and support the continuation of Indigenous intellectual traditions, a lot more has to be done than simply finding books and texts. We have to make space on the shelves for these works and we also have to make space within library categories.
- Fourth, what is considered Indigenous literary production has to encompass more than written text so that it can include multimodal storytelling encoded in Indigenous artifacts and traditions.
- Fifth, the Euro-western library fails to accommodate Indigenous protocols regarding private or sacred information.

3 I am not trying to argue that all narratives function the same way, that we access them the same way, or that any form of narrative tells us exactly the same thing. But they all are of value. Whether it's the words of a family story or the words of a noted Métis writer like Campbell or the words of Cree intellectual Stan Cuthand, they are valuable for the information that they encode and they are citable, as we try to make meaning by drawing connections between a variety of narratives. And all value "reading," whether it is Kohkum's ability to read dreams or Campbell and Cuthand's ability to discern the difference between bad and good medicine.

4 A specific thank you to Kristina Bidwell, who once alerted me to the fact that the Saskatchewan provincial archives had a lot of Ahenakew material, which I gathered in 2013, although I did not really read the cursive thoroughly until I had SSHRC funding to allow research assistants to transcribe the lot; thanks also to Donald Smith, who alerted me to the fact that historian and librarian Brendan Edwards was working with Ahenakew's great-niece Heather Hodgson to bring the novel to publication; and a special thank you to Brendan Edwards, who we discovered had worked to transcribe about half of the manuscript but had to abandon it due to his work responsibilities and who shared what he did with us in 2015. Thanks also to Iñupiaq editor Rachel Taylor and Yurok and Diné doctoral student Natalie Knight for completing and proofreading the transcription as part of *The People and the Text*.

5 At the time that the novel was written the Deputy Superintendent of Indian Affairs was Duncan Campbell Scott, who worked in this role from 1913 to 1932.

6 I was also motivated by an experience in graduate school when I attended one of Manuel's jointly authored plays, *Missing Lives*, and in subsequent conversations with the Helping Spirit Lodge Society, copies of the plays were shared with me. While it has taken me too long to be able to find a way to cast light on their work, I hope this publication can be one of many gestures to support them.

CHAPTER TWO

"I write this for all of you": Recovering the Unpublished RCMP "Incident" in Maria Campbell's Halfbreed (1973)[1]

Deanna Reder (Cree-Métis) and Alix Shield

"I write this for all of you," announces Métis author Maria Campbell in her 1973 autobiography *Halfbreed*, "to tell you what it is like to be a Halfbreed woman in our country" (8). Campbell describes her life growing up in extreme poverty in northern Saskatchewan in the 1940s and 1950s—a poverty created by the 1885 defeat at Batoche that pushed Métis claims aside in favour of European settlement. After her mother's death, and a short, failed marriage at age fifteen in a thwarted effort to keep her younger siblings together, Campbell drifted West, scrabbling together a living by whatever means she could. After two suicide attempts and a nervous breakdown, she decided, at the age of thirty-one, to confront everything that had happened to her and began to write her life-story.

Her publisher, McClelland & Stewart, suspected that the book would be successful, but never anticipated that the initial print-run of 4,500 copies[2] would immediately sell out. They ordered an additional 4,000, then another 2,500,[3] and struggled in that first year of publication to keep up with demand. Professors from across Canada lobbied for a paperback edition to teach in their classes.[4] Universities at that time had little, if any, Indigenous content, and certainly nothing from a Métis perspective.

Deanna Reder

Few understood before Campbell's book that Métis people were shunted literally to the margins of society, to the sides of the roads called Road Allowances where the land had no price and no value. They were left, writes Campbell in *Halfbreed*, with "no pot to piss in or a window to throw it out" (26). By using her autobiography to give an account of the often-forgotten tales of Métis resistance against unwinnable conditions, Campbell inspired a generation of Indigenous writers to tell their own stories. Delaware playwright Daniel David Moses called her "the Mother of Us All" (Lutz 83).[5]

So it is with some hesitation that I declare that this book is special to me and my family because many would say the same. However, my ties to this book are strong, not just because I am Métis and Campbell was born in the very same part of the world as my mother, in the very same month and year—April 1940—but also because it is the only book I ever remember my mother reading. She was excited to recognize the descriptions of places, ways of living, and people, like Métis leaders Jim Brady, who lived for a while in her hometown of La Ronge, and Malcolm Norris, whose son she had briefly dated as a teenager. Looking back, I realize that this demonstrated to me how Indigenous people rarely see our lives accurately depicted in mainstream media, so that finding a book written by someone who looks and lives like us is validating and precious.

I can even go so far as to credit Campbell with inspiring my current research on the neglected and understudied canon of Indigenous writing in Canada. My doctoral work focused on Indigenous autobiography in Canada, and as a professor at Simon Fraser University I have taught *Halfbreed* often over the years.

In April 2017, I attended an international conference in Dublin where Maria Campbell had been invited to speak. Called "Untold Stories of the Past 150 Years," the conference marked Canada's sesquicentennial by gathering together scholars, poets, and storytellers to share examples of neglected histories. For many of us, Campbell was the highlight of the event. *Halfbreed*, after all, is one of the most famous Indigenous autobiographies published in Canada. The book explains how the state used social institutions—schools, police, media—to make Indigenous peoples ashamed of their cultures. As Campbell's great-grandmother, Cheechum, states in the book: "They make you hate what you are" (90).

To my surprise, I ended up being seated next to Campbell herself; on the other side of Campbell was my research assistant and settler scholar, Alix Shield. Hoping to write on the publishing history of *Halfbreed* as a case study in her doctoral research, Alix asked Campbell about her manuscript that we had heard had been handwritten on hundreds of pages of foolscap. Campbell explained that she hadn't seen any need to keep these papers and had probably burned them. Knowing that Alix was about to go on a research trip to Ontario that fall, I asked Campbell if there might be early drafts in the

McClelland & Stewart fonds at McMaster University. She was encouraging. We promised to let her know what we found.

Alix Shield

In October, six months after our meeting in Dublin, I was visiting the McMaster University archives in Hamilton as part of a month-long research trip. Around the same time, news was breaking of the Harvey Weinstein scandal; women were coming forward with allegations of sexual assault, coercion, and harassment against the film producer. And it was only the beginning of a movement that would gain momentum over the next several months.

Deanna and I already knew, thanks to the important archival work of historian Brendan Edwards, that a particular "incident" involving the RCMP appearing in Campbell's manuscript had been deemed by publishers as too "libellous" to include in *Halfbreed* and was removed prior to the book's publication.[6] We had also heard that Campbell's autobiographical text had been revised from around 2,000 hand-written pages to less than 200 (Lutz 42). After several weeks in the archives, I set aside a day to explore Campbell's files in the McClelland & Stewart fonds. I sat down with a pile of manuscript pages, and began skimming them for any editorial notes. Some of the names had been scratched out and changed, but otherwise the editorial marks were very minimal. About a hundred pages in, I came across a page and a half that had been struck out with a giant red X. The excised passage contained a story from Campbell's childhood, taking place when she was only fourteen years old[7]:

> During all this time Dad worked for Bob and poached on the side, and as usual the Mounties and wardens were often at our house. We were eating fairly well, as Dad made good money from the sale of meat. One day he was away and Grannie and I were drying meat in the bush. We had a tent set up about a mile from the house and all the children were with us. I raced home to get something we'd forgotten just as three R.C.M.P. drove up in a car. They said they were going to search the house as they knew Daddy had brought meat home the day before. I let them in and said that everyone else was at the store, and prayed that no one would come from the camp. While one Mountie was upstairs and another in the barn, the third followed me into the kitchen. He talked for a long time and insisted that I knew about the meat.
>
> Suddenly he put his arm around me and said that I was too pretty to go to jail. When I tried to get away, he grabbed my hair and pulled me to him. I was frightened and was fighting back as Robbie came running into the room.

He tried to hit the Mountie but was knocked to the floor. I was nearly to the door when the other one came in. All I can recall is being dragged to Grannie's bed where the man tore my shirt and jeans. When I came to, Grannie was crying and washing me off. I must have been in a state of shock, because I heard everything she said but could not speak or cry despite the pain. My face was all bruised and I had teeth marks all over my chest and stomach. My head felt as if my hair had been pulled out by the roots.

Grannie was afraid that Dad would come home, so she helped me upstairs and put me to bed. She told me not to tell Daddy what had happened, that if he knew he would kill those Mounties for sure and be hung and we would all be placed in an orphanage. She said that no one ever believed Halfbreeds in court; they would say that I had been fooling around with some boys and tried to blame the Mounties instead. When Daddy came home she told him that King had gone crazy and had thrown me. Dad sold King because he was afraid that I might be crippled or even killed next time. I don't know what Grannie told Robbie. After that, he always hated the police, and when he grew up he was in trouble all the time and served prison terms for assaulting policemen. My fear was so great that I even believed they would come back and beat me to make sure that I told no one. For weeks afterwards, if I heard a car coming into the yard, I would be sick to my stomach with fear. (Campbell, "Halfbreed Woman")[8]

The significance of this passage was immediately clear. I phoned Deanna soon after, whispering through the phone from the library basement. I explained that I was still in the archives and urged her to read the pages that I was about to send.

Deanna Reder

I was very familiar with the chapter in question because of the dissonance I experienced when first reading the book. I now realized that the gap I noticed in the narrative was created by the decision to simply X out the rape. Chapter Twelve, and indeed the whole book, shifts when you learn that Maria, on the brink of womanhood and growing in competence and confidence, is violated. The result is a blow to her and to her family. While in the published version there is no explanation for Robbie's subsequent rebelliousness that saw him placed "in fifteen foster homes" before eventually moving to Alaska (147), the excised passage could explain his lifelong hatred for the police and his later convictions for assaulting them.

In a 1989 interview with Hartmut Lutz, when Campbell complains that this passage was removed, she states: "That whole section makes all of the other stuff make sense. And you can almost tell at what point it was pulled out. Because there is a gap" (Lutz 42). Earlier in the story, when the family suffers the loss of their mother, Grannie Dubuque arrives to take care of the children. This relieves Maria, the eldest, from the burden of providing child-care. Now, with this missing passage recovered, one can imagine the trauma the grandmother went through, acting as a surrogate mother, having to both care for her granddaughter after a sexual assault and hide this news from her son-in-law. Her subsequent and unexplained departure resulted in the breakup of the entire family, when they couldn't manage without her.

Also, it is in this excised passage that we read that there is a disruption in Maria's memory when she recalls being dragged to her grandmother's bed but nothing else, describing what she calls a "state of shock" that causes a sense of disassociation in which she "heard everything [Grannie] said but could not speak or cry despite the pain." With Grannie Dubuque gone, Maria had little opportunity to express her grief, so she suppressed it, dismissing her emotions by minimizing what happened: "I had so much to do that I seldom had time to be sorry for myself" (88), she writes in the book. While the passages that follow don't lament the loss of her grandmother, Campbell describes going to the school dance with her new housekeeper, Sophie, and insulting her. Asked by friends if her chaperone was her mother, Maria responds: "'That old, ugly Indian?'" and describes feeling "shame and hatred for her, myself, and the people around me" and "wanting to cry so badly, but not being able to" (90). Her lack of legal or social outlets to speak about the rape compounds her inability to voice her anger and pain until it erupts in self-damaging ways. In fact, her unmentioned physical and sexual assault by the police troubles the rest of the narrative.

Alix Shield

The excision also changes the book right from the beginning. In the Introduction to *Halfbreed*, Campbell writes about the difficulties of returning home to Saskatchewan, and explains how writing this book was part of coming to terms with her past: "Like me the land had changed, my people were gone, and if I was to know peace I would have to search within myself. That is when I decided to write about my life" (7–8).

That Campbell was even willing to share the rape publicly is extraordinary. Yet when reading the archival correspondence between members of

McClelland & Stewart's editorial team, I began to realize how insistent they were about removing this passage, even though, as Campbell states, "I had insisted it stay there" (Lutz 42). When the *Halfbreed* manuscript was first sent over to McClelland & Stewart by Jim Douglas (of Vancouver publishing house Douglas & McIntyre), the editors agreed that significant revisions were required in order for it to be published. The manuscript was submitted under Campbell's legal name, June Stifle, but was to be published under the pseudonym Maria Campbell; this name was chosen for sentimental reasons, after her great-grandmother, and not as a means of hiding her identity.[9] The manuscript changed hands several times, and eventually landed at the desk of Jack McClelland. A memo, provided by Jim Douglas, accompanied the manuscript and described it as follows:

> This is the story of her life and a grim life it has been ... A life of violence and meanness on the part of her men and her church and the police. Her first sexual experience was to be raped by RCMP officers in her own home—and it goes down from there. It is the round of indignity and degradation that sociologists write about. Here, an articulate, intelligent half-breed tells us what it is really like. (Douglas)

After reading through the manuscript, McClelland responds to Douglas' endorsements with skepticism:

> I'm afraid that I don't agree with your assessment as to how we should proceed. Aware as I am of your usually realistic and discerning eye when it comes to manuscript evaluation, I have concluded that you must have been overwhelmed by the author's personality, by your meeting with her and possibly unduly influenced by her agent (or whatever his function is) who I suspect maybe [sic] prone or susceptible to the same influence. (McClelland, Letter to Douglas)

McClelland goes on to outline the significant revisions and excisions necessary before the project could proceed. This included expanding the childhood material, and condensing the later "Vancouver" section. Even in these early stages of manuscript consideration, McClelland identified the sexual assault incident as one that he believed could pose problems:

> One point that really bothers me is her experience with the RCMP. I don't know, because I haven't checked with a lawyer but my suspicion is that this

could not be used. The RCMP could almost certainly get an injunction stopping the distribution of the book and they almost certainly would. Then it would be up to her to prove the incident. I presume that this would be almost impossible and a messy business that she wouldn't want to be involved in ... I haven't any doubt about the incident itself. I am sure it occurred just as I know it occurs today, but I think the only time one can do anything about it is when it occurs. (McClelland, Letter to Douglas)

While McClelland suggests that the rape scene is not worth such legal complexities and is therefore dispensable, his approach fundamentally opposes Campbell's own reasons for writing the book "as a kind of therapy to purge myself" (qtd. in Woods). As part of the book's "Preliminary Publishing Plan," McClelland & Stewart proposed a strategy for marketing the book in which Campbell would play the role of victim to emphasize the "major theme of injustice to be promoted personally by the author" ("Preliminary"). Yet the injustice of her sexual assault, despite her insistence at its importance, wasn't allowed to be mentioned.[10]

Upon examination of the original submission, McClelland decided to move forward, under the strict condition that Campbell provide a revised draft following his recommendations, including the removal of the rape scene. But that didn't happen. Instead, Campbell sent the manuscript back early the next year with minimal changes, prompting Executive Director Anna Porter to question her progress: "Has she in fact revised it since your correspondence with Jim's query[?] if she has, the revision has been completely unsuccessful" (Porter, Letter to McClelland). At this stage, the "RCMP Incident" was proving a point of contention between the author and her publisher.

After receiving several partial revisions from Campbell over the next ten months, editor David Berry writes a letter to Jack McClelland in November 1972: "I thought you should know that she has re-inserted the Mountie-rape incident in the revised manuscript. Her own lawyer apparently thinks this is OK, but as we might feel differently about it I thought you should know." Several days after this memo was sent, McClelland writes a letter to his lawyer, Mr. Robert I. Martin, asking for advice: "Sometime [sic] ago we discussed a problem relating to a book by a Métis woman ... We concluded jointly that we could not safely include this incident. Her lawyer tells her that we could. I would like to include it if we can, but I am still of the opinion that it could lead to an injunction."

Over the next two months, McClelland & Stewart pushed to get the book finished and into production. In a letter dated January 12, 1973, David Berry writes to Campbell with an update: "We made very few changes in the manuscript, and since there was a big rush to get it to the printer I didn't think it would be worthwhile to send it back to you." Several days later, Berry would send Campbell another letter, including the updated page proofs. In this letter, he notes, "I don't know if Dianne or Jack McClelland told you that we are taking out the incident with the Mounties. We'd like to keep it in, but our lawyer advises us that unless it could be proved the RCMP could get an injunction to stop the sale of the book."[11] At this point, an internal memo was sent around McClelland & Stewart stating that they were to "drastically advance the schedule on this book" and that "we had all better give this title special attention whenever possible" (Scollard). It's difficult to know at this stage if Campbell was being deliberately left out of editorial conversations. By the time the master proofs were arranged in February of 1973, the entire page-and-a-half had been crossed out with red pencil, and was never mentioned again.

Deanna Reder

In January 2018, we emailed Campbell with news of Alix's discovery of the excised passage. "Wow you actually found it," she replied. "I didn't think [Jack McClelland] kept it because when I asked him for it he said he had destroyed it so I wouldn't get into trouble" ("Re: research after Dublin").

We arranged to visit her at her home in Saskatoon in late February. As we sat at Campbell's dining room table, Alix presented her with a prayer tie—tobacco wrapped in red cloth—and I gave her some sweetgrass and a small gift. Campbell brought us tea and prepared the meatloaf she was making for our lunch. Once she was seated, Alix showed her the scans of the missing passage. Campbell shared how, when she received her author's copy by mail in 1973, she went directly to the point in the book where the passage should have been. That's when she discovered it had been removed.

Campbell encouraged us to write about our findings, but did not want to be involved. Now seventy-eight, she is busy as a teacher and an activist with little interest in going back to talking about those days. As our visit was drawing to a close, Campbell shared a story with us. When she was a girl her family would get assorted books for twenty-five cents a box, and she remembers that sometimes there would be a book by poet E. Pauline Johnson in the batch. Her favourite poem by Johnson was "The Cattle Thief." Campbell remembers falling upon the poem with pride—the thought that an Indigenous woman could be a writer amazed her. She used this example to explain how often in her life she had received awards, but the awards themselves were never important. What convinced her to accept them was the thought that such acknowledgments might set an example for young Indigenous girls to believe in themselves.

Halfbreed became a bestseller, and arguably remains "the most important and seminal book" written by an Indigenous woman in Canada (Lutz 41). Had this passage not been removed, the effect is, of course, impossible to say. It would have allowed the author to publicize a rape she never reported out of fear she would have been disbelieved; this might have inspired an earlier generation to consider the mechanisms that silence women. Campbell lays bare the racism that continues to complicate an Indigenous woman's account of sexual assault—as Grannie Dubuque warned in the excised passage, "no one ever believed Halfbreeds in court." Campbell's description of the sexual assault might have raised awareness and conversations that now, amidst today's National Inquiry into Missing and Murdered Indigenous Women and Girls, are coming into public discussion. In the Lutz interview, Campbell is asked if she would ever like to re-write *Halfbreed*. She responded: "Yes, some day. I don't think I'd make changes. What I would do with the book is, I would only put in that piece that was taken out. I wouldn't want to touch what's there, because that was the way I was writing then, and I think that it's important it stays that way, because that's where I was at" (47). Only now, with the recovery of this excised passage, forty-five years since its first publication, can a reissue of Campbell's book be done as she originally intended.

NOTES

1 This article was originally published on the canlit.ca website in May 2018. Maria Campbell supports the publication of the article and has granted *Canadian Literature* permission to publish it and to reproduce the original excised manuscript pages on the web and in print. Since the problems surrounding the excised pages came to light when this article first appeared on the journal's website, there has been renewed interest in the book. Over five thousand people read the article in the weeks after it was published; according to *Canadian Literature* editor Laura Moss, by 6 October 2019 it had been read online over 11,000 times. A new edition of *Halfbreed* was released in November 2019 with McClelland & Stewart. It includes the missing passage, a short introduction by Kim Anderson, and a conclusion by Maria Campbell. Further, M&S has also issued an audiobook, read by Maria Campbell herself.

2 See Porter, Letter to Witmer. In this letter, Anna Porter, Executive Director at McClelland & Stewart, suggests to Glenn Witmer (and copied to other M&S staff including J.G. McClelland, L. Ritchie, and D. McGill) that in this initial print run

of 4,500 copies, books should be sold for $5.95. This same letter also states that *Halfbreed* "has great magazine potential," and that they plan to send a set of galleys to *Weekend* magazine for possible publication.

3 See "Re-print Purchase Order for 'Half Breed Woman'" and "Delivery Required by September 26th." Both of these purchase orders are addressed to the Alger Press (Oshawa, ON) and are signed off by Peter Scaggs, of McClelland & Stewart's Production Department.

4 See Audley, Letter to Porter and copy to Glenn Witmer and Don Roper, 31 Aug. 1973; Audley, Letter to Porter, 28 Sept. 1973; Porter, Letter to Dave McGuill and copy to Paul Audley, 17 Oct. 1973. These letters discuss the possibility of McClelland & Stewart issuing a quality paperback version of *Halfbreed*, citing requests from professors at the University of Toronto and Brock University who expressed interest in teaching *Halfbreed*, especially if the book were offered at a lower price point.

5 In an interview with Hartmut Lutz, as recorded in *Contemporary Challenges: Conversations with Canadian Native Authors* (1991), Lenore Keeshig-Tobias credits Daniel David Moses for this quotation.

6 See his article in McMaster University's *Historical Perspectives on Canadian Publishing* digital series, titled "Maria Campbell's Halfbreed: 'Biography with a Purpose.'" This "incident" is also discussed in Hartmut Lutz's interview with Campbell in *Contemporary Challenges*.

7 The authors have decided to reproduce this passage as Campbell wrote it before further edits, except for one name change to correspond to the names in the published book.

8 We are grateful to Maria Campbell for giving us permission to reproduce these unpublished pages from the original typescript manuscript.

9 See Berry, Letter to McClelland. In this letter, McClelland & Stewart editor David Berry explains to Jack McClelland that although they having been working on the *Halfbreed* manuscript with June Stifle, she has expressed that she would actually prefer "to use the name Maria Campbell as her professional nom-de-plume, but doesn't care about concealing her real identity and would not object to the use of a photo on the jacket or to in-person promotion."

10 A clipping from the *Globe and Mail* titled "RCMP Harassing Indians, Committing Sexual Acts against Women, Head of Group Charges" was found among the McClelland & Stewart "Halfbreed Woman" correspondence at McMaster University, addressed to the attention of editor David Berry. This article was published on January 13, 1973, only months before the publication of *Halfbreed*. Also in 1973, the same year that *Halfbreed* was published, the RCMP celebrated their organization's centennial anniversary.

11 See Berry, Letter to June Stifle, 15 Jan. 1972. Shield would like to acknowledge an error that appeared in the May 2018 canlit.ca web article (and subsequent print version) concerning the publishing timeline of events for Campbell's *Halfbreed*; this version of the article has been corrected. Where Shield had initially noted that David Berry addressed a letter to June Stifle dated 15 January 1972 (where Berry writes, "I don't know if Dianne or Jack McClelland told you that we are taking out the incident with the Mounties"), she has since realized that this letter was likely dated by Berry in error and should have read 15 January *1973*. In further tracing Berry's involvement as an editor for the Halfbreed project, Shield realized that he was only assigned to the book in the fall of 1972, around which time he wrote to Campbell to introduce himself as her editor (see Berry, Letter to June Stifle, 7 Sept. 1972 in Box 2CA84 of the M&S fonds). Furthermore, this letter logically follows his previous letter to June Stifle, dated 12 Jan. 1973, in which he states that he will soon send the printer's proofs onwards to her. For a more detailed analysis of the publishing timeline for Campbell's *Halfbreed*, please see Chapter 4 of Shield's PhD dissertation (titled *Kwaskastahsowin ("Put things to right"): Case Studies in Twentieth-Century Indigenous Women's Writing, Editing, and Publishing in Canada*), available through the sfu Library.

CHAPTER THREE

Telling Harm: Time, Redress, and Canadian Literature

Benjamin Authers

"Redress" has become the exemplary means by which claims for breaches of the rights of minority groups by the state are articulated in Canada. In the past three decades, redress processes have seen government apologies and remedies offered for acts including the forced removal and abuse of children under the Indian residential school system, the discriminatory "Head Tax" imposed on Chinese migrants, and the internment of Japanese Canadians in the Second World War. Defined as "[a] discursive formation frequently organized around the pursuit of reparations for specifiable historical injuries and for reconciliation of social divides framed as stemming from those injuries," redress has been an at-times productive space for the activism of minoritized groups seeking recognition and remedy for particular government acts and policies (Henderson and Wakeham, *Reconciling Canada* 6). It has also been rightly critiqued for the ways in which it manages such activism, limiting its scope and forms. Notably, redress practices in Canada have also been profoundly lacking as a meaningful response to the ongoing harms of colonialism.

This chapter examines the temporalities of what Jennifer Henderson and Pauline Wakeham term the "culture of redress" in their co-edited volume, *Reconciling Canada: Critical Perspectives on the Culture of Redress* (2013). Taking the 2008 Harper government apology for residential schools as an example, I read redress through its fitful relationship with time, both the ways government responses seek to contain wrongs as past and harms as redressed, and how this is disrupted by the persistence of the harms caused by these wrongs. Building on the long relationship between literature and the culture of redress, I suggest that literature can give greater presence to wrongs and harms as part of a temporality that recognizes their continuity. Offering an additional dimension to the unruliness that already characterizes the time of redress, Jeanette Armstrong's novel *Slash* (1985/2007) and Kerri Sakamoto's *The Electrical Field* (1998) emphasize the unremediated nature of harms caused by government wrongs. Through this, they suggest that although meaningful responses to wrongful state acts are necessary, the harms caused by these acts may nonetheless persist. These novels urge their readers to recognize the potential *im*possibility of redress as a closure of the past, whether at specific moments of agreement and apology or during more generally celebratory tellings of the state, such as in the marking of Canada 150.

In this chapter, I move between discussions of the Japanese Canadian Redress Agreement and the apology for the Indian residential school system, and I end by thinking through *Slash* and *The Electrical Field*, something that, I am aware, risks collapsing two distinct histories and political projects. I want to stress that there are numerous differences between the claims of Japanese Canadians over the Second World War internment and subsequent dispersal, and the multivalent campaigns for redress and reconciliation by Indigenous peoples—First Nations, Métis, and Inuit—of which the Indian Residential Schools Settlement is but one aspect. At the same time, there are important questions to be asked about the connections that might exist between movements for redress. These may include anti-colonial alliances in the relational space "between a social body constructed as 'Asian' and a social body constructed as 'Indigenous' in a Canadian national context" (Lai, "How to Do 'You'" 12), alliances to which literature might contribute by "challeng[ing] us to imagine the ways in which dialogue and interaction could spark deeper understanding of our interrelatedness" (Wong, "Decolonizasian" 166; see also Phung). As events like the 1994 Writing Thru Race conference demonstrate, political and literary alliances between Indigenous and Asian-Canadian peoples (and, indeed, other minoritized communities) may simultaneously make differences between communities apparent (Lai, "Other Democracies"; Gagnon, *Other Conundrums* 71). A comprehensive examination of the connections and disconnections between Japanese-Canadian and Indigenous redress movements is beyond the scope of this chapter. Instead, the following discussion of the temporalities of redress reveals common political and literary concerns, as well as dissimilarities arising from distinct experiences of racism and colonialism, that provide productive insights into the possibilities and limitations of the culture of redress in responding to government wrongs against Indigenous and non-Indigenous peoples.

The Culture of Redress in Canada

After decades of activism by members of the Japanese-Canadian community, on September 22, 1988, the "Terms of Agreement between the Government of Canada and the National Association of Japanese Canadians" (the Redress Agreement) was signed by Art Miki, President of the Association, and Canadian Prime Minister Brian Mulroney. In it, the Canadian government acknowledged that the forced removal, internment, and dispersal of Japanese Canadians during and after the Second World War was "unjust and violated principles of human rights as they are understood today" (Government of Canada and the National Association of Japanese Canadians, "Terms of Agreement" 339 [s. 1]). The Redress Agreement attempted to acknowledge and remedy these wrongs, and contained a pledge to prevent such a violation of rights from ever reoccurring (339 [s. 2]). It also made financial, legal, and political recompense to internees, their families, and the Japanese-Canadian community, by way of "symbolic redress" (440).[1]

The symbolic recompense in the Agreement reflects the process by which the Japanese-Canadian community sought remedy for the government's actions. As Roy Miki argues, redress activism rearticulated Japanese-Canadian identity "to incorporate the more inclusive language of 'citizenship' and 'human rights' that constitutes the liberal democratic values of the Canadian nation" (264), a reading of Japanese Canadians "into the nation as 'citizens'" (323). Within the political discourse of redress, this framed the harms committed against Japanese Canadians and their communities "as a national issue," something that required "'settlement' by the federal government, the authority responsible for the violations" (264). Here, as elsewhere, redress is not simply the Redress Agreement. Rather, it includes a spectrum of documents, words, symbols, and political, legal, and cultural acts and meanings that cumulatively denote the harm committed by the state, the case for its recompense, and the form of that recompense.

This short summary of Japanese-Canadian redress is not intended to establish the Redress Agreement, nor Canadian redress processes more generally, as ideal mechanisms for responding to historical harms. They are not. And Miki (along with other writers on the community's seeking of redress) notes that there are limitations to what redress did in this instance and what it might achieve overall, as illustrated by the ambivalent ending of Joy Kogawa's novel *Emily Kato*, a rewriting of her more triumphal *Itsuka*. As an early, notable example of a redress campaign and agreement, however, Japanese-Canadian redress does provide one point from which to begin to unpack the meaning of redress in the contemporary Canadian state and the blend of political, legal, and cultural discourses that circulate through it.

Redress agreements, with their political (and politicized) apology and often generalized financial remedies, are, of course, not the only means by which marginalized communities and the individuals who compose them might seek remedy for state wrongs. Notably, the capacity to gain recompense for human rights violations committed by states has increased in domestic and international law, including through the expansion of rules about the standing of individuals to sue for rights violations and the ability to claim non-monetary forms of compensation (Menkel-Meadow 624–26, 630; Antkowiak passim). Legal processes, which are frequently expensive, conservative, and unable to recognize certain kinds of claims and harms, are not a panacea to the political difficulties faced by groups seeking redress for state abuses of human rights. Rather, they can form part of the range of approaches to redress, potentially offering a distinct and valuable kind of remedy (N. Saito). Even when it does not take place in the juridical space of the court, the law influences redress, with many of the aspects of its processes shaped and co-opted by "legal language and requirements," as Carrie Menkel-Meadow notes (635).

Acknowledging the influence that the law has on redress in Canada, this chapter views redress as a broadly conceived set of ideas and practices. In addition to specific remedies, redress is also about the multivalent forces and processes that shape agreements, and determine what wrongs can and cannot be redressed. As Henderson and Wakeham suggest, speaking of a "culture of redress" attempts to reflect these multiple meanings, and to emphasize that redress in Canada must be understood as more than a simple relationship between state and claimant group:

> As a range of cultural, political, and pedagogical practices enacted by heterogenous agents, the culture of redress shapes particular notions of history and the political, establishes what can count as a group injury and indeed what it is that can be injured, solidifies a sense of the "national state," and potentially naturalizes government responses as well as the contingent identities of those groups forming themselves to make demands upon the state. The culture of redress does not simply amount to a dynamic of demand and response though which scores are settled, debts repaid, and apologies delivered; it effects a much wider epistemological restructuring, one that is not managed from any single vantage point or locus of control. (*Reconciling Canada* 10)

The culture of redress in Canada thus constitutes a way of producing knowledge about state actions and the possibility of recompense for them, as well as what constitutes "appropriate" modes and interpretations of that knowledge. Henderson and Wakeham argue that this has "disciplined [the] discursive forms" by which redress might be sought, naturalizing "a specific kind of political culture, within which it currently makes sense to pursue social justice and future equality" (*Reconciling Canada* 17). The culture of redress may thus constrain the processes that can be undertaken to seek apology and recompense from the state, the wrongs that can be remedied, the remedies sought, and the finality with which remedies are treated. Notably, while redress activism originates in marginalized communities, in its dialogue with the state, it can become "a manifestation of a desire for closure," with "a particular emphasis on history and the imperative of 'moving on,' as well as a renewed emphasis on legalistic conceptions of injury that conceive of harm explicitly or implicitly in relation to liberal individuals and property" (7). The culture of redress may thus result in a state failure to acknowledge certain, often ongoing, systemic wrongs and their attendant harms, notably those stemming from colonialism (Menkel-Meadow 636, Dominello 299).

Time and the 2008 Apology for Indian Residential Schools

From the 1870s, the Canadian government had been involved in developing and administering residential schools in conjunction with churches; most ceased to operate in the 1970s, and the last one closed in 1996. Indigenous children in these schools were subject to systemic abuse and neglect. The schools were also intentional sites of cultural genocide, enabling assimilationist policies that forbade Indigenous languages and broke the transmission of culture between generations of Indigenous people. On June 11, 2008, then Prime Minister Stephen Harper apologized in Canada's House of Commons for the government's role in the Indian residential school system. This was not tied to the announcement of a specific agreement between the government and Indigenous groups, as had been the case with Japanese-Canadian redress, but was rather part of a larger process of redress and reconciliation that was predated by the Indian Residential Schools Settlement Agreement approved in May 2006, and implemented from September 2007 (Government of Canada, "Indian Residential Schools"). The Settlement Agreement did not apply to all students of residential schools in Canada, however, and September 28, 2017, saw the approval of a further agreement for students of Newfoundland and Labrador residential schools, with an apology delivered by Prime Minister Justin Trudeau on November 24, 2017 (Government of Canada, "Newfoundland and Labrador Residential Schools"). That Harper's apology predates a further apology, as well as coming a decade after the 1998 "Statement of Reconciliation" delivered by Jane Stewart, then Minister of Indian Affairs and Northern Development (Stewart 323), underscores the difficulty of producing closure in such a complex matter. Harper's text similarly demonstrates that the language of official apology often manifests multiple meanings, including temporal ones.

In the apology, which Harper offers to "former students of Indian residential schools" (335), the government's actions are framed as historical wrongs that have had, and that continue to have, significant consequences. Residential schools, Harper states, were intended to assimilate Indigenous children into a hegemonic Canadian culture. The schools had "a lasting and damaging impact on aboriginal culture, heritage and language" (335), intergenerational effects that are acknowledged as leading to systemic "social problems that continue to exist in many communities today" (336). The apology thus acknowledges publicly the wrong committed, the culpability of the state in that wrong, and the harm that continues to come from it, what Paul Huebener terms "a rather remarkable acknowledgment of temporal responsibility" (62). As it is framed here, the wrong of residential schooling is of the past—the apology is addressed to "former students" and their communities, and states that the residential schooling policy "was wrong"—while its harms are of both the past and the present. From an apparently more enlightened contemporary position, Prime Minister Harper renounces the policy as having "no place" in Canada, through a seemingly timeless formulation of the nation-state and what it stands for that is nonetheless characterized by the purported values of the present. Thus, "[t]oday we recognise that this policy of assimilation was wrong, has caused great harm, and has no place in our country" (335; this echoes the statement in the Japanese Canadian Redress Agreement that the government's actions were "unjust and violated principles of human rights as they are understood today"). It is in the present that the apology is made, in order to redress "a sad chapter in our history" (335); as Harper goes on to reiterate at multiple points, it is because "[w]e now recognise" the wrongs done and the harms caused that "we apologize" (336). This progression, ahistorical in its assumption that these wrongs were not known to be wrong when committed, sits alongside a temporality in which rights breaches are only acknowledged, and can only start to be resolved, in the present. There is thus an articulation of the time of state wrongs as past and of present resolution in the apology, ultimately extending this progressivist logic to articulate a new, ongoing relationship with Indigenous peoples.

Harper also posits the importance of apologizing itself, noting that the failure to apologize has been, historically, an impediment to healing and reconciliation (336). An apology is, Michael Murphy writes, "both a means of recognizing that an injustice has been done and a means of accepting responsibility for the harm and suffering brought about by that injustice" (53). An apology may be an important means by which governments can offer recompense, including for actions that were enacted legally at the time, and where a government acknowledges responsibility this can be significant for victims and begin to repair the harms done (Murphy, Robbennolt, and Wexler 557). Apologies may also create a historical record of the human rights violations committed by the state, and serve to bring the group who suffered the wrong into symbolic belonging to the nation (Miki 323; Dominello 283, 285). However, apologies may also be qualified, or serve yet other rhetorical functions; government apologies to Indigenous peoples in particular can "be less about benefitting Indigenous peoples and more about serving as an exculpation mechanism for white modes of power" (Giannacopoulos 339).

Notably, and unlike many other official apologies, the 2008 government apology does allude to the dialogic nature of apologizing, stating that "[y]ou have been working on recovering from this experience for a long time, and in a very real sense we are now joining you on this journey. The Government of Canada sincerely apologizes and asks the forgiveness of the aboriginal peoples of this country for failing them so profoundly" (Harper 336). Rhetorically, this apology thus constructs a future relationship between the state and Indigenous peoples; coupled with the Indian Residential Schools Settlement, Prime Minister Harper posits that it "gives us a new beginning and an opportunity to move together in partnership" (336).

Despite this apparently dialogic stance, however, elsewhere in the apology is the presumption that ultimately reconciliation will occur. Before asking for forgiveness, Harper asserts that with the apology the government is "now joining" Indigenous peoples in healing from the residential school system, and later states that strengthened Indigenous communities contribute "to a stronger Canada for all of us" (337). In his doing so, the necessity of asking for forgiveness is glossed over and the temporal terms of this relationship are determined for Indigenous peoples, with the state now present in Indigenous healing and their incorporation into a "stronger Canada" as the future. Assuming the acceptance of the apology refigures the relationship of the nation-state to Indigenous peoples and the past, allowing "the imagined community of Canada to see itself as one step closer to expiating the racialized colonial encounters of the past" (Mackey 49; see also Chrisjohn et al. on refusing the apology). Indeed, in its focus on specific assimilatory policies rather than the ubiquitous wrongs and harms of colonialism, the apology gives the impression that residential schools were an "aberration" (Dominello 295), a misleading and exculpatory rhetorical move that situates the "wrong" in bad laws and "situates bad laws in the past" (Giannacopoulos 341). As in many other official apologies, the statement of contrition functions temporally to manage "the present and future by prescribing an idealized teleology of national healing through which the state's performance of contrition demands performative responses from those marginalized subjects it addresses—responses that reduce forgiveness to acquiescence to the colonial status quo" (Wakeham 6). In offering apology unilaterally, the state determines the terms of its regret for its actions and how they are to be understood and remembered. In assuming the apology's acceptance, it also seeks to articulate what the relationship between the state and Indigenous peoples looks like both at the time of apology and in its wake.

How then might the time of redress be understood differently, challenging the state's unilateral articulation of its progression from unenlightened past to redeemed present and unified future? How might redress be read as something that, despite acts of rhetorical containment, is nonetheless capable of being opened out for more contested relationships by those groups being apologized to? Henderson and Wakeham are careful to note that the culture of redress "might also serve as the site wherein these norms are questioned, reconfigured, and disputed" (*Reconciling Canada* 10), and I want to suggest that this might occur through the "temporal fitfulness" of the language of redress. In her discussion of the time of international human rights law, Fleur Johns notes that human rights, much like aspects of the culture of redress, have encouraged "a progressive temporality marked out in human rights terms ... moving away from rights-infringing pasts towards rights-respecting futures" (56). At the same time, aspects of rights discourse, including documents such as the International Covenant on Civil and Political Rights, also work to disrupt such progressivist logics. Human rights law demands that states stop certain actions and that they undertake others; it alternates between immediate rights compliance by states and more vague, future expectations (52), or it frames rights concerns as timeless, while also presenting rights ideals as not reflected in the present (44). Rather than a simplistic progressivism, then, Johns suggests the possibility of reading human rights law through its "temporal fitfulness," the ways in which it simultaneously "links, sequences, and periodizes; elsewhere it seeks to arrest a temporal flow" (41).

Such thinking echoes certain Indigenous perspectives on time. Mark Rifkin, for example, suggests the reparative possibilities for Indigenous peoples of "contest[ing] the inevitability of time's singularity" (47). Arguing instead for an attentiveness to "temporal multiplicity" (ix), he posits how a focus on Indigenous frames of reference in the experience of time might decouple Indigenous peoples from a colonizing settler time, and so foreground Indigenous temporal sovereignty. Grace Dillon also describes a more complex, non-linear idea of time in her notion of "Native slipstream." Drawing the concept from Indigenous science fiction, Dillon describes Native slipstream as viewing "time as pasts, presents, and futures that flow together like currents in a navigable stream" ("Imagining" 3). Rather than a progressivist trajectory, Native slipstream posits the simultaneous co-existence of multiple modes of temporal experience. Native slipstream also, Dillon suggests, raises possibilities for alternate world-making, as it "allows authors to recover the Native space of the past, to bring it to the attention of contemporary readers, and to build better futures" ("Imagining" 4; see also Dillon's "*Miindiwag*"). Acknowledging this, Dillon suggests, like Johns and Rifkin, the possibilities that an attentiveness to temporal multiplicity, fitfulness, and disruption can offer for conceiving time differently, and so for responding to forms of what Huebener terms "temporal discrimination, the entrenched belief that one particular model of time is natural, desirable, and superior to other models of time" (69).

Temporal fitfulness is, I would argue, also present in the language and practices of redress, and offers a possibility for understanding differently the time of redress as more temporally complex than an act of closure stemming from the move between "past" wrongs, "present" acts in remedy, and "future" redressed relationships. Such a reimagining was the focus of comments made in response to the Prime Minister's apology by Beverley Jacobs, President of the Native Women's Association of Canada. Jacobs gives thanks for the apology, but she also demands recognition of the consequences of colonialism and holds the government to account for responding to these consequences in the future. Disrupting the potential for redress to manage wrongs and render them as past, she claims the right to an ongoing partnership with the government to address colonial harm—a right that invokes the mutuality of treaty ignored in the apology and that disrupts any presumption of foreclosure—and demands to know "[w]hat is it that this government is going to do in the future to help our people?" (339). Such a rethinking of the time of redress does not assume progression and resolution: Jacobs holds as an open question whether or not there is indeed a future relationship between Indigenous peoples and the state, post-apology. The Calls to Action issued by the Truth and Reconciliation Commission of Canada frame past and ongoing harms through future-oriented "calls" to a multiplicity of bodies and institutions to urge reconciliatory actions. While the term "colonization" is used only once, in reference to the role of church parties to the Settlement Agreement, the Commission's calls nonetheless address a range of the consequences of colonialism in Canada, at once speaking to the expansive legacy of residential schooling and the present, future, and contingent actions necessary to begin to enable redress. Progression is reframed here too; as a "call to action," a redressed future cannot be assumed. Instead, there is a hope, or a demand, but not an inevitability. The Indian Residential Schools Settlement Agreement similarly challenges, at moments, this presumption of closure. While the time of financial compensation is legalized and limited (Government of Canada, "Indian Residential Schools"), other aspects, notably of "Health and Healing," underscore a nexus with "former" students of residential schools, while also emphasizing that harm to these students is ongoing and has extended throughout families and communities, producing an "intergenerational trauma" (Government of Canada, "Indian Residential Schools Resolution Health Support Program"). Residential school survivors thus occupy a position at once in the past, present, and future; the wrongs they have suffered similarly cannot only be located in them as individuals. The Harper apology itself undertakes aspects of this fitfulness, moving, despite its vision of a redressed, "stronger Canada" (Harper 337), to acknowledge the atemporality of intergenerational harm and the potential irresolution of redress as a "journey" (336). In both its state and non-state manifestations, then, the culture of redress offers different ways of conceiving of recompense and remedy, ways that are not necessarily delimited by the ideological and temporal rhetorics of official apologies—indeed, ways that may challenge these from within—and ways that can at times rupture an otherwise progressivist or foreclosing discourse.

Literature and the Time of Remedy

In the space remaining, I suggest extending these complicating temporalities of redress by considering how certain literary works have represented the harms caused by state wrongs in ways that do not uncritically relegate them to "sad chapters" of history. Literature has long formed a central part of the culture of redress. In parliamentary discussions at the announcement of the

Japanese Canadian Redress Agreement, for example, the leader of the New Democratic Party, Ed Broadbent, referenced Kogawa's novel *Obasan* to illustrate the "profound, serious human suffering" of the internment (Canada 1986–88, 15: 19501); in turn, Kogawa's novels *Itsuka* and *Emily Kato* represent both the parliamentary announcement of redress and Broadbent's speech. There is, of course, a great deal of cultural meaning contained in such statements, notably that literature will make people more understanding of, and perhaps more empathetic to, the suffering of others. As Suzanne Keen notes, the novel's vaunted capacity to produce empathy, and so the social benefit of empathy for an often distant other, "offers an almost magical guarantee of fiction's worthiness" (62). Such a "heavy freight" (64) perhaps also forms part of the motivation for the "#IndigenousReads" aspect of the Canadian government's reconciliation program (notably, the Truth and Reconciliation Commission also had a reading list, including fiction and nonfiction works). #IndigenousReads promotes literature by Indigenous writers with the stated aim that "the Government of Canada hopes to encourage reconciliation by increasing Canadians' understanding of Indigenous issues, cultures, and history" (Government of Canada, "About #IndigenousReads"). There may well be that potential, but the government's uncertain declaration of futurity, that this is a hope, is a necessary one—it cannot be assumed that a literary work *will* do this.

Nonetheless, literature might work to imagine the culture of redress differently, through its representation of the causes and consequences of state harms and story's imbrication with temporal experience (Rifkin 34). Supplementing, but also interrogating, the more "official" forms of redress, literature can undertake the critical role Len Findley posits, acting as an alternative "where redress can and should be pursued in multiple sites and media, and in registers ranging from the sober to the impassioned" (217). As *Slash* and *The Electrical Field* demonstrate, literary works offer such an alternative by illustrating state wrongs and the harms they have produced in individuals and communities, resisting the rhetoric of closure that is often a part of the culture of redress by insisting on the persistence of those wrongs and harms.

Okanagan author Jeanette Armstrong's novel *Slash* engages with the experience and consequences of residential schooling by placing the schools within the larger context of colonialism and emphasizing their pervasive personal, communal, and intergenerational effects. At the beginning of the novel, the protagonist, Slash, then Tommy Kelasket, is warned that residential school "made people mean inside from being lonely, hungry and cold. He said that kids were even beat up for talking Indian. He told us some other stuff about what happened to some of the girls that was real bad" (Armstrong 3). This fleeting, early reference to residential schools serves as a frame for the narrative that follows. A symptom of colonialism, the more immediate harms of residential schooling—the abuse, "being lonely, hungry and cold"—are also entrenched, persisting across time in the individual, social, and intergenerational harms of people made "mean." Armstrong's argument, to which she returns throughout the novel, is that the wrongs of colonialism are both specific and cumulative acts and harms, and continue to be exacted on Indigenous peoples. Thus, they are incapable of being simplistically, singly, or definitively redressed. As the activist Elsie argues, speaking of the diseases that decimated Indigenous communities after contact, "the colonizers used it to their advantage and continue to use the disadvantaged conditions as a means of control. It is oppression being exercised on a people weakened and defenceless. That did happen. That continues to happen" (72).

This recognition of the multiplicity of wrongs and harms (of diseases and ongoing oppression, of being abused and being made mean) and of a corresponding temporal collapse of the causes of these harms ("[t]hat did happen. That continues to happen") illustrates what Nancy Van Styvendale describes as trans/historical trauma: "[c]umulative, collective, intergenerational, and intersubjective ... [it] exceeds any attempt to fix its location or define its event, even as it demands our attention to historically specific atrocities" (203). For Van Styvendale, the term *trans/historical* allows attention to the manifold nature of the traumas inflicted by colonialism, "repeated in multiple epochs and, in this sense, exceed[ing] its historicity, conventionally understood as its singular location in the past" (204). What *Slash* illustrates, in its insistence on the permeating, persistent presence of colonial wrongs, including but not limited to residential schools, land theft, the imposition of capitalism, and the abrogation of Indigenous sovereignty, is the impossibility of an easy location of colonial wrongs as past. Rather, they are multiple and extensive, suggesting the impossibility of simplistic means of redressing them and so of definitive closure. Hostile to discourses of rights as assimilatory tools (Armstrong 205), *Slash* suggests instead its own, more temporally complex, response, by turning back to an Indigenous past from the perspective of the present. It is not an ahistorical break like the one that characterizes Harper's contemporary recognition that actions undertaken by past governments were wrong; *Slash* suggests instead a productive, critical temporal continuum: "[t]here were young people who were very aware of what was Indian and what wasn't. They were rebuilding a worldview that had to work in this century, keeping the values of the old Indian ways. To me that was more important right than anything else" (191). Faced with trans/historical wrongs that are impossible to render only as single events, *Slash* suggests something equally temporally complex and meaningful, an Indigenous culture that is simultaneously of the past and present. Notably, it is also a response that cannot be contained within the closure of official apology and redress; rejecting the place of the state, it neither asks for state sanction nor offers forgiveness.

Kerri Sakamoto's novel *The Electrical Field* offers another way of conceiving differently of the relationship between state wrongs, harm, redress, and time. Published ten years after the signing of the Redress Agreement, but set in the 1970s, the novel paradoxically evaluates Japanese-Canadian redress from before it happens. Rather than assume a post-redress position of closure, the expectation, as Marlene Goldman writes, that "Japanese Canadians are expected to relinquish their attachment to an unjust past that is supposedly over and done with" (384), Sakamoto instead stresses the ongoing nature of the harms created by internment and the possibility that redress may not be capable of providing remedy for them. Sakamoto's protagonist, Asako Saito, lives an isolated existence in Ontario. Interned as a child, she repeatedly returns to her experience of the camps, and her brother's death there, from the novel's present. For Asako, despite her claim that "[w]hat's past is past," the past of the internment never is: she immediately notes that this is a "meaningless phrase" and another character, the redress activist Yano, urges that she "[n]ever say that. Never" (22). Instead, the internment constantly returns to Asako and other Japanese-Canadian characters in the novel, a temporal disruption that suggests the impossibility of confining the past to the past, and the necessity of "the need to revisit the internment and re-evaluate our current responses" (Visvis 68).

From its position post-redress, *The Electrical Field* warns against a forgetting about the internment that may come with "an evolutionary continuity that encourages audiences to assume the past is past, that it is part of an anachronistic moment, and so fails to have any relevance to the present. This ... brings to a halt the ongoing social dialogue between the past and present, a dialogue that innately encourages remembrance" (Visvis 71). Redress in *The Electrical Field* is rather a site of contestation, constantly under scrutiny. For Asako, the public nature of redress will do little to close or remedy what has happened:

> I had no wish to share in his anger, or to make others share in mine; to blame
> the government, the camps, the war, the man they may or may not have named

that hill after [William Lyon Mackenzie King]. For what life did or did not give to me. There would be no end to it.

My bitterness belonged to no one but myself. I did not share it with strangers; I did not hold them accountable. For these were private matters; family matters. (Sakamoto 110)

Even as she refuses to engage with redress activism, refuses to hold the government to account, Asako acknowledges the pervasive consequence of the internment, recognizing that there can be "no end" to that accountability. Seen as a private matter, the harms of the internment foreclose the possibility of both community activism and community healing. Redress must always be incomplete; it cannot provide resolution to either individuals or a community riven by the wrongs of government action. Instead, *The Electrical Field* suggests the necessity of constantly revisiting the internment and its harms, of recognizing that "the wound endures; for some, justice, redress, and personal and social harmony are not an option, and the interment and its effects remain an ongoing reality with which we need to engage" (Visvis 77). The novel's engagement, from temporal positions both before and after redress, insists upon the necessity of returning to these harms, of resisting the finality endorsed by the casual and careless—"People say it wasn't so bad"—by simultaneously questioning and insisting: "But it was bad, wasn't it, Saito-san?" (Sakamoto 258).

Generic differences are important; literature cannot supplant law's institutional entrenchment, just as law struggles to produce the representational complexity of harm that literature may more successfully mediate, and neither operates in quite the same manner as the broad, overtly public space of political discourse. Despite their differences, however, these multiple aspects of the culture of redress underscore the temporal complexity that characterizes redress and the conflicting discourses that compose it, such as how redress may manifest a state desire to resolve the past and to articulate from that a national future. At the same time, the culture of redress also offers the temporal ruptures that can provoke more complex understandings of the nature of the wrongs committed by the state, of ongoing and intergenerational harm even at the moment of apology, and of personal, communal, and national stories that tell these wrongs and harms differently, as pervasive and unresolvable. These ruptures underscore the apparent impossibility of achieving redress where it is postulated simplistically as closure. They further emphasize the necessity not only for the state to recognize and respond meaningfully to the harms it has caused, but also for this to form a perpetual part of the stories Canada tells about itself, including, importantly, in times of national celebration and in rhetorics of the national future. An attention to the temporality of redress, then, establishes the need for such fitful under-standings of the time of wrongs and harms as a means of recognizing and rewriting rhetorics of closure. And it demonstrates the necessity of an atten-tiveness to the many stories that compose the culture of redress, told and untold, in any attempt to articulate and to respond to the violence on which the Canadian state is formed and persists.

NOTE

1 See sections a–f for details of the agreement's specific terms.

CHAPTER FOUR

Modified Seeds and Morphemes: Going from Farm to Page

Laura Moss

Upon the occasion of the 150-year anniversary of Confederation, the Government of Canada invested a total of $610 million in incremental funding in programs that "celebrated what it means to be Canadian" ("Canada 150"). The Canadian Heritage website for "Canada 150" proudly proclaimed that, during 2017, alongside an emphasis on "engaging and inspiring youth, celebrating diversity and encouraging inclusion, [and] establishing a spirit of reconciliation with Indigenous peoples" was a focus on "discovering Canada's natural beauty and strengthening environmental awareness" (Canadian Heritage). It is this "environmental awareness" that I want to pursue in this chapter, particularly as it relates to agricultural, specifically seed, practices and biotechnology. I hazard a guess that for many environmentally aware people in Canada who recognize the dangers of climate change, over-logging, oil extraction and transportation, hydro-electric expansion, water pollution, factory farming, and the genetic modification of food, "strengthening environmental awareness" means something rather different than what it does for Canadian Heritage during Canada 150 events. The celebratory tone of the Canada 150 material contrasts markedly with the sharply critical tenor of many community groups, activists, and artists who were and have been well aware of the effects of changes to resource management on the environment long before the sesquicentennial and who are likely more interested in climate justice than in the platitudes of government programming.[1]

In this chapter, I turn to three writers whose work impugns such platitudes, as they consider seeds and changing seed practices critically and creatively. I focus particularly on literary forms—specifically palimpsests, linguistic modification, and direct quotation—to show how artistic engagements can draw attention to a competing multiplicity of perspectives on environmental issues and to open space for strong critique. I begin with Robert Kroetsch, who, in the mid-1970s, recognized the poetic potential in the rather unpoetic topic of seeds and family farming, as he set the historical object of the seed catalogue underneath personal history; I turn next to Rita Wong, who, thirty years later, modified morphemes in her poetry collection *forage* to mimic, and thus excoriate, the genetic modification of plants and to hold corporate agribusinesses accountable; and finally, I consider how in her verbatim docudrama *Seeds*, Annabel Soutar lays bare the patent infringement case of chemical giant Monsanto against Saskatchewan farmer Percy Schmeiser to expose the complexities of intellectual property rights. I want to consider the relationships between environmentally conscientious writing and agriculture, and the intersections of, broadly, biotechnology and art. Examining creative depictions of seeds helps us consider stories that need to be told about changing local environments and their relationship to big business. To do so, I travel 535 kilometres from Kroetsch's Heisler, Alberta, and 551 kilometres from McKenzie Seeds' Brandon, Manitoba, to Percy Schmeiser's Bruno, Saskatchewan.

The call for papers for the Untold Stories of the Past 150 Years conference, held at University College Dublin in April 2017, asked us to "consider those narratives that, until recently, have been suppressed or held considerably less attention in public forums and debate" ("The Craig Dobbin Chair"). Forty years ago, when Kroetsch published *Seed Catalogue*, he was driven by a similar mandate. The narratives he saw as suppressed were those of the places and people of his youth in western Canada. In his essay, "On Being an Alberta Writer," Kroetsch makes an impassioned case for the need to root the untold stories of settlement and farming in local sedimental layers of land and history. "I had to tell a story," he says, "I responded to those discoveries of absence, to that invisibility, to that silence, by knowing I had to make up a story. *Our story*" (73, emphasis original). In *Seed Catalogue*, Kroetsch rendered into poetry what he saw as the untold stories of settlement and farming, family and community, local land and natural history. "The garden gives us shape," Kroetsch argued as he approached these stories through the extended metaphor of seeds (qtd. in W. Campbell 17). Voices that span generations haunt Kroetsch's long poem as the speaker lovingly recalls his mother in the vegetable garden—"bring me the radish seeds, my mother whispered" (11). The poem asks variant questions: *"How do you grow a gardener?"* (15), *"How do you grow a prairie town?"* (23), and several times, *"How do you grow a poet?"* (29, 31, 33), ending with *"How/do you grow a garden?"* (45). Seeds resonate, both figuratively and literally. *Seed Catalogue* palimpsestically imposes the pages of the *McKenzie Seed Catalogue* source text under personal memories, tall tales, facts, legal documents, and family stories. In the process of bringing together what Kroetsch has called the "particulars of place," he narrates layers of rural Alberta and prairie history with 1970s-style postmodern incredulity and aplomb. The poem is powerful in its assertion of presence and the validity of storytelling in this context.

When Kroetsch set out to render his farm, his family, and his province in poetry, other stories remained quiet. While *Seed Catalogue* records, quite gleefully, the absence of European art, philosophy, and environmental landmarks on the prairies—repeating *"the absence of ... "* twenty-two times in one stanza (23–25)—Kroetsch elides other kinds of silences. It is ironic, but not surprising in its historical milieu, that in a poem so intent on detailing the absences of Albertan history, Kroetsch neglects to acknowledge the Treaty Six territories where his Heisler farm was located. Further, he problematically fails to recognize complicity in his homestead's displacement of Indigenous populations, to question the naturalization of settlement and farming in that land, to consider the voices of those who came before his own in that place, or to think of Indigenous contemporaries elsewhere. The passing references to Indigenous people in *Seed Catalogue* come in the form of a racial and gendered slur and in the speaker's brief attempt to decipher historical traces left on the land. Since the publication of *Seed Catalogue* over forty years ago, many Indigenous and non-Indigenous writers (including Maria Campbell, Marilyn Dumont, Marvin Francis, Louise Bernice Halfe, and Gregory Scofield, and Lorna Crozier, Aritha Van Herk, Suzette Mayr, and Hiromi Goto, among others) have told stories of places that overlap geographically, if not always experientially, with those of Kroetsch. While Kroetsch worked hard to carve space for more voices from rural Albertan farmscapes in his poetry and fiction, he also ended up silencing Indigenous and other voices. With so many voices to choose from, I had not considered *Seed Catalogue* for years. I recently returned to it, however, to take seriously the seeds of the title and to compare Kroetsch's approach with current representations of seeds: pre- and post-introduction of the genetic modification of organisms (GMO). I am not arguing that Kroetsch was a proto-environmentalist in *Seed Catalogue*, but rather that in this 1970s poem, environmental awareness is about asserting presence on the land, even if we now recognize the limitations of such an assertion.

When Turnstone Press published the first 1,000 copies of Kroetsch's long poem in 1977, the words were set in twelve-point Baskerville, printed in green ink on "Byronic Blue Brocade" paper. In the background of those original copies are screened reproductions of images, printed in the colour of burnished copper, from the McKenzie seed catalogues of 1916 and 1922 (*Seed Catalogue* 75). In its very production, the original poem asks readers to consider the materiality of the catalogue and the routes the seeds travel. Seeds and their direct market sales are present as the first layer of Kroetsch's palimpsest of origins (both figurative and literal) as the words are set on top of the commercial publication. *Seed Catalogue* opens with these lines from the poet's inspiration text, the 1917 *McKenzie Seed Catalogue*:

> *No. 176 Copenhagen Market Cabbage*: This new introduction, strictly speaking, is in every respect a thoroughbred, a cabbage of the highest pedigree, and is creating considerable flurry among professional gardeners all over the world. (4)

Consider, now, the *McKenzie Seed Catalogue* copy (online only) from 2017:

> Cabbage Early Copenhagen Market
> One of the largest early producing cabbages with wonderfully formed heads weighing 1–1.5 kg (2–3 lbs) at maturity ... An established favorite among gardeners that will continue to be loved over time for its consistent production and superb taste.

And this, Bean Improved Golden Wax (Bush), also from 2017:

> One of the most popular wax beans with very high yields on compact, bushy plants. String-free 15–18 cm (6–7") long beans with a mild buttery flavour. Rust resistant. Delicious when frenched, then steamed. [...] Sensational! Sow seed directly in soil once all danger of frost has passed.

The promissory tone of seed marketing language embedded in *Seed Catalogue* is still evident in the McKenzie catalogue a century later: continuity guaranteed, fecundity ensured. Opulent growth will come after the danger of frost has passed. Sensational! The diction of the 1917 version, with an emphasis on the "thoroughbred" nature of a cabbage that is of the "highest pedigree," suggests the pervasiveness of a colonial attitude to a social hierarchy—extended to vegetables—and the purity of breeding. This Canadian cabbage can compete on a global stage. The twenty-first-century copy is more humbly aimed at the gardener, rather than the professional gardener, and excises such hyperbolic language. Still, the main difference in catalogue copy introduced over the course of a hundred years is the presence of logos at the top of every web page that proudly state: "Packaged with fresh seeds NON GMO" and "Since 1896 Depuis 1896" arched over a red maple leaf with all its nationalist connotations available.

While the catalogue copy for McKenzie Seeds has remained remarkably consistent over the century—with the notable addition of the assurances of non-GMO—the company itself has transformed. According to the "Company History" page of its website, Albert Edward McKenzie began the "Brandon Seed House" in 1896 "from a flour, grain, and feed business he inherited from his father." It was incorporated in 1906 to become A.E. McKenzie Seeds Co. Ltd. In a 1945 post-war gesture, A.E. McKenzie gave 90 percent of the company shares to the Government of Manitoba, through the McKenzie Foundation, for the "benefit of higher education," to go toward building Brandon College (later Brandon University). In 1975, the final shares were given to the government of the province so the company could be run as a Crown corporation. In 1994, the Manitoba government sold McKenzie Seeds to Regal Greetings, a non-retail mail-order catalogue company. Less than a decade later (2002), Regal sold A.E. McKenzie Co. Ltd. to the unspecified McKenzie Management Group, who in turn sold it to a Norwegian company called Jiffy International AS (2006), and it continued to operate as a division of Jiffy until 2012, when it was sold to Seed Holdings Inc. The history of McKenzie Seeds, following a trajectory from local family business to public Crown corporation to multinational conglomerate, parallels many other economic stories in Canada, and indeed across the globe. Over the 125 years that the company has been in business, there has been massive environmental change alongside economic globalization. That the company still proclaims its Canadianness in the maple leaf logo points to the desire to market the company in its history rather than its present. In so doing, it obfuscates the layers of corporate history and presumably sets out to capitalize on the connections gardeners have with local land and place. Such naturalized nationalism only tells part of the story though. When McKenzie Seeds proudly declare their products to be "NON-GMO," they are tapping into pervasive concerns about the security of genetically modified food and popular discussions of food purity and food safety. The fact that there is a law regulating that all seeds sold for the home market in Canada must be non-GMO is beside the point in marketing terms. Their safety is proclaimed to reassure customers.

Conversely, poet Rita Wong is emphatically not reassured by such proclamations in her poem sequence on GMO foods from the 2007 collection *forage*. In an interview with poet rob mclennan, Wong explains her motivation for the collection: "I want to understand what it means to act ethically in a globalized world." She asks the important question: "How do I reconcile my intent (to work toward peace and social justice) with my consumption patterns as a citizen in North America?" (mclennan). She often asks ethical questions about the relationships between science, technology, the land and water, human and non-human inhabitants, and consumer culture. Indeed, while poems such as "opium" and "sort by day, burn by night" engage contemporary ecological and global politics from the colonial history of the drug trade to the carcinogenic waste of computers and technology ("what if your pentium got dumped in guiyui village? / your garbage, someone else's cancer?" [47]), it is in the poems about the genetic engineering of seeds that Wong is especially poignant in her critique in this collection. Wong taps into concerns about the dangers of allowing corporations—explicitly, the agricultural giant Monsanto—excessive power over food, farming, and food development.

In "the girl who ate rice almost every day," dual poetic columns tell dual stories: one of a girl named "slow" in the near future who subversively farms "slow-cooking rice" fertilized by her own toxic beet-stained feces in underground sewers, and one cataloguing, verbatim, recent US patents on rice (19). This is seed cataloguing of another kind. Unlike Kroetsch's poem, Wong's poem, even when nestled in dystopic fantasy as in "the girl who ate rice," recognizes Indigenous land rights and Indigenous presence: "She wanted to know what a grain of rice grown on the land where she lived, the land of salish, musqueam, halkomelem speakers, would taste like? How could it grow?" (18). Wong locates the poem's narrative firmly in the unceded territories of the Salish and Musqueam peoples of British Columbia. The dystopic language of the left column contrasts the legal language of the patents in the right column. The act of juxtaposition reinforces the manner in which the regimentation of food on the right could indeed lead to the imagined world on the left and remediates the two.

In "the girl who ate rice almost every day," Wong employs two distinct registers of language to create linguistic subversion through abrogation of scientific language. In "canola queasy" and "nervous organism," she effectively critiques the hegemony of multinational agribusiness through linguistic mimicry with verbal and visual reflections on the genetic modification of food. Her modified language in these two poems illustrates how quickly a few key changes can render a word, or a cell, unrecognizable. Verbal splicing mimics cell splicing. In a poem surrounded by a hand-written quotation from Northrup Frye, which makes the block poem visually reminiscent of the walls of a cell (and symbolically reminiscent of a garrison), Wong begins "nervous organism" with the uncapitalized (anti-capitalist) words "jellyfish potato/ jellypo fishtato/ glow in the pork toys/ nab your crisco while it's genetically cloudy boys/" and ends with "jellypish for tato smack/ your science experiment snack yields slugfish arteries brain murmurs tumour precipitation whack" (20). The slashes are in the original, and they paradoxically offer the reader both distance and proximity at the beginning of the poem (separate but together). With the absence of the slashes in the final line, Wong speeds up the tempo of the poem to render the confusing merger of spliced elements more immediate. The seemingly absurd opening conjunction "jellyfish potato," further modified throughout the poem, is, in fact, a reiteration of an actual modified hybrid of a jellyfish and a potato. By the last line, however, it is as mutated and unrecognizable as "jellypish for tato smack" (20). In a few words, Wong powerfully spells out the health-related safety concerns of genetic modification with "slugfish arteries" and tumours alike (20). That the poem is difficult to read out loud reinforces the inarticulability of the series of changes being catalogued. To balance the abstractions of the linguistic modifications, Wong grounds the poem in political and geographic context, referring to countries and states by name and trade agreements by acronym: "hasta nasty nafta through mexico, california, oregon, washington, canada" (20). In the end, Wong condemns the mobility of "industrial food" from "basketballs of lettuce" to "avocado bullets" as mutations for profit, as she points to the artificiality of the food that is made to withstand transportation through modifications to its original genes (20).

Just as the concrete form of "nervous organism" resembles a mutating cell, Wong's "canola queasy" is surrounded by the words of Mae Wen Ho, which are visually reminiscent of a porous fence around a field of neatly planted rows of words. The framing passage from Ho reports how one variety of Monsanto's "herbicide-tolerant transgenic" genetically engineered canola seeds was pulled from the market when "unexpected properties" were found in it (qtd. in Wong 36). Wong's poem plays with the concept of "unexpected properties." Also uncapitalized, the poem begins with: "vulture capital hovers over dinner tables, covers hospitals a sorrowful shade of canola" as "false prophets hawk oily platitudes in rapacity as they engineer despair in those brilliant but foolish yellow genetically stacked prairie crops" (36). The opening image of hovering "vulture capital" ominously entwines GMO canola production, health management, and corporate greed. Instead of modifying morphemes in this poem as she does in "nervous organism," Wong modifies syntax to create run-on sentences replete with unexpected conjunctions (mimicking corporate mergers) and logical fallacies. She also reworks clichés, relying on the reader's recognition of their mutated origins: "don't shoot the messy angels with your cell-arranging blasts, don't document their properties in order to pimp them" (36). The direct address of the final line in the poem, "hey bloated monstrosity," invokes readerly complicity in the corporatization of farming (36). Genetically engineered canola in this context makes the reader queasy, meaning both unsettled and nauseous. It is in the very messiness of the language in this poem, where some of the conjunctions seem particularly nonsensical, that Wong embeds her criticisms of corporate agriculture, fears about health, and the ugly potential of modified seeds.

At the bottom of "canola queasy," held within the fence, we find this: "Dedicated to Percy Schmeiser, the Saskatchewan farmer harassed and sued by Monsanto because genetically engineered canola blew into his fields" (36). The tone is unflinchingly critical: "harassed" and "sued." Wong is fierce in her tactical biopolitics here. In 1997, Percy Schmeiser was sued for patent infringement, after Monsanto claimed that he had violated their intellectual property when he was found to have used their patented genetically modified canola seeds without a licence. Plants containing Roundup Ready resistance were found on a section of his farm. Monsanto owns the patent for the individual gene within the seed cell that resists Monsanto's own herbicide Roundup. Schmeiser argued that he did not knowingly retain Monsanto's patented seeds in 1997 when he harvested canola from his fields and kept back seeds to sow for the following year. Schmeiser lost in three successive court decisions, including at the level of the Supreme Court of Canada in 2004, with a 5–4 decision in favour of Monsanto. Paul Gepts asks a key question in his writing on this case: "Who owns biodiversity and how should the owners be compensated?" (1295). The question of whether living organisms, seeds, plants, and genes can be owned and protected by corporate patents on intellectual property has since been taken to the Appeal Branch of the Supreme Court.

Even though Monsanto won its patent infringement case against Schmeiser, the media has often cast the story of the small prairie farmer who takes on the giant multinational corporation as a version of the biblical David and Goliath. Monsanto sees it differently. In addition to a detailed list of seven key ways they are helping to feed the world (in keeping with their name: *Mon santo* translates to "my saint") and contributing to a sustainable planet, Monsanto's corporate website (USA) also features under the heading "Just Plain False" and subheading "Myth: Monsanto Sues Farmers When GMOs or GM Seed Is Accidentally in Their Fields" and sub-subheading "Percy Schmeiser," a page dedicated to the farmer: "He's become something of a folk hero in some circles, playing the role of David to Monsanto's Goliath. He ... is a frequent speaker around the world at events hosted by groups opposed to agricultural biotechnology. / The truth is Percy Schmeiser is not a hero. He's simply a patent infringer who knows how to tell a good story." While Wong abrogates the language of science in her poetry to comment on its potential dangers, Monsanto uses the language of narrative, framing Schmeiser as a good story-teller—but "not a hero"—to take control of the narratives of biotechnology.

Annabel Soutar's documentary play *Seeds* takes up Schmeiser's good story and the question of his heroics. In the form of verbatim theatre, however, *Seeds* assumes more of the posture of objectivity than either Monsanto's web-site or Wong's poems, although reliability of fact and precarity of positioning are challenged throughout. Soutar uses the words of Schmeiser and Mon-santo's representatives, among others, to ask questions and provoke debate. In "A Note on the Text," Soutar points out that the text is "made up primar-ily of verbatim language from interview testimony, court trial transcript, and newspaper articles" that she has sampled and incorporated into the dialogue of *Seeds* (xi). Each of the main actors in the law case has a part in the play and each remains on stage at all times. Percy, his wife, Louise, neighbours, sci-entists, lawyers, and spokespeople for Monsanto all interact and speak. The only non-verbatim sections of *Seeds* come from a character aptly named Playwright, a pregnant journalist. That she is pregnant with her own grow-ing seed highlights the fact that even verbatim playwrights can't escape the seed metaphor. Playwright conducts interviews on stage and fills in know-ledge gaps with research from beyond the play, but she also speculates on the unborn baby's potentially impeded growth and the uncertainty of its future with a diet of GMO food. She guides us through information and mediates from both inside and outside the story. Other than the artistic interventions of Playwright, in keeping with the form of "verbatim theatre," the exact words of the original utterances are replicated (but sometimes reordered). The play relies on this reordering, juxtaposition, and remediation to create points of conflict and to highlight unusual conjunctions. By creatively juxtaposing partial facts and challenging elided knowledge, Soutar tactically pushes ques-tions around biosecurity and food safety without fully supporting Schmeiser individually. Ethical engagement trumps individual heroism here.

Act One of Soutar's play begins with Percy telling his story in the kitchen of his farmhouse. He seems like a humble farmer who has been treated unfairly by an agrochemical giant. During the first act of the play, narrative sympathies lie with Schmeiser. In the second and final act, the playwright introduces ambiguities into Percy's testimony. She also juxtaposes his testi-mony with that of several scientists, neighbours, and acquaintances who call his reputation and motivation into question. The play leaves the audience with many more questions than answers. In an interview with Soutar, Chris Nuttall-Smith notes how he found Schmeiser's character to be "weaselly" and how "it wasn't clear by the end if maybe he did just plant those seeds and then lie about it" (Nuttall-Smith). Soutar responds by pointing to the benefits of aesthetic engagement with fact: "for me, that was gold in terms of storytelling. It's a much more interesting and theatrical story if someone who you think is a perfect hero at the beginning of the play turns out to potentially have fabricated this entire story. I love endings like that, where you're just not sure, because it forces the viewer to do their own research, to make their own assessment" (Nuttall-Smith). She adds, "But was it frustrating to activists who got behind him? Absolutely." It is important for Soutar to draw attention to the artistic nature of the play and to show how it is not simply anti-GMO activism masquerading as docudrama. It is about raising questions, productively, through storytelling. By provoking questions, Soutar attempts to bring awareness to important environmental issues without being overly prescriptive.

The artistic director of the Crow's Theatre in Toronto and the director of the 2012 production (as a co-production with Porte Parole, Montreal), Chris Abraham, maintained an emphasis on questions by having actors in lab coats approach audience members with queries as the patrons entered the theatre. Joel Fishbane describes how the cast introduced themselves using their real names, as the viewers took their seats. Echoing the question asked by the Supreme Court, patrons were asked, "What is life?" and the answers were projected onto a screen that stretched across the back of the stage. Abraham notes, "I wanted the audience to understand the role the media had in the transmission of the story ... Multimedia was a window into the way we ourselves were re-constructing reality" (qtd. in Fishbane 83). Breaking the fourth wall so early in the theatre experience reinforced the audience's inescapable participation in the conversation around intellectual property, GMO food, and farmers' rights. The effect was to break down distance between the subject, cast, and audience and to reinforce communality and even complicity. As Fishbane notes, "Often, in verbatim theatre, we are asked to pretend the actors are the people they're quoting. This imposes a form of fictional reality on the piece, one which may distance us from the facts being presented. With Abraham's technique, however, this fiction is instantly dismissed. The actors *admit* they're actors right from the start: they present themselves as a group of friends who have been altered by a story and are now telling it to us because it's something they think we should hear" (83). This admission of performance also powerfully draws in the audience. No one is outside the play. By basing an artistic experience on a case from the news and high-lighting its artificiality, its performance as documentary theatre, the 2012 production ensured audience proximity to the topic and raised awareness without being prescriptive.

When *Seeds* was first produced in 2005, the story focused on Schmeiser. For the 2012 production, Soutar updated the play to reflect advances in science. Between the original staging and the subsequent production, more scientific evidence came to light and was added into the play by Soutar. As Soutar notes, the epilogue "includes information about events in the summer of 2012 relating to the global debate about genetically modified seeds" (xi). In the printed script of the play based on the 2012 version, Soutar directs future productions to update the science of biotechnology and the GMO debates before each new staging. "This information should be modified ... to describe events that are current at the time of production and relevant to present-day audiences" (xi). This is key. It is a fluid play, a play in process. Soutar asks future directors to be responsible for evolving knowledge about food science. Telling untold stories, we need to recognize how the stories come to us, how we sit in relation to them, and how they change over time.

With *Seeds*, Soutar participates in a long tradition of documentary theatre. The form has often been used as a space for social commentary and to bring ethical issues in contemporary stories to light. Soutar is self-reflexive in her use of the genre, as she compares documentary theatre to biotechnology.

> PLAYWRIGHT: (*to audience*) I've become interested in the parallels between the work I do making documentary theatre and the work that biotech companies do making genetically modified seeds.
>
> To begin with, we are both in the business of ... life. We use life as raw material and we modify it in order to produce something that we then call our "invention."
>
> We both describe our mission as "making the world a better place"—Monsanto by feeding a hungry and growing world; me by telling stories in which a multiplicity of voices reflects something I perceive to be important about the world. But we are also both susceptible along the way to ... outside influence. (71)

By recognizing structural parallels here, Soutar again breaks the fourth wall and shares responsibility, even the possibility of complicity, with her audience. Although she is outwardly sympathetic to Monsanto by finding commonality in "invention," she ends with a warning about susceptibility to "influence" (71). The undefined word "influence" sits heavily at the end of this speech as the next lines turn to Playwright, who is having an ultrasound to discover the sex of her baby. One suggestion is perhaps that she is influenced by a concern about the future, about the effects of modified invention on her growing seed. Another suggestion is that she recognizes her own potential to be influenced by both sides of the GMO debates. In her work on *Seeds*, Tania Aguila-Way argues that Soutar infuses the documentary play with an "ecological form of avant-garde experimentalism" in order to create a different kind of space to call multiple perspectives into question. For Aguila-Way, the addition of avant-garde aesthetics to the documentary theatre form helps to create a public sphere forum where the "fears and concerns of mainstream anti-GMO activism can not only be acknowledged and debated but also brought under scrutiny to create a more nuanced understanding of the stakes involved in the seed sovereignty debate" (22). Soutar recognizes the dangers of influence even when telling stories in a multiplicity of voices. No story is neutral.

The passages highlighting the modification process of invention with both documentary theatre and biotechnology also remind us that even with verbatim speech, the presentation of voices is mediated and the knowledge it accesses is remediated. Soutar's play lays bare the insidiousness of "outside influence" and in effect points out the unreliability of transmitted and modified fact. I want to pause here to think about Soutar's work through the lens of agnotology, a study that comes from the history of science and technology: "the study of culturally produced ignorance or doubt and the manufacturing of inaccurate or misleading scientific data ... [that] is concerned with censorship and suppression of knowledge through willful intention, neglect, or forgetfulness" (qtd. in "A Conversation with Ruth Ozeki"). I was introduced to agnotology in an interview with novelist Ruth Ozeki, author of *All Over Creation* (a novel in part about the dangers of big business and farming). In reference to her novel *A Tale for the Time Being*, she notes that, "although agnotology usually is concerned with scientific data, I think it applies nicely to the documentation of women's history, or the lack thereof. We can learn a lot by studying what isn't. It seems important to me to leave the gaps and holes, rather than trying to fill them in" (Ozeki). This is a kind of return to valuing postmodern gaps and aporia, reminiscent of the work of Kroetsch, in fact, to provide incredulity to master narratives. We see it productively in *Seeds* as well. By juxtaposing partial speech and quoted facts, Soutar's play illuminates how individual speech can be implicated in censorship through omission. It is up to each member of the audience to decide if we hear the words of Monsanto and Schmeiser agnatologically.

Theatre historian Attilio Favorini argues that "documentary theatre is highly relevant and resonant in societies that create and consume contemporary news as aggressively as we do" (n.p.) While the genre of documentary theatre tends to foreground documentary elements over aesthetic concerns, Soutar reminds us that the documentary evidence is still aesthetically mediated in a play. With the advent of "alternative facts" and "post-truth," the conjunction of art and politics in a play such as Seeds resonates now as it asks how much you can trust even verbatim speech, if out of context, and calls conceptual objectivity into question. Not only does the play build awareness about the issues raised in biotechnology and agriculture, it also asks us to consider our own positioning and to take information that is shared as fact, but modified, with a grain of salt.

Fishbane observes in his discussion of the 2012 production of Seeds that "Schmeiser and Monsanto argued over the plant a seed grows into, but the script is more interested in the seeds themselves—and the impact they have on those who sow them" (83). I too am interested in the seeds themselves and on how they circulate in and under creative writing in Canada, often to afford a meta-commentary for critical biopolitics. The creative works under consideration here each offer a productive way into heightening the environmental awareness championed in the Canada 150 directives, but each does so through specifically literary means. Kroetsch and Soutar layer seeds, family stories, and facts, palimpsestically, with modified gaps left for what is still unknown, while Wong layers modified scientific language to mimic scientific manipulation of life forms. Together these three writers help tell some of the untold stories of environmental change and the corporatization of agriculture, important stories for 2017 and well beyond.

The necessity of telling stories of environmental urgency was recently brought home when, on August 16, 2019, Rita Wong was sentenced to 28 days in prison. She had been found to have violated a court injunction as she sat in peaceful protest at the Trans Mountain pipeline gates in Burnaby, British Columbia, in 2018, and she received the maximum sentence allowed for such an offence. At her sentencing, Wong issued a statement:

> I did this because we're in a climate emergency, and since the Federal government has abdicated its responsibility to protect us despite full knowledge of the emergency, it became necessary to act. We are in imminent peril if we

consider the rate of change we are currently experiencing from *a geological per-spective*—we are losing species at an alarming rate and facing mass extinction due to the climate crisis that humans have caused. This is the irreparable harm I sought to prevent, which the court, the Crown, and corporations also have a responsibility to prevent. (cited in Smith)

Wong justifies her embodied activism, and continued presence at the Trans Mountain site, with a defence of necessity in the face of a climate emergency. Such an argument is entirely consistent with her creative work and has long been an important part of her artistic expression. In her poetry, she writes about individual responsibility to the environment and to the communities in which we live, whether affected by GMOs or pipelines. Wong's artistic practice and her community engagement, even so far as she puts her body on the line in protest and imprisonment, are indelibly linked. She effectively uses both her art and her physical presence to raise awareness of the current environmental emergency and the fact that it is, as she says, "necessary to act." Wong's effort to prevent climate destabilization and destruction through the complement of public protest and poetry strengthens environmental awareness as no government program could ever do.

NOTES

An early version of this research was presented at the Untold Stories of the Past 150 Years conference in Dublin, Ireland, in April 2017. Thank you to the organizers, particularly Linda Morra and Paul Halferty, for the opportunity to share this work and for organizing an important collection of untold stories. Further drafts were presented at the Mikinaakominis / TransCanadas: Literature, Justice, Relation conference held at the University of Toronto in May 2017 and at the invitation of the Centre for Creative Writing and Oral Culture, and the Centre for Globalization Studies, at the University of Manitoba in October 2017.

1 Since the Canada 150 celebrations, the government has continued to present a contradictory stance on environmental issues. For example, on June 17, 2019, the House of Commons passed a motion to declare a national climate emergency in Canada and the very same week the Liberal government approved the $9.3 billion Trans Mountain pipeline expansion project, which many argue will lead to increased greenhouse gases, a sevenfold increase in tanker traffic, and an increase in danger to the marine environment on the BC coast.

SECTION TWO

Unbecoming Narratives

CHAPTER FIVE

Landscape, Citizenship, and Belonging

Shani Mootoo

1.

I'd like to use my personal journey from landed immigrant on arrival in Canada, to present-day Canadian citizen to explore what it might take—and what it might mean—for people like me, a first-generation immigrant writer of colour, to write fiction in Canada and have it published here, and what "belonging" and "outsiderness" might mean today to, and for, diasporic writers who've made Canada their home, their base.

Right away, I'll say that, short of writing what would have to be a big book on the subject, there is bound to be confusion about this notion that immigrant writers are outsiders. The generalization is made suspect by the number of us who recently have been on prizewinners' lists, who have been on juries for prizes, and who have sat on funding juries in the arts. Many of us have positions of tenure at universities. Many are at the dinner tables of the big parties. And yet, I maintain that the subjects of our work, in general, tend to hearken back to the places from which we come. This makes me think of us as having no more than a foot in the door—not the door of the literary scene or industry, but the door of the country, the door of the land in which we have chosen to make our home.

Out of what may seem at first like disparate thoughts and snatches of this and that, a bit of history, and a recalling of periods of activism, I hope to cobble together a picture of what it has been like to juggle one's identity in an age when ideas, rights, permissions, and (what were long-standing) norms are shifting daily, and just about everything is being re-sorted and challenged, day by day.

I grew up in the Caribbean island of Trinidad, and lived there for the first twenty or so years of my life. It has been close to forty years since I left that island in the Caribbean, and I have been living and working since then as an artist and writer here in Canada.

All my books, six so far, were written in Canada. The primary publishers of all my works, save for my second novel, were Canadian publishers. I live in Ontario in a house I own with my partner; I pay taxes here; I have my medical history recorded in the health care system here; and I pay attention to what official Canada does to its variety of citizens and how it performs in the rest of the world. I enjoy the rights afforded to citizens of this country. I vote whenever I am called upon to do so, raise a placard, sign petitions, march in the street, sport a Canadian flag on my luggage when I travel, cheer for Canada during the Olympics, and feel proud when Canada and Canadians support refugees from oppressive countries, or speak out against oppressive regimes. I am affected when the rights of other Canadians are violated right here in Canada.

And yet, the place in which I've explored the themes in my writing— themes of love, friendship, family, belonging, and "outsiderness," to name a few—is primarily the one in which I spent my formative years and in which I grew up, Trinidad, the place, to reiterate, I chose to leave in my early twenties when I emigrated here. It wouldn't be far-fetched to say that my novels have been love songs to that island, a place that now no longer exists, for as I have grown and changed, so has the Trinidad I once knew so intimately.

Is it any wonder, then, that I am often labelled a Trinidadian-Canadian writer, and even, sometimes, simply as a Trinidadian writer? I can count on half the fingers of one hand the number of times I've heard and seen myself referred to as a Canadian writer.

Judging from the works of a good number of other immigrant writers, this kind of hyphenated identity labelling pertains not only to me, but to many— not all, but to many—of us who were not born here, but who have made this place home: Cecil Forster (*Independence*), Pamela Mordecai (*Red Jacket*), and Dionne Brand (*At the Full and Change of the Moon* and *What We All Long For*) come to mind, and so do Ramabai Espinet (*The Swinging Bridge*), Ana Rodriguez Machado, Anita Rau Badami, Shyam Selvadurai, Madeleine Thien, and Rawi Hage, to name a few. Often, our books are set in our respective "back-home" locales but, even when the setting in which our characters live is Canada, our characters' stories tend to be predicated on what they left behind, or turn on trips they've recently taken back to their country of origin, or on dramas from back home, rehashed on the ground here in alienating environments that attempt to replicate those from afar.

When set in Canada, the stories by first-generation immigrants of colour in this country tend to have as their backdrops the underbellies of cities

(I think here of Rawi Hage's *Cockroach* and the literal underground subway rides of Dionne Brand, the cafés, and restaurants), or the city's edges, suburbs where protagonists congregate in high rises or ghettoes occupied by other immigrants. Mostly conducted in indoor spaces, it is only in these carved-out neighbourhoods, and only to themselves, that the characters, sometimes generations of them in a single house, are visible three-dimensional entities. Invariably, they are constantly trying to outrun their pasts or the confines of traditions, cultures, and families that they have travelled here with, wrestling with family secrets, or the need to be examples, or to recognize what are supposed to be opportunities unavailable to them back-home, yet almost out of reach here, or they are fighting each other and the world at large, to eke out some kind of acceptable living in a place where they are, in a word, invisible and/or suspect, outsiders. The landscape of these novels tends to be interior spaces.

Set in Canada, place is not incidental, but it is not physical and tangible either. Canada tends to be an idea. It is a land in which the novels' characters include the invisible workforce that oils the machinery that makes its cities tick, the mother, as the mother in Chariandy's *Brother*, who travels far afield to work as a janitor to make ends meet for her and her two sons; yet, it is a land in which the characters themselves cannot easily rise to the surface. The city, when portrayed, is itself a kind of insular interior space. There is no Canada except for that shown in these kinds of portrayals. The fact of the truths revealed in such scant portrayals is enough to make "Canada" an important idea, yet the language used to describe it is often shorthand, dashed-off simplistic words like snow, cold, winter jacket, mittens, scarf—signifiers for the apparent inhospitality of the new country. Weather and the accoutrements of cold-weather dressing are added-value metaphors for an oppression known in the bones by these characters, yet almost otherwise inexpressible in novels that are not meant to end up sounding like theses on immigration, race, and class.

At the same time, the simulacrum of "back-home" is shored up by the use of remembered endearing colloquialisms from our places of origin; we name foods, the aromas of foods cooking, and even shortcuts that work effectively to make communities out of characters who, in their particular back-homes, might not have cared to know one another.

To my mind, we are, in effect, all writing love songs or laments to our disappearing back-homes. If anything gets said about Canada, it is that, in this land of plenty, to which so many travelled with great hopes, success has been, for the majority, elusive. But, in these books that make it onto the general reading lists, this latter is almost incidental. It is what was lost on leaving back-home, and what of back-home was brought to this new country that are of focus.

It is often said to people who are new to the art of writing fiction, "write what you know." Perhaps this is indeed, simply, what we—those writers I mentioned, and I—are doing: merely writing what we know. The places in which we grew up have surely determined our sensibilities; they are the foundation of who we are as we are now. I suspect that it is partly for these reasons, precisely because of what we gave up, lost, or left behind, that we return always to them, that we write to and for our homelands and to the people we left.

At the same time, and in some ways, many of us authors, like the characters in our books, have yet to land truly here in Canada. It makes sense that if we, the writers, remain tied to the stories of our pasts, and of our specific communities, our roots here in Canada will remain shallow.

But is belonging here a condition that's entirely up to us to make happen? What might it even look like? How can this country ever be more than a backdrop or caricature—can it be a place in which one can immerse oneself, inhabit the trees and streams, the farmlands, the small towns, the asparagus fields, the vineyards, the locks of the Trent and Rideau Systems? Can it even be in a topic—for instance, the wind turbines debates, or land rights, or mercury poisoning in the water of Indigenous communities?

To speak of inside and outside is to create another kind of fiction. Any society has both, and these exist in a relational, contradictory, and ever-shifting way. We define ourselves as "x" in relation to "y"—which is to say that "x" (the inside) could not exist without "y" (the outside), against which it constructs its identity. There's what happens in everyday life—are you treated well or badly in a shop?—that marks your position, but that doesn't change the reality that the outsider is also inevitably a kind of insider, because his or her presence serves to construct the inside. I think here of African Americans in the USA. There's a tendency for whiteness to be defined as something monolithic in relation to, and in opposition to, blackness. We've seen this idea exploited by politicians like Trump. That such a false monolith has racist roots is a given, but it also doesn't allow room for the variation and complexity that exists in white society. Sadly, that is beside the point here. The point is that whiteness exists, and it exists as a force only because Blackness also exists, and because those who buy into such a monolithic idea of identity attempt to oppress those outside.

Lately, I have come to see the sliding-over of the land of Canada in my own fiction as emblematic of yet another kind of loss. It is the loss of a present, of the present time, because I am always living in the past, and a past that does not stretch across space and might be consequently reached by airplane, but a past that is only reached today through the imagination. If we write that past well, it might be because, I would say, that language is at its most lyrical and poetic when it is put to use to describe and conjure up that which is missed or longed for, and is that much more potent when there is a sense that that which is missed was unfairly taken from you. I may have left my back-home voluntarily, but even there I would likely have been an outsider—outside of what is acceptable, outside the norms of the place, the cultures, traditions, the notions of family, and the role of a good Indian woman in society. So, we are, as I see it, always pleading, explaining, trying through our characters to understand the ultimately un-understandable of why exactly we left—whose fault was it, ours, our families', the country's? And how we left—did we run, did we go willingly, happily, full of hope? Where we currently are—did we make the right decision, can we ever? Should we one day go back?

Nowadays, there are other related questions I ask myself: how much of what I write is fueled by my own nostalgia? How much of it is political, a form of activism, the need to tell through stories and characters of the conditions in which many immigrants live in Canada? Can one ever stop being an immigrant? Who does it serve for us to remain immigrants, to remain outsiders, even after we've been here for decades, and regardless of how many books we have published? Have writers like me learned that publishers and readers expect and want us to offer glimpses of difference, of the exotic, and subconsciously, do we give in to this expectation?

These are not academic questions, nor do they hinge on mere suppositions. I would like to use my second novel *He Drown She in the Sea* to explain. My protagonist is a Trinidadian man named Harry. The novel begins in Trinidad, where he is the son of a maid. He has become a small businessperson, but he is in love with a young woman whose family was served by his mother. Their class difference makes any romance between them impossible. Harry wants to leave Trinidad to escape this pain of love, but he won't leave until his aged and ailing mother dies. When she does die, he makes the leap. In Canada, he moves up the chain from taxi driver to owner of a thriving landscape design and maintenance business. In Canada, he transcends his original class through his accomplishments, and the rest of the story is about how he reconnects with that love of his youth, who has come to Canada for a visit, and how here they manage to bridge their class difference. She leaves her husband, and she and Harry end up together.

When I submitted my manuscript to my then-publisher McClelland & Stewart, the publisher at the time, the late Ellen Seligman, by whom every writer wanted to be published, suggested I change my story. I could keep Harry, but I should ditch, she suggested, the love story, and have Harry come to Canada; yes, that was acceptable, but have him come for economic reasons, and don't kill off the mother; have Harry leave his ailing mother in Trinidad, and let the story be about how he pined for her, his regrets about leaving her; let there be letters between them in which he tells her about his life and how he is trying to make ends meet with the hope that he could bring her here. Asked why these suggestions were being made, I was told that it would make a better story, that it would make for a story *that would sell.*

This was not my story, and my insistence on writing the story I had in mind led to it being moved from McClelland & Stewart to Grove Atlantic in the United States, where it was edited and published. But the struggle for me personally was more complicated and, in some ways, more private than a simple move from one publisher to another. On the surface, the move was so that I might stay true to my vision. Beneath the surface simmered implications of why my version might have been unacceptable, and why the suggested version was imagined to be more palatable to a mainstream Canadian audience.

I'm not accusing my then-publisher of anything except trying to help me write a book that would sell—she and others in the industry were well aware of the market in the early 2000s. As professionals, they knew what audiences were enjoying, what was selling best, and what was not. But I believe my publisher's advice is worth unpacking—why is it that an immigrant novel focused on nostalgia for back-home, an immigrant's struggle with what was lost by coming to the new country, would have sold better than one in which the immigrant triumphs—in business and in love—despite the obstacles that were to be faced? Is it possible that, in the mind of a mainstream reader, the beloved Hollywood story of triumph does not belong to, or rather does not suit, the immigrant, or at least the immigrant of colour? The preferred storyline reflects better the audience's imagined immigrant, a displaced person, someone who always longs for the place he or she left, who can never really land in this new place. In this sense, the nostalgia signalled by the writer and the writer's characters is mirrored by another kind of nostalgia that resides inside the reader who is being catered to. That reader's nostalgia is equally layered, and might include, for example, a tropical landscape in which they are indulged tourist-lords and ladies, and for a Canada where an immigrant remains an outsider, or—to be blunter—for a Canada that is white.

For many immigrant, raced, and queered artists and writers, self-identifying has not long been a privilege. Identity has been, more usually, imposed on one by others, and pertinent to the subject at hand, by the publishing and curatorial industries—very particular expectations are made of us and, in order to survive in our careers, we end up fulfilling them. By them, we are defined, and so we agree to define ourselves, for to survive we must conform and affirm the role of citizen outsider—here, but not here, unsettled, always taking off, but never arriving. For myself, it has long been as if I have been living in the belly of an airplane that is in the air, yet not moving, not allowed to land, all this for the entertainment of others.

Taking a page from my early life in Trinidad, and another from my first home in Canada, in Vancouver, that is, when hiking and outdoor recreation gave me a sense of purpose and fuelled the content of my early paintings, I firmly believe that an actual connection to the land in which one lives, to the ground beneath one's feet, to the trees and shrubs and weeds, to the birds and the bees and wild animals, is a conduit to a sense of belonging. It is not everything, but it is a large part of it, perhaps even a foundation. To have access to the land, to know and respect its occupants, is to create a sympathetic bond with it. And perhaps "sympathetic" is key.

André Alexis, a Canadian of Trinidadian background, gives me a glimpse of what arrival here might look like in his *Fifteen Dogs*. The book spans Toronto from the Beach neighbourhood to High Park, the Park being the main setting in which the story takes place. One who knows the Park may say that his portrayal of it is not exactly accurate, but it is still intimately drawn out in a way that gives breath and breadth to the landscape—it is the hideaway, the home, the playground of the dogs, and so a place that must be detailed by the author for it to be believable. To do so, the immigrant author needs to immerse her- or him- or themselves in the nature of the place. One of the things I admire about Alexis' book is that the author disappears as a man of colour, as a Trinidadian man, as an immigrant; instead, we are taken to a place that is brought abundantly alive by knowledge of, and an ability to create believably its nooks and crannies, its flora and fauna.

2.

I don't know what makes some individuals determined outsiders and others feel only its pain. My partner, who came of age in the Vietnam War era in the United States, is disdainful of the desire to belong. She says the outsider is free. That "belonging" is a trap. You're only an insider if you play by the rules. If you don't, she says, you're out. And since it's not really about you, you might as well please yourself.

What makes her think this? And what makes me long for the validation that I would hope is a result of this thing I call "belonging," the enracinated belonging to a particular place that we see in Alexis' novel? My own longing is no doubt material for the couch, but the origin of these individual quirks in each of us is what creates the kinds of societies in which we live, where some people thrive, some scrape along, some have the ability to lead and others are more comfortable following, some to tear down walls and others to fortify them.

The contradiction I see in my partner's thinking is that one must actually inhabit a particular locale in order to be an outsider in it. To choose to be an outsider is a kind of privilege. An artist who has the wherewithal to make such a choice can benefit from announcing this status, take advantage of being in constant flux, run with new ideas, never gathering moss, applauded, like the Shakespearian jester for daring to speak truths that society at large does not want to hear.

An outsider—in the sense my partner understands the term—who has chosen to be an outsider is given that status by the fact of such choosing, the opportunity to live openly and, one hopes, to be respected for having made such a choice. It may not be entirely perfect, but the respect one gains reflects an openness in the culture.

3.

Unlike many refugees today, risking limb and life of themselves and family members to flee imminent persecution or annihilation in their homelands, I was not in any literal physical danger when, in my early twenties, I left Trinidad. At the same time, presented with the opportunity, I was open to leaving because I had come to understand that Trinidadian society was not welcoming to a person "like me." And, once I left, I could have returned any-time—well, up to a point in time, which I'll soon address—but I chose not to return.

Being able to live openly and honestly has always been as necessary to my practice as a visual artist and writer as oxygen is to life. In childhood, I knew I was "different" or "odd," and that in Trinidad, accumulating experience as the years went by, I would not be able to express myself honestly either in work or in daily life. As an aside, let me say that forty years later, homosexuality remains a criminal offence in Trinidad and Tobago. If the laws that make criminals of us are a holdover from the days of British colonialism, politicians today have gone out of their way to uphold them. When a country votes in its first female Prime Minister, one imagines that society has grown up and is exhibiting broadmindedness. One takes it for granted that a female head of state will recognize discrimination for what it is, and make every effort to banish it wherever it rears its ugly head. After all, so many other countries have enshrined protections based on gender and sexual orientation.

And yet, given the opportunity to begin the process toward striking down the law criminalizing homosexuality, and to include gender and sexual orientation as protected in the constitution, Trinidad's first female Prime Minister refused to allow debate on the subject, saying that the time was not right for such debate in Trinidad.[1] Even if the damning law were not soon to be struck down, nor protection enshrined for decades, public debate (no doubt in some cases with attendant further discriminations deployed) would actually have brought further awareness to the subject, and public conversation and education might have been initiated. Two steps forward and one step back is still movement forward and, in some instances, all that could be hoped for.

But life in Canada was not entirely smooth for a person like me either. Living in Canada since my early twenties, I became involved in the long fight for LGBTQ rights here. It is because of those early fights that, at this stage in my life, and in the gay rights life of Canada, I am free to walk out on the street with my partner and, like a heterosexual couple, hold hands with her. I expect most people will not even notice. But legislation only goes so far. The heart isn't easily legislated; it's certainly possible for someone to hurl an abusive remark our way, but we are protected by the country's hate laws, which are taken seriously and imposed when necessary.

I could not have written my particular novels while living in Trinidad and expected the kind of reception that a writer wishes for. Had I had the courage, the subjects of my books would have been considered taboo and offensive, and I might well have exposed myself to discrimination and violence from acquaintances and strangers alike. From the relative safety of Canada, and from my relative anonymity here, I was able to develop a voice to tell stories from my point of view and experience, to speak truths, to write toward Trinidad, to sing to the country I left, and to shout at it. I have always needed the freedom to express myself honestly and openly, and I would not have found it in Trinidad back then.

Put this way, Canada sounds like the queer and immigrant writer's dream. But time has been moving so fast these last twenty to forty years that with so much work now published internationally by writers of colour, not only those living diasporically, but those who live and work in their homelands of origin, it may be forgotten that it was only in the 1990s, after much hard activism against racism and various other kinds of discriminations on many fronts, that such work started being actively sought after, published, reviewed, nominated, awarded prizes, and read. Support by progressive changes in federal, provincial, and municipal arts funding helped bring access and visibility to waves of new voices that spoke of multiple new landscapes of back-homes that hovered inches above the map of Canada.

Writers from minority communities, seemingly and suddenly freed from having to highlight only the good, began to tell personal stories, and to reveal aspects of life that were not necessarily complimentary to those communities. Being published meant that our works would be available not only to outsiders but also to our communities, who were patting us on our backs for the delight of being able to see their lives in print. Notions of intended audience, however, were not simple. We wrote along a thrilling line that meandered between the various landscapes, and the political and social groups we imagined as constituting our potential readership.

In this sense, race activism, and the eventual hard-won responses to it, created a particular kind of work by writers and artists of colour. Space was created not only for our literary and artists' voices, but also for the voices of a public that had been itself invisible. We were giving a glimpse of our lives to ourselves and to those who couldn't previously imagine us. Race activism also made room for a new generation of critics, teachers, and arts administrators of colour to have their voices heard. These latter might well have brought to their fields, like anyone else, solid academic credentials, but their common experience seemed to be that their skills were once undervalued. Now suddenly academics had, like us, added value by dint of their personal life experience and skin colour. They were at once translators and ennobled native informants. They would enjoy this new currency and credibility, but, for some, this lasted only as long as they stuck to the subjects of which they were partly a reflection. Many of us may still be unwilling to admit that we were not simply placed in a ghetto, but that we were complicit in the formation of one.

4.

In 1957, my parents, both of Indo-Trinidadian origin, were in Ireland because my father was a student in Dublin at the Royal College of Surgeons, one of the top medical schools at the time that attracted foreign students from around the world. I was born there, in Daddy's second year. I wasn't there for long. I only spent the first three months of my life there. I was taken at three months to Trinidad and left in the care of my grandparents, while my parents returned so that Daddy could finish his degree. I would step foot in Ireland only much later, first at the end of the 1990s for no more than an overnight jaunt in Dublin, and then again in April 2017, when I spent several weeks contemplating what it means today to have been born there.

For the sake of brevity and focus, I will skip decades in my story, save for a few words about emigrating in 1981 at age twenty-four from Trinidad to Canada. In Canada, as a landed immigrant, I existed in a kind of limbo, with one toe tentatively dipping into Canada, the rest of that foot and the entire other wading through Trinidad. I had a kind of easy-come easy-go, fair weather relationship with both places. It soon became clear to me that it was in Canada that I was more likely to find my true voice in the visual arts. But an art practice would involve soliciting grants to fund my projects from programs administered by the federal and provincial arts councils. And filling out a grant application for arts funding was something I couldn't bring myself, as a landed immigrant who had not committed fully to the new country, to do. So, in 1986, I applied for and was granted citizenship. It never occurred to me, however, that in doing so I would lose my Trinidadian citizenship.

I found out about this loss quite a while after I became Canadian, on a visit to Trinidad, when I joined the queue for residents at Immigration at Piarco International airport. The officer asked why I had lined up in the residents' queue. I answered that I had dual citizenship. He asked what two countries I thought I was a citizen of. I said, as if he were daft, Trinidad and Canada. He informed me that, as I was born in Ireland, I had Irish citizenship automatically and, when I chose to take out Canadian citizenship, I gave up my Trinidadian one, as Trinidad only recognized dual citizenship. I stood there for a while not really understanding what he was saying. The previously harmless curiosity of an accident of birth was suddenly a rock in my shoe.

A kind of immigrant writing for a person like me in Canada was necessary at a particular point in time. I believe that that time has evolved. And what I lament is the kind of enracinated citizenship that is the privilege of one born and brought up in a place, rather than a constantly negotiated citizenship that is the result of having arrived from elsewhere and taken an oath of loyalty in the new country. But to approach that kind of experience, one has not only to dare to stray from the safety of a niche that permits a single note kind of voice, but also to unlearn the well-practised and well-rewarded psyche of outsider. And, above all, one has to learn how to "belong."

5.

If I strip away my perceived need to perform skin colour, immigration, queerness, I am at heart, in my deepest heart, stirred by nature, by land and seascapes. But when in the past I bicycled through the mountains of British Columbia and Alberta, where I once lived, or now in the countryside of southern Ontario, I could see the land only in its broad sweep, overwhelming

scenes apprehended only in passing, their details a blur and incomprehensible, not because they were actually incomprehensible, but, as I see now,
because I had not stopped "being a tourist in the land in which I was living."

Living in the countryside, as I do now, one is obliged to face the elements,
to deal with snow storms that leave you stranded for days, with ice so thick
you are house-bound, tornadoes, Lyme disease, chipmunks that enter your
home, rabbits that jump into the fenced-off enclosure that is your vegetable
garden and give birth there, squirrels in the walls of your house, coyotes yip-
ping as they trek through your backyard at night. One is forced to watch, to
listen, to act in markedly different ways than in a city.

It is this, all of this, in one's present life that one wants to write about and to
paint and photograph.

But to see and to be able to vocalize the language of such a landscape, the
perennial immigrant needs to enter it in a new way, to "feel" it to learn it.

I was recently awarded an Ontario Arts Council Chalmers Fellowship,
which has allowed me to embark on a year-long idealistic exploration of "the
poetics of naturalization." The project is to develop a new imagery of citizenship, a new vocabulary of belonging, a language of affinity and connectedness
that transcends the little piece of paper on which my birth has been recorded
or the card that records citizenship, and engage with those subjects—landscape and nature, love, and desire—that have always stirred me in my depths.

Oddly, and not so oddly, a methodical enquiry into a poetics of naturalization began, for me, in Ireland. Ireland is, not so oddly—and oddly—the
least complicated place to which I belong. To be certain, it is a bureaucratic
belonging but, nevertheless, it raised the question of what the fact of my
birth there, the fact of an Irish birth certificate, might mean to me if I were
to roam the land of Ireland mindfully. Might I there approach some sense in
my body I'd not encountered elsewhere—either in Trinidad where I grew
up, or in Canada where I've lived most of my life—a sense of personhood, of
belonging?

The three weeks I spent in Ireland turned out to be deeply affecting. I was
not there as a descendant of Irish men and women who fled Ireland after the
1840s and went to the Americas. I was not there to trace or reclaim ancestry. I
have no ancestry there. Still, I travelled with my 1957 birth certificate and my
Irish passport and, I have to say, I noticed I walked about the various locales
in which I spent time with a pleasant, hoped for, yet strange, new kind of ease
and comfort. It is not just that the place of birth is so affecting, but nowadays
the rights of citizenship naturally acquired is one of the few certainties we can
rely on.

In Dublin, when I visited the Easter Uprising exhibit at the General Post Office, I felt as if I were for the first time learning the history of a country to which I had ties. But there were unexpected nuances. The kinship I felt with the men and women rising up against British rule was not because I am Irish, but because I am also Trinidadian. I grew up in a country, a region that, when I was a child, had been subject to the heavy thumb of the British, and I felt empathy for that urgent desire for liberation.

Some years ago, I visited India and, save for the very same colour and texture of skin and hair shared with Indians, and despite my desire and expectations, I felt no kinship with all that was around me; I felt oftentimes baffled and ignorant and saw that, to Indians in India, I was a foreigner, one of those Indo-Trinidadians who come in search of roots, but whose brand of Indianness was tediously imitative to them of old ideas regarding a Mother India. I did not find in India what I was able to achieve in Ireland. Perhaps it is because the one-note belonging of looks turned out to be a trick played on me; I was too-much faced there with my own lack as an Indian, with my difference. At the same time, it was my difference from the mainstream Irish, mingled with the visibility/invisibility of the visitor, that made room for me to feel a welcome there. I could publicly explore under the guise, on one hand, of tourist, the country, its people, its culture, and yet inside of me, I would know that because of an accident of timing of my birth, I absolutely had irrevocable rights in that land, rights the same as its citizens.

Walking through Dublin wearing a cloak of belonging, a piece of paper attesting to place of birth in my pocket, attempting to locate some sense of right, somewhere in my psyche and in my body, was a kind of performance. My hope was that, on returning to Canada, the fictional cloak would have seared itself onto my skin like a protective shield, that facing inland in Canada, a sense of self discovered in Ireland—a sense of being a person with myriad rights—would remain lodged inside me, and I'd be freed to see and to write about and paint and photograph the land without the sword of immigration, colour, or sexuality dangled above my head.

And, sure enough, when this past summer I travelled up the Rideau System, from Lake Opinicon just north of Kingston to Westport, photographing and painting the land from a boat on the water, I felt more at home, more real than I have in the city. I was born surrounded by water, grew up surrounded by water, and currently live on an isthmus surrounded by water. But the water of the lakes of Canadian Shield was new. It was inland, and it was fresh, and, out in the open, it was obsidian black. Lakes Opinicon, Sand, Newboro, Indian, Clear, and Upper Rideau, on which parent loons bobbed teaching their young to fish. The waters brought me to the edges of the land, where they lapped against four-billion-year-old Precambrian igneous and metamorphic rocks, copper coloured, and salmon coloured rocks with striations of dancing quartz. Pileated woodpeckers in the white pines and ospreys in the naked-topped spruce, beaver dams divvying up the lake, kings of the water—the trumpeter swans, herons in calligraphy flight spelled their relation to dinosaurs, and on fallen trees half slipped into the water basked rows of Northern Map turtles.

Now my intention is to put language to what I have seen and felt in this Canadian womb. To put the landscape inside my mouth. To see what a conversation between a person like me and the artists of the past who have painted these waters and trees might sound like.

It must be said, at the same time, if only in a few words, that I will have to be careful how I incorporate this new connectedness to Canada, as I've learned in my almost forty years here as an activist that the North American landscape does not belong—and never has truly belonged—to newcomers. That all recent newcomers—any of us, in other words, who have arrived in the last six hundred years—are guests in these territories. Indeed, any notion of land, and what land is good for, must be tempered by Indigenous knowledges and understandings, which, for me, requires a willingness to hear such understandings, and to be an ally to Indigenous land rights activists. This raises the question of the extent to which, after the Columbus years that brought us the age of "discovery," imperialism, and various forms of migration, any attempt at belonging by settlers to these territories is indeed fiction.

Belonging is, for someone like me, inevitably, a failed project. I am not unaware of this, but artists know that failure and struggle are our work's friends. We flirt with failure, especially to break down boundaries. Experimentation and spontaneity are, I believe, where art and questions and unexpected answers exist.

NOTE

1 In 2018, the High Court of Justice in Trinidad and Tobago ruled that the country's laws criminalizing same-sex intimacy between consenting adults are unconstitutional. It would appear therefore that homosexuality has been decriminalized, and has been legalised. There are, however, no laws explicitly protecting LGBTQ people from discrimination or hate crimes. Transgender people remain particularly vulnerable—as yet, there has been for them no legal gender recognition.

CHAPTER SIX

Untold Bodies: Failing Gender in Canada's Past and Future

Kit Dobson

Almost as an addendum to the Canada 150 celebrations, in late November of 2017, Liberal Prime Minister Justin Trudeau offered an apology on behalf of the federal government for the past persecution of LGBTQ2 people in Canada. More specifically, Trudeau apologized for the ways in which the federal government and its intelligence agencies had, more or less from the postwar period through the AIDS crisis, sought to locate and expel members of queer communities from roles in the military and civil service.[1] Describing past governments as having been guilty of creating "laws, policies, and hiring practices" that labelled queer people "as less than" (Trudeau), the Prime Minister sought to apologize to "all the LGBTQ2 people across this country who we have harmed in countless ways" and pledged to make a better present and future in Canada for all. Although critics might rightly suggest that Trudeau's apology is simply the latest in a series of government apologies in Canada that seek to contain the past by demarcating it as having been in error[2]—and implying, in turn, that the present has solved this particular historical wrong—it is, at the same time, an important one to examine critically. Rhetorically, Trudeau's statement is an interesting manoeuvre when it fails to complete the clause that I cited above, the "less than" of the apology. Less than what? Trudeau does not disclose more. The context suggests that persecuted queer people were held to be "less than" other Canadian citizens, but how else might one complete that statement? The apology might render queer Canadians more equal to their fellow citizens; however, I would like to hold on to the openness of Trudeau's statement, because there remain, I will argue below, many ways to remain "less than," while nonetheless achieving formal recognitions of equality.

In a lengthy list of those who have faced discrimination and persecution in this context, Trudeau singled out "transgender Canadians," who are, the Prime Minister noted, "subjected to discrimination, violence, and aggression at alarming rates. In fact, trans people did not even have explicit protection under federal human rights legislation until this year" (Trudeau). Trudeau is here referencing Bill C-16, An Act to amend the Canadian Human Rights Act and the Criminal Code. This Bill, given assent on June 19, 2017, amends the Human Rights Act to protect gender identity and gender expression, making both prohibited grounds for discrimination. This legislation, too, demonstrates a commitment on the part of the current federal government to take action on issues of gender discrimination. But what of the lengthy history for which Trudeau is apologizing? In their book *The Canadian War on Queers*, Gary Kinsman and Patrizia Gentile study the specific history for which Trudeau was apologizing. Examining how agencies like the RCMP worked to uncover, expose, and eliminate queer members of the military, police, and civil service, they document an insufficiently known history, right down to the so-called research that led to the creation of "the fruit machine," the pseudo-test designed to root out queer people "empirically." Kinsman and Gentile's in-depth, thorough research and interviews with people who lived through these purges—purges that Trudeau references explicitly in his apology—demonstrate what was at stake for those impacted by the government's homophobic and transphobic policies. Their interviewees also, significantly, report the sensation of feeling themselves to be "less than": "I was treated like the enemy," one survivor reports, for instance (149). The history for which Trudeau apologizes continues to have impacts on the present, as lives and livelihoods were disrupted and lost to a bureaucracy that reflected widely held prejudices.

Coming in the aftermath of Canada 150, this present volume focuses upon past, present, and future untold stories in Canada. I view this framework as an important one because of the lens it provides us. This lens gives us space to think through narratives—this is a book that is, in one way or another, about stories—and about the untold. In their narrative of Canadian history, Kinsman and Gentile argue that "injustices are an integral part of the ideology and practice of national security" (xiii). What injustices remain? How do they continue into the present and future? What stories are not told due to unjust gender relations in Canada? What is untold, in my view, is important to consider and to honour, particularly when the untold is that which is rendered invisible by the frameworks of both "the ideology and practice" of the everyday that are in place in Canada. An increasing body of critical work notes that queer and trans inclusion in Canada remains highly fraught terrain, and it is important to recognize this tension.

This chapter takes up, in particular, a consideration of the persistent inequalities of Canada's shifting gender politics. I offer it here as an index, not only of some of my thinking, but also in a spirit of openness and, I hope, compassion for anyone who might feel bound and betrayed by the limited notions of the human that late capitalist society offers. While the legislation of same-sex marriage in Canada's 2005 Civil Marriage Act—alongside the 2017 protection of gender identity and expression, as well as Trudeau's apology—may have appeared to settle the country's past inequities concerning queer and trans people, what remains? I am interested in the ways in which the unruly presence of the gendered body pushes back against not only heteronormative discourses, but also, in the wake of Canada's inclusive, liberal-minded legislation, the growth of what Jack Halberstam, Judith Butler, Michael Warner, Lisa Duggan, and many others have recognized in other contexts as a growing set of homonormativities.[3] What stories will be the legacy of the next 150 years? What new normativities is Canada producing when it comes to the gendered body? In her 2013 book *Reproductive Acts*, Heather Latimer argues that the gendered body in Canada and the United States remains a site of contestation and normalization under neoliberal modes of governance, and she sets out, in concert with other critics, to queer the available scripts. Rinaldo Walcott, in a similar vein, argues that "homo-rights follow in a long tradition of national containment, wherein more peoples and their practices are brought into the national body who then come to perform more expertly the brutal forgetting of the post-Enlightenment, modernist organization of human life, which can otherwise go by the name 'global colonialism'" and that, in turn, it is necessary to find "ways of organizing life and belonging beyond capitalist modernity" (vii).[4] What happens when the body refuses to be or cannot be normalized according to dominant scripts of "inclusion" or "accommodation" within the capitalist modernity against which Walcott agitates? Through a reading of the collaborative project *Gender Failure*, by trans writers and performers Ivan E. Coyote and Rae Spoon, I argue in this chapter that the progressive narrative of gender inclusion in Canada continues to fail particular, non-conforming bodies, and that it does so with increasing force in a neoliberal economy that seeks to define and delimit the ways in which some bodies are deemed more human than others, particularly under the rubric of human rights discourses. Gender trouble was great; however, now it is time to speak about gender failure.

We can begin to think about gender failure by bearing witness to the ways in which critical thinking has moved in recent years. I think that their growing familiarity might provide us with a way to track contemporary concerns. That Lauren Berlant's concept of cruel optimism, for instance, has become so very widespread and been translated into many different contexts suggests not only the malleability of her claim that many contemporary forms of optimism for the "good life" have become corrosive to human animals' abilities to thrive, but also that it is a shared concern in a world that remains deeply invested in organizing and codifying bodies and determining which ones are more economically and socially fit than others. Those bodies that are determined by others, and by interlocking systems of oppression, to be more fit—the more normative-bodied—are often deemed to be more fully human, and the consequence is that everyone's humanity is policed to greater or lesser degrees. In that respect, Berlant's arguments are relatively consonant with those that Judith Butler has made since the War on Terror began, about which bodies are deemed worthy of commemoration (even though they may disagree on how to address the cruelty with which optimism persists and with which the body is policed). Jack Halberstam's arguments, in *The Queer Art of Failure*, might allow us to witness the ways in which queer bodies are deemed to have always-already failed to have adhered to scripts of the good life. "What comes after hope?" he wonders (1). What happens, that is, after our hopes for success or for having our dreams fulfilled are crushed in one way or another? Rather than accepting blame and defeat, Halberstam argues, a queer argument might allow instead for a celebration of failure. He observes that "failure allows us to escape the punishing norms that discipline behavior and manage human development with the goal of delivering us from unruly childhoods to orderly and predictable adulthoods" (3). Such a celebration of failure pushes back against the ways in which "success in a heteronormative, capitalist society equates too easily to specific forms of reproductive maturity combined with wealth accumulation" (2). That is, the terms of something like success are not ones that can be easily defined by subjects for themselves in the contemporary world. The terms of engagement have been predetermined according to heteronormative and capitalist teleologies, and to fail to fit those norms is dangerous. Yet to succeed, too, might mark a different form of failure: a failure of the imagination, and a failure of the subject to be inclusive, open, and expansive when encountering forms of difference that do not easily equate to something like the liberal human subject—perhaps especially as that subject is described and then deconstructed by Rosi Braidotti and others seeking to bring posthuman subjectivities into view.

The possibility of celebrating failure, or of celebrating oneself from precisely where one exists in the present, is, in many ways, corrosive to capitalism's demand that one's life is in need of constant improvement—improvement that comes from selling one's labour (body / time) in exchange for a purer form of existence. Alexis Shotwell, in her 2016 book *Against Purity*, argues strongly in favour of rethinking cultural attitudes toward such purity in order to live ethically in these environmentally, politically, and socially messy times. For Shotwell, to pursue ethical living means recognizing one's ethical compromises and one's complicities. Life remains necessarily imbricated in suffering, in being the agents of the suffering of other beings, and to live well may mean an honest recognition of the situations in which we find ourselves. To articulate matters somewhat differently, Maggie Nelson, in *The Argonauts*, asks the following: "how to explain, in a culture frantic for resolution, that sometimes the shit stays messy?" (53). Why can't the shit stay messy? A culture of normative success seems to rely upon tremendous repressive powers, sublimating, repressing, and expelling all things that do not tidily fit into the heteronormative category of success. I am reminded of the architecture of contemporary North American houses, which grow larger and contain more and more bathrooms as time goes by: it seems that we do not want the shit to stay messy. The message in contemporary domestic architecture is that society wants the shit to be gone. The pervasive anxiety around bathrooms—readily observed also in, to me, the utterly perplexing difficulty Western society has in creating gender-inclusive public bathrooms—is just one more index that to fail, to leak, to be messy, all of these are the things against which normativity mitigates and agitates.[5]

The thinkers I have mentioned concern themselves, then, in different ways, with how normativities assert and reassert themselves. These thinkers, too, centre their concern upon bodies that lie outside of normative frameworks, bodies for which dominant conceptions of "success" or the "good life" may not be fully available. It remains important, following Berlant, to note that the scripts of success and the "normal" life are simply not available to everyone: those scripts are dependent upon many pre-existing sets of normativities, as Sara Ahmed analyzes, too, in her trenchant analyses of the normativities attached to dominant happiness scripts. How to respond remains the crux of my concern here.

Rae Spoon and Ivan Coyote recognize precisely how damaging and dangerous these scripts are in their collaborative performance and book, *Gender Failure*. *Gender Failure* began onstage, as an outgrowth of a previous collaborative performance by Spoon and Coyote, *You Are Here*, in which they minimized the queer content of their work as an experiment in order to see how much recognition it might bring (their response: they felt that it brought a lot more success than their queer work up to that point [see 11–12]). For *Gender Failure*, the two writer / singer / performers decided to foreground their everyday struggles with the binaries of gender, in order to "shine light" on what they term their "true trans selves" (15). In an interview with Moynan King while the work was still in the process of being created, Coyote stated that "it's gonna be our show, for our people" (48). In *Gender Failure*, viewers and readers witness how Spoon and Coyote's struggles are frequent, or even constant, as queer trans artists. Julian Gunn argues that, in their work, Spoon and Coyote "delineate the separation of bodily and social being enforced by the gendered prohibitions built into collective spaces, and the struggle to rec-oncile, or even to express, this division" (150). Their spatial struggles come back to issues of embodiment and how their bodies—perceived as unruly—relate to space. As a show that toured and was then recorded on the page, it is important to consider it as a performative work in this context, because of the spatial nature of performance itself.[6]

The book version of *Gender Failure* operates as a series of short pieces, written alternately by Spoon and Coyote. Both funny and tragic, the pieces offer "down-to-earth" perspectives (as Kate Bornstein put it in one of the reviews blurbed on the book) from two artists who have had to struggle in order not to be rendered invisible in the multiple communities in which they travel. "I get really tired of being mistaken for a monster," Coyote writes (210), itself a line that can be read as one possible complement to Trudeau's "less than" statement. *Gender Failure* documents, in sometimes very pain-ful detail, the ways in which both the artists and their communities have been judged, threatened, and, at times, dismissed from the world around them. Spoon writes that they thought they were "a failure" for being "a per-son who couldn't conform to what was expected" (17). They write that they "did want to succeed" as a girl, and then later as a trans man, but that gender "wasn't like learning how to play the guitar or to rollerblade," because it was something that Spoon "could never really learn to do well" (46). Coyote, in turn, observes the biopolitical means through which trans people are evalu-ated and disciplined, noting in their discussion of seeking top surgery that "the government will pay for you to get fixed, but only if they decide you are broken in the right way" (70). One problem with this system, they add, is that "there is no box to check for not wanting a box at all. No one knows how to fix that" (70). Spoon agrees, asserting both that governments have appointed themselves the role of being "the ultimate authorities in deciding the legal distinctions between male and female" (119), but also that, "if being a man is something that required a person to tick off a bunch of boxes, not many people would make it through" (105). Governmentality functions through codifying and classifying their bodies; whether or not they wish to participate, disciplinary forces ensure that they do nonetheless. Moving into queer communities that push back against such disciplinarity, however, has proven fraught too. Spoon notes that "there are so many rules placed on physical bodies in the gay community" (179), where homonormative assumptions can hinder and hurt just as heteronormative ones do (as we read, perhaps most poignantly and awkwardly, as Spoon attempts to navigate their way through Grindr, or as Coyote negotiates using bathrooms with cisgendered queer women as well as straight ones). The trans body is not only governed from above, but also through daily interactions that constantly remind Spoon and Coyote of their difference and noncompliance.

Many of the struggles recorded in *Gender Failure* are ones concerned with pronouns and the ways in which bodies are storied—when and if they are storied at all. Both artists are very clear that they use the pronoun "they," but they are repeatedly misgendered, even in communities in which they might expect respect and understanding. In Ivan Coyote's recent book, 2016's *Tomboy Survival Guide*, they propose taking the conversation on pronouns one step further: "I would like to phase out the use of the phrase 'prefers the pronouns' she, he, or they, (or any other) and replace it with 'uses the pronoun'" (211). The reason is that, Coyote writes, "[w]hen someone writes that a person 'prefers' a particular pronoun, it implies that there is a choice there for everyone whether to respect that wish or not," whereas "not having their pronoun respected is hurtful" (212). Every instance of being misgendered, as they put it, leads to "a tiny little sliver" of their disappearance (246); these acts wear upon them and remain a clear site of struggle. Spoon argues in *Gender Failure* that "language is a living thing, and I find the attempts to preserve it from the threat of gender-neutral pronouns to be a transphobic reaction" (203). The capacity for language to shift, alternatively, provides a potential for an opening and possibility that is only very unevenly realized in the present.

There are many threads of *Gender Failure* that deserve analysis, but I am particularly struck by the ways in which both Spoon and Coyote integrate their own failures into their work. One especially unflinching element related by Coyote discusses their relationship to Trans Day of Remembrance, a day that they critique for lacking in-depth understanding of the particular trans people who are dead or missing from their stories (52). In a recuperative stance, Coyote sets out to tell one of the missing stories, that of Rosie. Coyote sets out Rosie's story as follows:

> Rosie disappeared, never to be seen again, over twenty years ago now, shortly after being diagnosed with terminal cancer. She had been told by her doctor that he could no longer ethically prescribe hormones to her, as he suspected that long-term heavy estrogen use while she saved up money for the many sur-geries that at that time were not covered by our province's health care plan had been a contributing factor to the tumours growing in her stomach and intes-tines ... Rosie had disagreed. She packed up one suitcase, socked away all the remaining hormones she had been stockpiling, and vanished. (53)

Coyote goes on to concede that, by the time of writing, they are "forced to assume that she is dead" (54), while the missing persons case that they and their friend Rachel opened on Rosie remains unsolved. The ways in which Rosie's body has been governed by others—by doctors and by medical sys-tems—appear to have led to her death, and Coyote approaches her as such.

Coyote continues by giving Rosie a fuller story. We learn that Rosie was from Quebec and was Métis, but, more to the point, that Rosie "made the best baked beans ever ... and taught [Coyote] how to refinish furniture" (55). Rosie is bawdy, funny, tough, and sad, a survivor of a set of challenging circumstances, but also someone who laughed, loved, and lived. Coyote wishes both to celebrate and mourn her. At first, however, Coyote strug-gled to understand Rosie: "I had never met any other woman quite like Rosie before," they say, in part because "her voice was low ... and her bare skin above her black bra was covered in five o'clock shadow and painted with now bleeding-edged and sailor-flash faded tattoos" (35). Rosie's gender non-conformity is confirmed when Coyote's friend, Archie from Red Deer, a gay man, comes for a visit and dismisses Rosie as "the ugliest drag queen" that he has ever seen (38). Archie's response, however, is but a more callous mirror of Coyote's own initial struggles with Rosie. As they slowly get to know each other, Coyote observes that

> [i]t took me months, slowly, slowly, to get her to smile, and then chat, and then one day, accept my third or fourth invitation to come in for a cup of tea. I referred to her as "he" only once, early on, I didn't know, I was still so small-town back then. I used the word "he" for her only once, and it was barely out of my mouth when she caught it in one manicured and muscled fist and tossed

it back at me. She wasn't mad, just certain. "Don't ever call me 'he,'" she said calmly. "Ever. I hate it. I am a she. Her. Hers. Got it, kid?" (36)

Coyote's own culpability in this moment demonstrates a dawning trans awareness. As they put it, it "seemed simple to me. And it is. I loved her already. I wanted to make her happy. Call her what she wanted. Call her what made her happy to hear" (36). Coyote's own past experience of misgendering their friend, in turn, demonstrates their own failure, not simply at gender, but also at being a friend and at compassion. It shows a growing awareness and the possibility for change. It provides space for viewers and readers to accept Coyote and Spoon's own gentle requests for openness and understanding, for unravelling the normative scripts in which readers are themselves imbricated. In the process of retelling this initial encounter, then, Coyote gently observes the importance of pronouns in discussions of gender and acknowledges their own past complicity with hegemonic behaviour patterns.

Rather than only occupying the role of the imperfect, failing, unhappy queer, however—and here I am thinking of the term as theorized by Sara Ahmed—Spoon and Coyote seek spaces of solace and refuge, and find them, within the struggle of recognizing that the normative model of the human articulated under liberalism does not fit all bodies, and perhaps their bodies in particular. For Rae Spoon, solace is found in gender retirement. "When I retired from gender," Spoon writes, "it was because I came to the realization that the gender binary was what had been failing me all along" (17–18): "in gender neutrality, I decided to refuse the model of body characteristics denoting sex and gender altogether" (201). Gender retirement animates much of the hope that Spoon expresses in Gender Failure. For Coyote, solace comes from celebrating unruly queer and trans lives. Contemplating Rosie's life and passing, they write:

> I refuse to reduce her life to nothing more than a name on a list of the deceased. I want all of who she was to be remembered, to be honoured. I want it to be known that Rosie's life also contained joy, and laughter and friendship and love, in addition to despair and poverty and cancer and death. (54)

The reason, Coyote writes, is that "you cannot fight despair armed only with more despair" (54). In many respects, a core theme of Gender Failure is concerned with how despair can be turned to joy, or how failure can provide one with unexpected victories. Spoon's gender retirement provides precisely one such victory:

I am a gender failure. I failed at the gender binary, unable to find a place in being either a man or a woman with which I felt comfortable. But ultimately I believe that it's the binary that fails to leave room for most people to write their own gender stories. (242)

At moments like this one, Spoon and Coyote's gender failure becomes a strength above all else. It is a struggle, absolutely, but a struggle that provides an exit, a momentary escape from the structures of domination within which they find themselves enmeshed.

"Fail again. Fail better," I hear Samuel Beckett saying (a line that Halberstam quotes [24]). "The queer art of failure," Halberstam asserts, "turns on the impossible, the improbable, the unlikely, and the unremarkable. It quietly loses, and in losing it imagines other goals for life, for love, for art, and for being" (88). We remain vulnerable to hurt; living beings suffer. Perhaps that one thing might bind us together in imagining possibilities for different narratives. Kinsman and Gentile argue that "we need to challenge existing social forms such as marriage, which have historically been based on our [queer peoples'] exclusion and marginalization as well as on the oppression of women, and we need to focus more on how to transform oppressive social relations and how to build social alternatives" (xvii). As this project envisions the stories that remain untold in Canada's past, present, and future, looking past Trudeau's apology and toward, instead, the embodied lives that queer and trans folks inhabit, I suggest ways in which stories remain untold, not simply because they have not been recorded, but also because of how they are not ones that Canada has yet been able to witness. Stories might celebrate ways of being that Canada has not yet been ready to accept as the successful, joyous celebrations that they might become. These narratives might undo parts or the whole of what Canada has sought to be and force a more radical reconsideration of colonial, neoliberal capitalism. "Some days the whole world seems to want to disappear dudes like us," Ivan Coyote notes (124). The telling of their untold stories, however, ensures that that disappearance does not, and will not, happen, and may prompt the reconsideration, questioning, an even dismantling of the master narratives that make up what it means to lead a daily life.

NOTES

1   Although the term is not without its many challenges, in this chapter I will use the term *queer* in order to indicate LGBTQ2S+-identified people.

2   I have in mind here, in particular, Jennifer Henderson and Pauline Wakeham's *Reconciling Canada: Critical Perspectives on the Culture of Redress* (2013), an edited collection that examines previous apologies in Canada, which Ben Authers takes up in this volume.

3   Naomi de Szegheo-Lang offers a good summary of the concept of homonormativity by summarizing it as a term that signals "practices that belong to a privatized, depoliticized gay culture based in domesticity and material consumption" (71). I follow de Szegheo-Lang in deriving much of my understanding of homonormativity in turn from Lisa Duggan's thinking.

4   There is a lot of additional critical material that one could discuss here. A recent, important starting point is OmiSoore H. Dryden and Suzanne Lenon's *Disturbing Queer Inclusion: Canadian Homonationalisms and the Politics of Belonging* (2015).

5   Yes, I am also thinking of Slavoj Žižek's recurring rants about different national types of toilets, as in the following: https://www.youtube.com/watch?v=8mtZmBvat4k.

6   In that spirit, I encourage readers to seek recorded versions of performances online, such as the following: https://vimeo.com/76738781. This particular recording is a trailer for the show.

CHAPTER SEVEN

Thresholds of Sustainability: Cassils' and Emma Donoghue's Counter-Narratives

Libe García Zarranz

"Ethics consists in reworking the pain into the threshold of sustainability, when and if possible: cracking, but holding it, still. It is a mode of actualizing sustainable forms of transformation."

—Rosi Braidotti, 2006

"It was unsustainable."

—Cassils, in conversation with Catherine Wagley, 2011

We live in an era of "sustainability."[1] We hear repeatedly of the desire to develop sustainable cities with sustainable energy to enable the living of sustainable lives, particularly in the context of contemporary societies in the West. And yet, the ongoing war in Syria, the plight of refugees, and the rise of neofascisms in the United States, Canada, and Europe are only some instances of the current intensification of unsustainable practices of power that thrive on inhumanity and precariousness.[2] Particularly after 9/11, the strategic intensification of surveillance, militarization, and racial profiling has branded certain subjects—the migrant, the refugee, the trans[3]—as debilitated and thus disposable entities that need to be extirpated from the socio-political sphere under the name of security and protection.[4] Donald Trump's policies and rhetoric in the United States only accelerated this "biopolitics of racism" (Moore 173) to unprecedented levels, deeply shattering the sustainability of what critical race theorist Rachel C. Lee calls the "minoritized subject" (235). The politics of indifference that seems to characterize this historical juncture extends to other contexts, such as the Canadian one in which the problematic 150 anniversary celebrations in 2017, with their perverse discourses of

nation-building, prosperity, and growth, abounded at the expense of addressing continuing histories of colonization, racism, sexism, and transphobia. This
failure to take responsibility affects the everyday sustenance of communities
whose urgent pleas systematically remain unheard.[5]

How does this culture of indifference co-exist with the imperative to live
and lead sustainable lives? To borrow the words of comparative literature
scholar Haun Saussy, sustainability has become "yet another consumer desirable" (213), a buzzword that is often co-opted by corporate powers. This is
what I call the rhetoric of sustainability. Part of the motivation behind this
chapter emerges from the ethical imperative to trace the paradoxical asym-
metry between this *rhetoric of sustainability*, which has become a popular
discourse among normative structures of power, and an *ethics of sustainability*, which stands as a counter-discourse that seeks to dismantle the shortcuts
proposed by those very same structures. The urgency to problematize these
exclusions, these cuts, remains at the heart of feminist and trans writers and
multimedia artists in Canada, as I seek to demonstrate here.

In "The Ethics of Becoming-Imperceptible" (2006), feminist philosopher Rosi Braidotti draws on Benedict Spinoza and Gilles Deleuze to offer
an ethical account of the sustainability of bodies. Sustainability, Braidotti
claims, "is about how much of it a subject can take and ethics is accordingly
redefined as the geometry of how much bodies are capable of" (136). The
"thresholds of sustainability" (142) of a particular subject, that is how much
a body can take, necessarily relies upon material, biopolitical, and affective
variables, together with historical ruptures and violences. The sustainability
of bodies then necessarily becomes intimately intertwined with the question
of viability. Which populations and communities are viable—that is, which
populations and communities have the capacity for living under certain
conditions? Contributing to this discussion about viability and the biopolitical, transgender studies scholar Susan Stryker explains how "[t]ransgender
phenomena—[that is] anything that calls our attention to the contingency
and unnaturalness of gender normativity— ... constantly flicker across the
threshold of viability, simultaneously courting danger and attracting death,
even as they promise life in new forms, along new pathways" (40). This
threshold of viability that Stryker rightly points out acts as a marker of sustainability understood as a complex assemblage of bio- and necropolitical[6]
forces with important ethical repercussions.

Given that bodies are formed "within the crucible of social life" (Butler
2004) and, as such, always presuppose a public dimension, what happens to
those bodies—physical and textual—that are rendered unviable by normative

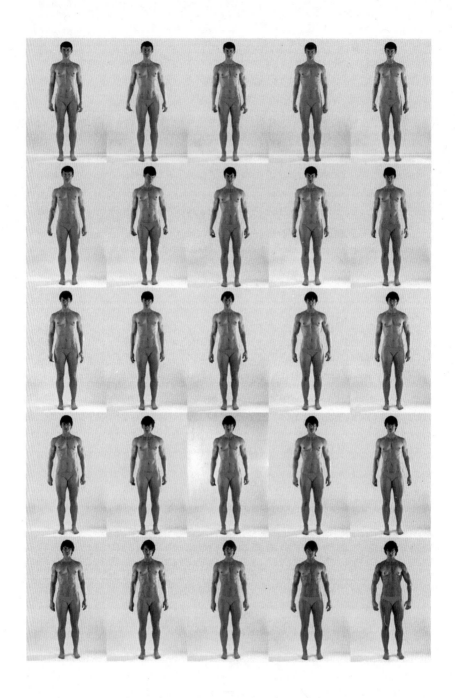

FIGURE 7.1 Cassils, *Time Lapse,* (Front) and (Left), 2011. Archival pigment print, 60 × 40 inches. Edition of 3. Courtesy of the artist and Ronald Feldman Gallery, New York.

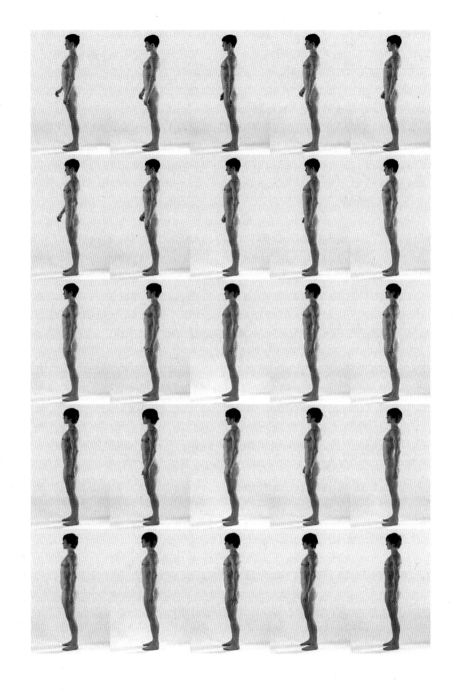

structures of power? What happens to those stories that resist intelligibility, that do not make sense? What happens to those audiences who refuse to practise more ethical ways of seeing? This chapter examines the thresholds of sustainability and viability in the work of Cassils, a Montreal-born, LA-based gender non-conforming trans-masculine visual artist and bodybuilder, and Emma Donoghue, an Irish Canadian queer writer and literary historian. Drawing on feminist philosophy and transgender studies, I put Cassils' durational performances, *Cuts: A Traditional Sculpture* (2011–2013), *Tiresias* (2010–2013), and *The Powers That Be* (2015), in conversation with Donoghue's novel *The Wonder* (2016). I focus on how the acts of bodily transformation represented in their written and visual texts—from carving, to cutting, to fasting—address and interrogate the sustainability of deviant bodies. Simultaneously, I look at Cassils' and Donoghue's work as counter-narratives, which I understand as forms of representation that put ethics at the centre of enquiry to interrogate received conceptualizations of the body politic and consequently, often remain silenced, unheard, and/or untold. In different ways, Cassils' and Donoghue's counter-narratives reflect the urgency to problematize these exclusions, these cuts, mobilizing an ethics of sustainability for this era of indifference.

"It was unsustainable" (Wagley): these were Cassils' words upon completion of the durational performance *Cuts: A Traditional Sculpture*.[7] Testing the thresholds of sustainability of their body, the artist gained twenty-three pounds of muscle in twenty-three weeks by taking male hormones and subjecting themselves to a severe diet and bodybuilding regime. Cassils recorded their bodily transformation by taking four photographs a day from four vantage points, as can be seen in Figure 7.1. The performance, on the one hand, is inspired by Cassils' everyday experiences as a body trainer in LA, working closely with actors who need to build muscle for film roles. *Cuts*, on the other hand, responds to Eleanor Antin's 1973 performance *CARVING: A Traditional Sculpture*, for which the feminist artist crash-dieted for over a month. Antin, as seen in Figure 7.2, was photographed naked in the same four stances to record the bodily transformation over thirty-seven days. Slowly moulding her own body, Antin's performance redefines the act of carving, both a metaphor and a literal activity, with a colonial masculinist history.[8] Antin thus challenges traditional aesthetics by becoming her own self-made feminist Pygmalion.[9]

The desire for self-construction is also a pervasive theme in Cassils' performances: "I see my body as a material, just like paint or clay" (qtd. in Iannacci par. 1). Yet, *Cuts* goes a step further than Antin's *CARVING*: it tests the

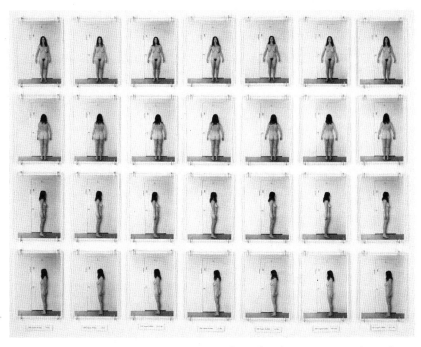

FIGURE 7.2   Eleanor Antin, *CARVING – A Traditional Sculpture*, 1972. 148 silver gelatin prints & text, 7 × 5 inches each. From the collection of the Art Institute of Chicago. Courtesy the artist and Ronald Feldman Gallery, New York. Courtesy of the artist.

thresholds of sustainability of those trans bodies that, as Stryker contends, "become vulnerable to a panoply of structural oppressions and repressions; [bodies that] are more likely to be passed over for social investment and less likely to be cultivated as useful for the body politic" (40). These trans subjects and communities, I add, are systematically cut out of normative systems of recognition and intelligibility. With their body in its peak condition, and in collaboration with photographer and makeup artist Robin Black, Cassils staged a highly stylized trans self-portrait (see Figure 7.3). Their provocative work, which pays homage to American visual artist Lynda Benglis and her 1974 *Advertisement*,[10] poses important ethical questions about the aesthetic representation of trans bodies, while tackling "the tensions between visibility and invisibility, inclusion and exclusion" (David 82).

Cassils' bodily experimentations in *Cuts* and *Advertisement: Homage to Benglis* (2011) certainly challenge readers to question hegemonic ways of seeing; they push audiences to reorient our gaze, in Halberstam's sense,[11] and look at bodies that are largely rendered invisible, while simultaneously marked by multiple violences. As performance studies critic Emily Hella

FIGURE 7.3

Cassils, *Advertisement: Homage
to Benglis*, 2011, c-print,
40 × 30 inches. Edition of 3.
Photo: Cassils with Robin
Black. Courtesy of the artist and
Ronald Feldman Gallery,
New York.

Tsaconas explains, Cassils' project unravels "the threat of radically unknow-
able raw physical capacity ... The stated structure of the project begins to
sketch out a map and dares to ask where—in the pursuit of maximum capacity—a body might go" (201). This mapping of non-normative bodies traces
a genealogy of feminist, queer, and trans cultural producers that insist on
resisting traditional forms of artistic representation. I here agree with gender
theorist and curator Jeanne Vaccaro when she contends that "representation
is not an unequivocal sign of inclusion or political progress; it can be a tactical effort at surveillance and control" (115). By saturating their installations,
photos, and performances with bodies that have been rendered illegible, Cassils shatters the limits of representation, disorienting viewers' normative ways
of seeing and feeling, and disrupting acts of surveillance in the process.[12]

To find out about thresholds, Braidotti contends, "we must experiment, which means always, necessarily, relationally or in encounters with
others. We need new cognitive and sensorial mappings of the thresholds of
sustainability for bodies-in-processes-of-transformation" (137). In related
ways, and as I argue at length elsewhere (2017), Emma Donoghue's feminist and queer fictional experimentations are often propelled by alternative
mappings of corporeality and affect, for which the subject is constantly in
process. It was the publication of the novel *Room* in 2010, since translated

into thirty-five languages and turned into an Oscar-winning movie (2015), that consolidated Donoghue's reputation, not only in the Irish and the Canadian literary contexts, but also in the global literary panorama. Declaring herself "Irish Canadian," meaning she's "totally Irish" (Cumming), Donoghue systematically works across literary genres: she has written "coming out novels," revisionist fairy tales, screenplays, literary criticism, historiographic fiction, and, most recently, children's literature. Common denominators in Donoghue's work include a constant preoccupation with how bodies, material and textual, are archived, read, and rewritten across temporal and spatial boundaries. The fact-based historical novel *The Wonder* (2016), which is now being adapted into a movie, follows a similar critical stance, while simultaneously posing a number of ethical conundrums around the thresholds of sustainability of non-normative bodies. Based on the nineteenth-century phenomenon of the fasting girls, *The Wonder* is set in 1859 in the Irish Midlands. As Donoghue explains, "I'd set it in Ireland, of course—not just because that's my homeland, but because ever since the Great Famine of the 1840s, we've defined ourselves as a people intimate with hunger" ("The Wonder" n.p.). While belonging to the Irish literary genre of famine narratives (Harkin par. 6), I argue that the novel exceeds the boundaries of the nation, inviting readers to consider how colonial and patriarchal discourses have historically functioned to regulate women's bodies, while simultaneously silencing their stories.

The Wonder introduces Anna O'Donnell, an eleven-year-old girl who claims to have survived without consuming food for over four months. Referred to as a "living marble" (29) and an "extraordinary wonder" (30), Anna has become a celebrity and her body a source of spectacle: she receives visitors from all over the world, who often leave money for the church in exchange for looking at her. A committee decides to hire Mrs. Elizabeth (Lib) Wright, an English nurse, with the sole function to watch and report her observations. Having worked for Florence Nightingale, Lib's sense of superiority is linguistic, bodily, and moral, which contributes to considering herself "a better class of nurse" (6). As Harkin contends, having internalized the discourse of the British Empire, her arrogance makes her feel equipped with a superior, colonial gaze, to examine Anna, her object of study. Lib is hired to watch for a fortnight, alternating her eight-hour shifts with a Catholic nun. As part of her observation, Lib records all the developments in Anna's health in her memorandum book, measuring the length of the body and the arm span, among other things. This act of surveillance performs a similar function to Cassils' photographic grids: it works as a way to trace the bodily transformation, while testing the girl's thresholds of sustainability. Apart from taking notes, Lib has to touch the patient: "She pushed her finger into the girl's calf, like a sculptor forming a child out of clay" (38). This moment of touch allows her to begin to carve an emotional relationship with the girl. As such, touching here becomes an ethical moment in that it enables Lib's response-ability.

Response-ability here entails being able to respond, while simultaneously being accountable for your actions.[13] Queer science studies theorist Donna J. Haraway, for example, who has written extensively about shared suffering and responsible conduct, aptly contends that we need to "open passages for a praxis of care and response—response-ability—in ongoing multispecies worlding on a wounded terra" ("Awash" 302). In related ways, material feminist theorist and physicist Karen Barad discusses this formulation in terms of agency: "agency is about response-ability, about the possibilities of mutual response, which is not to deny, but to attend to power imbalances" (Dolphijn and van der Tuin 55). I am interested in unravelling the many shapes a praxis of response-ability can take, including the ruptures, paradoxes, and tensions that emerge when response-ability is represented in feminist, queer, and trans texts.

In Donoghue's novel, Lib's response-ability for Anna is initiated when she begins to respond to the child with a sense of accountability: "*A delight-ful dying child.* It was as well that Lib knew the truth, she told herself; now she could act. But for Anna's sake, she had to proceed with the greatest care" (192). In contrast, Anna is also exposed to the scrutiny of various male physicians, doctors, and priests, biopolitical authorities who have histor-ically regulated female sexuality as a source of perversion. Dr. Standish, for instance, uses his instruments to poke and prod the girl's naked body: "The child shuddered on the woven mat, hands drooping by her sides. Angles of shoulder blades and elbows, bulges of calves and belly; Anna had flesh on her, but it had all slid downwards, as if she were slowly melting" (106). Touching here subjugates the child, hence becoming a moment of violence.

I put this description of Anna's body alongside Cassils' durational per-formance *Tiresias* (2010–2013), in which the artist's naked body is pressed up against the back of a neoclassical Greek male torso carved out of ice (see Figure 7.4). Like the blind prophet of Thebes, who is transformed into a woman for seven years, Cassils uses their body heat to melt the ice slowly, momentarily blurring the boundaries between masculine and feminine, making them indistinguishable. *Tiresias* once again explores the thresholds of sustainability by using Cassils' own physical body as a vehicle for testing

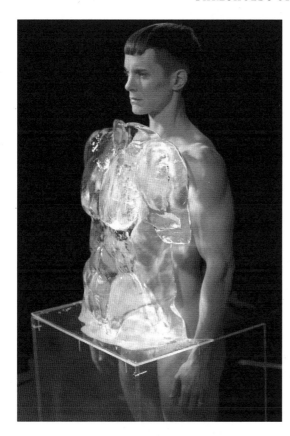

FIGURE 7.4
Cassils, *Tiresias*, 2013.
Performance for the
Camera. Photo: Clover
Leary. Courtesy of the
artist and Ronald Feldman
Gallery, New York.

corporeal and affective borders. As the artist explains, the performance, which lasts four to five hours, seeks to show "the instability of the body and our desire for a certain unsustainable physique" (n.p.). I claim that *Tiresias* also enables a moment of what could be called "transgender touch,"[14] with important ethical consequences. Following Barad,

> [a]ll touching entails an infinite alterity, so that touching the Other is touch-ing all Others, including the "self," and touching the "self" entails touching the strangers within ... Touching is a matter of response. Each of "us" is con-stituted in response-ability. Each of "us" is constituted as responsible for the other, as the other. (214–15)

Touching in Cassils' performance becomes an ethical moment in that it demands the audience to care, to respond, and to be affected, while simul-taneously stressing a sense of accountability and responsibility for the Other—in this case, the transgender subject.

In contrast, the contact between the doctor and Anna in Donoghue's novel increases the child's vulnerability and reduces her threshold of viability, in Stryker's terms. The doctor diagnoses Anna with hysteria, thus criminalizing her decision not to eat, and then suggests resorting to force and to using a rubber tube. Note how this violent technique was also used in prisons to subdue the suffragette hunger strikes at the beginning of the twentieth century and the Republicans in Ireland in the 1920s. In similar ways to what she does in the collection *The Woman Who Gave Birth to Rabbits* (2002), Donoghue seems to be tracing a biopolitical genealogy of deviant bodies that are deemed dangerous by the state, and therefore subjected to perverse strategies to turn them into docile bodies. Lib, nonetheless, refuses to terrorize the girl, given that bearing witness to Anna's deteriorating health slowly changes her attitude from suspicion to caring for the child. They are running out of time, however, as Anna's body becomes debilitated. Tapping the child's belly, Lib explains how "[t]he body's a kind of engine, ... Digestion is the burning of fuel. Denied fuel, the body will destroy its own tissues ... [T]he engine can't run much longer without proper fuel, do you see?" (211–12). Lib's response-ability for Anna entails an explanation of the thresholds of sustainability: how much can her body take?

As Braidotti suggests, if "the production and expression of positive affects is what makes the subject last or endure" (135), in Donoghue's novel it is the act of storytelling that makes Anna endure. Anna and Lib are constantly telling riddles to each other, which slowly contributes to developing a sense of trust between the two. Hence, I argue that touching also occurs through the act of sharing stories, activating response-ability. Sharing stories becomes a joyful act that helps Anna and Lib develop a sustainable affective community; in other words, telling one's story can activate sustainable affects understood as those emotions and feelings that become viable modes of action with the potential to reorient the system. This proto-feminist community thus provides a safe environment for the child to voice her story at last in discontinuous stages: Anna had been raped by her teenage brother when she was nine under the pretence of "marrying" her in the night. When he unexpectedly dies of a digestive complaint, the girl is terrified given that her brother had had no time to confess his sins, so she decides to starve and offer her life to save his soul in exchange. Consumed by guilt and shame, Anna reorients these unsustainable affects into religious devotion. Her drive to fast and die has therefore been propelled by external causes, in this case, living with trauma as a result of sexual violence. The novel suggests, nonetheless, that it is the act of sharing untold stories that may ultimately activate the girl's ability to respond toward her body's needs in a sustainable way.

Cassils' work, I argue, is not invested in producing or reproducing positive affects to define or redefine subjectivity. Instead, their performances cause frictions, tensions, and breaks. They elicit an affective response from the audience, making us feel uneasy, uncomfortable, accountable, but perhaps also mobilizing compassion, empathy, and response-ability. In the live performance *The Powers That Be* (LA, 2015), Cassils collaborates with choreographer Mark Steger to stage a fight between the artist's naked body and an invisible force. As stated by the artist in their personal website, this piece seeks to explore "the radical unrepresentability of certain forms of trauma and violence" (n.p.). The bodily convulsions and spasms signal, in my view, the direct and oblique oppressions and microaggressions that non-normative bodies are exposed to in everyday life—bodies that, as Stryker claims, "cumulatively erode the quality of psychical life and [that] also encounter major forms of violence, including deliberate killing" (40). *The Powers That Be* helps visualize an intensive subject, which is defined by Braidotti as one "that endures sustainable changes and transformation and enacts them around him/herself in a community or collectivity" (135). Disrupting the binary in Braidotti's articulation, the intensive subject in Cassils' performance reacts to fast and slow violences, while struggling for survival, in similar ways to Anna, in Donoghue's novel, as can be seen through the girl's bodily and affective battle.

Despite myriad obstacles, the girl has been trying to form her subjectivity by subjugating her body to extreme changes—and yet surviving. The intimacy developed between Lib and the girl then allows for one last transformation: Lib is able to convince the girl to drink a spoonful of "holy milk" that would turn her into a different girl. As a result, Anna would die, but eight-year-old Nan would survive. Anna finally chooses to drink, perhaps "longing for a different story" (274), as Lib puts it. This performance of death, which is also a common trope in Donoghue's novel *Room*, represents Anna's encounter with what could be called the ultimate threshold of sustainability. Braidotti contends that "'[e]nough,' or 'not going too far' expresses the necessity of framing, not the common-sense morality of the mainstream cultural orthodoxy. 'Enough' designs a cartography of sustainability" (153). Anna's transformation is her way of saying "enough": a moment of autopoesis and self-stylization from which she begins to map the road into becoming a sustainable subject.

Challenging religious value systems and indoctrination, the novel avoids a moralistic resolution. *The Wonder* ends with Lib and Anna in transit: in exile, arriving as new migrants in Australia. The open ending conveys a sense of hope for the future, represented as an imaginary space in which transformation is championed, enabling the possibility of a new life. Processes of change and transformation, Braidotti reminds us, "are so important and necessary, that they have to be handled with care" (133). Many trans populations, however, often live unsustainable lives with no access to care, something that Cassils problematizes and denounces by putting risk, violence, and unpredictability at the centre of their work. Cassils' performances also remain open-ended and are certainly more invested in process than in outcome. In her discussion of *Cuts*, Tsaconas aptly points out how "the artist did not set out with an explicit quantitative goal ... but instead was guided by the diffuse and intangible notion of arriving, eventually, at the point of the body's 'maximum capacity'" (201). In this sense, it could be argued that Cassils' bodily experimentations further follow Stryker's call for transgender studies to resist complicity with the biopolitical project itself. In different but related ways, Donoghue's and Cassils' counter-narratives raise intricate questions about the thresholds of sustainability of non-normative bodies, while fleshing out an ethics whereby subjectivity and agency can only be understood in their "infinite alterity" (Barad 207). By doing so, they firmly challenge the current cultural politics of compliance and indifference that perversely governs our contemporary world.

In the book *Staying with the Trouble*, Haraway characterizes our current epoch as one of urgency. With razor-sharp wit, Haraway contends that these are times "of great mass death and extinction; of onrushing disasters ...; of refusing to know and to cultivate the capacity of response-ability; of refusing to be present in and to onrushing catastrophe in time; of unprecedented looking away" (35). I remain with Haraway's words during these final remarks to consider the ethical implications of this refusal—a refusal to know, to respond, to take action, and to be accountable—particularly to reflect on the current state of Canadian literature as an institutionalized assemblage of power relations, alliances, and ruptures. I am thinking here of the untold stories, unheard voices, unacknowledged feelings that permeate the sides of CanLit, moving forward sideways, growing from what is to the side of it: the feminist, queer, and trans narratives of BIPOC and migrant writers and artists. I here also echo the concerns expressed by the editors of the timely collection *Refuse: CanLit in Ruins* (2018), who voice a collective "no" to the "serious inequities, prejudices, and hierarchies that exist within Canadian literature as an industry ... and an area of academic study" (McGregor, Rak, and Wunker 9). With recent debacles such as the Appropriation Prize or UBC Accountable,[15] it is more important than ever to pause and listen, to think about the stories we tell, the stories we borrow, and the stories that simply do not belong to us. As Joshua Whitehead pertinently puts it in his incisive essay "Writing as a Rupture: A Breakup Note to Canlit" (2018), "storytelling is a synonym for accountability" (191). Cassils' and Donoghue's counter-narratives align with Whitehead's ethical imperative when they enjoin their audiences and readers to stay with the trouble, to look directly into trauma and sexual abuse, and to consider how these forms of violence make the lives of many populations unsustainable.

McGregor, Rak, and Wunker further contend that to refuse can also mean to "re/fuse," that is "to put together what has been torn apart" (9). This, in my view, involves desire. As teachers, academics, and students, how can we turn the refusal to which Haraway refers into a desire to participate, to contribute to change, to act responsibly, to be present, and to look right into the trouble? A turn to response-able ethics then may not only be a timely and urgent lens from which to analyze this particular historical juncture but may also open up a discussion of past and ongoing legacies of colonization and future genealogies of resistance, simultaneously. "What is ethics, then?" Braidotti pertinently asks. "Ethics," she continues, "consists in reworking the pain into the threshold of sustainability, when and if possible: cracking, but holding it, still. It is a mode of actualizing sustainable forms of transformation" (139). I find Cassils' and Donoghue's ethical experimentations crucial to comprehend the complexities and paradoxes of the time in which we live. It is a time of inhumanity, no doubt, that demands utter response-ability from us; a time of divisiveness that makes it imperative for us to keep forging alliances between feminist, queer, and trans literary communities; a time of uncertainty that urges us to think within and beyond the borders of the possible to continue questioning or interrogating academic practices, while building feminist, queer, and trans methodologies. It is our response-ability then, as participants in this contested and troubled terrain of CanLit, to listen, attentively, to those counter-narratives that resist received versions of the body politic, in its multi-faceted iterations.

NOTES

1 This chapter was originally conceived as part of the panel "A Turn to Sustainable Feminist Affects: Unheard Histories, Untold Stories," organized by Susan Rudy (Queen Mary University of London), and in collaboration with Erin Wunker (Dalhousie University) and TL Cowan (University of Toronto). Part of this introduction draws on the rationale that we wrote collectively. I am deeply

grateful for their permission to reproduce it here, together with their insightful comments on how to think about sustainability within and beyond normative methodological frameworks. Research carried out with support from the projects 'Bodies in Transit: Difference and Indifference (Ref. FFI2017-84555-C2-2-P) and 'Cinema and Environment: Affective Ecologies in the Anthropocene' (Ref. PID2019-110068GA-I00 / AEI / 10.13039/501100011033), both funded by the Spanish Ministry of Science and Innovation.

2 Founded in 2017, the Canadian Nationalist Party is one of the many far-right parties that have emerged in the last few years worldwide. Their dangerous rhetoric, while masked under the "revival of national discourse," spreads hate and reinforces exclusionary practices against LGBTQ+ and other communities in Canada.

3 I here follow Pitts-Taylor and Schaffer in their rather expansive rendering of the prefix "trans-" in their "Editors' Notes" to the 2008 special issue of WSQ: "Trans-: Transgender, transnational, transspeciation, translation, transformation. Trans- as connection: shared space and time, transatlantic, transhistorical. Trans- as violation: transgression, transsection. Trans- as both assemblage and dissassemblage, as folded into structures of power as well as a movement of *becoming.* Most significantly for us, perhaps, *trans- as a way of seeing and thinking*" (9, emphasis added). I am particularly interested in teasing out how visual artists such as Cassils propose novel ethical ways of seeing and reading trans bodies in their work.

4 Gender theorist Margrit Shildrick claims that neoliberalism strategically produces and sustains bodies as debilitated "and therefore susceptible to a range of market commodities that hold out the promise of therapeutic interventions into the relative failures of physical, cognitive and affective embodiment" (11). Shildrick continues: "To be debilitated—to never reach the putative security of corporeal, affective and cognitive standards of flourishing—just is the condition of life" (14).

5 According to government data, there are currently fifty-nine long-term drinking water advisories that affect the everyday life of numerous Indigenous communities. Their continuous pleas for the right to clean water co-exist with Canada's national mission for sustainability. See further information regarding the data here: http://www.aadnc-aandc.gc.ca/eng/1506514143353/1506514230742.

6 See Achille Mbembe's "Necropolitics" (2003) and Jasbir Puar's *Terrorist Assemblages: Homonationalism in Queer Times* (2007) for an in-depth discussion on the workings of necropower.

7 *Cuts* appeared as part of a group installation in the show "Los Angeles Goes Live: Performance Art in Southern California 1970–1983" at the Los Angeles Contemporary Exhibitions (LACE, 2011–2012).

8 Carving metaphors abound in anglophone Canadian literature, with reference to nation-building projects, discovery, and exploration, but also in Indigenous and Inuit traditions. See Morley Callaghan's *The Loved and the Lost* (1951) and Jane Urquhart's *The Stone Carvers* (2001), among others.

9 As stated in the Art Institute of Chicago website, "The artist's idea of 'carving' her own body was inspired by an invitation from the Whitney Museum of Art for its biennial survey exhibition, which at the time restricted itself to the established categories of painting and sculpture, though this work was considered too conceptual for the exhibition" (http://www.artic.edu/aic/collections/artwork/144356).

10 See Nicholas Chare and Ika Willis' "Introduction: Trans-: Across/Beyond" (2016) for a detailed analysis of Cassils' homage to Lynda Benglis.

11 For an examination of the "transgender gaze," see Jack Halberstam's *In a Queer Time and Place: Transgender Bodies, Subcultural Lives* (2005).

12 Ana Horvat also discusses how disorientation works in Cassils' durational performance *Becoming an Image*. As Horvat claims, "the disorientation of the audience is not only an assault but also a process of dismantling preconceived ideas of what constitutes the trans experience and trans body ideals" (409). A similar argument could be applied to Cassils' *The Powers That Be*.

13 I here use the hyphen, following feminist and queer philosophers such as Donna J. Haraway and Karen Barad, who have disentangled the subtleties intrinsic to the term *responsibility*, now spelled *response-ability*.

14 Halberstam talks about the "transgender gaze," but I would like to offer a glimpse of how to theorize a form of "transgender touch" through representation.

15 For a detailed account of some of these scandals, see Alicia Elliott's "CanLit Is a Raging Dumpster Fire" (2017), originally published online in *Open Book*.

CHAPTER EIGHT

Unsustainable: Lyric Intervention in Vivek Shraya's
even this page is white

Erin Wunker

"Yet in this time of both full-blown terror and low-level ongoing anxiety, I have consistently found it valuable to risk putting the present moment into writing and to keep documenting the confusion of what is not yet known."

—"9-1-1 Every Day," Ann Cvetkovich

When do you stop documenting the present? You don't. I don't. As Ann Cvetkovich writes, "I have consistently found it is valuable to risk putting the present moment into writing and to keep documenting the confusion of what is not yet known" ("9-1-1 Everyday"). But it is exhausting, this documenting. It requires a shoring up of both the mind and the heart. And, I think, it requires working in in-between spaces and aesthetic modes that have not yet been solidified. Berlant writes that the "activity of living demands both a wandering absorptive awareness and a hypervigilance that collects material that might help clarify things, maintain one's sea legs, and coordinate the standard melodramatic crises with those processes that have not yet found their genre of the event" (*Cruel Optimism* 4). I think about that wandering awareness as my hand wanders to my phone to text my friends. To check in. To care and be cared for. To ask if an idea is good or a fever dream. What is the genre of this kind of friendship event that takes place so regularly through mediated technologies? I think it might be a poetics of sorts. I know that for me it is a praxis.

"*Trouble* is an interesting word," writes Donna Haraway. Stemming from a thirteenth-century French verb, its root means "to stir up, to make cloudy, to disturb." Trouble, for Haraway, is the word for our current moment. The task, as she sees it, is "to become capable, with each other in all of our bumptious kinds, of response" (*Staying with the Trouble* 1). I have come to think of that question about the troubled present in Canada, and in Canadian literary culture, as a question that has galvanized my sense of how friendship—specifically politicized and feminist friendship—is of vital importance to the now as well as to contextualizing intersecting and complex histories of oppression in a given time and space. My space is Canada, my time is the present. There is a great deal of work to be done. What might a praxis of friendship look like, especially when that praxis is one of solidarity and critique of the national context from which the poet does her work? How can poems critique white supremacy, misogyny, transphobia, and colonial violence as a gesture of friendship? These are questions I find at the heart of Vivek Shraya's *even this page is white*, and the text in which I would like to settle my thinking.

Vivek Shraya is an interdisciplinary artist. At the time of writing this chapter, her growing body of work includes short films, albums, children's literature, a novel, a collection of poetry, and a work of creative nonfiction. A four-time Lambda Literary Award nominee, Shraya is also the founder of VS. Books, an imprint of Arsenal Pulp Press aimed at the mentorship and publication of emergent Indigenous writers, Black writers, and writers of colour under the age of twenty-four. Her first novel, *She of the Mountains*, was a *Globe and Mail* best book, and her book *I'm Afraid of Men* was published in the fall of 2018. As a writer and editor, she works specifically to make space for BIPOC writers, while her film and music address issues such as sexual identity and mental health. It is not a stretch to say that Shraya's writing and pedagogical praxis are predicated on community building. In thinking about writing that takes place under the sign of the nation in the contemporary moment marked by Canada 150, I will focus my attention on Shraya's debut collection of poetry, *even this page is white*, which was long-listed for the 2018 CBC Canada Reads and won a Publisher Triangle Award. As I will go on to argue, *even this page is white* uses conceptual and lyric conceptual poetics to address the ongoing effects of colonial violence in the contemporary moment. Framed by a poetics and praxis of friendship, the collection offers both scathing critique and, I think, alternative models for navigating our unsustainable present.

The dedication of *even this page is white* reads as follows: "for anyone who has lost a friend from saying the word race." This acknowledgment of the difficulty of accountability and intervention—of saying "race" to a friend—is followed by two epigraphs. This first, an excerpt from Sara Ahmed's "Phenomenology of Whiteness," asks, "if whiteness gains currency by being unnoticed, then what does it mean to notice whiteness?" The second epigraph comes from correspondence between former poet laureate George

Elliott Clarke and Shraya. It reads, "Vivek—the page is always white because it is a void—'a voidance'—until ink cometh to make it right—and blankness is destroyed—and black words dance." Together these epigraphs train the reader's eye to look for what is both marked and unmarked. Put differently, in asking the reader to notice both whiteness and where and when the void is filled with black words, the epigraphs function as signposts for the collection. *even this page is white* is composed predominantly of investigative lyrics where, to build on Paul Naylor's definition, investigative here is reserved for those poetries that examine their cultural contexts, pose challenges to boundaries that exclude, work to name and critique the systems of power at work in the creation of meaning, jam up myths of progress, and deliberately and self-consciously engage in politics. The poems that make up the collection range from aphoristic to documentary, but they never lose sight of the unsustainability—of racism, of homophobia, of transphobia, of white supremacy—that continue to mark the present a tense one. The dedication and epigraphs train the reader's eye to witness whiteness—that void/ a voidance—which is the subject of Shraya's lyric interventions and investigations. The hinge of Shraya's poetic practice—her praxis—is friendship.

I find myself thinking of this dedication and epigraph often, lately, as I have spent time this past year using affect theory to write and think about recognition and friendship. Specifically, I've been thinking about friendship between women, and so the reading I've done has hinged on gender. As my friend and colleague Dr. Libe García Zarranz writes, one of the aims of feminist critics is to train our eyes and hearts—our feminist epistemologies and ethics—onto those "minoritized bodies" (qtd. in Lee) and experiences deemed increasingly cut out of or restricted by the state. In her keynote lecture to the members of the Association of Writing Programs in 2016, Claudia Rankine addressed the centrality of whiteness in the North American imaginary as an "amorphous discomfiture." The dis-ease that accompanies most discussions of race—especially with "good white people"—is, Rankine observes, understandable: "Conceptions of whiteness have been made and then propped up with eugenics and propped up with false science and false rhetoric and maintained through the justice system in every way. They become invisible" (qtd. in S.W. Thrasher). Shraya's dedication and the epigraphs that frame a doorway into the text seem, to me, to do some work of sketching the contours of living through white supremacy. Using her lived bodily experience to inform her poetic questions, her work walks a line between confessional and conceptual that draws whiteness, misogyny, and heteronormativity into conversation with brownness, colonial violence, and queer desire. Shraya's work,

I contend, asks readers to think through our individual relationships with visible and invisible privileges and oppressions.

In the opening to *Unmarked: The Politics of Performance,* performance scholar Peggy Phelan writes, "what we see is in every way connected to what we can say" (7). Otherness, difference, *differance*—Phelan locates them all in a Western-European ontology based on translation, of either self-reproduction or of otherness. One of the many insidious effects of this translation—of other into same, of other into self—is that it reproduces brokenness as a symmetrical relationship: "the relationship between self and other is a marked one," she writes, "which is to say it is unequal" (6). For Phelan, both live performance and intimate art construct the possible conditions for a "reciprocal gaze," which, in her view, casts light on the broken symmetries of our relatings. Reaching back to Rankine for a moment, live performance and intimate art construct possible conditions for drawing the invisibilized conditions of social structures into view. The possibilities Rankine flags are, I think, similar to what Phelan points to when she writes of the "broken symmetries between self and other, and the possibilities this break affords for rehearsing the political consequences of our acknowledgement of a failed inward gaze." For Phelan, "representation always shows more than it means: in the supplement one can see ways to intervene in its meaning" (27). In other words, whereas the Western-European traditions of philosophy and psychoanalysis tend to explain the individual's experience of another as one of translation (from other to same) or failed translation (uncanniness), Phelan here suggests a possible cog that can be thrown in that wheel. Certain kinds of artistic encounters crack the mirror. One such crack in the imagined community of Canada is, of course, race.

In his study of the ways in which civility—specifically, a white British notion of civility as a mode of conduct—undergirds "Canadian-Canadian society," Daniel Coleman posits that most of the nation's citizens are under a trance. Reminding readers that a trance is, in part, the repetition of a mantra, Coleman suggests that white civility is both cultural and structural. Positioned in opposition to Walcott's formulation of Black affect, white civility is figured by Coleman as doing both internal and external management (30). Building on the work of Jennifer Henderson and Pauline Wakeham, who note in *Settler Feminism and Race Making in Canada* that "race has been attached not just to bodies, but also to forms of conduct" (18), Coleman tracks civility as an unsustainable but prevalent affect of Canadian culture as well as policy. In short, white civility takes as foundational—as the "real"—both whiteness as the racial "norm" and "civility" as the racialized, whitened affect of national feeling and being.[1] Some practical results of this unsustainable affect are the homogenization of a national literary canon, or the inverse—what Ashok Mathur calls transubracination in which a few writers of colour "stand in" for a diverse and inclusive CanLit. But, as NourbeSe Philip wrote in the *Toronto Star* in 1990, when multiculturalism was becoming policy in Canada, "multi-culturalism is *not* anti-racism" ("Why Multiculturalism" A21). Indeed, as many writers and critics have suggested, multiculturalism has done much to reinstate whiteness as the emotional common denominator. Whiteness in Canada has much in common with Berlant's notion of an *impasse*; in Berlant's formulation, an impasse is not a moment of torpor or dithering, but rather a contradictory temporal expanse—a kind of mythological expanse—in which the individual moves through the world with "a sense that the world is at once intensely present and enigmatic" (*Cruel Optimism* 4). The impasse requires that the individual straddle the distance between immediacy and enigma. One feels she must be hypervigilant *and* allow her awareness to wander. The impasse, for Berlant, is a marker of the present.

We experience an impasse in many of the more traditionally lyric poems of *even this page is white*. Shraya's collection is broken into five sections: "white dreams," "whitespeak," "how to talk to a white person," "the origins of skin," and "brown dreams." Most of the poems—whether lyric or conceptual— are huddled in the bottom left or right corner of the page, leaving an expanse of white above and beside them. To unpack Shraya's lyric intervention, I want to linger for a moment on the second poem of the collection, "indian," which moves between traditional lyric page poetry and, when Shraya performs, spoken word. "Podium mic on," the speaker reminds "them" of the audience that "this land is not ours" (18). Shuttling between the distancing *they* and the collective *ours* moves the reader or listener from complacency to complicity until, at the end of the first stanza, we are shifted again into a different mode of address. "are you even in the room?," the speaker asks and, unless the reader is hailed by the signifiers of the title—"indian"—suddenly the circle is drawn more tightly around who is speaking and who is invited to listen. As the speaker grapples with the ways that "indian" is read onto her body and her mother's, complicity becomes the absent referent of systemic racism and colonial violence. The speaker recalls being in a car with her mother who "accidentally drove near a reserve / the only time I have seen her afraid." The double-bind of being marked by race is a system that privileges whiteness: "strange to be Indian with the sound of car locks / to be synonymous with indians" (19). Intergenerational trauma is layered onto learned behaviour when, upon interrogating the sustainability and ethics of territorial acknowledgments without restorative action, the speaker admits her own complicity in anti-Black racism: "last year Baltimore intersection black man / approaches once again a finger reaches for car / lock except this time the finger / is mine" (18). If the traditional circuitry of the lyric is, as Sedgwick and others argue, male in its gaze and homosocial in its movement, I suggest Shraya's more traditional lyrics intervene in the habitual lyric.

In Shraya's lyric, the masculinized "I" is troubled and doubled—two women, a mother and a woman-identified child with "m" on her birth certificate and a "woman inside [her body] who refused to buckle" (99)—both experience and perpetuate systemic racism. The speaker owns her own learned complicity in anti-Black racism, while asking Indigenous readers and listeners whether her territorial acknowledgments are "social justice or social performance" (17). The white supremacy undergirding modes of social relating on the lands called Canada (and, indeed, beyond those borders) is drawn from margin to centre. Blankness here is not avoided. Rather, the void at the centre of the lyric triangle is self-consciously crossed, called out, and rewritten in an attempt at ever-more ethical modes of relating. To recall Phelan, "broken symmetries between self and other" afford new possibilities ... Representation always shows more than it means to; in the supplement one can see ways to intervene in its meaning" (27). If white civility functions as a kind of Spivakian "sanctioned ignorance," then one tactic Shraya employs in the traditional lyric is to interrupt its habitual transmission. The blunt force of her own naming—of her body, her gender, her experience of and complicity in racism and the legacies of colonial violence—jams the flow of the lyric and, momentarily, the impasse of the current moment is brought into focus.

In her work on noticing and naming whiteness, Ahmed also suggests that a politics of recognition is one that hinges around definition work: "If we recognize something as racism," she writes, "then we also offer a definition of that which we recognize" ("A Phenomenology" 1). This work of naming and defining is, for Ahmed, the work of production as well: in naming and defining, we "delineate the boundaries" of what gets recognized as given. While Shraya's traditional lyric poems literally name and define realities that are other than those of white civility, her conceptual poems work to draw the reader's ideological impasses into the fore by other means. Shraya's poetics are also conceptual for a number of reasons, although I focus here on the question of gender and identity. The female subject is of central concern to conceptual writing. Robert Fitterman and Vanessa Place describe conceptual writing as "writing that mediates between the written object (which may or may not be a text) and the meaning of the object by framing the writing as a figural object to be narrated" (15). Unlike the traditional lyric structure, conceptual writing exaggerates the reading process insofar as its "excessive textual properties refuse ... the easy consumption of text and the rejection of reading in the larger culture" (Fitterman and Place 25).

While the ethics of conceptual poetry have, for very important reasons, been called into question and called out in recent years (I am thinking here, of course, of the work of Kenneth Goldsmith and Vanessa Place, and their respective albeit different appropriations of Blackness and Black embodiment), I contend that Shraya's conceptual poems are more properly working with what Sina Queyras coined as the lyric conceptual mode. Lyric conceptualism brings "excessive textual properties" into intimate proximity with the lyric subject. Here are a few aphoristic tenets set out by Queyras in "Lyric Conceptualism: A Manifest in Progress":

> Lyric Conceptualism accepts the tension between the self and the poetic sub-ject, wrestling always with the desire to give over to the poem and to be the poet in the poem.

> The Lyric Conceptualist looks longingly at those who enjoy the benefits of community but turns away from the gated community.

> The Lyric Conceptualist is not necessarily a feminine body, but it has the stink of the impure, a certain irreverence for the master, therefore it is by default, feminine in construction. (Wunker 118)

In short, I understand Queyras' tenets as encouragements: there is room in the lyric conceptual to bring together the avant-garde with the political. Indeed, the lyric conceptual mode is capacious enough to make room for both embodiment and experiment. Although Shraya employs the lyric conceptual mode intermittently throughout the collection, it is in the second and third sections, "whitespeak" and "how to talk to a white person," respectively, that the lyric conceptual mode is most prevalent. "whitespeak" opens with a poem entitled "a lover's bookshelf," which is a catalogue of the names of 124 authors. Only a handful of the authors are writers of colour. "white pride sounded like june 24, 2015 *for jennicet a hero not a heckler*" is composed of three columns of text (39). On the left, justified, is the transcript of President Obama's response to Latina trans activist Jennicet Gutiérrez's demands that the President cease deportations of LGBTQ people of colour from the United States. The President's response reads as follows: "hold on a second.

No. You're in my house. Shame on you. You can either stay and be quiet or we'll have to take you out." On the right, also justified, is the ambient noise of Gutiérrez being silenced. "Shhh. Boo. This is not for you this is for all of us." Centred and unjustified are Gutiérrez's own words: "I'm a trans woman / I'm tired of the abuse / I'm tired of the violence we're facing / not one more deportation" (39). Flanked on either side by the textualized refusal to witness, much less validate and make sustainable, her own lived bodily experience, Jennicet Gutiérrez's words are rendered lyric. Shraya centres the voice of a Latina trans woman at the White House and relegates to the sidelines the words of the Commander in Chief as well as the mainly white heteronormative audience.

The result, I think, is layered: the tools for recognizing President Obama and the audience are removed. Only the pagination and justification signal that this is sanctioned speech. Meanwhile, the lyric testimony of Gutiérrez is central, but not necessarily recognizable. Mimicking the lyric voice and typographical choices of Shraya's traditional lyrics—no capitalization, blunt statements of affect—it is more than possible for the reader to misrecognize Gutiérrez's speech as Shraya's. If "what we see is in every way bound up in what we can say" (Phelan), then Shraya's conceptual lyric recreates the conditions of our unsustainable cultural impasse around whiteness and witness. These conceptual lyric interventions construct moments of mis/recognition over and over. Poems such as "54,216 Signed a Petition to Ban Kanye West from Playing Pam Am Games Closing Ceremony," "#oscarssowhite," and "Miley, What's Good?" use conceptual practices of found text to reframe white civility against the "minoritized subject" deemed unacceptable by the "rising biopolitics of racism" (García Zarranz).

As I have been trying to sketch messily, central in this project is an ethical act of intellectual friendship as praxis. What I have been working to show are some of the ways in which Shraya's lyric and lyric conceptual poetics both intervene in these paradoxical asymmetries of discourse and counter-discourse of friendship as praxis. *even this page is white* employs the lyric "I" to interrupt the white supremacy and white civility (Coleman) of Canadian culture. Shraya's lyric conceptualism builds a poetics that demand intervention and accountability from both reader and speaker—it is a poetics of intimacy that offers a kind of friendship to the reader.

In an interview entitled "Friendship as a Way of Life," Michel Foucault is invited to consider desire—specifically gay desire—as a frame for his writing. Foucault's response informs my reading of Shraya's lyric conceptualism as a kind of praxis of friendship. In his response, he shifts from thinking about desire as primarily a sexual force and instead positions desire as a mode of organizing one's attention on another. Desire, in his formulation, becomes a mode of subverting the hegemony of compulsory heterosexuality, for example. Desire, figured as friendship by Foucault, becomes a way of being open to a range of intimacies that have been forbidden by hetero-patriarchy. The desire for these things—vulnerability, embrace, proximity—is, for Foucault, a desire for a new way of life.[2] What I see in Shraya's work, then, is this same refiguration of desire as friendship, as world-making praxis.

The final poem of the collection and the last poem of the section, both titled "brown dreams," returns to a more traditional lyric structure. Centred on the page, the poem asks questions without ending—there are no question marks, only the inflection of interrogative speech:

> How often you must prove your pigment
> when your entire body is painted bronze
>
> have you ever heard white question its colour
> snow moon salt milk tooth chalk
>
> what if there is no right way to be brown
> besides the brown you are
>
> soil nut clove wheat bark pluto. (107)

Here, though, like the shifting personal pronouns of "indian," the intimate reach of "you" is specific. This is not for me, a white cis-gendered settler-reader, although I am certainly invited to read and listen. Rather, this lyric extends to "you" with tender deliberateness. "You" are the central longing, the beloved of the traditional lyric. I am the witness, but I am not the participant or the longed-for loved one. And that disruption, that intervention holds me accountable. The poem works, but only if I do my work too. No longer void or avoidance, the page becomes a place to trouble the paradoxical asymmetries of narrative that relegate "minoritized subjects" to the margin. *even this page is white*, which intersects traditional tenets of lyric poetry with anti-racist action and intersectional feminist theories of situated knowledge, interrogates and ultimately rejects whiteness and heteronormativity. These are unsustainable affects. Instead, what emerges is a polyphonic work of witnessing whiteness that calls for individual and collective accountability in the project of anti-racism and reconciliation in Canada. In short, I suggest

Shraya's collection is a poetic enactment of a politics of recognition that works against ongoing colonial violences and invites and models an ethical mode of accountability predicated, in part, on friendship.

NOTES

1 See also Ahmed, "A Phenomenology."

2 I have written and been thinking about Foucault's essay for a while. This is a slight reworking of an excerpt from "Notes on Friendships," from my own *Notes from a Feminist Killjoy: Essays on Everyday Life.*

CHAPTER NINE

Untold Stories of Slavery: Performing Pregnancy and Racial Futurity in Beatrice Chancy

Kailin Wright

Slavery in Canada threatens to remain an untold story. Canadian history often celebrates Nova Scotia as a safe haven for freed slaves. There was a time, however, when slavery was legal in what we now call Canada. As George Elliott Clarke reminds us, "a mass ignorance exists about the conduct of slavery" in Nova Scotia (*Beatrice Chancy* 7). Speaking to and with Canada's unheard voices, Clarke's verse play *Beatrice Chancy* (1999) specifically tells the story of a female slave in early nineteenth-century Nova Scotia. The play, which recounts the factual account of a sixteenth-century woman, Beatrice Cenci, who murdered her sexually abusive father, dramatizes the untold story of pregnancy under systems of slavery. While *Beatrice Chancy* premiered in 1997 as a staged reading at Toronto's Theatre Passe Muraille, the publication of the play in 1999 marked the 400th anniversary of the real Beatrice Cenci's death.[1] Inspired by a range of source material, Clarke alters the historical narrative by setting the play on a slave plantation in Nova Scotia at the turn of the nineteenth century: Clarke's Beatrice is a Black slave, while Chancy is her white father and slave owner.[2] After discovering Beatrice's affection for a fellow slave named Lead, Chancy rapes his daughter; she becomes pregnant, murders her father in revenge, and is subsequently hanged as punishment while she is five months pregnant. Clarke's play thus brings a much-needed racial lens to the enduring symbol of reproduction in Canada and its prehistory.

Beatrice Chancy is only one example of how plays perform reproduction as the symbol of a future, or lack thereof, on stages across Canada; all too often, when a woman does not reproduce, she is treated as a figure that fails to participate in a future. In adding the context of slavery, Clarke complicates the rape, pregnancy, and execution by making them racialized acts.

Beatrice Chancy, for instance, presents the future as the repetition of past racial injustices, when Chancy abuses Beatrice just as he did her mother. For the pregnant Beatrice, her execution means that she will not have to bear her child-sibling and his slave: she invites God to "[s]hatter this penitentiary of flesh" and the chorus sings of death as a gateway to freedom while she hangs (144). An examination of the performance of pregnancy in *Beatrice Chancy* may increase awareness of this sensitive issue, foster a discussion about the racialization of the future, and challenge the representation of the death of a pregnant woman as a symbol of a failed future. Ultimately, for her fellow slaves and the audience, the death of the pregnant Beatrice is not only a site of mourning but also a locus of revolution that resists the white slave owner, the perpetuation of his lineage, and the increase in his slaves.

Through an examination of Beatrice's pregnancy and execution, I demonstrate the importance of critically discussing reproduction in order to combat negative portrayals of the end of a pregnancy as a racialized failure. After contextualizing scholarly and legal debates about reproduction, I focus on how *Beatrice Chancy* uses her death to reject white reproductive futurism. Ultimately, I argue that Beatrice critiques the structural racism of futurity that excludes Black families by harnessing her death and the end of her pregnancy as a political refusal to bear a white master's child and sustained abuse.

Racial Reproductive Futurity

Clarke's protagonist, Beatrice, conceives of her womb as a symbol of reproductive futurity—or the quantity and quality of a future—that privileges whiteness and precludes the possibility of a Black family. Lee Edelman theorizes the concept of futurity in *No Future*, examining the Child as a political symbol of a heteronormative temporality that excludes queer identity.[3] *Beatrice Chancy* makes a similar critique of the Child as an exclusionary figure but concentrates on the Child as a racialized symbol of white futurity.[4] Edelman begins *No Future* with an analysis of American politics in order to establish how political rhetoric uses the Child as a symbol of a national, shared futurity that unites citizens in "a fight for our children" (3). *No Future* defines this rhetoric of "reproductive futurism" as "terms that impose an ideological limit on political discourse as such, preserving in the process the absolute privilege of heteronormativity by rendering unthinkable, by casting outside the political domain, the possibility of a queer resistance to this organizing principle of communal relations" (2). Edelman suggests that the "politics" of the "Child" positions queerness as "the side of those not 'fighting for the children'" (3) and responds to this rhetoric by rejecting futurity altogether. As Mari Ruti explains, the "thesis of [No Future] is that instead of seeking to dismantle the homophobic representation of queers as death-driven, unproductive, and socially disruptive, queers should embrace these negative stereotypes … Queers should, in other words, take it upon themselves to embody the threat to the social fabric that they, whether or not they so wish, always already signify" (113). Edelman invokes the death drive in order to challenge pronatalism as homophobic, just as Beatrice willingly goes to her death in order to rupture the slave system that enables rape and makes her the bearer of future slaves. Beatrice does not choose her execution, but she does make a revolutionary choice about how to narrate her death and the end of her pregnancy as the failed futurity of her white slave master and father.

Whereas Edelman focuses on queer resistance, Hortense Spillers examines racial resistance to reproductive futurism that privileges the white, freed maternal figure. In her discussion of the "Black Family" during times of slavery, Spillers asserts that "'Family' as we practice and understand it 'in the West'—the *vertical* transfer of a bloodline, of a patronymic, of titles and entitlements … in the supposedly free exchange of affectional ties between a male and a female of his choice—becomes the mythically revered privilege of a free and freed community" (218). Ericka Miller similarly distinguishes "motherhood as defined by white feminists" and by "black women" in contexts of racial inequality, because "black mothers live with the knowledge that no matter how nurturing and attentive their mothering, it cannot protect a child from the brutality of race violence" (82). In Upper Canada at the end of the eighteenth century, for instance, enslaved women could not protect their child from slavery. The Upper Canada Abolition Act in 1793 was established "to prevent the further introduction of slaves" into Upper Canada, but it only "reaffirmed the property rights of existing slaveholders" (Wigmore 441) and stated that "any child born of a slave mother" would not be free until "the age of 25" (Reese 209). In her work on reproduction and laws under slavery, Dorothy Roberts demonstrates the continued state control of Black women's bodies, concluding that "[f]or slave women, procreation had little to do with liberty. To the contrary, Black women's childbearing in bondage was largely a product of oppression rather than an expression of self-definition and personhood" (23). Spillers, Miller, and Roberts examine how reproduction has been used as an agent of slavery. This "brutal domination of slave women's procreation," Roberts reminds us, "laid the foundation for centuries of reproductive regulation that continues today" (23). The Child and Family, it seems, has a history of reinforcing white privilege particularly in the United States and Canada. *Beatrice Chancy* reveals how slave systems in Nova Scotia enshrined the whiteness of the symbolic Child, which denied Black women like Beatrice access to a Family and a nationalist "fight for our children" (Edelman 3).

In Edelman's examination of heteronormativity, queer resistance, and the figurative Child, mothers are almost completely absent from his criticism. The mother, however, is the bearer of the Child and, as a result, of the symbol of futurity. Tackling Edelman's neglect of mothers and their diverse socio-economic experiences of reproduction, scholars such as Anca Parvulescu note that *No Future* "left untold the other story of reproduction" (89), including experiences of the poor (José Esteban Muñoz), migrant women (Parvulescu), disabled children (Alison Kafer), and racial and ethnic groups (Mari Ruti). Edelman, in short, responds to and resists a white middle-class discourse of the American Child under conditions that "allow parents to cherish their children" and reap "the political 'capital' that those children will thus have become" (112). In addition to the diverse range of families who may not see the economic or social benefits of parenthood, I argue that many women experience the inverse of Edelman's concept of social and cultural capital when a pregnancy does not result in a normative Child. Speaking to this use of reproduction as a symbol of failure, Mark Fisher asserts that "it is women, not men, who are queered by reproductive futurism: scandalously, it remains the case that women are made to feel like failures if they do not reproduce. It may turn out, then, that the most productive use of Edelman's ideas will occur in feminism" (2). Taking up Fisher's call, I use an intersectional feminist approach to Edelman's theory of futurity in order to consider how women are used as symbols of a failed racialized future.

The end of a pregnancy and women who do not reproduce are often treated as negative symbols of loss—whether it is the loss of heterosexual normalcy or of futurity. Merrill Denison's *Marsh Hay* (1923), Gwen Pharis Ringwood's *Still Stands the House* (1938), and Sinclair Ross' *As for Me and My House* (1941) reveal how a sudden end to a pregnancy, the death of a pregnant woman, and infertility have been used to represent not only individual loss but also Canada's threatened futurity.[5] In Clarke's play, Beatrice's stepmother and Chancy's white wife, Lustra, "beg[s] Christ to fill / my vacant womb" (74) and interprets her "fallow" womb as a negative, a "barren" vacancy that she longs to fill (53). Chancy blames the fact that she has not borne children as the reason for his mistreatment of her, hurling insults as he asks, "Who craves a dry, dull, empty, sonless wife?" (53). Lustra, then, concludes that women who do not reproduce are targets of blame.

Beatrice, however, complicates this symbolism of maternal failure by highlighting the different experiences of reproduction for free and enslaved women, describing "markets splitting mother and child" as they are sold to different masters (31). For slaves, as Beatrice says, "childbirth is sinning and pain" (142), because the Black Child serves a white master, a white futurity. In denying Beatrice access to Western definitions of family and maternity, slavery denies her of futurity. Just as Edelman's *No Future* encourages queers to embrace the death drive that they always already signify, Clarke's *Beatrice Chancy* embraces the interpretation of women who do not reproduce as a symbol of a lost white future. Accepting that "it took violence" to spread "the perfume of liberty" (147), Beatrice proudly declares "I suffer what I must" (140); as Deal, a freed slave, exclaims at Beatrice's hanging, "Gone—the horse of a whip cracking my back" (146). In transforming her death into a symbol of resistance, Beatrice not only rejects her slave master's lineage, she also works outside of white reproductive futurism.

While I examine Beatrice's treatment of death as a radical rejection of white futurity, the play (and my reading of it) could be controversial and interpreted to support arguments about the control of Black women's reproduction. In using her hanging and the feticide to usher in an end to slavery, *Beatrice Chancy* invites a comparison with other women who commit infanticide to protect their children from slavery in works such as Angelina Weld Grimké's "The Closing Door" (1919), Toni Morrison's *Beloved* (1987), and Lawrence Hill's *The Book of Negroes* (2007). As with key figures in Grimké's, Morrison's, and Lawrence's works, Beatrice intimates that she would be willing to commit feticide to end slavery when she explains to her beloved, Lead, that she would "annihilate this world— / This womb of horrors" (138), thereby intimately connecting her impulse to "annihilate this world" of slavery with the annihilation of "this womb." An important distinction, however, is that she does not kill a child or choose to end her pregnancy. Grimké's mother figure, for instance, kills her newborn son in order to protect him from being the victim of racial violence and lynching. Grimké's short story first appeared in a special issue of the *Birth Control Review* dedicated to "The New Emancipation: The Negroe's Need for Birth Control," but, as Layne Craig argues, was ultimately addressed to white women readers. Craig recounts how "birth control advocates enabled and even publicized" the "figure of the African American woman who refuses motherhood in a racist society" through "Grimké's work" (20). Whereas Gloria Hull critiques "The Closing Door" for supporting the sterilization of Black women and eugenic movements, Miller argues that the story "emphasize[s] the different implications of maternity for white and non-white women" (80).[6] I interpret Beatrice's patricide and execution in this vein as a story about the different implications of maternity and pregnancy for white and Black women, for the freed and enslaved.

In exposing the unrelenting whiteness of futurity in Canada, *Beatrice Chancy* challenges historical narratives of Canada as a place of freedom. Slavery, after all, was legal in Nova Scotia during the late eighteenth and early nineteenth centuries until the Slavery Abolition Act abolished it in most parts of the British Empire in 1834—a little known or perhaps willingly forgotten part of the pre-history of Canada. "It is important to note," Harvey Whitfield says, "that many Africans and New World Africans were brought into Nova Scotia in bondage" ("African" 102). As Renford Reese reminds us, "Many British and British Loyalists that fought and lost the [American Revolutionary War] migrated to Canada with their slaves" and, during the late eighteenth century, "over 2,000 slaves arrived in Canada: 1,232 slaves were brought to Nova Scotia" (Reese 210). Gregory Wigmore similarly explains that, "[e]ven when historians acknowledge these slaves [in Canada], they rarely mention that many found freedom by crossing the border to the United States—which contradicts Canada's later reputation as a haven from slavery" (439). In reminding its audience of Canada's troubled racial past, *Beatrice Chancy* debunks the national myth of Canada as an enduring place of multicultural harmony. Clarke's play, then, critiques the continuing structural racism that privileges a white perspective in national narratives about the past as well as the future. Clarke introduces his play by explaining that he does not have access to his heritage because, "being a Nova Scotian of African-American origins (i.e. an Africadian), I will never know the furthest origins of my African heritage," but "I do know that is was disrupted by a ship and ruptured by chains" (8). Slavery denies Clarke his past and Beatrice her future. Given the political use of the Child as a symbol of national futurity, Clarke's play asks crucial questions about the race of the symbolic Child in Canada. Through these opening remarks about Canada's history and in setting the play in Nova Scotia, Clarke encourages a reading of the play that connects Chancy's abuse of Beatrice to national racial violence and restrictions on Black mothers. *Beatrice Chancy* is more than a play about the sufferings of one woman; it dramatizes Black women's historical lack of choice when it comes to fundamental rights of reproduction and maternity in Canada.

Performance Contexts

While some scholarly works consider reproduction in American and Canadian literature, Canadian theatre has not devoted such critical attention to the subject.[7] Canadian theatre, much like fiction and film, has a long history of staging reproduction, abortion, miscarriage, non-normative pregnancy, and the death of a pregnant woman, including Denison's *Marsh Hay* (1923), Ringwood's *Still Stands the House* (1938), Michel Tremblay's *Les Belles-Soeurs* (1968), Tomson Highway's *Dry Lips Oughta Move to Kapuskasing* (1989), Margaret Clarke's *Gertrude and Ophelia* (1993), Robert Lepage's *The Seven Streams* (1994), Djanet Sears' *Harlem Duet* (1997), and Catherine Banks' *It Is Solved by Walking* (2012), to name a few. In response to the scholarly focus on American and Canadian fiction, this chapter turns to the theatre and its powerful embodiment of pregnancy.

Beatrice Chancy's dramatization of racial reproductive futurism was performed in the wake of the Supreme Court of Canada's *R. v. Morgentaler* case in 1988 that struck down the previous abortion law (1968–69) as unconstitutional and enabled women to retain an abortion without any legal restriction. In addition to legal debates on reproductive rights, the late 1980s and 1990s were also a time when Toronto theatres worked on acknowledging racial diversity as exemplified by the change to Nightwood Theatre's mandate from a focus on "women-centered work" in the early 1980s to "the focus on women of color" in 1989 (Knowles 145). Plays such as Clarke's *Beatrice Chancy*, Sears' *Harlem Duet*, and Highway's *Dry Lips Oughta Move to Kapuskasing* premiered at Toronto theatres and spoke to the issues of the late 1980s and 1990s by integrating arguments of pregnancy, race, and ethnicity. These plays feature feticide, abortion, miscarriage, and "damaged" pregnancy as tropes that warn of the lost futurity of Black and Indigenous families (Highway 207).

Despite the political and symbolic significance—not to mention the audiences' shock at the visceral scenes—scholarly criticism and theatre reviews tend to overlook performances of reproduction that do not result in a normative child. Scholars have analyzed *Beatrice Chancy* in terms of identity politics and intertexts—a fitting area of investigation given that Clarke uses Canada's history of slavery to frame his retelling of Beatrice's patricide.[8] Maureen Moynagh contributes an insightful exploration of *Beatrice Chancy*'s representation of slavery and argues that Beatrice exemplifies what Lauren Berlant terms an act of "diva citizenship," by calling for a radical change to the dominant social order and accepted practices of citizenship (223). I would add that Beatrice's rejection of her pregnancy and the Child is yet another example of this diva citizenship because, as Edelman points out, "that figural Child alone embodies the citizen as an ideal" (11). In embracing the end of the pregnancy and the loss of the symbolic Child, Beatrice performs what Edelman would describe as a "queer" pregnancy that enacts "a threat not only to the organization of a given social order but also, and far more ominously, to social order as such, insofar as [she] threatens the logic of futurism on which meaning always depends" (Edelman 11). Emerging out of an important time for reproductive rights and diversity, I argue that pregnancy is key to *Beatrice Chancy*'s representations of racial identity, because it calls attention to the threatened futurity of the Black family. Beatrice, after all, cannot live out her fantasies of domestic life with her Black beloved.

Replacing the Womb with the Tomb in Beatrice Chancy

Turning to the play more closely illustrates how the issues of reproduction, race, and futurity are mutually constitutive. *Beatrice Chancy* begins and ends with slaves "*leapshouting*" about freedom and asking "O King Jesus" to "Slay slavery!" (12). Clarke's play draws attention to the often-overlooked period in history when there was slavery in Nova Scotia's Annapolis Basin before the Slavery Abolition Act of 1833 that outlawed slavery. Beatrice, whom Clarke describes as a "*martyr-liberator*" (10), eventually helps to win freedom for her fellow slaves as she struggles with her two conflicting identities as the white master's (Chancy's) daughter and as his slave. In sending her to a convent to be educated as a lady, Chancy seems to view her more as his daughter than as his slave. Yet both roles, whether she is daughter or slave, posit Beatrice as a type of object. Chancy, after all, plans to "graft her / On some slavery-endorsing Tory / To fat my interests in the Assembly" (28). Moynagh examines the doubleness of Beatrice's role and of Chancy's relationship to her as at once slave master and father:

> The ambiguity of Beatrice's status emerges in the contradiction between Chancy's plans for her, which position her as daughter, and the language he uses to convey those plans, which is at once crudely biological ("I'll graft her") and economic—more appropriate to a slave, in other words. Strictly speaking, under slavery, any child of a black mother was black. Thus, Chancy's efforts to remake Beatrice in his own image ("I dispatched Beatrice to Halifax / To shape her more like us—white, modern, beautiful" [52]) suggest a deliberate rework-ing of kinship in a way that exposes its racial subtext. (111)

The racial kinship and Chancy's ownership of Beatrice are reinforced through the rape, because she is not only Chancy's familial object (daughter) and eco-nomic object (slave), but also his sexual object.

Slave laws further reinforce the racialization of reproduction and rape by serving to protect Chancy and dehumanize Beatrice; as Lustra warns Bea-trice, "you forget your low place. Troops shield White Women" (77). Roberts recounts how "[t]he law reinforced the sexual exploitation of slave women" by "fail[ing] to recognize the rape of a slave woman as a crime" (29). Chancy's rape of Beatrice functions as a legal way to enforce his paternal and racialized hold of her. As Chancy exclaims, "I considered you as my daughter" but "[y]ou mock my love by loving dung!" (55). Chancy thus fears that she will no longer be his daughter in two ways: first, because she will belong to her husband not her father, and second, because she will be joined to a Black man and not a white master. Beatrice's marriage to Lead would undo her ties to her father in terms of paternal and racial relations. Chancy's rape claims his kinship to a slave-daughter by making Beatrice "his" in a sexual way. When she cries out in fear and asks for "Lead! Lead! O my sweet Lead!," Chancy casts himself as Lead's replacement because "[i]nstead, you feel your father's hands" (86). Chancy refuses to sell Beatrice, which would render her a slave and daughter to him no more, choosing instead to rape her and thereby maintain her dual role as at once kin and property.

While Chancy's rape of Beatrice upholds slave laws and asserts his ownership, Beatrice's patricide at once denies structures of kinship and slavery. The control of women's bodies and reproduction was essential to the slave system and its perpetuations. As Roberts asserts, "the social order established by powerful white men was founded on two inseparable ingredients: the dehumanization of Africans on the basis of race, and the control of women's sexuality and reproduction" (23). Her patricide, however, rejects the social order of family, slavery, and gender. As Moynagh explains, Beatrice "violates social law, not only by killing a member of her society but by striking at the kinship structure itself and its gendered organization. For in rising up against her father, Beatrice does the unimaginable: the object of exchange becomes an agent in her own behalf" (107). Chancy's legal objectification of Beatrice as daughter and slave magnifies the impact of his violence as well as her revolt.

The rape raises the stakes of my argument about the importance of an inclusive racial futurity and a Black family: slavery, rape, and incest are the markers and mechanisms of a system that does not recognize a Black family, Child, or futurity. Beatrice's child, as Moynagh points out, would be Black under the system of slavery. Chancy's paternity of the child, as a result, would be unacknowledged and his role as slave master would trump familial ties. Beatrice, however, would also be denied her maternal role, because the child would be born a slave and Chancy would have the right to sell the child. In raping and impregnating Beatrice, he reinforces her enslavement by forcing her to beget more slaves and by denying her of the maternal rights to care for or raise the child: the child would be born into slavery rather than into the Western notion of a Family (as described above by Spillers). "Here lies one of slavery's most odious features," Roberts explains, "it forced its victims to perpetuate the very institution that subjugated them by bearing children who were born the property of their masters" (24). Beatrice's pregnancy is a threat to her, precisely because it represents the future tense—the future propagation of the trauma of her rape and Chancy's progeny. His paternal role doubles the violence of his crime: he commits incest as well as rape. As he himself claims, "I'll beget son and grandson / While she gets son and brother" (97). The pregnancy, then, exacerbates the sexual violence and incest by threatening to bring it into the future tense, as Chancy's living lineage and as Beatrice's "son and brother." In her analysis of the history of slavery and the significance of Black bodies, Spillers considers whether the "phenomenon of marking and branding [slaves] actually 'transfers' from one generation to another" (207). For Spillers, racial trauma and slavery can be passed on from generation to generation, and Beatrice's pregnancy threatens to do just that: her enslavement, incest, and rape will live on into the future through her Black child-sibling. As Beatrice exclaims, "I breathe his corruption by breathing air" (117).

In rejecting these laws of slavery and her reproductive work for the slave master, Beatrice's pregnancy represents the death drive. After Chancy rapes her, she embodies the impulse to kill Chancy and the death drive, as she longs to "gouge out his heart" (108), to "obliterate / Him" (129), to "[become] a devout killer" (140), to fill "the O of a noose" (145). In Jacques Lacan's, Sigmund Freud's, and Edelman's theories, the death drive and queerness are interrelated, because they both oppose social order and break things apart.[9] Her murder of Chancy and subsequent execution do just that—they oppose the order of slavery and it is only through these deaths that she is "free" (131). While "queerness," as Edelman says, "can never define an identity; it can only ever disturb one" (17), "the death drive names what the queer, in the order of the social, is called forth to figure: the negativity opposed to every form of social viability" (9). Just as Edelman opposes narratives of the future as merely "fantasies [that] reproduce the past," so Clarke suggests that Beatrice's pregnancy threatens to repeat the cycle of tragedy and slavery, because she would give birth to her father's child-slave just as her mother did before her. In her willingness to "annihilate" her "womb" (*Beatrice Chancy* 138) that bears her master-rapist-father's child, Beatrice anticipates Edelman's argument that "the Child as futurity's emblem must die" (Edelman 31). She welcomes death as a way of escaping the reproduction of slavery (or a slave) and as her last act of protest, exclaiming, "Slave days is over!" (126).

The death of Beatrice while she is pregnant, however, does not perform the complete negation of a future—and here is where my analysis diverges from Edelman's argument for "no future"—because her death only negates white futurity and the reproduction of the slave system. She is critical of her role as child bearer under the slave system—she opposes the reproduction of her slave master-father and his system of enslavement. She does not, however, necessarily oppose reproduction. By extension, she challenges the futurity of her white rapist-father and his slave business, but she does not oppose futurity altogether. The death of pregnant Beatrice disrupts her chains of slavery by releasing her and any progeny from slavery. As a result, she does not choose to die, but she ushers in her "*Death*" (80) as the failed futurity of Chancy and the potential futurity of the freed slaves. While the pregnancy amplifies the violence of the rape and her enslavement by making her the begetter of a child-sibling and a slave, the hanging of the pregnant Beatrice concomitantly increases the freedom gained in death because, as she frames it, her death frees herself and ensures that she will not "calf bastards" (109).

Whereas the end of a pregnancy all too often symbolizes a mother's failure or a doomed future, the execution of the pregnant Beatrice is a revolutionary act of freedom from slavery. Her death and her murder of Chancy, after all, help to set the slaves free, and she joins them in rejoicing their new freedom. In murdering Chancy, she has helped ensure that "Governor Wentworth … freed Chancy's slaves" (144). In the final scene, as she hangs, the chorus of "Slaves/Liberateds" invoke the pleasure of the grave by singing of death as a radical act of freedom from slavery:

> Oh freedom, oh freedom,
> Oh freedom over me.
> And before I'd be a slave,
> I'd be buried in my grave,
> And go home to my Lord and be free. (148)

Although the play ends with Beatrice's death, Clarke presents this death of a pregnant woman as a symbol of "freedom" from living slavery. As Clarke himself explains in an interview, "I knew I wanted to write a tragedy and not one where there was going to be any easy sort of resolution at the end. She does take action; it's good action, positive action. At the same time, it results in her own destruction" (Compton 151). This uneasy ending may be why the play has yet to receive a professional production—although the large cast and poeticism might also be a factor. Beatrice's dying pregnant body—a potentially powerful embodied performance to be sure—is the site of action, revolt, and freedom from slavery.

While narrating the colour black and Beatrice's Black pregnant body as poetic and dramatic vehicles for revolution, *Beatrice Chancy* racializes love and hate as black and white, respectively. White represents "lies" and loathing, as Beatrice's lover, Lead, proclaims:

> Hear me, I'm sick—sick of whiteness:
> White pine white spruce white sheets white wine
> White lies whitewash white lightnin white
> Verse white sugar white meat white smoke
> White this white that. Let black *Death* troop! (80, emphasis Clarke's)

Lead is "sick" of slavery and the "whitewash" of his surroundings—surroundings of nature ("White pine white spruce"), domestic life ("white sheets white wine"), and cultural oppression ("White lies" "white / verse") (100). The exclamatory end to this speech, however, is not "white" but rather "black *Death*," as he invites death to "troop!" over whiteness. He here establishes "*Death*" as a vehicle for "black" revolt, setting up Beatrice's death and her pregnant Black body as a protest to oppressive "whiteness" (100).

After hearing of the horrors that Chancy has inflicted upon Beatrice, Lead and his fellow slaves Deal and Dumas gather to talk of revenge. As Lead proclaims that Chancy's "death be our freedom!" (101), Dumas' speech on "black" as "loving" serves as the mirror scene to Lead's "white" speech and seems to pick up right where his monologue ended. While Lead ends with the imagery of "white smoke," Dumas begins by "loving black smoke":

> Loving black smoke and black currants,
> Loving blackbirds and black-eyed Susans,
> Loving black sheep and black whisky,
> Loving black rum and black pepper,
> Loving blackest night and black women,
> Loving black black and blackish black,
> Loving ... Death grows clearer, clearer. (100)

Dumas colours love and the act of "loving" as "black": the racialization of "loving" heightens, as he goes from "black" to "blackest" and finally to "black black and blackish black"—a climactic line that repeats "black" four times (100). His monologue, however, not only ends in this "blackest" of imagery, but also nurtures "Death" as it "grows clearer, clearer." The idyllic arrival at "black black" is also an arrival at "Death." Dumas' monologue foreshadows the play's radical conclusion and use of death as a liberating escape from white oppression and slavery. Death, then, is the impending arbiter of Black trooping over slavery.

These speeches set up Beatrice's Black body as a foil to slavery. Spillers, however, explains that slaves' physical scars and marks of abuse, like Beatrice's swollen abdomen, are often read as "a kind of hieroglyphics of the flesh" (207) that further render the bodies as property. As Spillers says, "The anatomical specifications of rupture, of altered human tissue, take on the objective description of laboratory prose—eyes beaten out, arms, backs, skulls branded, a left jaw, a right ankle, punctured; teeth missing, as the calculated work of iron, whips, chains" (207). The specific abuses of the enslaved at once reflect and render the body as captured object. Examining rape as a method for dehumanizing female slaves, Roberts explains that "the fact that white men could profit from raping their female slaves [by forcing them to beget more slaves] does not mean that their motive was economic. The rape of slave women by their masters ... was an act of physical violence designed to stifle Black women's will to resist and to remind them of their servile status" (29–30). Spillers argues that the "African female subject, under these historic conditions, is not only the target of rape—in one sense, an interiorized violation of body and mind—but also the topic of specifically externalized acts of torture and prostration that we imagine as the peculiar province of *male* brutality and torture inflicted by other males" (207, emphasis Spillers'). While the female body is sexualized as an object of rape or sexual violence, it is also, in what Spillers describes as "stunning contradiction" (206), rendered as "ungendered" through the "*male*" brutalization of the flesh (207). The rape of Beatrice, then, threatens to undo her femininity as well as her subjectivity. Despite her narration of her swollen belly as a visual reminder of the rape and of the ongoing weight of her sufferings, the play does not reduce her agency by anatomizing her body. Beatrice presents her womb as "a fractured vase" (94) and "stew of vinegar and blood" (95), but she remains an active speaker of her own suffering and refuses to "Bear his jagged incesting" (109). In the end, Beatrice's interpretation of her death as a radical act overwrites the "hieroglyphics of the flesh" (Spillers 207) that threaten to mark her as object and slave.

Beatrice, together with Lustra (Chancy's wife), is hanged for the murder of Chancy, but the play's different treatments of their deaths further underscores Beatrice's agency. Whereas Beatrice remains an active subject to the end, Lustra's white body is objectified through the anatomization of her death. Clarke takes care to note that "*chunks of precious flesh have been torn, wholesale, from Lustra's flesh*" (*Beatrice Chancy* 148), illustrating what could be described, in Spillers' terms, as a typical "scene of unprotected female flesh" and death (Spillers 207). As Clarke's stage directions note: "*When Lustra is hanged, she plummets two yards, jerks. She suffers a shock-like seizure, a pressing pain that gnashes her jaws so tightly, she can feel the nerves in her face and in her teeth. Then, her neck ligaments rip apart, separating the bones in her spinal column. Red leaps from her mouth*" (148). Chancy's white wife, Lustra, becomes a captive body in death through the brutal anatomization of her "*jaws*," "*face*," "*teeth*," "*neck ligaments*," and "*the bones in her spinal column*" (148). Beatrice, by contrast, bears "*no mark upon her skin*," because she has resisted and rewritten the narrative of her flesh, the meaning of her body.

In dying five months pregnant and keeping "*Love's* sun / steeped in our tombs" (147), Beatrice will not deliver a slave child or be forced to propagate her father's rape into the future tense. Her final words before she dies speak to the power of the tomb: "Lustra, my sterling Lead, I'll keep *Love's* sun / Steeped in our tombs in endless Thanksgiving. / It's all but all" (147). Beatrice's articulation of the tomb of "endless Thanksgiving" references her "endless" pregnancy, which betrays the sequential rhetoric of reproductive futurity and with it a Child or future. In a rare positive articulation of her pregnancy, she claims, "This innocent is blessed: / It'll not breathe our infested air" (143). In dying pregnant, then, Beatrice finds a loophole in slave law: the Child can remain "innocent" and "blessed," because the "endless" pregnancy will never produce a slave. In this way, she challenges racist patrilineal reproduction that ensures the future of its father-slave owner and participates in the "dismantling of such a logic" (Edelman 22). The welcomed death of the pregnant Beatrice is a radical conclusion that works outside of reproductive rhetoric and Chancy's slave system.

Beatrice Chancy replaces the white futurity of the womb with the fatality of the tomb. The "undertaker" Reverend Peacock hopes that "[t]he extra weight in her belly'll hang her *straight*" (10, 146, emphasis added), but pregnant Beatrice proudly marches to her death as a form of Black resistance to white futurity. As Beatrice explains, "My life's a prison that *Death* will unlock" (140, emphasis Clarke's). Deal, "*a heroic slave*" (10), is shocked that Peacock is sending a pregnant Beatrice to the gallows: "My God!—to hang a pregnant woman / And on Thanksgiving, as if it were war" (145).[10] Beatrice, however, interprets her death as a battle won when she says, "Don't weep! We'll seize Paradise today" (146). She reconfigures the tomb as a not-womb of freedom: instead of a heterosexual womb impregnated by Chancy or Lead, she imagines "our" shared resting place with Lustra, thereby revolutionizing their "tombs" as a bed of racial resistance. I describe the tomb as a locus of her resistance, because she opposes her enslaved and nonconsensual role in reproductive futurity by embracing her death. As Edelman explains, queerness and the death drive "*should* and *must* redefine such notions as 'civil order' through a rupturing of our foundational faith in the reproduction of futurity" (16–17, emphasis Edelman's). For Edelman, the queer embodies the social order's "traumatic encounter with its own inescapable failure" (25–26) and a "resistance to futurism" (27). She enacts resistance but she resists reproductive futurity as a racial temporality and narrative that privileges whiteness. Reverend Peacock and her hanging, as a result, fail to set her "straight" (146). Her tomb replaces the womb as a symbol of hope and functions outside of the framework of "a fight for a [white, patriarchal] future" (Edelman 2).

Beatrice does not participate in Edelman's negation of "the Child," but rather the negation of the racialized Child as a symbol of an exclusionary white futurity. While her death ensures that she will not bear Chancy's "bastards" (109), she is able to "keep" her imagined "sun" (or son) that was created out of "*Love*" and that will remain "in our tombs" (147). This imagined "sun" of "Love" further reinforces her rejection of Chancy's Child as a symbol of white futurity rather than her rejection of any Child. Beatrice, after all, invokes the desire for a Black family: she "is hungry to be wed" to Lead and, as Lead himself says, "[w]e're both natural happy in our love" (54). She and Lead even discuss "our wedding" and plans to "[s]cape to Halifax," so they can be together (64). In reaction to her absence of choice about reproduction and marriage, she revolts against a markedly white futurity that violently excludes a Black family. Beatrice chooses the tomb over her womb as a symbol of hope.

The Future Stops Here

Beatrice Chancy exposes Black women as the symbolic bearers of a collective racial futurity, but, with the historic rapes of slaves, it is all too often a futurity that does not belong to the Black mother. Dramatizing the circularity and repetition of a racial futurity that excludes Black, Chancy's cyclical raping of female slaves begets more children and thus more slaves and more violence. The death of the pregnant Beatrice warrants critical examination in the ongoing battle over reproductive rights, because it calls attention to the use of a woman's body as a public symbol of collective and racial futurity. A woman who does not reproduce or a pregnancy that does not result in a child should not be used to symbolize a failure, whether it is a personal failure of the mother and couple or a public failure of a race and nation.

Ultimately, Clarke's play is a call to arms to change the exclusionary racialization of futurity and of the symbolic Child as white in Canada. The play, in this way, necessitates a reconsideration of pregnancy as a symbol of national racial futurity that strips Black women of agency. Beatrice's pregnant body is a site of resistance against slavery that encourages the audience to align with this empathetic character and her political protest as she willingly "*graces the scaffold*" (*Beatrice Chancy* 146) in order to "insist that the future stop here" (Edelman 31).

NOTES

1 For the libretto version, see "*Beatrice Chancy*: A Libretto in Four Acts." All quotations from *Beatrice Chancy* refer to the play version.

2 The afterword to the published verse play, which Clarke titles "Conviction," lists multiple and diverse source materials for his version of the story of Beatrice Cenci, including plays, film, opera, photographs, and even a restaurant. For Clarke's discussion of his adaptation process, see "Embracing Beatrice Chancy."

3 The word "Child" is capitalized throughout this chapter in order to reference Edelman's notion of the figurative "Child" as a symbol of futurity. Edelman draws on Lauren Berlant's examination of the Child as the ideal American citizen in *The Queen of America Goes to Washington City: Essays on Sex and Citizenship* (1997).

4 For critiques of Edelman's articulation of the Child and futurity in the context of race, see José Esteban Muñoz's *Cruising Utopia* (2009) and Jasbir K. Puar's *Terrorist Assemblages: Homonationalism in Queer Times* (2007). Muñoz maintains that Edelman "accepts and reproduces this monolithic figure of the child that is indeed always already white" (*Cruising* 95); Puar suggests that Edelman "ironically recenters the very child-privileging, future-oriented politics he seeks to refuse" (210–11).

5 See Kailin Wright's "Failed Futurity: Performing Abortion in Merrill Denison's *Marsh Hay*" for a consideration of how Canadian plays in the early twentieth century use pregnancy to warn audiences about the future of rural Canada.

6 See Grimké's article "'Rachel' The Play of the Month: The Reason and Synopsis by the Author" in the *Competitor* (January 1920) for her defence against accusations that her work supports "race suicide."

7 Karen Weingarten's *Abortion in the American Imagination: Before Life and Choice, 1880–1940* (2014) and Linda Myrsiades' *Splitting the Baby: The Culture of Abortion in Literature and Law, Rhetoric and Cartoons* (2002) examine abortion and reproductive law in American literature, making them compelling companions to

Heather Latimer's consideration of abortion in American and Canadian literature in *Reproductive Acts* (2013). See also Sandra Sabatini's *Making Babies* (2003) on the changing treatment of the child in Canadian literature.

8 Katherine Larson (2006) concentrates on *Beatrice Chancy*'s many intertexts and paratexts, while Linda Hutcheon (2006) uses the play as an example of how "power can be adapted—that is, destabilized, disrupted" (175). In considering Clarke's treatment of the "seldom-discussed history of slavery in what is now called Canada," Donna Heiland (2007) approaches Clarke's play as "a Gothic drama about slavery" (126).

9 Ruti offers an analysis of Edelman's version of Lacanian negativity and under-standing of the death drive in relation to Slavoj Žižek.

10 The hanging takes place on Thanksgiving—another date that gestures toward the false narrative of cultural harmony in Canada's prehistory, but this time between Indigenous peoples and colonial settlers.

CHAPTER TEN

Authors and Archives: The Writers' Union of Canada and the Promulgation of Canadian Literary Papers

Erin Ramlo

For the last two years, I have hunted through The Writers' Union of Canada's archives, as well as early Union members' archives dispersed across Canada, to look for letters, articles, and missing links that will help me build an institutional and critical history of the organization. Founded in 1973, The Writers' Union of Canada envisioned itself as an integral advocacy organization for the rights and freedoms of authors in a quickly emerging national literary industry. The organization's advocacy and lobbying were aimed at professionalizing their industry: establishing important fiscal interventions in Canadian publishing, including Access Copyright and the Public Lending Right; creating equitable professional practices, from standard contracts to sales reforms; and opening up opportunities for Canadian authorship, in everything from reading tours, to educational programs, and counts of Canadian book reviews. From its beginnings as a discussion among friends frustrated by a lack of fair industry practices, the Union grew into an effective instrument of grassroots political and cultural change that eventually came to deeply influence Canadian cultural policy. The Writers' Union of Canada's own archival files that trace the development of these many initiatives are immense—at 268 boxes and counting, and organized thematically by committee, their structure and scale has seemed almost impenetrable. Trying to search out the as-yet-untold story of the Union, I have necessarily taken a sideways route into archival work—what Carole Gerson might call "oblique" (15)—as I also use the papers of individual members, particularly of women and people of colour, to reveal their personal labour around important events, and then turn back to the Union's institutional archive for more structural details.[1]

In 2016, I found myself in the University of Calgary's archives, perusing the Writers' Union files in the fonds of several early Union members. As I explored Mordecai Richler's files dedicated to the Union, I was struck by a curious little document. It was titled *Authors and Archives: A Short Guide* (Skelton). Printed on The Writers' Union of Canada letterhead, it read as a how-to guide for Canadian authors who wished to sell or donate their papers to archival institutions. Divided into sections ranging from "Selection of Archival Material" and "Tax on Archival Material," to "The Market for Archives" and "Archives and Copyright," this five-page guide was published by the Writers' Union in 1979 as an educational resource for its members.[2] *Authors and Archives* is a significant reminder that the Writers' Union was deeply aware of, and interested in, the political and cultural potential of the archive, as it demonstrates the Union's interest, not only in the material labour of Canadian authors, but also in authors' symbolic capital as artistic producers, and in the cultural relevance of preserving their papers. In this chapter, I use *Authors and Archives* as a case study to explore the entwined fiscal and cultural advocacy that The Writers' Union of Canada engaged in on behalf of Canadian authorship. I consider why the Union esteemed archival preservation so highly—as providing both immediate material and imagined future critical value—and examine whether or not this document actually worked to strengthen archival holdings of member authors for the use of future researchers. Moreover, given the theme of untold stories that underpins this volume, I argue that, by encouraging their membership to stake out archival space and authority and by valuing their literary production and the preservation of their materials, the Union enabled the future exploration of untold stories, as they tacitly advocated for the value and importance of women, rural, and economically marginal authors' archives.

Before delving into *Authors and Archives* itself, it is perhaps best to take a step back and consider the politics and intentions of the Writers' Union more broadly. According to Christopher Moore, after arguing about the importance of Canadian authorship before the Ontario Royal Commission on Book Publishing, a small group of authors gathered at Toronto's Park Plaza Hotel for hot dogs and beer in early 1971. This group, including June Callwood, Graeme Gibson, Margaret Atwood, Ian Adams, and Fred Bodsworth, shared their dismay at the lack of fair professional practices in the Canadian publishing industry, and articulated their mutual desire to do something about it. Also in 1971, Gibson wrote a series of letters to Canadian authors, soliciting their involvement in a new organization. In an October 1971 letter to Timothy Findley, Gibson asked if he would be "interested in a Union of Canadian writers?"[3] Gibson had been discussing the possibility with other prose writers, and he therefore noted, "so far we've all felt the emphasis should be on the word UNION." Gibson's emphasis on this particular word reveals the ideological underpinnings of the fledgling Union—they intended to create an organization that not only brought together disparate authors from across the country, but one that, like a trade union, challenged industry and governmental structures, as it advocated for the labour of literary practice. Gibson's letter continues: "We anticipate it being a political thing, not a club." This group of friends and colleagues, then—mostly emerging Canadian authors at the time—came together to confront the challenges they faced in the burgeoning moments of the CanLit movement. They set out, over the next several years, to build a politically minded coalition of authors who would advocate for the material value of their labour as cultural producers.

A series of informal meetings that took place through 1971 and 1972—sometimes held in Marian Engel's living room—led, eventually, to the official founding of The Writers' Union of Canada in November of 1973, as sixty-three prose writers from across the country came together in Ottawa to ratify their constitution. Economic stability for emerging authors was a key component of the Union's early work, as were goals to set up standard contracts with publishers, copyright reforms, and the Public Lending Right, a program that compensated authors for the use of their books in libraries (and which still does today). According to Margaret Atwood, "the Union was initially comprised of a small number of authors who felt that writers must work as a unified group if they were to gain any measure of control over the economic conditions influencing them" (n.p.). Recognizing the need for equity and accountability in a quickly expanding Canadian literary industry, members rallied to demand fair compensation, representation, and recognition for what they saw as the vital artistic and cultural work of their community. According to Atwood, they would thus be able to "take collective responsibility for the decisions which affect[ed] the ways in which they were seen and treated" (n.p.) by the publishing industry, by the media, and, more widely, by Canadian culture.

It is important to remember that interventions like this one, while aimed at improving the material valuation of Canadian authorship, were also deeply entwined with the nationalist agenda that underpinned the structure of the developing organization. The newly formed Union's first official press release, for example, published on November 4, 1973, made their nationalist intentions quite clear, as they called for the Canadianization of the book trade, which had hitherto been dominated by American interests.[4] The press release clearly articulated that, while the aim of the new organization was to "transform completely the system of book publishing and distribution in this country" for the financial betterment of Canadian authors, the Union also positioned this work as fulfilling a particularly nationalist agenda. "National survival," the press release proclaimed, "demands that our people have access to books written by Canadians about Canada … both for the sake of the survival of Canadian writing, and for the sake of the survival of Canada."[5] This clear nationalist framing reverberates throughout the organization's founding documents, rooting the very core of the Union's operational impetus in the construction and dissemination of narratives that were invested in forwarding a national agenda.

Broadly, then, the Union's concerns were twofold: that literary authors be valued, first, materially, but then also culturally, for their artistic labour. While this work consistently occurred within a nationalist context, what I wish to signal here most is the entwining of cultural capital and financial concerns. As the Union encouraged the growth of Canadian literature through programs like reading tours, review counts, authors in schools, and, for my purposes here, archives, they were always, ultimately, also invested in the material valuation of artistic production. This entrenched institutional goal of supporting initiatives that fostered financial security was, however, a circular process: gaining some measure of symbolic capital bolstered fiscal security, which, in turn, supported the continued production of more Canadian literature, and thus, contributed to the continuance of the discipline's symbolic, material, and nationalistic value.

So, while the Union aimed most of their efforts at fiscal reform, they were also interested in the futurity of members' presence in the Canadian cultural consciousness. In 1977, the Union made their investment in that continuance of Canadian authorship quite clear, establishing an Archives Committee, helmed by author Robin Skelton. The committee was charged with exploring the state of Canadian literary archives and making recommendations to members about their potential as both fiscal and critical opportunities. To do so, the committee initiated a substantial study into the state of literary archives, sending out questionnaires to three branches of the Canadian literary archival industry: writers, publishers, and the archival institutions themselves. Seeking information on how archives were managed from these three separate but related locations, the committee sought to understand how their concerns intertwined or diverged. According to the committee's files, housed in McMaster University's Archives and Research Collections,[6] writers were asked, for example, if they had sold their archives and for how much, or if they would ever consider doing so. If they had donated their papers, did they receive tax relief? Had they placed restrictions on their papers, or were they fully accessible to researchers? Publishers were asked how they managed documents: did they return manuscripts to authors or keep them in their own files? If they kept them, did they plan to donate them to an archival institution, sell them, or destroy them? The archival institutions were asked about content: What kinds of archives did they currently collect? And did they have any Canadian literary holdings already?

The information from hundreds of questionnaires was distilled into an internal report, and then, later, into the how-to document that caught my attention in Calgary. The internal report notes that of the nearly 200 surveys sent out to member authors, fifty-six authors replied regarding their experiences with archival institutions. Fifteen respondents had sold their archival collections already, and another eleven had donated material, making for a total of twenty-six member authors with archival holdings in 1977. The experiences of survey respondents varied so wildly—from what they felt was exploitation to great financial success—that, the report concludes "it seems necessary to work out a guide to handling the personal archives of writers, or at the very least to draw up a list of do's and don'ts" for members.[7]

This impetus drove Skelton and the archives committee to draft their archival call to action, which culminated in *Authors and Archives: A Short Guide*. The guide offered members advice about everything from appraisal information, sales strategies, and tax relief regulations, to copyright rules, executions of wills and bequests, and potential restrictions on materials. *Authors and Archives: A Short Guide* was distributed at The Writers' Union of Canada's annual general meeting in May of 1979 and mailed to other members thereafter. It was submitted to major libraries nationwide and available to non-members from the Union's office for a small fee. By this point, the Union's membership had grown considerably from its initial thirty-seven author-friends to 357 professional writers (French, "Writers' Dramatics" 18). A significant community of cultural makers was educated, then, through this document, about navigating the Canadian literary archival landscape. Moreover, they were encouraged to invest the time and energy to nurture, organize, and value their own material documents and ephemera, a concept that was relatively unheard of in a fledgling industry of emerging writers.

The *Authors and Archives* guide thus characterizes what constitutes "archival material": what that material actually includes, how to collect and organize it, and how to have it appraised (see Figure 10.1). Challenging the traditional assumption that privileged manuscript collections, Skelton tried

The Writers' Centre
24 Ryerson Avenue
Toronto, Ontario M5T 2P3
(416) 868-6915

AUTHORS AND ARCHIVES: A SHORT GUIDE

ARCHIVAL MATERIAL

Few people understand the nature and utility of archival material. They think
that it consists only of manuscripts, worksheets, and corresepondence with important people. This is not the case. A full archival collection will include
photographs, tape recordings, press cuttings, diaries, signed copies of books,
records of house purchases, mortgages, insurance policies, and all the written,
printed, photographed and recorded material relating to the person or persons
concerned, even including such memorabilia as walking sticks, jewellery, and objets
d'art. Whatever can shed light, however obliquely, upon the subject of the archive
may be useful to those who, in the future, intend to write a biography or survey
of the life work of a person. Of course, few libraries are willing or able to
house all that a biographer might find fascinating, especially bulky memorabilia,
such as an author's desk or his or her favourite armchair. Nevertheless, this
material should always be considered in selecting archival material. It is helpful for a biographer to actually see objects that he or she may have to describe,
rather than to rely upon second hand reports. Material of no apparent significance
may also turn out to be helpful. A clearly marked envelope, with no letter inside
it, may help a researcher to establish where the writer was on a given date and
help in dating other material. A picture postcard saying merely, "Wish you were
here" may save the worker a great deal of research. Bills and account books are
also helpful in this fashion.

GATHERING MATERIAL

The majority of Canadian Publishers will, if asked, return to the author the original manuscript of their books. Some will also return correspondence. In signing
a contract with any publisher it is wise to ensure that the publisher agrees to
return this material to the author for his personal archive. Magazine Editors may
or may not return this material. Those magazines attached to colleges and universities are inclined to give this material to their own libraries as part of
the archives of the magazine itself. Others find it simply impossible to cope with
the additional work involved in sorting out the material. There is, however, no
harm in asking editors to return materials. Some people make a practice of returning letters to the writers of them if these letters seem to be of interest, though
this is often done by bequest after the recipient's death. Nevertheless, it is
worth while considering the possibility of enlarging the correspondence section of
an archive by asking for letters to be returned.

2/. . .

FIGURE 10.1 *Authors and Archives: A Short Guide* by The Writers' Union of Canada,
1979. McMaster University, William Ready Division of Archives and Research
Collections. Used with permission of The Writers' Union of Canada. Photo courtesy of
Erin Ramlo.

to instruct members to broaden their point of view about what archival material could actually include. He wrote that "a full archival collection will include photographs, tape recordings, press cuttings, diaries, signed copies of books, records of house purchases, mortgages, insurance policies, and all the written, printed, photographed and recorded material relating to the person or persons concerned" (1). In short, Skelton argues, the records of one's everyday life are important and ought to be prized and preserved.[8] Although one might not consider one's own materials valuable, Skelton notes that "whatever can shed light, however obliquely, upon the subject of the archive may be useful to those who, in the future, intend to write a biography or survey of the life work of a person" (1). He repeatedly appeals to his readers to consider their poor beleaguered researchers who will be obliged to navigate these archives. He observes that "material of no apparent significance may turn out to be helpful ... a picture postcard [for example] saying merely, 'Wish you were here' may save the worker a great deal of research" (1). Note the implication of utility, labour, and assistance in Skelton's words— indeed the idea that archival preservation will be "helpful" and "useful" to an imagined future researcher is repeated throughout the document. I also like the invocation of the term *worker*—this is, after all, a Union, and their rhetorical bent to valuing the professional labour of writers is striking. Moreover, note the text's expectation that CanLit's archives will one day become an important site of biographical and critical study. By preserving their own archives, Union members could make a contribution to future critical scholarship, and, what's more, they could assist future researchers—the next generation of Canadian scholarly writers—with their own production. By encouraging members to create archival collections, the Union was implicated in a developing critical consciousness of the field of Canadian literature, and, by extension, in the nurturance of collective cultural memory of and about the discipline.

There seems to be an element here of appeal to the always already present futurity of the construction and preservation of archival materials. Calling on Derrida, we might consider that, in *Archive Fever*, he asserted that "the question of the archive is not ... a question of the past," but rather "a question of the future, the question of the future itself, the question of a response, of a promise and of a responsibility for tomorrow" (36). Moreover, Derrida's famous assertion that "there is no political power without control of the archive" (4) feels relevant here for an organization that saw itself as making an important political investment in the future of Canadian authorship. In an article titled "Archives, Records, and Power: The Making of Modern

Memory," Joan Schwartz and Terry Cook similarly assert that archives "wield power over the shape and direction of historical scholarship, collective memory, and national identity, over how we know ourselves as individuals, groups, and societies" (2). *Authors and Archives* acknowledges that part of the project of crafting and establishing archival collections is in its possibilities to influence, guide, and assist future knowledge and understanding. We must also remember, however, as Helen M. Buss writes, that archives are not neutral sites, but rather "collections developed from specific social assumptions that dictate what documents are valuable" (2). The specific social assumptions that drove the Writers' Union's valuation of archival materials were based on a project of cultural nationalism, which has its own agenda and structure of power and privilege, tied primarily to the whiteness of the Canadian nation. Those who did not conform to that structure were almost invariably omitted from the archival record. While we ought to always be critical of archival practices, then, inasmuch as they have a very material potential to reify these structures of power, the details of a document like *Authors and Archives* helps to reveal the complexities at work in such archivization processes. In this particular case, those processes—paradoxically, perhaps, in view of the nationalist underpinnings of the Union's mandate—included several groups often on the margins of archival representation, as the document worked to bolster the inclusions of new, emerging, rural, or otherwise undervalued Canadian literary artists.

The latter sections of *Authors and Archives*, dedicated to the "valuation of archives" (2) and to "the market for archival material" (3), provide us with some clues regarding these intentions. The focus, here, turns back to the Union's overarching aim to support the fiscal and material security of their membership, offering "practical suggestions" for "making *some* financial profit" (3) from one's papers (my emphasis). Skelton advises members to break up their archival donations into several accessions in order to accrue "maximum tax relief" (2) from their donations. In trying to sell one's papers, he advises, do not offer "large collections: offer small ones with a valuation of below $1000.00" (3)—opting, for example, to try to sell the papers related to one novel rather than one's whole collection. In this way, an author might secure some small bit of material benefit—and moreover, might be able to do so over a series of years to the same archival institution—while ensuring that one's work be preserved. Consider that many authors were, at this point, struggling to make ends meet. One *Globe and Mail* report at the time cited that the majority of Union members made less than $3,000 per year (French, "Union Rejuvenated" 18). A $1,000 purchase of their archival papers, then, might make all the difference in their ability to keep writing.[9] If a collection were to be donated rather than sold, the tax relief offered by that donation might help offset the author's income for the year and similarly create some very material benefit for a practising writer. I draw attention to these financial sections of *Authors and Archives* because they demonstrate that the point of this document was not to help celebrity authors profit wildly from the sale of their archives, but rather to assist practising writers in the Union's membership to glean some additional bit of immediate material and future symbolic benefit from their production.

My research suggests that 63 percent of early Union members now have personal archives—as in, dedicated institutional archival holdings under their own names. Of the 191 authors listed in the Union's 1977 membership book, *Canada Writes!*, 120 of them now have archival collections. In the Union's initial survey of those same people, cited above, only twenty-six members reported having placed their papers with an archive at the time. This fourfold increase in the number of member archival holdings post-1977 feels like a significant shift. What is most interesting, for my purposes, are the ninety less-well-known or more regional members who are now represented in Canadian archival collections. People like children's author and translator Joyce Marshall, whose papers are in Quebec's Eastern Township Archives, or Newfoundland's nonfiction writer Cassie Brown, whose archives are at Memorial University. While the Union included a group of very prominent literary celebrities—Farley Mowat, W.O. Mitchell, and Sinclair Ross, for example—the less-well-known authors actually made up the bulk of the Union membership. They now also make up the bulk of member archival holdings, which are housed in a wonderfully varied set of institutions all across the country: from the University of Calgary, McMaster University, and the University of British Columbia's extensive Special Collections, to more locally based city or provincial archives, like the Mission, BC Community Archives, which hold Andreas Schroeder's papers.

It is also worthwhile to consider that the Union had a significant membership of women—36 percent in 1977—and, under the guidance of their first chair, Marian Engel, the Union sought to improve the position of women's authorship in Canada. As Linda M. Morra's *Unarrested Archives* reminds us, historically, institutional archives have often refused women's records and the records of people of colour, and there is a long history in Canada of the devaluation of their inclusions (3). As Helen M. Buss notes, the inequities of archival representation are revealed when we consider the records of "marginalized people, those not of the traditional white male elite" (1). Clearly, the Union was striving to work against this bias, if not entirely successfully. While far from creating gender equity in archival holdings, thirty-five of the Union's 1977 female members went on to establish archival collections of their work. Making up 29 percent of all 1977 Union members with archives, these women inscribed themselves and their stories into the nation's critical consciousness by way of archival presence. By extension, they made an important symbolic and material intervention in the cultural conscious-ness of the developing field of Canadian literature. The archives that this document encourages might thus be approached as a form of counter-archives,[10] of particularly privileged types, of course, given the fact that you had to already be a published author to become a Union member—but a series of alternative archives no less, that were worth time and energy to try to preserve. By providing members with a "how-to" guide for placing their papers in archival institutions, the Union was expanding opportunities for less-experienced, lesser-known, or more regional authors in their member-ship to create a space for themselves in cultural memory and future research, a space that had hitherto been reserved for those powerful elites. It is important to remember that The Writers' Union of Canada's process was not to create one cohesive archive of its own, nor did they encourage members to hom-ogenize their collections in particular curatorial ways; rather, *Authors and Archives* empowered members to value their own production and to find the correct avenue, process, and institution for the dispersal of their own archives.

While I do not intend to claim that *Authors and Archives* was directly responsible for a material shift in Canadian archival holdings, it is product-ive to consider how it interacted with a series of cultural developments in the late 1970s in Canada—like the increased attention on CanLit, for example, or feminist approaches to archival study and holdings, and broader projects of counter-archiving and co-operative arts advocacy. These developments bolstered the otherwise undervalued or untold stories of Canadian author-ship. One such intervention, on the Union's part, was this investment in the archival futurity of their membership and of their work. Ultimately, while I can make an informed suggestion that *Authors and Archives* affected the material holdings of Canadian archival institutions, the actual extent of that influence remains speculative, and a number of questions remain to be explored. In time, I hope to be able to construct a more detailed accounting of Union members' archival holdings through the years. As membership increased into the thousands through the 1990s, I wonder, did the creation of archival collections keep pace? How equitably, on a statistical basis, do Canadian literary archival holdings now reflect the voices of women, economically marginal authors, and authors of colour? While I have argued that the archives of female members of the Union are actually represented quite well, unfortunately, authors of colour have not had access to the same amount of space within Canadian archival holdings, nor within the structure of the Union itself. With only one person of colour, Austin Clarke, among the Writers' Union's founding members, and only a handful of Indigenous people and people of colour in the Union's membership up until the 1990s, the organization's nationalism operated in the service of a decidedly white image of the Canadian nation.

Through the 1990s and beyond, questions about racism and appropriation became central to critiques of the Writers' Union's structure and intentions.[11] Such critiques continue to this day, raised, in part, by the May 2017 publication of an editorial titled "Winning the Appropriation Prize" in the Writers' Union's *Write Magazine*. This Union-produced editorial, which prefaced a collection of work by emerging Indigenous authors, proclaimed: "I don't believe in cultural appropriation" (Niedzviecki 8). For an organization that has been implicated in discussions about racism and appropriation in Canadian literature for almost thirty years—since Lenore Keeshig-Tobias raised this issue in a Union panel on racism in 1989—the *Write Magazine* editorial was a revealing look at the ongoing hierarchies of racist inequity that are so often at the core of cultural institutions. As Karina Vernon and Linda M. Morra remind us in, respectively, "Invisibility Exhibit: The Limits of Library and Archives Canada's 'Multicultural Mandate'" and *Unarrested Archives*, the choice *not* to place one's papers under "house arrest" in public repositories can then, for some, be an act of resistance to the colonial structures of power upon which such institutions are built. In particular, Morra argues that Union member M. NourbeSe Philip's withholding of her papers from a formal repository "work[s] against … official archives that were apparently meant to represent a nationally imagined collective" (150), one that had, previously, "excluded her from representation because of her race and gender" (152). Such ruptures in the archive—its omissions or its lacks—have the potential to reveal just as much as its inclusions. Would considering Union members not included in institutional archival repositories, I wonder, reveal its own set of untold stories? Ones that, like Philip's, "critique the existing national arrangement of archives" (Morra 6)? Most of Canada's prominent archival institutions are currently directing their acquisitional changes and developments toward the digital—how to best preserve and share information within quickly changing digital landscapes. Looking forward, acquisitional equity will need to become a priority, as it has the potential to address such gaps in the record and represent the experiences of a broader spectrum of Canadian writers. Meanwhile, I'm still left wondering: Has Skelton's call to break up archival holdings into smaller accessions resulted in fractured or incomplete archives for some authors? And, could those fractures similarly be productive ones? More broadly, I still wonder, what drove the Union to set up an archives committee in the first place? Which members brought it to the table—and why? Did they position their concerns as a symbolic intervention for the futurity of CanLit, or primarily as a financial opportunity?

While *Authors and Archives* will remain, for me, a point of future exploration, a 1979 *Globe and Mail* article clearly highlighted what William French saw as the document's immediate potential. He noted that "[w]riters who have read the Skelton report will now be much more adroit in their negotiations" with archival institutions and will be able to navigate a process for which, until that moment, "the rules [had been] largely unwritten" ("Archives Want Bills" 16). The Writers' Union of Canada wrote those rules, French implies, which they have invited a significant generation of Canadian authors to consider, to learn, to follow, and to employ, both for their financial betterment and for their place in the Canadian archival canon. French concludes his article with a prescient quip about imagined future researchers by which I will conclude. He writes: "Skelton, presumably, has filed the original manuscript of his report among his other papers, awaiting that great Evaluation Day" (16). So he did, and so I found it—with the help of some exceptional archivists—right where he left it. And here we are, some thirty-five years after this document's production, evaluating, studying, and discussing the stories that these archives have to tell—Skelton's and The Writers' Union of Canada's imagined future researchers, materialized.

NOTES

1 I would like to thank Mary O'Connor, Peter Walmsley, and Margaret Boyce for their time, suggestions, and encouragement in reading early drafts of this chapter; Lorraine York for her support in wading through archival questions; and Linda Morra for her generous editorial advice and commentary. I would also like to thank The Writers' Union of Canada and the late Graeme Gibson for granting me permission to quote from their archival materials for this chapter.

2 See Mordecai Richler Fonds, University of Calgary, Accession No. 680/00.11, Box/File 15.56. I thank the staff of the Archives and Special Collections at the University of Calgary, particularly Allison Wagner, for their help and kindness. There is a lovely bit of archival synchronicity in the fact that I first stumbled upon

Authors and Archives in Richler's papers. Sold to the University of Calgary in 1974, reportedly for a then-unheard-of sum of $100,000 (W. French, "Calgary Leads" E1), this particular collection was likely part of what inspired the creation of *Authors and Archives* in the first place.

3   Timothy Findley and William Whitehead Fonds, Library and Archives Canada, Box 98, File 20. Gibson penned this letter to Findley to arrange the details of their upcoming interview for his book *Eleven Canadian Novelists*, placing the Union question as a postscript. All eleven novelists featured in Gibson's book would go on to become members of the Writers' Union.

4   See Rowland Lorimer's *Ultra Libris: Policy, Technology, and the Creative Economy of Book Publishing in Canada*, particularly Chapter 3, "Establishing a Book Publishing Industry: 1960 to 1990," and Roy MacSkimming's *The Perilous Trade: Book Publishing in Canada, 1946–2006*, for more information.

5   Austin Clarke Fonds, William Ready Division of Archives and Special Collections, McMaster University, First Accrual, Box 44, File 1.

6   See Writers' Union of Canada Fonds, William Ready Division of Archives and Research Collections, McMaster University, First Accrual, Box 64, Files 1–3, and Second Accrual, Box 104, Files 5–8. I thank the staff of McMaster's Archives and Research Collections for their ongoing assistance. Bev Bayzat, Renu Barrett, Myron Groover, and Rick Stapleton, in particular, have patiently guided me through the Writers' Union's administrative files over the last few years, and they have my sincerest gratitude for their contributions to this work.

7   Writers' Union of Canada Fonds, William Ready Division of Archives and Special Collections, McMaster University, First Accrual, Box 104, File 5.

8   Not everyone was pleased with Skelton's call to "build" one's archive. At the 1983 Annual Conference of the Association of Canadian Archivists, Jean Tener, then archivist at the University of Calgary's special collections, critiqued Skelton's instructions as having the potential to create "artificial collections" (229), i.e., collections that have been too mediated. She does concede, however, that "by setting up an Archives Committee and producing a Guide, The Writers' Union of Canada acknowledged that its membership needs advice about an issue of very real concern to authors" (231).

9   The member portion of the committee's questionnaire reveals a range of valuations for member collections. Less-well-known writers typically noted sales in the range of $500 to $1,000, while more noteworthy figures sat on the high end of the spectrum. Margaret Atwood revealed an initial $11,000 (1970) payment from the University of Toronto, while Pierre Berton noted a $50,000 (1974) payment from McMaster. Most respondents were located somewhere between the $3,000

and $5,000 range. See Writers' Union of Canada Fonds, William Ready Division of Archives and Special Collections, McMaster University, Box 64, File 2 "Archives Questionnaire to Writers, 1979."

10 Ann Cvetkovich develops the concept of affective counter-archives in "In the Archive of Lesbian Feelings," which draws on the important work done by the Lesbian Herstory Archives in New York City among many others. While Cvetkovich's focus is on the archiving of ephemera of LGBTQ histories and memories, and on the radical archiving of emotion and trauma to document intimacy and sexuality, her work has informed my thinking here, particularly due to its gestures to the archiving of grassroots political activism. For Cvetkovich, such archives "assert the role of memory and affect in compensating for institutional neglect" (241), as they insist "on the value of apparently marginal or ephemeral materials ... [to] propose that affects—associated with nostalgia, personal memory, fantasy, and trauma—make a document significant" (243–44).

11 See Elliott ("The Cultural Appropriation Debate"), Lai ("Community Action"), and Philip ("Race-Baiting") for productive critiques of the Writers' Union's structurally imbedded colonial and racial inequities.

SECTION THREE

Memories from Below and Beyond the Border

CHAPTER ELEVEN

The Vietnam Era Resisters Who Shaped Canada's Ceramic Heritage

Mary Ann Steggles

In the 1960s and 1970s, the "largest out-migration in United States history resulted in more than 100,000 Vietnam war resisters and draft dodgers" relocating north of the forty-ninth parallel (Hardwick 15). These political refugees, both women and men, were mostly white, urban, middle class, well educated, and privileged. Theirs was a life-changing decision. Some settled in Canadian cities, while others, seeking simplicity and self-sufficiency, purchased derelict farmhouses or acreages in rural Canada. The DIY lifestyle of these counterculture youth looked back to both the British and American Arts and Crafts movement. They not only critiqued mass production and consumerism as a form of political and cultural activism but were also environmental activists promoting sustainability. Dropping out was seen as freedom from a capitalistic system that was the root of society's ills.

These young people sought in every way possible to be self-reliant, to do it themselves. Most learned by doing as the majority of the Vietnam migrants were from urban areas with little or no knowledge of construction, animal husbandry, or solutions to the myriad of problems associated with living in rural Canada. Nearly half of the migrants purchased small acreages, some with derelict buildings. Having little funds, they quickly learned how to reuse, repurpose, and recycle. They built their own houses with found materials. They cleared land for vegetable gardens, learning how to companion plant to avoid the use of pesticides. The milk from the cows was separated; the cream was churned into butter for homemade bread while the strained liquid became yoghurt or starter for sourdough bread. Wood provided heat, fuel for kilns, and material for making furniture. Discarded machinery found new life. Old vacuum cleaners became glaze sprayers, while stainless steel milk drums made excellent mixers for clay slip. Discarded firebrick was used for kiln building. More than anything else they "hoped to replace what they saw as competitive, greedy, capitalist accumulation with sustainable economic models based on mutual support and subsistence" (Janovicek 9). Key to this was the making of handmade objects, which they hoped would be valued and passed down to future generations, instead of quickly going to the land-fill. Most were already trained in clay processes, many at the graduate level, while others learned these skills, once they had settled in Canada, to earn a living. For many, ceramics provided the framework for a new holistic lifestyle that involved rebelling against a growing greed and materialism, which they believed supported an immoral war in Southeast Asia (Janovicek 9). Some sought to elevate their practice above the status of craft, to have their work recognized as fine art, while others found inspiration in the writing of British potter Bernard Leach and his exaltation of the humble craftsperson and beauty in utility. Most worked diligently to organize pottery and craft associations at the local, provincial, and national levels. They taught at universities and art colleges, won awards, gave lectures and workshops, exhibited their work, and inspired others to become involved.

These artists are the focus of my research project: I have located and interviewed many individuals who immigrated to Canada, as a result of the Vietnam conflict, and who were ceramists or who became ceramists after they moved. To date, there are 117 individuals taking part in this project. Over a period of five decades, their immense legacy has been completely ignored and neglected. Why is this? This chapter looks at possible answers that include the rancour over perceived loss of positions in Canadian universities and colleges, threats to the lifestyle and livelihood of some Canadians, and an unwillingness by many to understand just how much of a debt Canadian culture owes to these American political refugees.

Social Unrest in the United States Brings Resisters to Canada

The Vietnam conflict officially began in 1959 and ended on April 30, 1975. Myra MacPherson, a writer for *The Washington Post* and author of *Long Time Passing: Vietnam and the Haunted Generation* (1984), stresses that "Vietnam was the most divisive time of battle in our country since the Civil War" (5). Many believed a government that told them their country was under threat from spreading communist ideology, whereas others viewed American militarism in Southeast Asia as imperialistic politics and a lucrative means of filling the pockets of the owners of American armaments companies. In 1964, while running for re-election to the presidency, Lyndon B. Johnson said that he would not escalate the conflict in Vietnam. The reality was vastly different once he was back in the Oval Office. In August 1964, an American destroyer, the USS *Maddox*, was leading secret missions in support of the South Vietnamese government from the Gulf of Tonkin (Dickerson 6). Reports of attacks on the USS *Maddox* by North Vietnamese gunboats provided an excuse for the United States Congress to pass the Gulf of Tonkin Resolution. That Bill essentially gave the President of the United States the authority to use all conventional military weapons at his disposal to halt communist aggression spreading to South Vietnam, or any other Southeast Asian country, without having to declare a state of war. The actual circumstances of any naval confrontations in the Bay of Tonkin at the time are unclear. Was there one incident or two? Real or fabricated? In the end, it did not matter; the result was the same. President Johnson dramatically increased the military presence in Vietnam, an act that turned individual resistance into mass protests across the United States.

Sit-ins and demonstrations that began on American college campuses moved to the streets to join the civil rights marches. As MacPherson notes, "With Vietnam, the smouldering sixties blew up into incendiary proportions" (43). America's youth felt the oppression of the era, the continual race riots, and the shooting of students by the National Guard at Kent State. One artist in this study, Sally Michener, recalls, "There had been a race riot the year we moved to Cincinnati. Martin Luther King had just died. Shortly before we left for Vancouver, the Kent State killing of students protesting the war by the National Guard had occurred. It was simply too much." Most did not trust the government in Washington who, under President Johnson, instigated surveillance and infiltration programs on anti-war activists. The goal of these covert and illegal actions was to disrupt and discredit American social and political groups and their leaders, such as the Students for a Democratic Society (SDS) and the Reverend Martin Luther King Jr., leader of the civil rights movement. The disillusion the youth felt intensified when they realized that "the country in which they thought they lived—peaceful, generous, honourable—did not exist and never had" (M. Young 3). Feelings of outrage and helplessness were exacerbated by evening news reports showing the bombardment of a small, underdeveloped Asian country by the most powerful nation in the world.

Wayne Cardinalli, one of the subjects of the interviews, remembers how his hopes were shattered:

I participated in the early marches on Washington to protest the war. Those were years of hope that we could stop the violence. Then came all those events that broke the bubble of innocence. John and Bobby Kennedy, and Martin Luther King were assassinated one after another in such a short period. There was no time to catch your breath. There were the Kent State killings and the women and children killed at My Lai. It was all too much. Janis Joplin and Jimi Hendrix overdosed and this added to a feeling of hopelessness. The last straw for me was when U.S. troops invaded Cambodia. It was at that point I decided that there might be better places to live.

As Cardinalli's recollections suggest, a significant form of protest was to leave the United States and move to Canada (Gower 40) (see Figure 11.1). For the individuals in this research project, their decision to leave the United States was not easy; instead, it was "bold, and often vocal, a statement about what was wrong with American society" (Rodgers, *Welcome to Resisterville* 181). Some parents told their sons: "I would rather see you dead than go to Canada."[1] A number left, therefore, without telling their family and friends, fearing someone would call the FBI and report them. Others abandoned established artistic careers. Once they had crossed the border, there was no promise that they would ever be able to return.

As new immigrants, these young people brought with them their social and political values about the environment, alternative energy, civil rights, women's rights, and nuclear disarmament. Many were enrolled in art schools during the 1960s and were part of an anti-establishment, anti-authoritarian generation. In refusing to support American imperialism, they arrived at the border already anti-American in their outlook. They were ready to embrace a new life in a new country whose values—equality, justice, and hospitality—they "believed" to be the antithesis of those in the United States (Braunstein and Doyle; Hardwick; Roszak). Walter Ostrom, distinguished professor of ceramics at Nova Scotia College of Art and Design (NSCAD), believed that Canada offered "the opportunity to achieve racial equality, educate the citizenry, Ban the Bomb and substitute a War on Poverty for the War on Viet-nam." Canada was, after all, "the land of Pierre Trudeau, a friend of Castro and draft dodgers, leading a nation of peace-niks" (Ostrom).

It would be wrong to conclude that everyone immigrating to Canada because of the Vietnam conflict was either a draft dodger or a deserter. A number who immigrated either were beyond the draft age of twenty-six, had already completed alternative service, or were women. The majority had landed immigrant status and were not "border hoppers." Albert (Bert) Borch, as one example, was designated a conscientious objector (CO), a status that allowed him to teach at a Quaker boys' school for two years instead of being

FIGURE 11.1   Wayne Cardinalli. Photograph by Jeanne McRight with permission by Cardinalli.

sent to Vietnam. At the end of his service, Borch and his wife, Ingrid, were so disillusioned with American foreign policy and the use of military force on Vietnam that they decided to move to Canada. They did not want their children ever to be subjected to military service. The couple also desired to live in a tolerant, peaceful country.

Byron Johnstad, as another, had just turned twenty-six when he crossed the border with landed immigrant status (see Figure 11.2). One of the first to arrive on Canada's West Coast with a graduate degree in ceramics, Johnstad had been hired to teach at the Vancouver School of Art. The processing of the paperwork took longer than expected and so, by the time he arrived at the School, the position had been given to someone else. With his landed immigrant status in hand, Johnstad chose to stay in Canada even so and, within a few months, had several job offers. During his time as a graduate student at the California College of Arts and Crafts (CCAC), Johnstad was actively involved with anti-war demonstrations and Joan Baez's Institute for Non-Violence. The opportunity of starting a new life in a country free from social and political discord appealed to the talented designer and ceramic artist.

Still, more than half of the new immigrants were women (Jones 51). These include wives, partners, sisters, and mothers of the young men who moved. In my interviews with the women ceramists, it became clear that the initial

FIGURE 11.2
Byron Johnstad,
Examining Work
Drying, 1969. Unknown
photographer, with
permission by Johnstad.

impulse to relocate to Canada was often theirs. Some did not want their sons to face the challenges of being a new immigrant alone, while many others did not want their young children, even infants and toddlers, ever to be drafted into the American military. Several said they would have come alone, even if their partners had refused.

The Counterculture and the Back-to-the-Land Movement

Approximately half of the individuals who immigrated to Canada in my study were part of the back-to-the-land movement. The majority of these settled in British Columbia. Often called "hippies" or "counterculture youth," the label encompassed a wide variety of individuals who chose to live in rural areas, often remote, away from the social ills of America (Coates 3; Janovicek 10). While some searched to find meaning in their life through psychedelic drugs, others looked to Eastern spirituality—or both—for answers. So Janovicek observes that "[d]rugs were a major conflict. People assumed all of the newcomers were 'druggies.' Although marijuana was common, back-to-the-landers tended not to celebrate psychedelic, drug-induced experiences. As radicals of the 1960s grew up and took on adult responsibilities, such as parenthood, many of them stopped using harder drugs" (13).

Counterculture youth wanted to transform the values of America; according to Theodore Roszak, author of *The Making of a Counter Culture*, their aim was both political as well as cultural. For many, it was an outright rejection of auspicious consumerism.

Many of the young men and women chose to live in rural isolation away from the urban centres and the watchful eye of the authorities for fear they would be arrested and returned to the United States (Coates 6). In British Columbia, the groups helping the young draft dodgers and deserters urged them to get as far away as they could from the large urban areas, like Vancouver, because the RCMP was known at the time to be working with the FBI (Carr). Two remote areas were the Gulf Islands and the interior regions of British Columbia, most notably the Slocan Valley and the Powell River area.

Whether they lived in communes or on small rural holdings, these social activists shared some common beliefs. They chose to live simply with few, if any, modern conveniences. In doing so, they rejected "the unsustainable waste inherent in capitalism" and mass production (Janovicek 9). Looking to the writings of earlier Utopian thinkers, such as Henry David Thoreau, they advocated a simple life, away from the military-industrial machine of the United States. To be successful and to survive, they needed to create small-scale alternative economies. In the West Kootenays and elsewhere, when someone from the back-to-the-land community opened a business or a service, other members worked to make sure that the venture was a success (Rodgers, *Welcome to Resisterville* 51). This might include spending what little cash they had for dinner at a new café or washing dishes in exchange for a meal. They helped one another build houses, the earliest made out of found materials and heated with wood rather than electricity. One benefit was that it kept the owners off the grid and away from the eyes of the bureaucrats.

One area of concern was food security. They planted organic gardens; some raised chickens either for meat or eggs or both, whereas others had larger livestock, such as cows for milk and cream. Still, it was difficult to be completely self-sufficient in Canada because of the harsh winters. The back-to-the-landers put their resources together and began buying in bulk; this led to the creation of food co-ops, many of which still exist today. Food and firewood were traded for childcare, carpentry skills for food or ceramics. In 1972, the bartering system was formalized into the Kootenay Barter Bank, an institution founded on the idea of "co-operation and mutual support" (Rodgers, *Welcome to Resisterville* 51). Here people could exchange their skills for other goods and services. Today, some of the most successful businesses in the West Kootenays are "the vegetarian restaurants, bulk food companies and organic produce farms," many started by the young American immigrants in the late 1960s and early 1970s (Rodgers, *Welcome to Resisterville* 169).

Craft production became an essential part of the alternative economy (Janovicek 9). Those trained in ceramics soon discovered that their work was highly valued. As part of a lifestyle that rejected mass-manufactured goods as well as plastics, handmade items, such as pottery, were in high demand. The vessels could be bartered for things the potter did not have but needed. Alternatively, the pottery could be sold for cash to tourists. The potters also taught. Sometimes they helped other community members learn a skill so that they could earn a living, or they offered workshops for community members for cash.

The immigrants helped to set up alternative sales venues, such as fairs and co-ops where individuals could learn, create, and sell their work. In the isolated region of the Slocan Valley in British Columbia, Elaine Hanbury, a potter from England, and her husband, Jack Anderson, a draft dodger from Texas, organized the first Kootenay Christmas Faire in 1973. Hanbury wanted to create a happening with musicians, a celebration of the talent of the artisans living in the area, while she simultaneously wanted to be able to sell her pottery (Alfoldy, *Theory and Craft* 12). The event was not without its controversies. The desire to make the cold basement of the civic hall more like an "organic outdoor experience" in late November or December violated many of the fire and food regulations (Alfoldy, *Theory and Craft* 13). As a result, there were constant threats by the local fire department (Alfoldy, *Theory and Craft* 13). In truth, the success of the fair, operated by local hippies, with more than 3,000 people attending and the artisans generating good sales, shocked the local businesses (Alfoldy, *Theory and Craft* 13). The festival continued in its original form, expanding to include events for children and dances on the weekend. In 1997, visitors totalled more than 8,000 with good sales for the artisans (Alfoldy, *Theory and Craft* 13). It is unclear precisely when the original iteration of the craft festival ended, but today it has fallen victim to high booth prices, so that many of the original vendors no longer participate (Alfoldy, *Theory and Craft* 2018). In Manitoba, counterculture youth and back-to-the-landers, some of whom were recent immigrants because of the Vietnam War, started the Pumpkin Creek Faire in Roseisle, a rural village in southern Manitoba, in the early 1970s. It, too, featured sales by local artisans as well as handmade food items and music. Others living on the Gulf Islands began organizing studio tours. One of the oldest is the Denman Island annual tour of the pottery studios on Canada's May long weekend. It is, in fact, one of the rare opportunities to see the studios and to meet the potters who have been working on the island since they arrived in the late 1960s and 1970s. Similar studio tours followed across Canada.

In studies about the reception of the back-to-the-landers in various parts of Canada, it is clear that not all were welcome by the long-term residents of the regions (Weaver, *First Encounters*; Hardwick). The use of drugs, nude swimming, and lack of respect for personal property were some of the issues. However, far more important were the political views of these young Americans: they were extremely critical of local industries that were seen to be destroying the environment. On Denman Island, there were demonstrations against logging and mining with calls to protect the island's water resources. Protests also took place in the West Kootenays and elsewhere. Many of the young arrivals were against clear-cutting and logging, while older established residents made their living in the forestry and mining industries. After five decades of living in Canada and wanting to continue to live meaningful lives and contribute to the good of the entire community, many of the resisters remain committed to protecting the local environment.

The Ceramics Revival in Canada

Craft historians and artisans will remember the late 1960s and early 1970s as a period of rapid change and institutionalization, a revival of interest in crafts nationwide. Up until this time, there were few places in Canada to get an undergraduate degree in ceramics. There was no place to study for an MFA in ceramics. One of Canada's renowned clay sculptors, the late Marilyn Levine, shares the implications of the lack of educational opportunities in Canada: "At the time there was no place in Canada to get a master's degree, so I was forced to go to the U.S. ... There, art departments were in universities and in Canada, they were in technical schools" (qtd. in Alfoldy, *Crafting Identity*, 134–35). Levine moved to California to study. She was not alone. Other significant clay artists in Canada, such as Vic Cicansky, had to travel to California to get a graduate degree.

For ceramics, the era included the founding of the Sheridan College of Applied Arts and Technology, commonly known as Sheridan College, in 1967 in Mississauga, Ontario. A few years earlier, the Winnipeg School of Art relocated to the Fort Garry Campus, where the late Charlie Scott, a recent immigrant from Massachusetts in 1964, set up the curriculum based on that of Alfred SUNY and the Rhode Island School of Design (RISD), his alma maters. He built the School's first wood fuel kiln, starting a trend of traditional wood firing and vessel making that continues today (see Figure 11.3). In 1969, the Nova Scotia College of Art and Design improved its studios as well as its curriculum, hiring draft resister Walter Ostrom to teach and take charge of the changes. Ostrom promoted the use of local earthenware clays such as the

FIGURE 11.3   Pamela Nagley Stevenson, Sitting in Studio in Winlaw with Work. Photo courtesy of Paul Galewitz.

iron-rich Lantz clays and majolica. Today, visitors to the studios of ceramists in Nova Scotia will see his influence on the beautiful tin white-glazed decorative ware being produced. By the end of the 1970s, the journal of the Ontario Potters Association, *Ontario Potter*, was able to report that there were five universities, fifteen community colleges, and another six institutions that offered full- or part-time educational opportunities in ceramics. Without exception, an American was hired at every one of these schools to develop the ceramics programs, ending decades of reliance on the British diploma system.[2]

Of the 117 participants in this study, at the time of their application for landed immigrant status, one young man was pursuing his PhD, twenty-one had undergraduate degrees, and twenty-four had master's degrees. Of those with MFA degrees, all were either teaching full time or part time in Canadian colleges and universities, if they chose to do so. Albert Borch was hired by the Alberta College of Art and Design (ACAD) in 1968. Their ceramic facilities were minimal, embarrassingly for Borch, after he had studied and taught at the School of the Art Institute of Chicago and the California College of Arts and Crafts. He worked hard with his colleagues to turn ACAD into a leading international institution for studying ceramics. He left a legacy that combined technical training with artistic practice, at the same time encouraging his students to grow in their direction instead of mimicking his style. Nearby, another American resister, Charles "Chuck" Wissinger, shaped the ceramics department at Red Deer College, while the late Tom Smith led the charge in Fredericton, where he introduced raku firing. Sally Michener immigrated to the Vancouver School of Art in 1973. Having received her MFA from the University of Cincinnati, she arrived at a time when the colleges and universities were growing, and when the "Baby Boomers" were demanding a university degree. Michener shaped much of the new curriculum at the Vancouver School of Art. She introduced artist talks and ceramic tours for students. She also reshaped the pedagogy by introducing hand building and more sculptural and conceptual approaches in ceramics informed by a wider sense of art history.

The late David Gilhooly began teaching at the University of Saskatchewan in Regina in 1969. He was part of an active exchange of ideas between California and Regina, beginning with Ricardo Gomez's arrival five years earlier. Gilhooly's whimsical approach to clay, mixing sculpture with function, inspired many. In fact, the celebrated Canadian sculptor Joe Fafard switched from creating kinetic sculpture to portraiture after being exposed to Gilhooly's papier mâché animals (Alfoldy and Steggles, 2007). Gilhooly moved to Toronto to take a position at York University in 1971. In 1977, he returned to the United States following President Carter's January 21, 1977, pardon for civilians who were convicted of violating the Selective Service Act. This short chapter is not, however, about individual styles or accomplishments, but rather about the enduring impact of a group of immigrants taken collectively. If it were, the list of American ceramic artists would be long, but the names of Canadian ceramists, teachers, curators, and students whom they influenced would be much longer at this critical time in the history of Canadian ceramics.

There is, however, one other individual who must be mentioned and that is the late Ruth Gowdy-McKinley. She accompanied her husband, Don, to Sheridan College in Mississauga, Ontario, in 1967. She was made resident potter at Sheridan, while her husband was in charge of furniture design. She built her wood kiln near the ceramics facilities. Known for her clean forms and glazes, she was the first ceramist elected to the Royal Canadian Academy of the Arts in 1976. Her influence still resonates through the Canadian ceramics community as the "mother of Canadian wood firing." Had her husband not chosen to accept the position at Sheridan, for both political and economic reasons, Canadian ceramics would have lost a great example of a potter who married beauty with utility. Moreover, even though she died very young, at the age of fifty, in 1981, her passion, her ideas, and her work continue to inspire.

At every Canadian college and university with a ceramics area that existed between 1963 and 1977, there was an American academic playing a significant role. Indeed, every one of the immigrants who accepted teaching positions at Canadian colleges and universities left an indelible legacy as their ideas became institutionalized in a way that has affected students for five decades.

At the same time, pottery and craft associations were being established or were modernizing. Membership in the Canadian Guild of Potters in Toronto expanded from ninety-five in 1945 to more than seven hundred members across Canada in 1970. By 1975, Ann Mortimer, head of the Ontario Potters Guild, realized that with the growing numbers of members across Canada, the organization was getting too large to be managed (Hopper). As a result, various provinces that did not already have a craft or potter's association began to formalize organizations of their own. Leading the call were often Vietnam resisters such as Duane Perkins and Steve Jorgensson in Manitoba, who helped found the Manitoba Craft Council in 1974, along with myself (another resister), Ione Thorkellson, Marilyn Foubert, and Kirk Creed.

The revival in craft, in general, and ceramics in particular, saw an increase in prominent collectors purchasing contemporary Canadian ceramics. In British Columbia, two of the most familiar were B.C. Binning, the founder of the UBC Festival of Contemporary Arts, and his wife, Jessie. The other was Geoffrey Massey and his wife, Ruth Killam Massey. Massey believed in good design and in the integration of life and art (Vaillant 20–23). In fact, Geoffrey Massey and his cousin Hart Massey began a collection of Canadian crafts in 1975. Members of the Massey Foundation travelled across Canada buying work that was eventually donated to the National Museum of Canada in Ottawa (Vaillant 23). On the West Coast, others like Doris Shadbolt, a curator at the Vancouver Art Gallery, began their own, and today, the Shadbolt collection of ceramics is part of the Morris and Helen Belkin Art Gallery at the University of British Columbia (UBC). Shadbolt observed the importance of such institutional recognition for this art form: "people's interest in handmade pottery was stimulated by the fact that it was being taken seriously by the Vancouver Art Gallery, the Vancouver School of Art, the University of British Columbia and the National Gallery" (qtd. in Vaillant 25). These individuals inspired others across Canada to begin to take the collecting of Canadian ceramics seriously.

It is not surprising that, as private and public collections began to grow, there were calls for recognizing those artists whose work was deemed to be excellent. To do so added value to objects in collections, both public and private. In 1977, the Saidye Bronfman Award for Excellence in Crafts was established; it was renamed the Governor General's Award in Visual and Media Arts in 2007. To date, two Vietnam resisters have received the Bronfman: Walter Ostrom (2003) and Peter Powning (2006). Ostrom was also inducted into the Order of Canada (2007), while four others were elected as members of the Royal Canadian Academy of the Arts. They include Ruth Gowdy-McKinley, David Gilhooly, Sally Michener, and Peter Powning.

This revival might be seen as a contradiction of Canada's search for identity. As Jessica Squires, author of *Building Sanctuary: The Movement to Support Vietnam War Resisters in Canada, 1965–73*, observes, "The Canadian government, like other governments, was, in the sixties, enduring a broader hegemonic crisis linked to widespread and global critiques of imperialism, colonialism, and capitalism. In Canada, this critique in part took the form of tensions around the concept of Canadian identity" (15).

The search for a Canadian identity was, in part, a means to demonstrate to Canadians and the world that Canada was a country distinctively different from the United States. This impulse also involved a call "to prioritize Canadian jobs for Canadians" (Squires 145). Canadians did not want to be like Americans, nor did they want American influence in their lives. One way that Canada could radically differentiate itself was to be a nation of peacekeepers. Ironically, this allowed for sympathy with the American draft dodgers and deserters during the Vietnam conflict, while paradoxically claiming that these immigrants, often well educated, would, in fact, be taking jobs away from Canadians (Squires 145). The concern over American influence in Canada's post-secondary institutions led, in the early 1980s, to a movement to hire Canadians first. As a result, in 1982, the federal government brought in new immigration legislation aimed at "giving preference to hiring only Canadian citizens for faculty positions in higher education" (Hardwick 19). This practice continued for two decades, until Canadian colleges and universities desired to become more international.

Conclusion

There is no doubt that the Americans who immigrated to Canada in the 1960s and 1970s, because of the Vietnam conflict, contributed to the history of Canadian ceramics. They helped to improve the offerings in ceramics at Canadian colleges and universities at a time when post-secondary administrators were anxious to replace the British diploma system with a four-year degree. They helped found associations, won awards, and taught locally, giving back richly to the communities in which they resided. Their influence is evident in the work and attitudes of the individuals who were once their students and are now artists or teachers, or both.

A few Canadian academics are beginning to write about the cultural contributions of this immigrant group. As one example, Martha Langford, an expert on contemporary Canadian photography, writes about the Baldwin Street Gallery in Toronto and the impact that the late John Phillips, a resister; Phillips' partner, Laura Jones; and the late Fletcher Starbuck, also a resister, had on Canadian photographic history. Her essay, "Hitching a Ride: American Know-How in the Engineering of Canadian Photographic Institutions," which appears in *Narratives Unfolding: National Art Histories in an Unfinished World*, unapologetically has an American focus in its evaluation of the cultural history of Canadian photography at the time; it was simply the reality (211). She notes that "Canadian photographic culture in the post-centennial years might be considered a primary example of US cultural colonization, given the prominence of the actors and their enduring influence" (211). The same might be said of the American influence on ceramics. When asked, my subjects said they were just bringing fresh ideas and working as hard as they could to make the student experience under their guidance exceptional. Almost everyone said that they did not think of themselves or their influence as being distinctly American. Two books on the impact of the war resisters on Canadian literature came out in 2008 and 2017. The first, *Crossing the Lines: Poets who Came to Canada in the Vietnam War Era*, edited by Allan Briesmaster and Steven Berzensky, is a collection of poetry by individuals who immigrated to Canada during the Vietnam era. Besides the poems, there is an excellent listing of the contributors and their literary accomplishments at the end. The second, *War Is Here: The Vietnam War and Canadian Literature*, by Robert McGill, examines how authors inject the Vietnam era into their writing and how those writers helped to continue the construction of the myth that Canada was liberal, hospitable, and humanitarian to the immigrants during the era. Still, the only publication that clearly examines the positive influence on Canadian culture is that by Langford. In addition to looking at the impact of the photographers who came to Canada and lived in the Baldwin Street area, Langford also discusses the organizations and documents that proved helpful to those wishing to immigrate.

Many of those coming to Canada in the 1960s and early 1970s relied on information from the Toronto Anti-Draft Programme (TADP; Langford, "Hitching a Ride" 225). Its counsellors encouraged them to assimilate into Canadian culture as soon as possible (Langford, "Hitching a Ride" 225).

They told them "to embrace the emerging movement of Canadian nationalism, precisely because it was an anti-imperialist movement" (Spira qtd. in Langford, "Hitching a Ride" 225). As a result, these American immigrants are recognized as having the most rapid Canadianization of any migrant group of Americans (Hardwick 15). Like Canadians, these Americans believed in individual diversity, strict gun controls, and universal health care. They wanted to live in a kinder, more peaceful, inclusive nation. Canada's lack of an aggressive military presence in the world was a key factor in helping the young people defend the values of their new country. Most did not call attention to themselves as Americans and, years later, their colleagues and neighbours were surprised to discover that they were American draft dodgers or resisters during the Vietnam era.

It is, thus, apparent that there are multiple overlapping reasons that the contributions to Canadian ceramics by this group were never recognized. First, the Americans whose society was divided by the Vietnam conflict are not interested in those who left their country (Matthews and Satzewich 165). In fact, they cannot imagine that anyone would want to give up "The American Dream" when so many want to immigrate to the United States (Matthews and Satzewich 165). Second, the Canadians, at the time, were celebrating a newfound nationalism following the centennial celebrations of 1967. Despite the fact that there were no qualified Canadians to fill the academic positions, there is still anger that these plum posts were occupied by Americans until they resigned or retired decades later. Third, while Canada is a country built on the hard work and ingenuity of its immigrants, few seem prepared to acknowledge just how much Canadian culture has been influenced by Americans. Fourth, the artists in my study did not understand their importance to the advancement of ceramics in Canada, and yet they rarely ever thought of themselves as Americans. Most remain humble about their work and grateful to be Canadian. Lastly, ceramics is simply not as prestigious as some other fine art mediums (Sorkin). In fact, quite a number of contemporary theorists and artists believe that ceramics have no place within contemporary art, nor should it be part of a university education. In other words, there is a bias against the discipline. Taken together, these are ample reasons that the contributions of these individuals, however extensive, have remained untold.

It is now fifty years since most of those in my study moved to Canada. Of the 117, 107 remain, a higher percentage than any other research on this migrant group (Hagan; Jones; Squires). All either have dual citizenship or have renounced their American citizenship altogether and only carry a

Canadian passport. The ceramists do not think of themselves as Americans, and have not for years, but rather as Canadians. Still, as one potter living in the Kootenays observed, "it is nice to be appreciated."

NOTES

1 My former mother-in-law, Sarah Ruth Martin, told my former husband this in 1969.
2 The late Susan Hardwick, Professor Emerita of Geography at the University of Oregon, describes the state of Canadian universities and colleges at the time as follows:

> A period of unprecedented growth in higher education occurred in both Canada and the United States during the booming post-World War II years. This growth was precipitated by the demands of growing numbers of undergraduate students interested in earning college degrees. In Canada, these demands were especially challenging due to the small number of Canadians graduating with PhDs in the 1950s and 1960s. (18)

Hardwick notes that by 1969, the number of Americans academics in the social sciences and humanities in Canadian universities had reached 41 percent (18). The number employed in the ceramics areas of colleges and universities was much higher.

CHAPTER TWELVE

Who Can Tell? Photographic Histories and Counter-Histories of Mennonite Communities in Canada

Martha Langford

The recent appearance of new national histories of photography[1] has caught the attention of Australian-born historiographer and theorist Geoffrey Batchen, who asks, "Could the writing of regional or national histories be a way of rethinking the history of photography as a discipline, threatening to transform it beyond recognition?" ("Beyond Recognition?"). In many cases, the new histories are simply expansions, refreshing the canon with worthy additions. Others are deliberately revisionist, re-reading their national photographic histories through different methodological lenses.

The Canadian situation is somewhat different. There is no authoritative story to retell, as a national history of photography has never been written. It exists only in the collective imagination, based on a substantial repertoire of texts by archivists, curators, critics, theorists, and photographers. Never consolidated—and never imbued with canonical authority—the *idea* of such an official history that must be countered has nevertheless inspired both critical practice and historiographical debate. Feminism, Marxism, gender studies, postcolonial, and settler-colonial theory have been applied,[2] approaches unified by a fine-grained analysis of power—its arrogation of knowledge—that subtends the work of Michel Foucault.[3] Carol Payne's critical history of the National Film Board of Canada's photographic program is pointedly entitled *The Official Picture*.[4] An informed reader will thus be alerted to an overarching system of control and resistance—ideologies that generated this important Canadian collection and a healthier skepticism arising now. Political philosopher José Medina efficiently describes this historiography of call and response as follows:

Official histories are produced by monopolizing knowledge-producing practices with respect to a shared past. Official histories create and maintain the
unity and continuity of a political body by imposing an interpretation on a
shared past and, at the same time, by silencing alternative interpretations of
historical experiences. Counter-histories try to undo these silences and to
undermine the unity and continuity that official histories produce. (14)

Although the lack of an "official history" has certainly impeded the
teaching of Canadian photography history, its delay might also be considered fortuitous (Langford et al. 305–308). It now seems possible, even
necessary, to write a photography history that entangles official stories in
counter-histories, that effectively narrates their reciprocal, if often uneven,
relationships. Such micro-histories already exist—the challenge is to write
a macro-history that relates the past in both historical and historiographical
terms. Simply put, the question becomes: why did certain practices flourish
in the past and how have they fared in the meantime? The story is complicated by theoretical and methodological shifts in photographic studies over
the past fifty years—cultural historians situating themselves in geopolitical,
social, and ethical debates. In the field of visual culture, considerations and
reconsiderations might be mapped as a series of hairpin turns.[5]

This is the level of re-revisionism that complicates the writing of a Canadian photography history. Counter-history, or the untold story, has
anticipated the official telling and clamours for revision at the gate. To this
curious situation, we must add the discipline's redirection of interest, from the
professional studio or art gallery to the scrapbook. In this shift, the divisions
between spaces of knowledge become clearer, even as they are breached. In
1967, Michel Foucault was beginning to think about sanctified versus desanc-
tified spaces, about "oppositions that we regard as simple givens: for example
between private space and public space, between family space and social
space, between cultural space and useful space, between the space of leisure
and that of work" ("Of Other Spaces" 23). Vernacular photography, once
sanctified by association with privacy and family, while debased by high culture and rejected by capitalist professionalism as a form of leisure, was both
revered and untouchable. It is now recognized as a—if not *the*—dominant
form of photographic memory and collective experience, one that trumps
the iconic visual image by activating other senses, including sound and touch
(Langford, *Suspended Conversations*; Batchen, *Forget Me Not*; E. Edwards).

Hierarchies are breaking down: artists, curators, and users of the Pin-
terest app now place iconic and domestic images on an equal footing. The

co-presence of "different sites"—different sets of site-defining relations—can be confounding until one sees them as interrelated, sites and counter-sites mirrored, as Foucault suggests ("Of Other Spaces" 23–24), or calling and responding to each other, as I am suggesting here. In the writing of national photography histories, digital collections are just the latest means of reproduction and circulation, reminding us of the permeability of cultural borders, first by printed matter, now in digital form. Canadian photographic history has always been silently transnational, its research and exposition emulating, supplementing, and occasionally talking back to Euro-American accounts. Historians now favour transnational approaches (Parsons; Langford, "Hitching a Ride"), which in the Canadian multicultural context, blend into transculturalism—exchanges between diasporic communities.

These complementary approaches cast Canadian photography history in relational formations that Michael Werner and Bénédicte Zimmermann call "histoire croisée" (31–33). The historian herself is also entangled; Werner and Zimmerman's insistence on self-reflexivity matches Donna Haraway's advocacy of "situated knowledge" as the only genuine objectivity ("Situated Knowledges" 583).[6] And just as we need to know ourselves, as subjects-information, we need to ask about the other subjects, behind and in front of the camera. Even in the most formulaic studio or ethnographic portraits, affect theory encourages us to seek signs of performative agency emanating from the subject—while they may be submitting to the camera, they are also actors in their own lives.[7] The official picture is thereby imagined as fragmented into unofficial versions. All of this makes for a very big historiographical brief.

Acknowledging his youthful sense of inclusiveness as a reaction to then-dominant methods, historiographer Christopher Dummitt finds that "[t]he inclusive history has become the common sense of the profession" (Dummitt and Dawson, "Introduction" xvi). He calls for a history that "blends these various strands of history into ever more complex and compelling narratives," that "builds even as it tears down" (Dummitt, "After Inclusiveness" 122).[8] Storytelling, as Dummitt tells us, remains the historian's highest calling; in constructing a Canadian photography history, the backstories cannot be neglected.

Inclusiveness, synthesis, and storytelling are not mutually exclusive, as I hope to show by creating dialogue between different photographic forms. My case study is the photographic representation of the Mennonites, an Anabaptist Christian movement that founded colonies in Canada and elsewhere. My starting point is a body of work with all the credentials of an official history. The maker is Larry Towell (b. 1953), a Canadian photojournalist and documentarian; 1994 winner of the World Press Photo of the Year Award; the first and only native-born Canadian member of the prestigious photographic cooperative Magnum Photos; and first winner of the Henri Cartier-Bresson Award (2003). These laurels alone would guarantee Towell a place in any comprehensive history of Canadian photography.[9] He attracted this attention for globe-trotting, trouble-spot photojournalism, notably in El Salvador, Israel, and Palestine, published in important magazines, such as *Life, Time,* and *The New York Times Magazine,* and consolidated in impressive monographs.[10] Simultaneous to this very public activity, Towell was also gathering and taking the family photographs that would compose *The World from My Front Porch* (2008), in which he contrasts the beauty and security of his farming lifestyle in Ontario with the trouble zones of violence and dispossession that he was recording elsewhere. His documentary project on the Mennonites, shot between 1989 and 1999, fits into this practice as a study of emplacement and displacement. Published in a deluxe edition by Phaidon in 2000, the book is entitled *The Mennonites: A Biographical Sketch.* Towell introduces it as a "personal book" of photographs and text.[11] *The Mennonites,* it needs be said, is a somewhat misleading title. In his opening statement, Towell identifies his subjects as *Old Colony* Mennonites that he photographed in rural Ontario and Mexico. The Old Colony is a branch of the Mennonites, with distinct, stubbornly defended values and corresponding struggles.

Towell's preface sketches the history of the Mennonites who founded Canadian colonies: their Anabaptist tenets and persecutions in northern Europe; their migration to Manitoba via Ukraine; their resistance to integrative schooling, which Manitoba sought to impose after the First World War; and the splintering of the community as a large segment of Old Colony Mennonites left for Mexico. This diasporic religious community, writes Towell, "is the most conservative and insular of the sixty or more diverse groups in existence today. In their Mexico colonies, faith and adherence to traditionalism are intertwined, represented by the horse and buggy for transport, steel-wheeled tractors for farmwork, and the rejection of electricity."

While the proven photogenic traits of simplicity and exoticism are writ large on these communities, Towell also draws them to earth, identifying their crisis as landlessness, which he represents in word and images, and identifying with their plight, which he empathetically imagines in contrast with his own deeply rooted life in Ontario. He creates, in effect, two spaces: his own utopic and the Mennonites' dystopic, as they reel from the effects of drought and diminishing resources. This dual approach is implicit

FIGURE 12.1   Larry Towell. Lambton County, Ontario, 1993. © Larry Towell/Magnum Photos.

in the subtitle of *The Mennonites* and explicit in his preface to *The World from My Front Porch*, in which landlessness is identified as the leitmotif of his oeuvre: "Wherever I travel, it is the identification of these displaced people that intrigues me most. From the landless of El Salvador to the Mennonite migrant workers of Mexico, I am drawn to their crisis ..." (145).

In *The Mennonites*, Towell establishes the start of his project in an encounter that emplaces this doubled identification: "I discovered them in my own back yard, land hungry and dirt poor." The Mennonites are explained as seasonal migrant workers, up from Mexico (Figure 12.1). "Back yard" should not be taken literally: the first encounter actually took place in his father's autobody repair shop, where the man, David Reddekop, was employed as a helper. He and his family were renting a run-down farmhouse not far from Towell's leased property. On his first visit to their temporary home, he learns that Reddekop's nine children like Canada "[b]ecause there is food to eat."[12] In *The World from My Front Porch*, this encounter is cast autobiographically:

> The first landless Mennonite I met was David Reddekop. From a colony in Mexico, he'd made the five-day road trip north, and was now sweeping the floor of my father's autobody shop for minimum wage. He and his wife Sarah had eight children, with several more to come. He'd just pulled out some of his own badly infected teeth, with a pair of pliers at his kitchen table and had set

his fourteen-year-old son's broken arm with cardboard and masking tape. He didn't trust doctors. David had no sense of how he should live in contemporary society, but he was sincere, and this sincerity attracted me. (153–54)

Towell calls himself a poet, as well as a photographer and videographer. His monographs and feature articles generally include his allusive text. Prefaced with a brief historical overview, *The Mennonites* is organized in chapters interlaced with what Towell calls "a train of thought composed of flashbacks and fixations drawn from diary notes and the silt of memory." He befriended some of these people, sleeping in their homes, sharing their food, interviewing the son of a man excommunicated for owning a vehicle, and travelling with one impoverished family on their re-migration from Canada to Mexico, a harrowing five-day journey across the United States.

For Towell, the meditative writer and social documentary photographer, an opportunity to join a family of migrant workers' trek across the United States must have been irresistible. Engine failure, flat tires, hunger, and fear of the authorities recall the struggles evoked in John Steinbeck's Depression-era novel, *The Grapes of Wrath*, and Dorothea Lange's documentary photographs of tenant farmers evicted from desiccated fields turning to dust.[13] Towell's "silt of memory" unquestionably includes these literary and photographic masterpieces, as well as their origin stories—stories invariably predicated on truth and trust. Phaidon's promotion of *The Mennonites* underlines Towell's "unique access" to a community that prohibits photography. As Towell writes, "[b]ecause I liked them, they liked me, and although photography was forbidden, they let me photograph them." He does so in a manner that exceeds documentary photography's quasi-scientific observational mode, crossing into the private realm, physically and affectively, communicating the survival of the sacred (Figure 12.2).

To forbid photography invests it with a certain power. The Second Commandment prohibits the graven image as idolatrous. The most conservative of the Anabaptists—Amish, Brethren, Hutterites, and Mennonites—invoke scripture to restrict photography in their communities. As Donald B. Kraybill explains, the proscription is not categorical, but reasoned. At issue is photography's enframing and potential strengthening of a subject-in-formation:

> The guidelines vary by group and family, but in general, members of Old Order communities are forbidden to consent to or pose for a face-on photograph. Photographs of animals, landscapes, homes, businesses, and even children

FIGURE 12.2 Larry Towell. Ojo de la Yegua Colony, Chihuahua, Mexico, 1992.
© Larry Towell/Magnum Photos.

who are not church members are less objectionable. Photographs of members taken by outsiders from a distance and side- or back-view photographs of
members are regarded as the moral responsibility of the photographer rather
than of the subject.

The taboo on posing for photographs is meant to discourage pride and
vanity; personal photos call attention to the individual and set the individual
above other members in the group. (186–87)

The Mennonites is brought to us as an exclusive—the hallmark of
prize-winning journalism and social documentary photography—based on
human relations. Nothing could be more mysterious. Towell insists on this
condition with a device whose necessity and visual power he has deployed
elsewhere, notably in Palestine. Wherever his photographs might—we
think—compromise the subjects or get them into difficulty with the authorities, the Old Colonists cover their faces with their hats or hands (Figure 12.3).
But we are still left wondering: if the price of being photographed is excom-
munication, how does he induce this level of cooperation?

The Mennonites whom he photographs are living in a state of emergency
that forces them, temporarily, to let an outsider in. This precariousness
has precedents; an earlier occurrence was recorded by sociologist Calvin

FIGURE 12.3   Larry Towell. Capulin Casas Grandes, Chihuahua, Mexico, 1999.
© Larry Towell/Magnum Photos.

Redekop in interviews with Old Colonists who had left Manitoba for Mexico
in the 1920s. The motive for leaving was not economic; it was founded on the
Old Colony's right to educate their children in their own religious schools—a
right they insist on to this day. This promise had been made to the Mennonites in 1873 by representatives of the Dominion government, then actively
recruiting European settlers for the Canadian west. Unbeknownst to the
Mennonites, the granting of separate education was not within the powers of
the Canadian government, but controlled by the province. In 1919, an assimilationist Manitoba threatened to exercise its constitutional right to send
Mennonite children to English-language schools. This decision launched
the Old Colony into a search for new lands. As interviewee Henry Neufeld
explained, interaction with people he called "worldlings" was rationalized
within the community:

> Sooner or later the break with the past must come. It seems to be in times of
> emergency or lack of alternatives that concessions are made. It is not con-
> sidered permissible for a brother to go along with a worldling [in a vehicle], at
> least in Canada before we moved. But when the Old Colony moved to Mexico,
> in the scramble to get moved, many of necessity availed themselves of the use
> of cars driven by worldlings. (Redekop, *Old Colony Mennonites*, 49)

FIGURE 12.4 Larry Towell. La Batea Colony, Zacatecas. Mexico. 1998. © Larry Towell/ Magnum Photos.

In the 1990s, in a renewed culture of crisis, Towell, unconsciously perhaps, slips into an established role as a worldly helper—in Mennonite culture, he is a "worldling." Still, Towell does more than drive the car.

In La Betea Colony, Zacatecas, Mexico, his recurring visits seem to create a photographic ritual. *The Mennonites* includes two images of young women posing in the sunshine with their straw hats tilted over their faces: first, in 1994, one girl alone and then in 1998, four young girls. In the first image, the girl poses with her back to the wall, in the space between house and outhouse. Her sole chaperone is the looming shadow of a windmill. In the later image, the four girls, divided in pairs, are spaced across a courtyard—a composition of figures and planes—in which furniture from the house is also on view (Figure 12.4). Eviction or migration is evoked, or remembered, in this surreal and sexually charged composition, perhaps prompted by house cleaning. Nothing is clear.

Kraybill's explanation of photographic control here becomes invaluable. Remember that children can be photographed face-on. It is only after baptism that they cannot, or they must take responsibility for their cooperation. Baptism is the doorway to adulthood, to becoming marriageable females. Rather than stretching the rules of their community, have these young women cooperated with Towell to work out a "modern" ritual to perform in a photograph that marks their passage to adulthood? Are they, in effect, setting aside face-on portraiture as a childish thing? Without pressing too hard on the parallel between a photographic device and the manifestation of the sacred, it is perhaps worth noting that ritual is understood by sociologists as one of "four mechanisms which sacralise identity on the personal and social level—objectification, commitment, ritual, and myth" (Hamm 19). A singular performance reinforces personal identity; an imitative performance reinforces the group, or in this case, the subgroup that is cooperating with the "worldling" photographer. The history of photography has been built on such symbolically charged and paradoxical expressions of desire and embeddedness. Only the subjects remember their circumstances.

An Old Colony Mennonite history of photography might be written from the perspective of photographic experience—its acuity at certain moments of disruption. In 1873, a Mennonite delegation from Russia was inspecting land around Steinbach, Manitoba. A photograph was taken by the authorities, and in the diary of Delegate Tobias Unruh, this event was recorded with shame:

> When we were ready to leave the three rigs loaded with people were lined up and photographed. This act grieved me seriously. We had come here as pilgrims and strangers, labouring in distress, seeking a home in a country where we could with our children together live according to the dictates of our conscience, and now we were, as it were, arrayed and classed highly. This photograph should reach the British authorities that they could see the warm reception that had been extended to us. Yet when I consider our miserable condition my eyes often run over. I cannot hide my face. My heart was deeply humiliated. (Warkentin 17)

As emigrants, seeking land and religious freedom, the Mennonite delegation needed to appear in a positive light. Photography threatened to reveal its vulnerability, to class the Mennonites as undesirable, thereby weakening their negotiating power with Canadian officials. Unruh's diary gives evidence of visual literacy and a solid grasp of photography as an instrument of propaganda. This is neither fundamentalism, nor superstition; it is evidence of photographic literacy, a realm of knowledge and feeling that can be entered empathetically through Towell's images, but also through other collections.

Thousands of photographs, including pictures of Old Colonists, have been amassed by the Mennonite Archival Image Database. Stylistically, there are very few points of comparison. Towell is a skilled photographer, with an expressive signature style; the archival photographs represent a range of photographic images, from the personal to the commercial. Standard photographic fare for the Mennonites is evoked by Abe Warkentin, who opens his review of Towell's monograph with the following: "This is not your typical Mennonite coffee table book brimming with photos of lovely homes and factories, prosperous farms, businesses and large churches. It is, rather, both a beautiful and gritty book" (Penner and Warkentin 259). Warkentin goes on to suggest that the mainstream Mennonite community has largely chosen to ignore Towell's book. They will not pay the hefty price, he claims, and "[t]he hardscrabble colonists who have lost their land and often even their faith and families in the tortuous journeys in and out of Mexico, can't afford it." He adds, "Tragically, even if they could, few would be able to read it" (Penner and Warkentin 261).

As befits the diversity of opinion in Mennonite society, Warkentin's review is published by the *Journal of Mennonite Studies* in tandem with another, written by Tom Penner of the University of Winnipeg. Penner engages with both word and image, finding the prose somewhat "over-stylized" and subjective, while "[t]he captionless pictures provide their own stark poetry and are something of a reprieve from the breathless intensity of the interstitial observations that accompany them" (Penner and Warkentin 262). Neither reviewer makes mention of a ban on photography. On the contrary, Penner writes that "Towell's subjects alternate between being camera-shy and self-aware, and the photographs consistently draw out hidden aspects of both individual and communal character" (Penner and Warkentin 262).

The thousands of photographs in the Mennonite archives tell many stories about the various communities. They represent "a spectrum of human responses," which is how historian Frank H. Epp characterizes the chapters of this sectarian history: the Reformation; the Anabaptist movement, and its further fragmentation into movements, such as the Menists, later Mennonites, who followed Menno Simons (1496–1561); and the "division and schism" that made a "'rainbow' of Mennonite groups" and continue to differentiate them today (Epp 33–34; Redekop, *Mennonite Society* 30). The Old Colony is a branch of the Mennonites that strictly enforces a traditional way of life as a means of perpetuating its formative values. As Calvin Redekop explains, "the goals of the Old Colony are personal salvation and dedication to the Old Colony way of life. These ultimate goals are to be achieved by separation from the world and acceptance by the young people of the Old Colony way of life" (*Old Colony Mennonites*, 123). Rubber tractor tires are forbidden, because they make it easier for young men to go to town and get drunk. Prohibitions are aimed at the survival of the colony. From this, one might deduce that one

FIGURE 12.5 Cornelius Krause. Six men standing beside a car, Mexico, 1923. Courtesy: Mennonite Heritage Centre.

reason that photography is forbidden—when and where it is forbidden—is because it brings the world into the Old Colony dwelling or schoolroom, to the detriment of cohesive isolation. The problem is not substantive, but functional: it is not photography per se that is the problem, but its circulation. Pictures make the Colony visible to prying eyes, thereby narrowing its separation from the world; photography heightens such invasiveness, placing images of the outside world before the eyes of restless, as yet unmarried, youth. Or so it appeared to Redekop in the 1960s, even though messages were mixed: cameras were contraband; books, newspapers, and magazines—all but the *Steinbach Post*—were banned; and old Montgomery Ward and Sears catalogues were permitted, as entertainment for children (*Old Colony Mennonites*, 142–43). In the 1990s, David M. Quiring was finding that "while the church still prohibits photographs, many do own some, often taken by outsiders." And he saw many picture calendars on display, rationalized by their functionality (*Mennonite Old Colony Vision*, 50). The spectrum of photographs in the Mennonite archives includes hundreds of consensual representations of Old Colonists in Canada, Mexico, and South America, returning to that same crucial "break with the past"—the exodus to Mexico of the early 1920s—when "worldlings" and "worldling" technology played a part.

The Cornelius Krause (1886–1968) collection, held by the Mennonite Heritage Centre in Winnipeg, shows photography in use at this time of

FIGURE 12.6
Cornelius Krause's face
framed by a cardboard
cowboy cut out, Mexico,
1923. Courtesy: Mennonite
Heritage Centre.

crisis and transition. The collection consists of negatives and high-resolution digital images made from 194 photographs provided by the land agent who travelled with Krause and other Mennonite delegates, as well as Krause's own pictures, showing places visited on the Old Colony delegation's 1923 prospecting trip in Mexico.[14] Portraits of the travellers and their hosts in front of cars document the mood of the mission: it is resolute and the men have nothing to fear from a camera (Figure 12.5).

There are numerous views of already established Mennonite settlements; pictures of tools, wells, and irrigation methods; anecdotally rich snapshots of delegates interacting with Mexican people; and groups of delegates facing the camera. Were these photographs contraband? Were they hidden? On the contrary, they appear to have circulated: there is much evidence of handling in the cracks, torn corners, and missing pieces of the prints.

The delegation's pictures were evidently taken and used to show something of the new land, its inhabitants, and cultural mores. But they are more than pragmatic: they give every indication of facility and enjoyment of photography, including its autobiographical and carnivalesque role-playing—Krause playfully inserted into the persona of a gun-toting *vaquero*, bandit, or revolutionary (Figure 12.6).[15]

From our current postcolonial perspective, it is especially fascinating to see Krause, the prospecting settler, looking at the other, playing at being the other—in this case, the Mexicans—as any tourist or ethnographer would do. Like any tourist, he photographs Mexicans selling items at the train station and other cross-cultural encounters.

Here photography also forms a spectrum, as Quiring reports that one of the earliest tribulations faced by the Old Colony Mennonites in Mexico was the requirement to be photographed for identity documents. He attributes this to "the prohibition against graven images" (*Mennonite Old Colony Vision*, 28), suggesting that appeals to scripture increased exponentially once the migration crisis was over. His own explanation of land ownership might offer a more practical reason: the Old Colonists kept individual names off their original land registrations as a way of controlling resale (*Mennonite Old Colony Vision*, 39). Identity documents with photographs would have made that harder to do.

In contrast with Krause's prospecting pictures, the Mennonite archives also document the post–Second World War production and circulation of photography. Benjamin Nobbs-Thiessen has studied photographs in *The Canadian Mennonite*, an illustrated magazine published in Manitoba from 1953 to 1971, finding mixed, sometimes contradictory messages. The pictures "describe Mexican Mennonite life in a kind of stasis" (24)—as "cultural museums separated by temporal as well as spatial divides from their more progressively minded brethren" (23). Enjoyed by progressive Mennonites, whose lives were increasingly entangled with the outside world, such images assert the distinctiveness of their movement and honour the idealism of its founders. Nobbs-Thiessen lingers on a set of photographs published in a 1947 article by Walter Schmiedehaus, "The Mennonite Life in Mexico." These photos set up a comparison between villages in Russia, Canada, and Mexico in a bald, ahistorical attempt at harmonization (Nobbs-Thiessen 23).[16] They are intended to foster connections, encouraging evangelical missions to reunite Mennonites worldwide and, specifically, to bring Old Colonists into closer alignment with their Canadian brethren.

This desire for unity was not universally shared. Quiring outlines the conflict arising from the persistent and, in many quarters, unwanted presence of Mennonite missionary and aid organizations, chronicling a campaign that began around 1946 under the aegis of the Mennonite Central Committee (MCC), then based in Akron, Pennsylvania. Driven out by the Old Colonists, the MCC resurged under Canadian leadership in the mid-1950s. Again repulsed, it returned to the charge in the 1970s, rebranded as the Kanadier Mennonite Colonization Committee, and later as the Kanadier Mennonite Concerns Committee. Abe Warkentin was its forceful director until 1995 (Quiring, "Intervention and Resistance" 87–88 and note 24; Quiring,

FIGURE 12.7 Photographer unknown. A Casual Picture of a Family sitting in a horse drawn wagon, Mexico, 1955. Courtesy: Mennonite Archives of Ontario.

Mennonite Old Colony Vision, 80–82). Each of these surges of interest in the Mexican colonies appears to have generated photographs, many taken in the observational snapshot mode of ethnography. The Mennonite Archival Image Database is now their central repository. A striking example is the 1955 photograph of a Mennonite family sitting in a horse-drawn carriage (Figure 12.7).

The *studium* of this image, as Roland Barthes termed photography's containment of knowledge, is the recorded presence of this family whose clothing and mode of transportation identify them as Old Colonists. Their awareness of the photographer is evident in the various reactions: the adult male stares out from under his hat, possibly impatient to get going; the woman smiles shyly; the three visible children look at the camera. There is at least one other person in that wagon, an older daughter, gauging by the rounded shape between the woman's hat brim and left shoulder; it is intriguing, if not necessarily pertinent, that this passenger is neither straining to see what is going on, nor trying to get into the picture. The photograph may have been snapped quickly, with the barest consent; no one, however, is hiding his or her face.

Like Barthes, I am attracted by other details, until ambushed by one (Barthes 53). The backdrop that frames the beautiful team of horses is a freestanding building, whose façade is emblazoned with painted signs for Mexican beer—Monterrey and Carta Blanca. This Mennonite family portrait is thereby firmly emplaced in Mexico, whose border has nevertheless been breached by American business. Mounted on both sides of the Casa's front door are bottle-shaped emblems of Coca-Cola. Can agribusiness be far behind? Foucault speaks of heterotopia's capability to juxtapose in a single real space several sites that are themselves incompatible—what he refers to as the paradise garden ("Of Other Spaces" 25). But the detail that stirs me—what Barthes called the *punctum*—is not this American colonization of an otherwise orderly Mexican/Mennonite scene, but rather the sight of the woman's hands lightly curling around, perhaps trying to steady, the shopping bag at her feet. There is something precious to her there, and this protective gesture, combined with her gentle smile for the camera, might be a repository of a counter-memory—a very good trip to town. It at least offers that possibility to the viewer who seeks chinks in the wall of the colony. The woman's expression is friendly and welcoming, and might be taken as encouragement to the missionizing Mennonites from the north.

A Mennonite Holiday Tour of 1956 produced many touristic and friendly snapshots, including one of the Canadian visitors with their Old Colony sisters: eight women convivially posing in an Old Colony village near Cuauhtémoc, Mexico. A photographic historian might fasten on the camera around the neck of the third woman from the right: a visitor, to be sure. More significant to the Canadian Mennonites, at least, was the sisterhood on display: the women were organized in a line, villager, visitor, villager, visitor, and so on, in a way that breached the boundaries of their colonies.[17]

There are innumerable family photographs and casual snapshots in Canadian Mennonite archives, some taken by social historians interested in the diaspora. In 1977, the Henry Bergen family of Durango Colony cooperatively lined up for researcher Bill Janzen.[18] Such a banal image—but I will return to it shortly (Figure 12.8).

Quiring's interviews, conducted in 1996 with Old Colony bishops and officials, capture the tensions within the various settlements. For decades, more progressive Mennonite settlements had been sapping the strength of the Old Colony settlements by accepting their excommunicated. By the 1990s, "the seasonal movement to Canada, when young families went north to earn money and then returned to the colony, represented a great menace" ("Intervention and Resistance" 87, 98). Noting that "leaders of relatively isolated and traditional colonies were the most receptive to taking aid from outsiders," Quiring suggests that "[t]his relative openness seemed partly due to having experienced less disruption from the actions of outsiders" ("Intervention and Resistance" 97). The "outsiders" in this case are other Mennonites, but his observation might also be applied to Towell's coincident presence.

FIGURE 12.8 Bill Janzen. Old Colony Mennonite family (Henry Bergen family of Durango Colony, Mexico), 14 April 1977, 1977. Courtesy: Mennonite Heritage Centre.

Towell's photographs are called poetic for good reason and his captions are lean, telling us nothing of the specific circumstances of a photograph. Breaking up his sequences to assemble the pictures by colony affords no meaningful distinctions. Likewise, reimagining his sequence in chronological order tells us nothing of his movement into the daily lives of the Old Colonists as he bodily contravened their highest principle, which is separation from the world. Oddly, it is in an image of intense crisis, the death of a child, that his role as a worldling becomes clear.

In 1998, the penultimate year of his project, in Durango Colony, Towell photographs three adults making final arrangements to a dead child in a coffin (Figure 12.9). The space is tiled, aspirationally antiseptic. The body is displayed as sleeping. A man and a woman work together to pin down the pleated coverlet, while a third woman, perhaps the mother or the sister, looks on.

In compositional terms, the dead child is the subject of this photograph. He or she is centred in the vertical or portrait composition, the attendants' bodies almost awkwardly cropped, working formally as *repoussoirs*. The effect of this framing is to draw the photographer, not visibly but functionally, into the scene. He can be felt standing at the foot of the tiny coffin. He is imagined, as theatre audiences imagine the fourth wall, as an embodiment of Foucault's line of separation that is also the threshold to displaced or hidden places such as cemeteries or colonies ("Of Other Spaces" 25, 27). In photographic theory and practice, Foucault's most utilized image of the heterotopia is the mirror—an

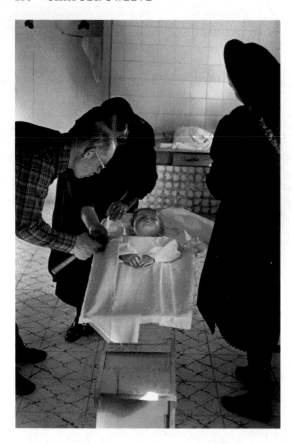

FIGURE 12.9
Larry Towell. Durango
Colony, Mexico, 1998.
© Larry Towell/
Magnum Photos.

instrument that delivers both a "placeless place" and its own intensified reality that allows its user to return ("Of Other Spaces" 24). It is another favourite trope for Towell, whose "biographical sketch" of his time with the Old Colonists is doubly emplaced as the "other world" from his front porch.

Like photography, the writing of history is a process of granting attention. Scholarly attention shifts in rhythm with the socio-political mores that pose supplementary questions and reframe knowledge. Attention to photographic experience means less attention to authorial claims, more to the sovereignty of another subject—that restless little girl, fourth from the left, in the 1977 Bergen family portrait, for example. She clasps her right hand to the side of her head; her left hand is open and reaching forward, not hanging obediently at her side; her feet are dancing. Will she know herself as a photographic subject in twenty years, when another photographer, possibly a "worldling," comes calling? Will she gaze into the camera, or will she offer up another unsanctioned version of herself?

My focus in this chapter has been on the distinction between told and untold stories, between official and counter-histories, essentially asking "which is which?" and what can be gained from their entanglement in an inclusive history. Official histories, as told or imagined, privilege the operator and the artist; vernacular photography has tended to be relegated to the margins, like folk art or storytelling. This chapter turns that notion on its head, suggesting that we might try to think about the production of a professional photojournalist, however authoritative or history-making in the cultural field, as the alternative or counter-history—as the one that a truly inclusive approach to Canadian photography history would be obliged to admit. This thought-experiment creates another spectrum, or perhaps an oscillation, between sources of "power/knowledge" that comes closer to Foucault's approach. As Medina interprets it:

> One may naively think that the opposite of power/knowledge would be powerlessness/ignorance, so that those excluded or marginalized in the discursive practices that produce certain epistemic and power effects would be simply subjects without any knowledge and any power, quasi-non-agents. But the pluralistic genealogical approach that Foucault sketches goes completely against those views that portray the oppressed as merely powerless and ignorant. In fact, this approach unmasks as an important misconception the view that the oppressed simply lack power and knowledge because of the forms of exclusions and marginalization they suffer. That distorted characterization plays in the hands of the dominant ideologies and grants too much to them: namely, it grants the very definition of what counts as legitimate power and legitimate knowledge. (13)

Emergent histories of photography acknowledge photographic experience as "what counts." My interpretation of the little girl's behaviour in the 1977 family portrait is just such a reading. It fits within a discourse of counter-history situated in the performances of everyday life. That said, we cannot neglect the heterotopic counter-histories, as they have fed our appetites for other spaces and unleashed the creator within. As real spaces of illusion that speak back to other real spaces (the mirror, but also the colony), heterotopias are photographic theatres of operation. They are counter-sites for the staging of counter-histories whose telling talks back to photographic power—the power that we are now investing in the archives. Freely circulating online, those everyday photographs are gaining in authority; they are often legitimized without a thought to their epistemological program. Disentangling their circumstances re-entangles them in the photographic history that we need now.

NOTES

1 The list includes Egypt, Indonesia, Japan, Denmark, New Zealand, the Netherlands, Norway, Great Britain, Australia, India, China, Italy, and the USA.

2 Among the many Marxist theorists and critical practitioners who shaped postmodern photographic discourse in the mid-twentieth century, Martha Rosler and Allan Sekula are noteworthy for their Canadian connections by dint of extended residencies at the Nova Scotia College of Art and Design, Canadian publishers, and, in Sekula's case, key texts (visual and verbal essays) "made in Canada"—"Photography between Labour and Capital" (1983) and *Geography Lesson: Canadian Notes* (artwork, 1986; monograph, 1997). In the 1990s, it was not uncommon to find Sekula misidentified as a Canadian.

3 Colin Gordon's afterword to *Power/Knowledge: Selected Interviews and Other Writings 1972–1977 by Michel Foucault* is a useful guide to this "strategic fulcrum" (233) in Foucault's thinking, as brought into English under these titles: *Madness and Civilisation* (1965), *The Order of Things* (1970), *The Archaeology of Knowledge* (1972), and *The History of Sexuality* (1978).

4 The National Film Board of Canada, Still Photography Division (NFB/SPD), was created to fulfil NFB founder John Grierson's vision of an effective wartime propaganda unit. The photographic unit developed its own nation-building program of photo essays and exhibitions. In 1967, it was given the mandate for the collection and circulation of contemporary Canadian photography, thereby becoming the Canadian institute of record for the emergence of photography as an art form and documentary practice. The NFB/SPD collection was transferred to the National Gallery of Canada (NGC) on the creation of the Canadian Museum of Contemporary Photography (CMCP) in 1984. The CMCP collection was for a while amalgamated with NGC's international holdings under the care of the Canadian Photography Institute of the NGC.

5 The crowded and unsettled field of "new visual studies" is ably addressed by Barry Sandywell and Ian Heywood in the introduction to their *Handbook of Visual Culture,* characterizing their interdisciplinary and (postdisciplinary) collection as "a site of provocations and reflective dialogues" (Heywood and Sandywell 3–7; citation 3).

6 I discuss this approach in my introduction to *Narratives Unfolding.*

7 Here I am thinking of the work of Julie Crooks, whose research on the Bell-Sloman emphasizes the agency of nineteenth-century Black subjects, posing for *cartes-de-visite.*

8 Christopher Dummitt's chapter, "After Inclusiveness: The Future of Canadian History" (98–122), is being glossed in this passage. See Dummitt and Dawson, "Introduction: Debating the Future of Canadian History: Preliminary Answers to Uncommon Questions" (x–xix) in their *Contesting Clio's Craft*.

9 Towell was nominated to Magnum in 1988, becoming a full member in 1993.

10 Towell's photojournalistic monographs include *El Salvador* (1997), *Then Palestine* (1998), and *No Man's Land* (2005).

11 *The Mennonites* is unpaginated.

12 *The Mennonites*, cited by Brett Abbott in *Engaged Observers* (176).

13 In his review of *The Mennonites* for *Journal of Mennonite Studies*, Tom Penner, University of Winnipeg, makes the same comparisons, although he judges Towell's work "less sure than Lange's or Steinbeck's about its attitude toward that suffering" (Penner and Warkentin 261–62). The other reviewer, Abe Warkentin, extols the qualities of one family portrait, claiming that "[p]overty just shouts from this picture and it could serve as the cover of John Steinbeck's classic, *Grapes of Wrath*" (Penner and Warkentin 260). For Warkentin, this takes nothing from its "realistic portrayal" (Penner and Warkentin 260).

14 It is noteworthy that these are not original photographs. In 2003, the Mennonite Heritage Centre in Winnipeg was given permission to copy photographs from the private collection of Jacob Doerksen, the grandson of compiler and photographer Cornelius Krause (1886–1968).

15 It is worth repeating that the photographs were only lent to the Mennonite Heritage Centre. The family plainly valued them as keepsakes and wanted the originals back.

16 Benjamin Nobbs-Thiessen cites Benedict Anderson's influential *Imagined Communities* (1983) to underscore the unifying force of print culture, as well as the extension of Anderson's theory by Timothy Mitchell (2000), who writes of modernity's space-time compressions (19–20).

17 The image is held by the Mennonite Archives of Ontario. The photographer is unknown. Cataloguing information is as follows: "Mennonite Holiday Tour of 1956. On a visit to the Penner family in an Old Colony village near Cuauhtemoc, Mexico, 4 women from the tour group stand with 4 Old Colony Mennonite women who wear hats and head coverings with their unique style of dresses." Published in *Canadian Mennonite*, vol. 4, no. 38, 1956[?], p. 7.

18 Born in 1943, Bill Janzen was then working on his doctoral dissertation, which he defended in 1981 and subsequently published as *Limits on Liberty: The Experience of Mennonite, Hutterite and Doukhobor Communities in Canada* (1991). See Mennonite Heritage Centre, "William Janzen collection."

CHAPTER THIRTEEN

Who Gets Remembered? Gender and Art in the Early Twentieth Century

Brian Foss and Jacques Des Rochers

In Canada, as in almost every nation, women constitute a slight majority of the population. Yet despite improvements over the last few decades when it comes to women's representation in the narratives of self-definition that Canada tells itself, much work remains to be done. This is as true in the arts and humanities as it is in politics and business. Interrogation of gender should therefore be very much to the fore in any stocktaking of overlooked or otherwise marginalized narratives during the many celebrations that mark Canada's sesquicentennial in 2017.

This chapter probes one aspect of the gendering of art production in Canada by focusing on the Beaver Hall Group: an artists' collective that was active in Montreal beginning shortly after the end of the First World War. The Group began fading from the historical record at the time of its dissolution in 1923, and continued to do so until the mid-1960s. Over the five decades beginning in 1966 it enjoyed renewed and steadily growing attention. Gender issues have been central to the Group's reputation—first to the dwindling of that reputation and then, for very different reasons, to its dramatic recent revival—over the nearly full century that has elapsed since the Group's founding. This chapter considers the ways in which evolving discourses about gender have positioned and repositioned the Beaver Hall Group within the canon of Canadian art.

The Beaver Hall Group: A Brief History

The Beaver Hall Group was founded in Montreal in the spring of 1920. A little more than four months later, two of its members, the artists Edwin Holgate and Adam Sherriff Scott, signed, with the financial backing of Holgate's father, a three-year lease on a building at 305 Beaver Hall Hill. That street runs north–south from the eastern edge of Montreal's current downtown shopping district, to the city's earlier downtown area in today's Old Montreal. In the early 1920s, it was in the process of being converted from a residential area of three-storey terrace houses (such as number 305) to more commercial architecture. It was the Beaver Hall Hill address that gave the Group its name. It consisted of four rooms intended for use as studio space and two rooms that were converted into exhibition galleries. It is known that the Beaver Hall Group held at least five exhibitions in the building. Unfortunately, whatever archives the Group may have accumulated have not survived. As a result there is much about its structure, budget, membership, operation and activities that remains obscure at best and, more usually, frustratingly unknown. The five exhibitions included three group shows (in November 1920, January 1921, and January 1922), a solo exhibition by member Adrien Hébert, and a display of pieces by Art Association of Montreal (AAM) students and by pupils of Anne Savage, herself both an important member of the Group and a major figure in the history of art education in Montreal. (The AAM is today the Montreal Museum of Fine Arts.) The Group ceased to function at some point in 1923 because of what Randolph Hewton, a particularly committed participant, described simply as "financial worries."[1]

As with so much other documentation that would have been produced by the Group, no membership lists are known to survive today. Nor do we know what criteria had to be met in order for someone to qualify as an official member. However, we do know that twenty artists took part in at least one of the Group's three members-only group exhibitions. In addition, another nine who did not take part in those displays were close friends or colleagues of the exhibitors, and were described—in their own reminiscences and/or in testimony by confirmed contributors to the exhibitions—as having had either actual or de facto membership status. The twenty-nine artists worked in painting, printmaking, design, and sculpture, and comprised fourteen men and fifteen women. Those numbers were groundbreaking in their importance: Beaver Hall was the first Canadian artists' group to achieve near gender parity. Jeanne de Crèvecoeur, Mabel Lockerby, Mabel May, Darrell Morrisey, Lilias Torrance (Lilias Torrance Newton, following her 1921 marriage), Sarah Robertson, Sybil Robertson, Anne Savage, and Regina Seiden participated in at least one of the three known large exhibitions, while Nora Collyer, Emily Coonan, Elsie Deane, Prudence Heward, Kathleen Morris, and Ethel Seath are not known to have done so. The male members who are known to have contributed work to at least one of the shows were James Crockart, Adrien

Hébert, Henri Hébert, Randolph Hewton, Edwin Holgate, A.Y. Jackson, John Johnstone, Hal Ross Perrigard, Robert Pilot, Adam Sherriff Scott, and Thurstan Topham. André Biéler, Albert Henry Robinson, and Stewart Torrance are not recorded as having been involved in any of the known exhibitions held at 305 Beaver Hall Hill, but are usually taken to have been associated with the Group in some significant way.

The artists affiliated with Beaver Hall tended strongly to have certain social and aesthetic characteristics in common. Almost all were Protestant anglophones. Only three—the painter Adrien Hébert; his sculptor brother, Henri; and the poorly documented painter Jeanne de Crèvecoeur—were francophones, and all three were Roman Catholic, as was the anglophone Emily Coonan. Regina Seiden was the only Jewish member of the Group. In addition, with rare exceptions all twenty-nine artists had middle-class roots, although Prudence Heward came from a comparatively wealthy background and Coonan from a working-class family. A majority of them had studied at the Art Association under William Brymner, who directed the art school there from 1886 until he retired in 1921. Brymner was not himself an artist who explored recent stylistic developments in his work. He was, however, committed to allowing his students to pursue their own interests: an openness for which he was fondly remembered by many of those students. Most important, all of the Beaver Hall Group shared an interest in modernist aesthetics, even if some, including Hal Ross Perrigard and Adam Sherriff Scott, were more sympathetic to visual modernism than they were actual practitioners of it. As just one example among many others, Sarah Robertson's formidable skills as a modernist colourist (skills that were greatly admired by A.Y. Jackson[2]) are on full display in images such as *The Blue Sleigh* (c. 1924; Figure 13.1), with its bright blue and red sleigh and its sky uncompromisingly painted in rich, velvety greens.

Visual Modernism and Gender: The Group of Seven and Beaver Hall

Perhaps the Group of Seven (1920–33), based in Toronto and long a dominant force in popular and critical understandings of the history of the visual arts in Canada, is the best starting point for examining gender politics as they were played out in the history of the Beaver Hall Group. The founding of the Beaver Hall Group was related, both temporally and logistically, to that of the Group of Seven, whose coordinated presence on the Canadian art scene dated from the spring of 1920. On May 7 of that year, their first joint exhibition as a seven-member collective opened at the Art Gallery of Toronto (now the Art Gallery of Ontario). The formation of the as yet unnamed Beaver

FIGURE 13.1 Sarah Robertson (Montreal 1891 – Montreal 1948), *The Blue Sleigh*, C.1934. Oil on canvas, 48.3 × 61 cm. Owen Sound, Ontario: Tom Thomson Art Gallery. Bequest of Norah Thomson de Pencier 1974 (1974.004.010).

Hall Group just two weeks later was due in no small part to the advocacy of one of the Seven: A.Y. Jackson. He had been born and raised in Montreal, and was the only Group of Seven member whose origins were in Quebec. In 1914, though, when in his early thirties, he had moved to Toronto in order to be closer to two other artists, Lawren S. Harris and J.E.H. MacDonald, who shared his thematic and stylistic interests. Six years later, Jackson, Harris, and MacDonald were joined by Arthur Lismer, Fred Varley, Fred Carmichael, and Frank Johnston to found the Group of Seven.

With his roots in Montreal, Jackson was acutely aware that modernist artists in his native city routinely faced the same obstacle that the Group of Seven battled in Toronto: the traditionalism of art institutions, art critics, and collectors. Montreal's two largest and most influential visual arts organizations, the École des Beaux-Arts and the Art Association of Montreal (the latter essentially an anglophone club), were dominated by conservative academicians. Although the city's critics and collectors had embraced Impressionism by the end of the first decade of the twentieth century, most strains of more recent work—everything from the Fauvism of Henri Matisse, André Derain, and Maurice de Vlaminck, to the Expressionism of Gabriele Münter,

Marianne von Werefkin, and other members of Munich's Blaue Reiter group, to the Cubism of Pablo Picasso and Georges Braque—remained beyond the pale for all but a tiny minority until well into the 1920s. In 1921, the frustrated Jackson complained that at Montreal exhibitions of contemporary Canadian art, "the mild stuff [is] always well hung, praised and often bought, and the intenser individual work skied [hung high up on the wall instead of at the more desirable mid-wall height], sniffed at and seldom purchased."[3] As late as 1927, four years after the dissolution of the Beaver Hall Group, he noted that its former members were avoiding the AAM's annual Spring Exhibition, with its sprawling display of recent Canadian work, because "it [the exhibition] promises to be worse than ever" in its catering to an often unappreciative audience consisting of "people who made their purchases elsewhere."[4]

Small wonder, then, that in 1920 Jackson encouraged his Montreal colleagues to band together, with a view to emulating the Group of Seven's use of group pressure to promote their art. Small wonder as well that two weeks after the opening of the Group of Seven's 1920 exhibition at the Art Gallery of Toronto, Jackson—a master polemicist and spokesperson—was voted by the Montreal artists the first president of the as yet unnamed Montreal collective. (The election was held more than four months before the October 4 signing of the lease on 305 Beaver Hall Hill.) The Beaver Hall Group's first known exhibition took place six months later, opening on November 20, and their first self-described "annual exhibition" was held two months after that, in January 1921. Jackson presided over the January 1921 vernissage, regaling critics from English and French newspapers with explanations about why the Group was such an important development on the Montreal art scene ("Public Profession"; Laberge).

Both the Group of Seven and the Beaver Hall Group hoped to use the coordinated force of multiple members as a publicity tool to build a broad audience for modern art. There were, though, crucial differences between the two collectives. The Group of Seven's 1920 exhibition catalogue, as well as their other public pronouncements, made clear their goal of employing bold colours, strong and simplified forms, and an underlying sense of design that took the wild variety of nature and subjugated it to powerful compositions, all in the name of representing the specificity of Canada as embodied in sparsely populated landscapes. The seven artists held that a distinctive national identity was essential if Canada and Canadian art were to achieve a maturity. To that end the members took as their touchstone the sketches and paintings of their mentor, Tom Thomson (1877–1917), focusing principally on northern Ontario landscapes, first in Algonquin Park and, following Thomson's drowning there in July 1917, the more rugged Algoma territory that stretched northward from Sault Ste Marie. Even more far-flung and demanding landscape subjects followed in later years, including the Rocky Mountains and the Arctic. As Jackson had written as early as 1914, "The Canadian who does not love keen bracing air, sunlight making shadows that vie with the sky, the wooden hills and frozen lakes. Well he must be a poor patriot."[5] Lawren Harris adopted a parallel stance in the foreword to the Group of Seven's 1920 exhibition catalogue: "No country can ever hope to rise above a vulgar mediocrity where there is not unbounded confidence in what its humanity can do ... If a people do not believe they can equal or surpass the stature of any humanity which has been upon this world, then they had better emigrate and become servants to some superior people" (n.p.).

Over the past century, art historians and critics have been justifiably active in pointing out that the Group of Seven's proposal for a national narrative tended to gloss over or omit the interests and lives of a host of population groups that did not happen to consist entirely of middle-aged white anglophone men living in Toronto.[6] The fact remains, however, that the Group of Seven was, with the support of institutions such as the National Gallery, remarkably successful in defining both Canadian art and Canada itself.[7] This was partly because its members produced art that was more obviously contemporary than what was available from more traditional Canadian artists, and partly because an interest in championing the uniqueness and the achievements of Canada was very much in the air in the years immediately after the First World War: a conflict in which the country had played an important role on the international stage. It was not coincidental that organizations such as the Canadian Historical Association and the Canadian Authors' Association were both founded at the beginning of the 1920s (Vipond; Cole). The Group of Seven artists' principal focus, however, was on sparsely populated landscapes. As the popularity and influence of their work became more and more widespread, "Canadian" art—and, to a significant degree, conceptions about the essence of Canadian life, experience, and identity—were increasingly associated with those landscapes in particular. (This was certainly not true across the country. For example, Quebec's conservative tradition of the close links between enduring rural settlement and French-Canadian identity problematized acceptance of the Group of Seven's vision in much of that province.)

Yet despite its indebtedness to the Group of Seven's force-of-numbers model, the Beaver Hall Group was very much its own organization. The most obvious difference was its nearly perfect balance between numbers of male and female members. The Group of Seven was an all-male phenomenon, and although three new members were inducted beginning in 1926, they, too, were all male: A.J. Casson, Edwin Holgate, and Lionel LeMoine FitzGerald. F.B. Housser, whose 1926 book *A Canadian Art Movement: The Story of the Group of Seven* was an important early document in the Group of Seven's hagiography, gloried in what Housser presented as the essentially heterosexual masculinity of the artists. According to Housser, the Group of Seven artist "divests himself of the velvet coat and flowing tie of his caste, puts on the outfit of the bushwhacker and prospector, closes with his environment; paddles, portages and makes camp; sleeps in the out-of-doors under the stars; climbs mountains with his sketch box on his back" in order to discover nature's "virgin mood unchastened by contact with man" (15).

Housser's overwrought prose aside, the gender gap between the Group of Seven and the Beaver Hall Group was not nearly as profound as their respective memberships suggest. In fact, the Group of Seven was highly supportive of other artists, both male and female, and specialists in a range of subjects that extended well beyond the Group's own concentration on rugged landscapes, including these artists in their annual exhibitions beginning as early as 1921. Beaver Hall's Prudence Heward, Mabel Lockerby, Mabel May, Kathleen Morris, Lilias Torrance Newton, Sarah Robertson, Anne Savage, and others gained valuable exposure through the exhibition of their work in Group of Seven shows during the 1920s and early 1930s. Jackson himself was a close friend of Prudence Heward, Mabel May, and Sarah Robertson, ardently supporting and promoting their work. Among the many examples of this was the laudatory and heartfelt tribute that he wrote about Heward ("one of [Canada's] most individual and gifted painters") in the catalogue for the 1948 exhibition that the National Gallery organized following Heward's death the previous year (Jackson 10). He even claimed elsewhere that he had wanted Heward to become a member of the Group of Seven, although that never happened—and, indeed, it is not clear how accurate that claim was (qtd. in Grafftey 72).

The Beaver Hall Group also differed from the Group of Seven in its choices of subject matter. Whereas the Group of Seven quickly established a reputation for favouring sparsely populated and physically demanding landscapes, Beaver Hall artists preferred urban themes. There were of course exceptions; Anne Savage, for example, was someone who often painted landscapes comparable to the vistas preferred by the Toronto artists. But the Beaver Hall Group identified closely with urban life in Montreal (then Canada's largest and most developed city), and used the city as a central theme in its art production. Adrien Hébert, for example, painted scenes from Montreal's bustling port as well as downtown shoppers along St. Catherine Street. Mabel May constructed views over rooftops as seen from the window of her studio. Kathleen Morris painted aerial views of automobiles making their way up urban streets, and also recorded horse-drawn sleighs waiting for customers in locations such as Dominion Square, in the heart of downtown Montreal. In her *Beaver Hall Hill* (1936; Figure 13.2), one of a series of her 1920s and 1930s street views, Morris minimizes detail in an attempt to suggest not the elemental power of nature (as in a Group of Seven canvas), but the sprawl and hum of urban life. Number 305 Beaver Hall Hill, which was adjacent to the Guarantee Building (the side façade of which is visible behind the upper branches of the tree on the right edge of the canvas) is unfortunately not visible in that painting.

Professional and Personal: The Beaver Hall Group and Friendship

An equally striking aspect of the work of the Beaver Hall artists was centred on portraiture and the human figure, in both of which the preference of the women artists was for female sitters. Moreover, a substantial proportion of those artworks shows family members and friends, including other members of the Group. There are, for example, portraits of Prudence Heward and also of Heward's sister, Honour Grafftey, by Lilias Torrance Newton; of Jeanne de Crèvecoeur by Emily Coonan; and of Sarah Robertson's sisters by Prudence Heward. The prevalence of portraiture by a number of Beaver Hall's women members does not imply that they had a monopoly on that type of subject matter. Most notably, Edwin Holgate frequently portrayed both identified and anonymous sitters in powerful canvases that are conspicuous for their use of modernist, often architectonic compositions. But the frequency with which the women members chose each other as models testifies to a core aspect of any discussion of gender vis-à-vis the Beaver Hall Group: the degree to which, for the women members, friendship was a basic component of their Beaver Hall experience.

This is evident in, for example, Heward's *At the Café* (Figure 13.3): a portrait of Group member Mabel Lockerby. Heward depicts Lockerby dressed in an arresting red garment with black sleeves, collar, and trim, and with a prominent red ring on her right hand. Lockerby's head and torso fill the surface of the canvas, suggesting a forceful personality, as does the robust modelling of her body and the contrast it forms to the much more sketchily presented male(?) figures who are seen behind and on either side of her. Her showy

FIGURE 13. 2
Kathleen Moir Morris
(Montreal 1893 –
Rawdon, Quebec, 1986),
preparatory sketch for
Beaver Hall Hill, Montreal,
1936 or before. Oil on
plywood, 35.5 × 30.3 cm.
MMFA, purchase, gift
of R. Fournelle and Joy
Sedgewick-Shannon
Memorial Fund. Photo
MMFA, Christine Guest.

clothing, her up-to-date short hairstyle, and her prominent ring (reminding the viewer that Lockerby, who wears no jewellery on her left hand, did not regard her unmarried status as a mark of impoverishment) all mark the sitter as a modern woman out for a night on the town. At the same time, though, her downcast eyes and serious expression propose an inner life that is at odds with the way more usual depictions of single women pandered to viewers' visual pleasure. Like many other portraits by women members of the Beaver Hall Group, *At the Café* is an intimate and complex psychological likeness of a professional colleague whom the artist valued as a friend.

The significance of the Beaver Hall Group as a venue for female friendship becomes clearer when the Group is placed within the larger context of women artists working in Montreal during the 1920s. Although they showed their work in the Art Association's Spring Exhibition, as well as in smaller shows held in places such as department stores and, less frequently, the city's few commercial galleries, women artists were ineligible for membership in the most influential anglophone arts societies: the Arts Club of Montreal and the Pen and Pencil Club. These were settings where visual artists, authors, dramatists, musicians, and patrons could, in relaxed settings, foster formal and informal links both professional and personal. Such networks were essential to building careers. Because women were excluded from both

FIGURE 13.3
Prudence Heward
(Montreal 1896 – Los
Angeles 1947), *At the Café
(Miss Mabel Lockerby)*,
1930 or before. Oil on
canvas, 68.5 × 58.4 cm.
MMFA, gift of the artist's
family. Photo MMFA, Jean-
François Brière.

the Arts Club and the Pen and Pencil Club, they were at a distinct professional disadvantage. The Beaver Hall Group helped rectify that shortcoming
by offering them opportunities to interact with other artists on a regular but
casual basis. Whereas for most of the men the Group was just one of various
avenues through which they could pursue their careers (especially because
with only three mixed members exhibitions during its three years of existence
it was not active enough to support a career singlehanded), for the women
it tended to be of greater personal and professional importance. Barbara
Meadowcroft's selection of a title for her 1999 monograph—*Painting Friends:
The Beaver Hall Women Painters*—was an insightful one.

Indeed, the relationships that most of the Group's women members estab-
lished and nurtured continued to be important in the long years after the
Group ceased to exist. This was especially true for Nora Collyer, Prudence
Heward, Mabel Lockerby, Mabel May, Kathleen Morris, Lilias Torrance
Newton, Sarah Robertson, Anne Savage, and Ethel Seath, all of whom maintained close and long-lasting ties with at least some of the others. This was
made clear thirty years after 1923, when Anne Savage recalled not only that
Beaver Hall had been "a small group of artists," but that "[s]trangely, they
were mostly women."[8] On the one hand Savage's misstatement seems peculiar; she had been an active member of the Beaver Hall Group rather than

having a merely tangential relationship with it, and so she might well be expected to insist that the Group contained almost exactly as many men as it did women. Conversely, however, her statement about the membership may be seen as confirmation of the fact that for women artists—excluded from full participation in the activities of both the Arts Club and the Pen and Pencil Club—the Beaver Hall Group was likely to have been seen principally as a women's group even during its lifetime. This ongoing sense of comradeship was no doubt reinforced by the similarity of most of the women's social backgrounds, and by their shared art training under William Brymner at the Art Association school. Equally important, most of the Beaver Hall women found their closest relationships outside of marriage because—like their female contemporaries elsewhere—they frequently had to choose between having a career and having a family, with all the social expectations and household demands that being a wife and mother involved. Significantly, only two of the Beaver Hall women ever married: Regina Seiden (who largely abandoned a professional career in favour of that of her artist husband, Eric Goldberg) and Lilias Torrance (whose twelve-year marriage ended in divorce in 1933, after which she pursued a high-profile professional career as a portraitist of elite figures, including Queen Elizabeth II and the Duke of Edinburgh [1957]).

The Revival of the Beaver Hall Group

The preceding sections have suggested reasons why, with the collapse of the Beaver Hall Group's financial situation in 1923, its existence faded from general public and critical memory over the next few decades. On the most basic level, the loss of whatever archive it may have accumulated has had a debilitating effect on the capacity of scholars and laypeople alike to become familiar with its history. In a similar way, the Group's short lifespan—just three years—was hardly sufficient time to establish an enduring legacy, especially because only two of its three members' exhibitions (in January 1921 and January 1922) garnered any press attention.

Another reason for the obscurity of the Beaver Hall Group has been the dominance of the Group of Seven, especially in English Canada. The two organizations came into existence in the same month in 1920, but the Group of Seven's positioning at or near the centre of much subsequent discourse about Canadian art can be credited to a combination of factors that the Beaver Hall Group did not necessarily share. Not the least of these was its emergence at precisely the moment when Canadians were searching for symbols of English Canada's national uniqueness and identity: symbols that the Group of Seven was ideologically determined to supply in the form of visually compelling artworks and that influential patrons, critics, and institutions were eager to support. The Beaver Hall Group shared the Group of Seven's dedication to visual modernism, but unlike the Toronto artists it lacked a publicity-friendly focus on a single subject, instead running the gamut from urban views to portraiture, the human figure, rural scenery, and (though far less frequently than the Group of Seven) unpopulated landscapes. Nor did it benefit from having anything like the Group of Seven's compelling message about national identity—especially the Seven's eagerness to explain their message in texts and lectures to anyone who would listen.

For all these reasons, the date of the Beaver Hall Group's closure in 1923 marked the beginning of its disappearance from public memory. Little was heard about it between the time of its dissolution and 1966. In the latter year Norah McCullough of the National Gallery, on the advice of Anne Savage, organized an exhibition of work by ten members of the Group (McCullough). McCullough was originally unfamiliar with Beaver Hall, but following Savage's recommendation she brought together work by Savage, Nora Collyer, Emily Coonan, Prudence Heward, Mabel Lockerby, Mabel May, Kathleen Morris, Lilias Torrance Newton, Sarah Robertson, and Ethel Seath. The result was the first Beaver Hall showing to be staged in more than four decades. McCullough organized her show without the benefit of archival documentation, relying instead on Savage's characterization of Beaver Hall as a collection mostly of women artists. However, just as the Group of Seven's formation in 1920 had fit perfectly into the post–First World War context of a burgeoning interest in defining Canada's identity and uniqueness, so McCullough's project was part and parcel of the blossoming commitment to writing art histories that were about more than just men.

McCullough's work aside, feminist art history was in short supply in Canada in 1966. In that same year, J. Russell Harper published his *Painting in Canada: A History*, a major undertaking conceived as a Canadian centennial project and the first detailed study of its type in English. Harper's coverage of the Beaver Hall Group is limited to a single paragraph. He mentions three men (A.Y. Jackson, Edwin Holgate, and Randolph Hewton) before observing that "[t]here were many outstanding women painters in this Montreal Group" and commenting briefly on four of them: Prudence Heward, Mabel May, Lilias Torrance Newton, and Sarah Robinson [sic; Sarah Robertson] (315, 318). Seven years later, Dennis Reid more satisfyingly allocated three pages to the Group in *A Concise History of Canadian Painting*, including remarks on six of the women "who dominated its membership." Those remarks comprised half-sentence references to Mabel Lockerby, Kathleen Morris, Lilias Torrance Newton, and Anne Savage, and more expansive descriptions of work by Prudence Heward and Sarah Robertson (186–89). The next year, however, Barry Lord, in his controversially Maoist study *The History of Painting in Canada: Toward a People's Art*, devoted only two sentences to the Group, whose members were "mostly English-speaking women [none of whom he named] whose portraits, landscapes and figure studies provided a thin cultural veneer for Anglo-Montreal society" (183). It was not until 1982 that a second Beaver Hall Group exhibition was organized, and it consisted of the same ten artists represented in Norah McCullough's 1966 display (Kollar). Barbara Meadowcroft also focused on women artists in her 1999 monographic study of the Group, as did Evelyn Walters in her 2005 book, *The Women of Beaver Hall: Canadian Modernist Painters*. Prior to 2015, only a 1994 MA thesis insisted on viewing the Group as having consisted of both men and women (Avon).[9]

No doubt one reason for at least some of the identification of Beaver Hall as a women's group had to do with the loss, decades earlier, of virtually all primary documentation about the Group. Also important, especially from the 1980s onward, in a Canada that was both more visibly and more officially multicultural, was a suspicion about the Group of Seven's definition of harsh landscapes as a *sine qua non* of Canadian art and identity. The dominance of the Group of Seven in twentieth-century Canadian art suffered accordingly. That questioning of the Group of Seven's status was also abetted by recognition that, as already noted, its wilderness-based aesthetic lacked resonance in Quebec, as well as by increasing pressure to recognize Indigenous title to large tracts of Canada's geography: something that did not necessarily sit well with the presentation of landscape as consisting of empty wilderness.[10]

Contestation of the legacy of the Group of Seven was not, however, sufficient in and of itself to account for the revival of the Beaver Hall Group. What was crucial in this regard was the contemporaneous impact that the second-wave feminist movement made on the practice of art history beginning at about the time of Canada's centennial year. The Beaver Hall Group presented a timely subject because the very thing that had made it so important for its female adherents—its provision of an environment in which they could compensate somewhat for the exclusions that they faced in institutions such as the Arts Club and the Pen and Pencil Club—was paralleled in such pivotal art history tracts as Linda Nochlin's influential 1971 essay, "Why Have There Been No Great Women Artists?" Nochlin itemized a range of social and institutional factors that had long impeded women's access to professional status.

The difficulties confronted by the women of the Beaver Hall Group fall neatly into the categories itemized by Nochlin. Further, a number of the artists had demonstrably done their best to circumvent or otherwise come to terms with those difficulties; they built careers as exhibiting artists, supported themselves as teachers (Anne Savage and Ethel Seath especially), explored companionship options outside of marriage, and joined organizations that fought for women's rights.[11]

Norah McCullough, in her 1966 exhibition brochure, seems to downplay those achievements when she describes her ten chosen artists as being "by no means careerists, but rather talented gentlefolk" (n.p.). Yet the most enduringly compelling of the artists have tended to be precisely those whose work rejected, in ways both subtle and blatant, McCullough's characterization. Lilias Torrance Newton, for example, was nobody's gentlewoman in the 1920s and early 1930s, even if her later career as a portraitist to members of the social and economic elite tended to impose restrictions on her art. In her 1926 portrait of Prudence Heward (Figure 13.4), she used intentionally awkward brushwork to build a likeness in which Heward looks morose and exhausted, with dark circles around her eyes and with almost nothing in the painting that might draw attention away from her face. Seven years later, Newton's *Nude in the Studio* (1933) nonchalantly presented an unabashedly contemporary nude, complete with lipstick, plucked eyebrows, and permed hair. It was removed from the Canadian Group of Painters annual exhibition the next year because its scandalous inclusion of pubic hair and green high-heeled sandals was taken as evidence that the model was too literally and unabashedly *naked* to be a proper *nude*. (When *Nude in the Studio* was later acquired by the Canadian diplomat Vincent Massey and his wife, Alice, the couple reputedly covered it with a textile whenever powerful prudes such as Prime Minister William Lyon Mackenzie King came to visit.)

Prudence Heward, too, had little interest in McCullough's "gentlefolk" category, thereby endearing herself to second-wave feminist theory. Heward's *The Bather* (1930, Figure 13.5), for example, is a flat-out rejection of the stereotype of the bathing beauty. Located in what might be taken for one of Lawren Harris' stripped down and semi-abstracted landscapes, and dressed in a rather ill-fitting swimsuit, the seated woman, her legs spread apart rather than kept together in stereotypically ladylike fashion, looks vacantly at nothing, while a strange plant grows at her feet. Heward frequently placed such plants, often somewhat suggestive of vulva imagery, in uneasy proximity to the bodies of the women and adolescent girls she depicted in her art. The incongruous placement of the plant in *The Bather* evoked merriment among

FIGURE 13.4 Lilias Torrance Newton (Lachine 1896 – Cowansville 1980), *Prudence Heward, c.1926.* Oil on canvas, 64 × 53.3 cm. Toronto, private collection. Photo MMFA, Christine Guest.

critics when the painting was hung in the 1933 Canadian Group of Painters exhibition at the Art Gallery of Toronto (Luckyj 43, 45).

Few artworks by Beaver Hall women could best the in-your-face audacity of Newton's *Nude in the Studio* or Heward's *The Bather.* Nonetheless, in the thematic and visual modernity of much of their work, and in the steadfastness with which they both acknowledged and offered alternatives to the Group of Seven, Newton, Heward, and the others laid the groundwork for a convincing revival of interest in their art in the late twentieth and early twenty-first centuries. In the wake of the almost complete overlooking of the Beaver Hall Group between the mid-1920s and the mid-1960s, that revival is a salutary reminder, during Canada's recent sesquicentennial, that the history of visual art in Canada—like the history of Canada itself—has its share of narratives and voices that we are the richer for remembering.

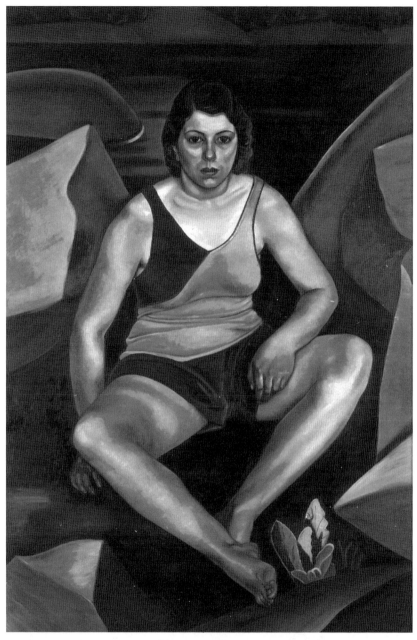

FIGURE 13.5 Prudence Heward (Montreal 1896 – Los Angeles 1947), *The Bather*, 1930. Oil on canvas, 162 × 106 cm. Art Gallery of Windsor, Purchase 1974, 974.10.

NOTES

1 Randolph Hewton to Eric Brown (National Gallery of Canada), 16 Feb. 1924 (National Gallery of Canada Library and Archives, Correspondence with artists, 7.1-H—Hewton, Randolph S.).

2 A.Y. Jackson to Sarah Robertson, 16 Mar. [1926] (National Gallery of Canada Library and Archives, A.Y. Jackson Correspondence with Sarah Robertson, File 1: 1926–1947).

3 A.Y. Jackson to Eric Brown (National Gallery of Canada), 18 or 19 Jan. 1921 (National Gallery of Canada Library and Archives, Correspondence with artists, 7.1-J—Jackson, A.Y., File 1).

4 A.Y. Jackson to Clarence Gagnon, 20 Mar. [1927] (McCord Museum, Clarence Gagnon fonds, P-116 D9, Correspondence).

5 A.Y. Jackson to Montreal art critic Albert Laberge, 25 Apr. 1914 (E.P. Taylor Library and Archives, Art Gallery of Ontario).

6 See, for example, Lynda Jessup, "Bushwhackers in the Gallery: Antimodernism and the Group of Seven."

7 See especially Charles C. Hill, *The Group of Seven: Art for a Nation*.

8 Anne Savage, handwritten text used in the preparation of her lecture "Women Painters of Canada" for the Canadian Club in 1953 (Library and Archives Canada, Anne Savage fonds: MG30 D374, Vol. 2).

9 In 2015, the Montreal Museum of Fine Arts retrospective Beaver Hall Group exhibition, co-curated by Jacques Des Rochers and Brian Foss, was grounded in the intention of dealing with the Group as a whole rather than with only some of its artists.

10 A representative selection of texts and art projects that question the ideological implications of Group of Seven imagery is included in John O'Brian and Peter White's *Beyond Wilderness: The Group of Seven, Canadian Identity, and Contemporary Art*. On disjunctions between the Group's vision of landscape and that of many French-Canadian viewers, see François-Marc Gagnon, "La peinture des anées trente au Québec."

11 See Kristina Huneault, "'As Well as Men': The Gendering of Beaver Hall," p. 265. Huneault's essay is the most thoughtful feminist analysis to date of the Beaver Hall Group.

CHAPTER FOURTEEN

German Internment Camps in the Maritimes: Another Untold
Story in P.S. Duffy's The Cartographer of No Man's Land

Jennifer Andrews

The year 2017 marks the 150th anniversary of Canadian Confederation; the
federal government also has held major celebrations of now century-old
Canadian military successes at Vimy Ridge and Passchendaele. But *The
Cartographer of No Man's Land* offers a more ambivalent and complex vision
of the ways in which Canada—and specifically Nova Scotia—has occluded
its own history of racism and racially motivated discrimination. Authored by
an American, P.S. Duffy, who summered in Mahone Bay for thirty years and
has Nova Scotian roots dating back 250 years, *The Cartographer of No Man's
Land* (2013) combines a first-hand account of one Nova Scotian man's experience of trench warfare in the months leading up to and including Vimy Ridge
with an exploration of his family's efforts to comprehend the effects of war
from their small fishing community, Snag Harbor, located on the south shore
of Nova Scotia, near Lunenburg. Angus MacGrath enlists in order to discover
the true fate of his brother-in-law Ebbin, who has been classified as missing in
action (MIA) during a tour in France.

As part of its multiple narrative strands, *The Cartographer of No Man's Land*
tells the story of a German immigrant, Avon Heist, who teaches at the local
school and befriends Angus' son, Simon. Heist is accused of spying on behalf
of the Germans from his Nova Scotia home because he has built a lookout on
his isolated property to observe bird species and passing boats; he is removed
from his position at the school, his home is searched by the RCMP, and he is
detained at "a former ironworks factory" in Amherst, Nova Scotia, with over
800 other men, including "sailors from the *Kaiser Wilhelm der Grosse*, sunk in
1915, sailors from other ships, various untrustworthy, roughshod Canadians,

and a large group of 'suspicious' aliens—many of German origin" (321). To protect himself while imprisoned, Heist abandons his allegiance to Canada and aligns himself with the communist movement in the camp, led by visiting internee Joseph Trotsky, even writing Simon to share this news, which devastates the boy who perceives this shift as a betrayal. Through the inclusion of Heist, Duffy rejects a resolutely positive portrayal of Canada, and particularly, the Maritime provinces; instead, she draws attention to the flagrant racism and classism of the period in the region directed at both Germans and select Canadians who were deemed undesirable.

This chapter considers the significance of the untold story of the Amherst Internment Camp and Duffy's role as an American writing about this obscured aspect of Canadian history. In doing so, I argue that Duffy's positionality as both insider and outsider to the Maritimes enables her to present a historical narrative about Canadian racism that while compelling is easy to dismiss precisely because she resides south of the Canada–US border. What does the story of Avon Heist's internment and its historical accuracy (which has been largely ignored in the Maritimes) say about regional and national ambivalence about acknowledging racism and classism, particularly given that it has been easy to view Canada as more inclusive and tolerant than its neighbour to the south? And how does Duffy's novel challenge what I am describing as the "fantasy" of Canadian exceptionalism[1] so prominent in the media in the era of a Trump presidency?

While there has been some research done on Trotsky's presence at Amherst in April of 1917, a detail in Duffy's novel grounded in fact, there has been relatively little attention paid to the German internment camps themselves, and in particular, the Amherst one, though the creation of the Canadian First World War Internment Recognition Fund, begun in 2008, has started to raise public awareness of these camps through its website and by funding over $8 million in grants to support research, curriculum material development, and artistic projects about the camps.[2] The website includes a digital map of the camp locations across Canada, including links to relevant newspaper articles published during the camps' existence, and ready access to free curriculum materials about the camps designed for students from middle school to the end of high school, including (in the case of the high school materials) a list of schools in Canada currently using the units in their classrooms—a group predominantly from western and central Canada. The Fund's mandate is national and much of the work done has focused on Ukrainian Canadians, a group that primarily immigrated to the Prairie provinces and Ontario; as a result, the Maritime camps warrant more careful examination.[3]

Even local acknowledgment of the internment camp in Amherst reflects an ambivalence about its history. Originally a critical part of the seasonal migration of the Mi'kmaq who "encamped each year on the southern ridge above the marsh, establishing a principal village site ... near the meandering tidal creek" (Furlong vii), the area also attracted Acadian settlers whose "unique system of dykes and aboiteaux" were ideal for managing the "tidal inundation of the salt marshes adjacent to the ... rivers of the Bay of Fundy" (vii). But the Acadian expulsion decimated the local communities, forcibly removing these long-established populations in a brutal fashion. In the aftermath, Amherst was reborn as a small village of under two hundred residents, most of whom were Irish; four Acadians remained. Amherst continued to grow. It was incorporated as a town in 1889, and by the turn of the century was a thriving industrial hub; with a railroad line running from Quebec to Halifax situated in its downtown core, and considerable strength in the manufacturing sector, the local economy flourished. Thanks to lobbying efforts of a federal minister from the area, and because of its proximity to Halifax, Amherst became the site of the largest internment camp in Canada during the First World War. Located in an iron foundry beside the railway tracks that were used to transport prisoners of war (POWS) to local work assignments, the camp housed 853 prisoners in the compound, surrounded by a barbed wire fence. After the camp was closed in 1919 it was revitalized to serve two different purposes, first as barracks for the North Nova Scotia Highlanders Battalion (as of 1939), and then later as the site of the annual winter fair until the buildings burned in 1958.

Today, Amherst is a small town of under 10,000 people and evidence of the existence of the POW camp is scarce. Like many Maritime communities, outmigration is all too common, and the economy is struggling, a pattern that dates back close to a century. As Donald Savoie explains in *Visiting Grandchildren: Economic Development in the Maritimes*, the adoption of a "National Policy" in the post-Confederation period meant that manufacturing gradually shifted to vote-rich central Canada, where urbanization far outpaced the Maritimes. The result was that between 1920 and 1926, manufacturing jobs in the region (including Amherst as a key hub) declined by 44 percent, and 150,000 Maritimers left the region. This pattern was exacerbated by the fact that the region was not the beneficiary of defence-related industries during the First World War. The internment camp thus functions as a historical pivot point for the shifting tide of Amherst's economic and political prosperity, a narrative that many would rather forget or refashion to suit their own purposes. For instance, a large plaque mounted on the side of the Casey

Concrete headquarters, where the camp was, acknowledges the significance of the site and describes the needless imprisonment of Ukrainians and other Europeans in the Malleable Iron Works between April of 1915 and September of 1919. However, locating the plaque is not easy. Casey Concrete is situated on the edge of the Amherst industrial park, and the sprawling yards behind include an aptly named "BONEYARD," piles of concrete blocks, and a sign promising large fines if caught trespassing on surveillance cameras.[4]

Other efforts to acknowledge the camp's existence vary from the 2001 installation of two granite headstones at the rear of a local cemetery recording the names of eleven of the thirteen prisoners who died at the camp, to performances of Cape Breton author Silver Donald Cameron's play about Trotsky's time at the camp, called *The Prophet at Tantramar* (1988) at Halifax's Neptune Theatre, which was later turned into a CBC radio play, and subsequently revived in 2014 by an Amherst theatre company as part of the town's 125th birthday celebration. An increasingly prominent part of local recognition of the camp has involved the cataloguing of photographs and postcards of the camp's occupants, in conjunction with the recovery of the intricate wooden carvings, handmade musical instruments, and artwork made by prisoners at the camp that were marketed and sold or given as gifts to community members during the internment as souvenirs of the POW presence. Many black-and-white photographs were taken of the prisoners engaging in theatrical and sports events, performing for locals, or gathering at work sites where the POWs made a considerable contribution to the infrastructure of Amherst by clearing land at the local experimental farm, establishing the foundations of Dickey Park, and labouring for the railroad; the postcards, printed locally, functioned as pieces of war propaganda, circulated by prisoners, Amherst residents, and travellers to the region as a record of the camp's existence that is benevolent, even arguably romanticizing camp conditions.

Likewise, the delicate and complex wooden objects produced by prisoners have become a central part of the small displays created to inform visitors about life in the internment camps at the Nova Scotia Highlanders Regimental Museum, focused on the efforts of serving men, and the Cumberland County Museum, which documents the history of the community dating back to the arrival of the first colonial settlers. Often labelled "souvenir[s]" by their creators and consumers—the local residents of Amherst—these objects, ranging from carved boxes, inkwell stands, and candle holders, to miniature models of boats, cannons, spinning wheels (see Figure 14.1), full-size card tables, trays, and even a full-sized working cello (see Figures 14.2 and 14.3), offer a way to humanize and redeem the prisoners, while still

FIGURE 14.1 Miniature Spinning Wheel. Cumberland County Museum Archives in Amherst, Nova Scotia. Photo courtesy of Jennifer Andrews, March 16, 2017.

FIGURE 14.2 AND FIGURE 14.3 Cello housed in the public exhibition about the regiment and the community at the Royal Nova Scotia Highlanders Regimental Museum in Amherst, Nova Scotia. Photos courtesy of Jennifer Andrews, March 17, 2017.

perpetuating what art historian Erin Morton calls "a fantastic sentimental alternative to troubling realities" (303). Both museums, which rely heavily on volunteerism and are chronically underfunded (a situation shared with most small museums across the country), continue to document and preserve these examples of craftsmanship. Nonetheless, the story of the camp remains unfamiliar to most residents of Atlantic Canada and more broadly, to Canadians.

In *Building Nations from Diversity: Canadian and American Experiences Compared*, Garth Stevenson probes how the two nations have historically differentiated themselves from each other. In the case of Canada and the United States, it is often summarized as the contrast between the cultural "mosaic" and the "melting pot." While the concept of the "melting pot" was borrowed from a play by Israel Zangwill, a "Jewish immigrant from the United Kingdom," first performed in 1908, in which Jews and Christians vow "to transcend their religious and cultural differences," the cultural "mosaic" emerged as a way of characterizing Canada's uniqueness in texts written about the country in the 1920s, the decade after the First World War, and then eventually displaced by a more inclusive synonym to reflect the federal government's public commitment, first declared as an official doctrine in 1971, to the idea of "multiculturalism" (4). As Stevenson suggests, this contrast has served as evidence of Canada's moral superiority over its nearest neighbour, creating a "cottage industry" in academia and the media focused on celebrating the nation's distinctive brand of multiculturalism (4). In doing so, however, it remains easy to overlook or dismiss historical narratives that counter this claim of virtuousness, among these the stories of interned people of German descent in rural Nova Scotia.

Paradoxically, a historical comparison of German immigration to both the United States and Canada provides an important framework for understanding why *The Cartographer of No Man's Land*—and the story it tells of the Amherst Internment Camp—has been marginalized. Writing in 2014, Stevenson points out that while "[w]hat happened in World War II is fairly well known, in its broad outlines if not in its details, and many who experienced it are still alive," "World War I, now almost a century past, has largely receded from memory or common knowledge" (123). He goes on to argue that "[n]either Canada's claim to be a tolerant multicultural mosaic nor the proud American boast that theirs is a government … of laws and not of men receives much support from a contemplation of these events" (123–24). In the case of the United States, German immigration and its influence on American culture were significant from colonial times to the twentieth century; between 1820 and 1917, approximately "five and a half million immigrants," including "ethnic and linguistic minorities," came from Germany to the United States, "more than any other country" (124). German immigration peaked in the 1880s, and then declined sharply, likely due "increasing prosperity" at home. Nonetheless, prior to the First World War, public school language instruction in German was permitted in eight midwestern US states, church services were delivered in German, and German-language newspapers and magazines were abundant, a situation that mirrors the prominence of Spanish in the United States today.

The German "imprint on Canada" was less significant, though Germans played a critical role in "the settlement of Nova Scotia in the middle of the eighteenth century" in an effort to populate the region, whose descendants Duffy portrays in her novel (Stevenson 126). There were small groups of Germans located across the country, ranging from Loyalists who moved to Upper Canada from Pennsylvania and neighbouring states to midwestern Americans who came northward in search of free land. Records of these groups were complicated by the fact that "the Canadian census, unlike the American, always enumerated people by ethnicity"—and being American was not considered a valid category (127). So "Germans" may have constituted "the fifth largest ethnic group (after the French, English, Irish, and Scottish)" in Canada, but that included a wide array of populations, among them descendants of immigrants, German-speaking minorities from central and eastern Europe, and religious communities like "the Mennonites and Hutterites, which tended to isolate themselves from the rest of the population, ... German or otherwise" (127). Because "Canada attracted very few immigrants from Germany in the nineteenth century," when compared to the United States, the "process of assimilation for most German Canadians had been in progress for well over a century" by the time the First World War began (126). Stevenson does highlight the fact that despite the scattered nature of small groups of Germans across Canada, there were "a few enclaves like Lunenberg (Nova Scotia) ... where elements of their German heritage survived" (127), but that presence was far more muted in the Canadian education system, for example, than in its US counterpart.

The advent of the First World War brought about a dramatic shift in the status and treatment of Germans on both sides of the Canada–US border, as a result of international law that allowed "the interning of people who are citizens or subjects of a state against which war has been formally declared" (127). While "some German citizens residing in Canada returned home in 1914, often for the purposes of joining the German army," many others remained, hopeful that they would not be rounded up because they had been loyal to their adopted nation (127). The numbers of interned Germans in Canada totalled close to 8,000 (including approximately 6,000 "Austrians," many of whom were ethnic Ukrainians). In contrast, in the United States, which joined the war effort in 1917, the number of German and German Americans interned was roughly 6,300, constituting a much smaller percentage of the national German-born population, which totalled over two million people (127). The internment may have impacted a relatively small group of people but it represented a much broader shift in public attitude, one of "hatred and hostility directed against every trace of German culture or heritage and against everyone who displayed evidence thereof, including persons who had been born in North America and had never seen Germany in their lives" (128), which was pervasive across the United States and Canada. The concept of the "melting pot" gained considerable traction when the United States entered the First World War, putting immense pressure on the large German American population to assimilate or else. Likewise, in Canada, "Germanophobia" was common (129). Persuasive British anti-German propaganda fuelled public expressions of hatred and led to anti-German riots and vandalism against local German-owned businesses and families. Fear of Germans also led to the disavowal of the legacy of German immigration to Canada; Berlin, Ontario, was renamed Kitchener after the "recently deceased British minister of war" who was featured on "recruiting posters throughout the empire"; the War Measures Act was invoked, which "disenfranchised those of 'enemy' origins" even if individuals had become British citizens in the fifteen years prior; and a ban of "all German-language publications" was instituted from 1918 to 1920 (129).

In *The Cartographer of No Man's Land*, P.S. Duffy explores the conflicted nature of Canadian multiculturalism in the decade prior to the coining of the term "mosaic" through the story of Mr. Heist, a "schoolmaster for the combined sixth, seventh, and eighth grades" in Snag Harbor, Nova Scotia, who uses the classroom to raise critical questions about the racism levelled at Germany and Germans in the local community during the First World War (51). When he first appears in the text, Heist has seized the end of the school day and his authority as a teacher to address a schoolyard fight in which German racial epithets have been used for "name-calling"—among them *"Kraut. Fritz. Hun"* (51). He claims to be presenting "A lesson in tolerance, if you will" (51), and gives the example of Mr. Fritze from La Have: "A loyal Canadian these many years, a Canadian of German extraction, he was not allowed to enlist. Volunteered and was *refused*. Barred because of his name—a name that evokes the worst sort of bigotry" (51).

Fritz, as Duffy explains in a recent interview, was an actual historical figure, whose tombstone was engraved with the ironic phrase, "Fifteen years a citizen" because despite his loyalty to Canada, he was not allowed to "join the Canadian army" (Andrews 149). The result, as Heist suggests to the students, is that even citizenship cannot guarantee recognition or inclusion of German Canadians, given shifts in political power.

Having provided this example of contemporary intolerance, Heist goes on to remind students that the Lunenburg area of Nova Scotia was populated in the eighteenth century by German Protestants "at the behest of the British ... To make settlements against the [French] Catholics" (51). In the same interview, Duffy explains that the recruitment of Germans was prompted by the governor general of the day, who feared that British imports could not build a community, describing them as "drunk ... and ... slothful" (4), and thus, turned to Germany as a source for hardworking labourers. Yet Heist mimics the same racist attitude he critiques when he probes the origins of German settlers by naming various German states, before eventually invoking "Prussia"

(53). He pointedly contrasts the "rich heritage of [German] letters, music, science, and philosophy," with the "arrogant, unlettered" Prussians whom he describes as being "against freedom ... Against culture!" and "Against parl-i-a-mentary government!" (53). In particular, Heist squarely blames Prussian leader Otto von Bismarck for subduing Germany, focusing only on military aspirations, and setting the stage for the outbreak of the First World War, much to the horror of "the peace-loving peoples of Bavaria" and "the rest of Germany" (54). For Heist, then, the Allies (including Canada) should be understood as a force of liberation, not only working to protect the rights of his students in Snag Harbor, but also bringing "freedom to the peoples of Germany" by crushing the legacy of the Prussian leader and his followers (54).

In *The Cartographer of No Man's Land*, Heist concludes his lecture by insisting that the racist discourse circulating on the school playground be understood as exclusionary and unacceptable, stating "*Krrraut* and *Hun, Bosch* and *Frrritz*! I will not tolerate this intolerance" and calling on the students to remember that though local men possessing a "peaceable German heritage from all up and down this province, are this very minute fighting in the Canadian army," others such as "*Fritze*," "A man as Canadian as you," have been "ostracized" and excluded from service (54). Duffy describes this moment in *The Cartographer of No Man's Land* as intentionally evocative of the paranoia of the era, a moment that may seem unbelievable to contemporary readers (including her own British editor), but which captures the genuine belief of the day that Germany could and would invade Britain if not stopped. The "florid language" drawn from "original source material" is coupled with Heist offering a self-serving and deeply ironic version of events (Andrews 149). Yet, for Duffy, the challenge of this scene in the novel is that the irony of Heist's stance "is lost ... on most readers" (150).

Given that as Linda Hutcheon has argued, irony requires the recognition of its doubled edge by the discursive communities it addresses, in this instance, what emerges is a shared and sustained experience of ignorance on both sides of the Canada–US border, though from different perspectives. Duffy notes that for American readers, the history of Nova Scotian settlement and Canada's contributions to the First World War are part of a broad lack of familiarity with the United States' northern neighbour. Canadians, depending upon their location, may not know about the German colonization of Nova Scotia but likely have been exposed to Canada's successes in the First World War through school curriculum content, education programs (such as the one run by curator Ray Coulson of the Nova Scotia Highlanders Regimental Museum who regularly visits classrooms in the region), and the public memorialization that occurs on and around Remembrance Day, though four provinces, including Nova Scotia, do not recognize it as a statutory holiday. However, most Canadians remain unaware of the existence of German internment camps during that same war.

In the case of Simon, for example, who is mocked by the bigger and older students for being Heist's favourite, the teacher's account of the First World War and later his letters about his imprisonment function as moments of confusion and potential revelation that Simon must negotiate in a place where British propaganda flourishes. Duffy uses Simon to explore the challenges readers face when forced to engage with the undesirable aspects of Canadian history, particularly when one is both enmeshed in and physically removed from the actuality of war because Simon may be too young to enlist yet his father is serving overseas, his uncle is deemed MIA somewhere in France, and his teacher and mentor is imprisoned as a suspected spy in a Canadian internment camp. On a daily basis, Simon is surrounded by images like those of "Little Belgium" who appears on a war poster prominently displayed in the window of the local grocery store. Identified by a friend of Simon's as "our girl," Little Belgium is strategically portrayed as wearing a grey cloak and red dress, reminiscent of the German Grimm Brothers' efforts to unite Germany through the folktales of figures like Little Red Riding Hood, but with a twist. Here, the country of Belgium is figured as a vulnerable young maiden in need of "rescue" by virtuous Allied soldiers, having been "raped and pillaged, houses burned, women dragged through the streets by their hair, children murdered by the swords of the advancing German hordes, exacting revenge on common citizens" (56). The diminutive stature and virginal purity of Little Belgium is explicitly contrasted with the images of violence and degradation depicted on the military enlistment cards distributed to men and boys throughout the British Empire. Simon, for instance, is obsessed with an enlistment card he has received, which shows a "crouching ape in his German spike-tipped helmet" and pointed fangs, clutching a "fainting maiden [with an exposed breast] in his brutish arm" with a "sinking navy ship and, beyond it, a town in flames" in the background. As Simon notes, the ape on the recruitment card carries "a spiked club with the word 'Kultur' dripping in blood on it," evidence for Heist's claim that "[c]ulture and decency [are being] dragged in the mud by the Prussians" (65). Of course, Simon hides his card in a book of poems written by Mr. Heist, concealing the brute force of nature with the promise of cultural sophistication.

But the distinction between and among German states that Heist makes in class is forcefully challenged when Simon accidentally drops the recruitment card in the midst of a local ladies' tea hosted by his mother to prepare comfort boxes for serving soldiers and to help the overseas war effort. The women in the group are horrified by the beastial image of a German monster yet equally quick to condemn Heist, despite knowing him personally. Local British aristocrat Lady Bromley most vocally criticizes the teacher for "splitting hairs over who is and is not the enemy" (66); she accuses him of "tricking our students" and labels him "[u]npatriotic" (66–67). Like Heist, who is "replicating the kind of rhetoric you see in [anti-German] recruitment cards" to differentiate himself from Prussian brutality, Lady Bromley employs her moral superiority as a community member with strong colonial roots and class status to counter his claims of innocence (Andrews 150). Here, propaganda triumphs over reason. Heist may relish the solitude of his cottage with a view of the bay, filled with books, "[n]ewspapers, manuscripts, articles, and stacks of letters, many in German" (179). Being a learned man, he naively believes that his status as a "loyal, upstanding member of the community … —fifteen years a citizen" and his role as a scholar and educator will keep him safe (308), despite Simon's repeated warnings that his behaviour is being read as suspicious by the community. However, his desire to watch local schooners and whales, his plans to build a lookout tower to better his view of the area's natural beauty, and his ritual of observing underwater life using a rowboat, perversely, become the basis for his firing, the search and seizure of his belongings, and his eventual imprisonment.

Simon's grandfather Duncan McGrath, who has become an adamant pacifist as a result of losing his brother in the Boer War and suffering through the drowning death of a son, counters the racist rhetoric of Lady Bromley by disbanding the tea and confronting Simon about his willingness to accept war propaganda as fact. He also models a version of resistance for Simon by standing up to local condemnation of Heist, when the teacher's house is searched by the RCMP, his belongings are seized, and he is sent off to the Amherst internment camp: "It was Simon's grandfather, not Mr. Heist, who had to be physically removed from the door of Mr. Heist's cottage; … his grandfather who got roughly knocked to the ground when he tried to wrest the telescope from their hands" (313–14). Heist, who is in a state of shock, remains seated quietly at his kitchen table. And in a more visible symbolic gesture, on the Sunday after Heist's arrest, Duncan, who is a member of the local Protestant congregation, stands up and accuses the members of "having turned on their own" before walking out with Simon by his side (314), pointedly recollecting Heist's lecture to his students about Britain's strategic use of Protestant German immigrants to counter the presence of French Catholics.

Duncan, who is not German and thus far less vulnerable to imprisonment, is able to expose the disposability of Germans as a model minority in the case of Canada based on the state of contemporary international relations.

Heist's time in the Amherst camp is mediated through the youthful Simon, whom the schoolteacher asks to care for his garden and borrow his books while he is being "[d]etained," which as the young boy soon learns "turned out to be a nice way of saying 'held prisoner'" and "'camp,' a nice way of saying 'prison'" (321). Heist is held there, despite being neither "an alien," "an enemy combatant," or an "enemy sympathizer" (321). Unable to produce his papers, he is confined to the camp in September 1917 and along with other prisoners finds himself "stacked up in bunks two deep and three high with hardly space to breathe," lines that closely echo the description of the camp offered by Leon Trotsky in his autobiography, *My Life*, having himself spent a month detained in Amherst in 1917 (321).

As Lubomyr Luciuk explains *In Fear of the Barbed Wire Fence: Canada's First National Internment Operations and the Ukrainian Canadians, 1914–1920*, life in these camps was typically harsh. Valuables were confiscated as soon as internees arrived, and often lost or stolen, never to be returned. The daily routine was strenuous and isolating as prisoners were "often denied access to newspapers ... [and their] correspondence was censored ... They were forced not only to maintain the camps but also to work for the government and for private concerns, and their guards sometimes mistreated them" (20). In the case of Amherst, for example, following a 1915 riot that was attributed to "poor" discipline (Furlong 86), prisoners were dispatched on a daily basis to clear over fifty acres of land at a local experimental farm and charged with building a pool in an Amherst park, labour that was paid for in the post-war period at a reduced rate. Trotsky's observations of Amherst are even more vivid:

> The ... camp was located in an old and very dilapidated ... foundry that had been confiscated from its German owners ... About eight hundred of us lived in these [cramped] conditions ... Men hopelessly clogged the passages elbowing their way through, lay down or got up, played cards or chess. Many of them practised crafts, some with extraordinary skill ... And yet, in spite of the heroic efforts of the prisoners to keep themselves morally and physically fit, five of them had gone insane. We had to eat and sleep in the same room as these mad men. (Furlong 87)

Trotsky's recollections bring to life the reality of POW camps. The size of the camp totalled a quarter of a mile in length and was one hundred feet wide, housing not only the prisoners using communal bathrooms and kitchens but also officers, guards, censors, and other staff, bringing the population within the camp to roughly 1,100 men, surrounded by a high barbed wire fence.

Much of the contemporary and retroactive coverage of the Amherst camp's history has been positive, stressing the habitability of conditions and the fact that prisoners were from 1916 onward able to work outside the camp, bolstered by the efforts made to create a place that was physically and culturally stimulating. The archived photos of the camp are predominantly populated with images of the prisoners in costume, before or after the performance of a revue, or involved in sporting activities. The images include men jauntily attired in bright white pants and muscle tanks with barbells in plain view for a weightlifting competition; prisoners lined up in elegant formations, wearing full fencing gear in the exercise compound; men playfully costumed in theatre garb—whether a knight in shining armour, a cross-dressed cowgirl, or a bewigged ballerina—and even a full-sized orchestra of suit-wearing prisoners complete with a piano in the midst of the outdoor exercise compound. Yet the "physical and mental toll" of imprisonment was great; the combination of limited activity in a crowded exercise yard, endless "waiting," and the constant confinement led to desperate attempts to escape at camps across Canada, including Amherst—despite the risk of being shot and killed (Luciuk 20–21). Given the physical proximity to the United States, which remained neutral for much of the war, Amherst prisoners were especially active in their efforts to escape. Notably, the United States served as a mediator for complaints made by the German government about the conditions of the camps, with the American consul travelling several times to Amherst to declare the state of the prison more than adequate, and External Affairs providing professional photographs of the men (the same ones collected by the Amherst museums) participating in camp recreation activities to demonstrate the quality of their treatment. However, in Appendix One of a 1921 federal government report filed regarding the internment camp operations, the list of ten prisoners who died or were wounded as a result of escape attempts included two names of Amherst detainees, Fritz Klaus and Kurt Becker, both of whom died as a result of gunshot wounds, the first in 1915 and the second in 1916; four others from Amherst are named as being wounded yet eventually recovered, suggesting that security was heightened at the Amherst location by the time the fictive Mr. Heist arrives.

Unsurprisingly then, Mr. Heist's letters to Simon growing increasingly desperate, revealing that he is "miserable and heartbroken" at Amherst, losing hope on a daily basis (344). Although he has been Simon's Greek tutor and initially encourages the boy to keep working on his translations, by November of 1917, "there was no reference to the suffering of Agamemnon or Troy, only to the suffering of Mr. Heist in the wretched conditions in which he found himself. He said the search for a single thing of beauty was fading" (345). To cheer him up Simon copies a meticulous sketch of the Morpho didius butterfly from a colour plate in Mr. Heist's bound volume, *Lepidoptera of North and South America*, an insect catalogue of species, which he first learned about while visiting Heist at his cottage. Morpho didius is a rare species, confined to South America, and named for its ability, as Heist explains, to undergo a "[m]etamorphosis" (182); with wings of iridescent blue on top and mottled brown on the bottom, this butterfly is a master of disguise and transformation, ultimately shifting, according to Heist, from "caterpillar, to chrysalis to ... butterfly, so light on its wing—that is pure beauty" (182). When Simon queries Heist about whether he collects butterfly species—or other specimens—the schoolteacher uses it as pedagogical opportunity to stress the value of observing the world and engaging with it rather than trying to control it. During the same conversation, Simon learns that Heist has "had three cousins killed in the war," losses that the boy later realizes must have "occurred on the other side of the line" (183, 185). However, the shift in perception that Heist's experience of the internment camp requires of Simon ultimately becomes too much to bear for the boy.

The final letter from Heist signals a fundamental betrayal that Angus, having returned from the war, recognizes as a critical survival strategy for the schoolteacher. Heist finds allies among his fellow prisoners, "Dymetro and Johann, two sturdy men who shared potato-peeling duty with him" and "rescued his spectacles when a fight broke out" (360). Like the Morpho didius whose wing colours camouflage and thus protect the species, Dymetro and Johann "mercifully" take the aging schoolteacher "under their wing" and provide sanctuary from what he describes as the "louts and bullies that populated the camp" (360).

Heist realizes that to ensure his survival necessitates aligning himself with his champions who become followers of Trotsky, who was imprisoned at Amherst for approximately a month in the spring of 1917 after being removed from a Norwegian ship that docked in Halifax while sailing from New York to Europe. Seen as potentially contributing to further unrest in Russia that might derail the country's commitment to the Allies, Trotsky was separated from his family in Halifax and sent to Amherst, where he encountered a captive audience, filled with men who had had little contact with the outside world and were eager to champion a cause. The result, as Silver Donald Cameron explains in his *Canadian Geographic* article, "Trotsky in Amherst," is that he became "a hero to the prisoners," providing an eloquent and persuasive vision of the value of revolution while also "vigorous in his complaints about the defects of the camp's administration" (4). For Heist and his friends, Trotsky becomes a symbol of "change," giving the schoolteacher what he describes to Simon as "the courage to survive" (Duffy 360). Moreover, Heist informs his young protégé that Simon "probably didn't realize how critical this moment in history was," noting that "[f]ew of your countrymen do" (360), a comment that devastates the boy, who views it as a betrayal of trust.

In anger, Simon tosses Heist's "books into the bay—his butterflies and Greeks. The key to his stupid cottage," taking the experience as a lesson that is impossible to truly know or rely on other people, the very opposite of Angus' and Heist's experiences when faced with the challenges of war (Duffy 361). He then heads out on the water with his teen friends in an unreliable boat and almost drowns. Fortunately, Simon is rescued by Angus, ensuring that the drowning Duncan witnessed of his own son, a tragic story he shares with Simon which clarifies why he is so adamantly against Angus serving in the war, is not repeated. For Duffy, Simon's impulsive reaction to Heist's perceived betrayal is juxtaposed with Angus' recognition that the German schoolteacher is motivated by self-preservation, the same strategy used by Angus' brother-in-law, Ebbin, who rather than face charges for having mistakenly shot a fellow officer on the battlefield transforms himself into a hero and postpones the inevitability of death, if only temporarily, by acquiring the name and tags of another soldier. The result is a novel that cultivates ambiguity in a deliberate attempt to raise questions about the moral and ethical complexities of the First World War, both overseas and at home in the Maritimes. By taking this approach, *The Cartographer of No Man's Land* rejects the often presumptively celebratory associations between Canadian national identity and the First World War, rhetoric that has been echoed in recent weeks with the anniversary of the Canadian troops' triumph over German forces at Vimy Ridge including free educational lesson plans posted on the Veterans Affairs site; a search of the site reveals a single photo of a Christmas Day celebration at an unnamed Canadian internment camp but no other records of this aspect of the First World War.

Instead, Duffy's novel prompts a closer look at the tourist souvenirs produced by those who were imprisoned, items that the curator of the Nova Scotia Highlanders Regimental Museum, Ray Coulson, describes in an undated talk to the Amherst Rotary Club as "made and sold for money that ...

[prisoners] could use at the Canteen" in the camp or given as gifts to local residents who brought them tobacco, passing it through the fence (3). In particular, the Regimental Museum houses a hand-carved working wooden cello and bow, an object of remarkable beauty, produced by a prisoner at the camp. Donated in 2007, the cello had been housed in an attic and mistaken for a fiddle, before being taken to be refinished by a professional cello restorer; it remains, as the framed explanation of the cello's origins outlines, "playable." Notably the head of the cello is carved in a unique fashion, portraying what could be described as a caricature of a human face with wide lips, a strong, flat nose, and piercing eyes, while the scroll of the instrument forms two ears. The same museum description explains that "[t]he head of the cello was carved in the likeness of a sergeant the prisoners did not like." When placed in conversation with *The Cartographer of No Man's Land*, the cello offers a powerful counter-narrative to the pervasive circulation of British war propaganda, which explicitly reduces the German population—including Mr. Heist—to the level of monstrous traitors, incapable of producing sophisticated cultural content, employing racist tropes to reconfigure and demean the camp sergeant through strategic visual representation.

In *Advertising Empire: Race and Visual Culture in Imperial Germany*, David Ciarlo notes that by the late nineteenth century, "[c]aricatures of black figures appear in the advertising of most nations that were colonial powers (and many that were not)" (2), typically depicting Black people as having "enormous red lips, oversized eyes and ears, and bumpy heads" (11). Advertising was employed to create and reinforce ideas of "nation—and race building" (137), relying on the "popularity of the 'science' of race … a broad fascination with an exotic 'Other,'" familiarity with the minstrel stereotype, and the "legacy of … slavery," to cultivate and sustain the most popular caricatured versions of Black people (2–3). In particular, Britain and the United States employed racial imagery extensively to advertise products, with American print ads often depicting extreme versions of African-American racial stereotypes that in turn spurred German advertisers and graphic designers (many of whom became globally known) to use similar images. The development of technology to create mass market newspapers and magazines in Germany and the fact that "[b]y 1914 a coherent version of racial differences was stereotypified and broadcast to virtually every person in Germany" (24) meant that "Blackness" became the defining "foil for the white German" (309). According to Ciarlo, it was "nearly impossible to find images of Black people that did not deploy" the ingrained conventions of racialization. Of course, Germany, like the Maritimes, had its own Black populations but these communities typically were ignored, enabling "highly visible constructions ... [to obscure] social complexity in powerful ways" (19). As Harvey Amani Whitfield has documented, slavery existed in the Maritime colonies, and despite the desire of Canadians to perpetuate a history of inclusivity, "Anti-Blackness" remains a foundational part of Canada as a nation and "continues to hide in plain sight" one hundred and fifty years after Confederation (Maynard 3). Similarly, Germany also drew extensively on the figure of the "African native" as a result of the Herero and Namqua genocides committed by the German military in Namibia in the early years of the twentieth century, which "literalized the extermination of blackness" in a colonial context (Ciarlo 276).

In *The Cartographer of No Man's Land*, every surface of Mr. Heist's cottage is filled with "newspapers, manuscripts, articles, and stacks of letters, many in German" (179), suggesting his familiarity with European, American, and colonial news and advertising, prior to entering the Amherst internment camp. While "German wartime propaganda generally eschewed the techniques of beastialization or demonization [of whites] deployed by the English, French, and (eventually) Americans," epitomized by the graphic rendering of German soldiers as monstrous on the enlistment card Simon finds, David Ciarlo explains that depictions of "non-whites ... were fair game" (315). During the First World War, Germans and Austrians took racial photographs and measurements of "the non-white French and English troops" in their prisoner-of-war camps to provide "empirical validation of racial stereotypes" (317). While Mr. Heist cannot be equated with the cello carver, his character provides important clues for understanding the racialized features of the cello head. It appears that German prisoners of war were using familiar representations of the Black "Other" to mock the authority of the camp sergeant, even while seeming to adhere to long-established racial hierarchies.

By carving the caricatured face into a cello, an elaborate and complex handmade musical instrument with an illustrious role within the development of classical music, the prisoners ensured that this explicit inversion of racial stereotypes employing familiar stereotypes of Black people in Africa, Europe, and North America would be framed and contained by an adherence to high-culture norms. The cello head rendered the sergeant monstrously unrecognizable to everyone except the prisoners, who were presumed to lack "the ability to consciously manipulate notions of visuality for their own purposes" (36), much like enslaved African Americans who, as Jasmine Cobb argues in *Picturing Freedom: Remaking Black Visuality in the Early Nineteenth Century*, frequently employed "deliberate representational practices" to challenge their bondage while trying to avoid potentially deadly repercussions

(76). Without equating the two populations or their situations, the cello is a powerful example of using one visual stereotype to counter another, creating a complex layering of meanings for the instrument's creator and his prison community. And of course, high-culture norms kept the cello safely stored for decades in a local attic, despite its unusual head, ensuring its survival because it appeared to adhere to predominantly white community norms.

Like the cello that remains tucked in a corner of a small chronically underfunded regional museum,[5] Duffy's narrative has been largely ignored by Maritime book reviewers and booksellers, despite being lauded throughout the United States and the rest of Canada. As Herb Wyile points out in *Anne of Tim Hortons*, the "commonplace idea that Canada as a federation is a kind of mosaic," fuelled by stereotypically bucolic images of "fishing sheds" in the "East Coast," has been fundamentally troubled by the uneven development of capital across Canada (8). Yet in order to survive economically, the region has trafficked in the rejection of "technological progress and mass consumption," creating what Ian McKay famously described as "a Folk society, natural, and traditional" (Wyile 148) including the production of "folk art," as part of a nostalgic vision of a "past of ethnic and cultural cohesion," free from "the burdens of sophistication" (E. Morton 19). *The Cartographer of No Man's Land* problematizes such efforts by exposing the contradictory dimensions of nationalism during the First World War and Canada's discomfort in acknowledging publicly a complex history of racism that stains, especially in the case of the Maritimes, a folk culture that is essential to its economic survival. Just as Angus recognizes Mr. Heist's shifting alliances while confined to the Amherst prison as a critical strategy of self-preservation, one that Simon struggles to understand, so too may Duffy's novel be read as cautionary tale for those who embrace Canadian exceptionalism in the era of a Donald Trump presidency, when it is all too easy to appear more inclusive and progressive. The cello and its carved head reminds us that so-called aliens, those who were confined to the Amherst internment camp, serve as an important rejoinder and a significant voice for better understanding the Canadian legacy of the First World War, particularly in Nova Scotia.

NOTES

Thanks to Nicole Richard and Ray Coulson, curators at the Cumberland County Museum and the Royal Nova Scotia Highlanders Regimental Museum, respectively, for their knowledge, time, and generosity during my visit in 2017. Gratitude as well to Rebecca Taylor at the Cumberland County Museum for her support and feedback.

Figure 1 is from the Cumberland County Museum Archives in Amherst, Nova Scotia. The miniature spinning wheel is one example of the fine-woodworking skills used by the prisoners to produce miniature objects they could trade or gift. Author photo taken March 16, 2017.

Figures 2 and 3 are of the cello housed in the public exhibition about the regiment and the community at the Royal Nova Scotia Highlanders Regimental Museum in Amherst, Nova Scotia. Author photos taken March 17, 2017.

1 The opening sentence of Lauren Berlant's 1991 *The Anatomy of National Fantasy: Hawthorne, Utopia, and Everyday Life* states that "[n]ations provoke fantasy" (1). While Berlant focuses on the American dimensions of this argument, I have argued elsewhere that the claim is readily imported to a Canadian context.

2 See http://www.internmentcanada.ca/index.cfm for information about this organization, which "exists to support projects that commemorate and recognize the experiences of all ethno-cultural communities affected by Canada's first national internment operations of 1914–1920." It is funded by a $10 million endowment, which was the result of a 2008 agreement between the federal government of Canada, the Ukrainian Canadian Civil Liberties Association, the Ukrainian Canadian Congress, and the Ukrainian Canadian Foundation of Taras Shevchenko.

3 The 2020 Annual Report of the Canadian First World War Internment Recognition Fund includes a description of the "Amherst Event" to mark 100 years since the closure of the local POW camp. The fund also supported the installation of a travelling exhibit from the Canadian War Museum called "Enemy Aliens: Internment in Canada" at the Cumberland County Museum in Amherst from July to October of 2019. See https://www.internmentcanada.ca/PDF/223824_Intern mentCanada_AnnualReport2020_WEB.pdf.

4 When I visited Amherst in March of 2017, I noticed that a professionally produced sign was posted at Casey Concrete, labelling the outside area in capital letters the "BONEYARD" to designate where concrete blocks are stored on the exterior of the building.

5 The Royal Nova Scotia Highlanders Regimental Museum in Amherst, Nova Scotia, was threatened with closure in August 2020, because of the aging state of the building in which it is housed. However, a vigorous letter-writing and advocacy campaign by supporters has ensured that the museum can remain in its current location; as of October 3, 2020, the museum had reopened its doors to the public by appointment. See https://www.facebook.com/nshmuseum/?modal=admin _todo_tour for more details.

SECTION FOUR

Rhetorical Renegotiations

CHAPTER FIFTEEN

The Story Behind the Story, or the Untold Story? John Coulter's
Perceptions of a Canadian Tragic Hero, Louis Riel

Krisztina Kodó

The 150th anniversary of the Canadian Confederation offers the opportunity to examine many stories that have not been fully told, or have been told merely to convey certain viewpoints that effectively suit mainstream political expectations. John Coulter's trilogy, *The Trial of Louis Riel, The Crime of Louis Riel,* and *Riel, a Play in Two Parts,* which retells the historical events of Louis Riel and his trial, and is based on actual records of the court hearings held in Regina in 1885, is one of these retellings. Indeed, Riel has captured the imagination of many authors and artists from the nineteenth century to the present, which has led to considerable literary production that is mostly biased either for or against Riel. In this sense, one may say that his "real story" has never been told; his is an untold story with "many shades of grey." According to Coulter, Riel is "the most theatrical character in Canadian history ... He rides the political conscience of the nation after nearly three-quarters of a century and is manifestly on his way to becoming the tragic hero at the heart of the Canadian myth."[1] This chapter examines whether Coulter can find the man—the tragic hero—at the heart of these events, and his relative success at revealing something about Riel's hitherto untold story. The article thereby seeks to explore John Coulter's perceptions of the Métis hero as a tragic hero in its classical definition.

John Coulter's name and person are well known within the field of Canadian drama and theatre. He was certainly one of the major proponents of the arts in Canada, and his role in the formation of the Canada Council cannot be denied (Anthony 30). An Irishman born in Belfast of Protestant parents, Coulter was "somewhat sadly deprived of the total recognition he deserved for penning at least twenty-five plays, the libretti for two operas, a biography of Winston Churchill, a book of poetry, one short novel, two major auto-biographical works, nine short stories and innumerable articles, essays and broadcasts for both the BBC in Belfast and London, and the CBC in Canada" (Gardner 1). During the years between the 1916 Easter Rising in Dublin and the Anglo-Irish Treaty in 1921, Coulter worked as a teacher of art in Dublin. But the happenings at the Abbey Theatre helped to shift his focus of inter-est toward drama. As a result, he gave up teaching in Dublin, immersed himself in drama and theatrical work, and returned to Belfast "to found a small repertory theatre company, an 'Abbey of the north'" (Gardner 1). This endeavour, however, was doomed to failure from the beginning. The original idea had been "to create an Ulster Theatre for the continued building up of an Ulster identity with plays for, and about, Ulster and its people" (Anthony 24). However, the Troubles flared up and Ireland was in the middle of civil conflict again by 1920. There is very little information available concerning Coulter's theatrical experiments in Belfast; some biographical sources do not even mention it at all, and it is therefore difficult to assess the relevance of his involvement at that time. However, his departure from Ireland certainly sug-gests that he was unable to realize his potential in Northern Ireland.

The fact that Coulter eventually left Ireland to seek new possibilities else-where is perhaps not surprising, since "emigration became a tradition in Ireland, not just a phenomenon, but actually a way of life" (O'Connor 130). From the early 1920s, he was already working in London, and then sometime later settled in Toronto, where he married the Canadian poet Olive Clare Primrose in 1936 (Benson and Toye 235). From 1938 onwards, he became involved in the development of Canadian theatre and drama, and wrote numerous articles and essays on the possibilities of creating a modern Can-adian theatre. As an Irishman, he compared this progress with that of the Abbey Theatre in Dublin and the importance of the Irish renaissance that helped to create an identity and a place to perform exclusively Irish plays by contemporary Irish authors. He considered the latter example worth follow-ing by Canadians.

By the time Coulter arrived in Canada, his name was already known to Canadians through the BBC shortwave radio programs that were transmitted from London. These included "Coulter's feature-program series 'the Home Counties' consisting of historical retrospects, folk songs, folk tales and drama of the English home counties" (Anthony 26). He was active in the cultural life of Canada from the point of his arrival, and he was among those artists responsible for the formation of the Massey Commission and, ultimately, the establishment of the Canada Council. Although his name is well established within these circles, his works cannot be called popular or successful. His name seems to have been altogether forgotten by the Irish, while his name in Canada has acquired greater recognition. The areas in which he did achieve success involved using "non-Canadian subjects" and "Canadian historical subjects with formal dialogue" (Benson and Toye 236)—as, for example, his Riel trilogy.

When Coulter "discovered the hero and rebel of Canadian history, Louis Riel," he felt this figure to be "so like the leaders of Irish conflicts ... with whom Coulter could truly empathize" (Anthony 32). The cause and the circumstances were similar to those in Ireland, a theme with which he could associate himself. As Geraldine Anthony writes:

> Coulter was therefore able at last to write a Canadian play that was hailed by critics as the first great historical drama in Canada. *Riel* emerged as a play that rose above the provincial and even national to a universal level. Oppressed people in every country could relate to this drama. (32)

Through the Riel trilogy, Coulter creates a production that "Canadians acclaimed 'Canadian'" (Anthony 32), the only irony being that Coulter is at heart a true Irishman, for whom W.B. Yeats and Synge were the great ideals of the Irish renaissance at the end of the nineteenth century. That renaissance launched a wave of Irish dramatic output, which Coulter considered the greatest theatre movement and development since the Elizabethan age (Anthony 35).

The spirit of rebellion against injustice is a familiar Irish theme with which Coulter was well acquainted from his own past in Belfast, Northern Ireland, and from Irish history. The idea of rebellion against an oppressor that brutally attempts to extinguish Irish culture and tradition dates back to the thirteenth century, when Henry II asserts his over-lordship of the territory and English presence is established in Ireland ("Henry II"). The resistance to colonial oppression therefore is inherent in Irish culture, which Coulter could adequately express through Riel's historical persona. In Coulter's interpretation, Riel becomes the Shakespearean tragic hero, whose isolated resistance to colonialism enhances the Métis' struggles for independence, identity, and self-expression. He creates from Riel a great national hero, who like those of Irish mythology willingly sacrifices his own existence. Ireland's relationship to England parallels that of the French to the English in Canada, and that of the Catholic Métis to the Protestant English ruling majority in Canada.[2]

Seen in this context, the Riel trilogy therefore acquires an international dimension, which I aim to illustrate through the figure of the tragic hero, Riel. This chapter focuses on *Riel, a Play in Two Parts* (1952; rev. 1975) and *The Trial of Louis Riel* (1968). The latter is a factual and realistic representation of the trial itself, in which Riel is allowed to speak and express his perceptions only at the very end; hence, Coulter does not give his hero ample opportunity to develop fully. The play assumes a documentary form, intent on preserving an authentic portrayal of the court hearings and verdict. Its main objective is to chronicle the events of the trial alone; therefore, the play begins with the court hearings and ends with the final verdict and death sentence of Riel. The play is not a fully comprised epic play in the Brechtian sense, but rather a blend of epic elements in which the actors mingle with the audience; the result is that "the sense of dramatic illusion is constantly voided by reminders from the stage that one is watching a play" (Jacobus 622). Also, the tense and dramatic atmosphere that is maintained throughout is only relieved when the jury, sheriff, and constable retire, and a few actors within the audience comment on the possible outcome of the trial. None are interested in Riel personally; rather, some of the commenters consider his loud prayers embarrassing. This particular episode helps to "jolt the audience into a consideration of the real issues being discussed" (Banks and Marson 288). What becomes obvious is that it is *not* Riel, the individual man, who is on trial, but rather the Métis, an oppressed minority whose rights are disregarded and whose attempts for any self-recognition are trampled upon by the governing English Protestant majority.

Riel, a Play in Two Parts, however, presents the two rebellions, in addition to the trial and execution, and portrays Riel, the isolated individual man, as a tragic hero. This is a play that is performed, according to Coulter's stage directions, "in the Elizabethan manner" (front, n.p. marking). This comment clearly shows that Coulter was intent on bolstering Riel's persona in order to create a valid Shakespearean tragic hero. The entire play centres on Riel, who achieves greater depth as the play progresses. This play also contains elements of the epic theatre, but, instead of focusing merely on the trial, we have thirty scenes that chronicle the events by way of linear narrative. The characters "represent political, religious, and racial elements who emerge necessarily as types, caricatures, and symbols" (Anthony 64). A typical epic element is the use of an ominous song's refrain; in the play, this refrain, "We'll hang him up the river with your yah, yah, yah" (Part I, scene 8, 39), helps to mark "breaks in the train of the play" as it unfolds (Banks and Marson 288). The refrain, in this instance, is a dramatic tool that provides a release from the intense and mounting tension, and shifts the focus toward a wider perspective, which ultimately helps heighten Riel's status as a tragic hero. Coulter also provides information on Riel's age, appearance, and manner of dress in his stage directions; through the dialogues, we are gradually acquainted with his deeds and speeches, and his intense religious beliefs. These are essential components that fortify his image, and further deepen and render the psychology of his character more complex. This portrait of Riel was based on the Riel myth that originates from the second half of the nineteenth century and has been maintained to this day.

From my perspective, Riel, the historical figure, seems to have found it more convenient to create a public image of himself, which may be considered the basis for the seemingly countless and varied portraits that emerge in most recollections. The astonishing display of works that treat the Métis leader range from plays to poems, novels, television dramas, Hollywood films, and sculpture. Interestingly, the characterization of Riel is divided, since some works are based on historical record, while others are a "figment of an author's colourful and sometimes lurid imagination" (St. Germain 49). Among the many stories of Riel, one early example from 1885 is J.E. Collins' publications *The Story of Louis Riel: The Rebel Chief* and *Thomas Scott's Execution*. Collins' works focus on the Riel icon, on the public image. However, Riel, the Métis and human being, is a less frequent source of study in any of the works on him; instead, the charismatic leader, whether a hero or a traitor, and murderer, has been treated as a symbol for the Métis by most writers, an image that Riel himself projected when he addressed the court at his trial. As he claimed, "I stand in this dock not as myself only, but as the chosen representative and leader of a whole people—the halfbreed people" (Coulter, *The Trial* 58–59). To enhance further and clearly define the source of and justification for his leadership, he added at the trial, "God ... made me his prophet. Prophet of the New World. God directed me to lead my people. I have led them" (*The Trial* 58).

Riel obviously fits the general pattern. The more he is used as a "symbol, the more the complexity of the man and his situation is simplified or ignored" (Osachoff 61). In defining the hero or heroic figure, the general idea that emerges, as noted by Sherrill Grace, is that it is a real individual who was given the status of hero for his contribution to some great cause or event that has historical significance. Heroic figures who become icons usually die at a young age and violently so, and they mostly live flamboyantly. Frequently, they are written about in biographies, histories, fiction, poetry, and plays, and have songs and films made about them (Grace 106). Interestingly, most of the earlier work, that is end of nineteenth century and early twentieth century, on and about Riel has been written by white writers and artists—not the Métis people. Today, however, there is substantial research available on Riel and the Métis by Métis scholars, as well. A noteworthy example is Albert Braz's work *The False Traitor: Louis Riel in Canadian Culture.* The work considers the many emotional responses the Riel topic still generates today, and in his introduction Braz defines Riel as "simultaneously one of the most popular and most elusive figures in Canadian literature and culture in general" (3). The Riel myth has been kept alive, mostly due to the fact, which Braz also maintains, that the sundry portrayals of Riel, the "Riel discourse" provides ideal subjects for the "invention" of icons rather than focusing on the actual biography of the main character. The obvious formula of the icon then has been placed on Riel. These ingredients define the icons as being non-conformists and outsiders, with their own particular flaws; they are considered eccentric, weird, and even mad. Perhaps the most important feature is the element of mystery that surrounds their whole being, which to some extent makes them outcasts, whom people in general either love with devotion or hate; there is no middle ground. They are in many aspects men or women ahead of their time, who must bear the burden of solitude, which for them involves a positive spiritual development in areas in which they may excel. Their detachment and reclusiveness is not understood by the general population. The further they retreat into their own world, the less we are able to learn about their personalities. This latter pattern perhaps explains the enigma that has surrounded and still encompasses Riel, the man. The "then-and-now" image of Louis Riel as a hero or villain, therefore, has remained unresolved to this day even though Métis scholars such as Adam Gaudry, Chris Andersen, Chelsea Vowel, Sherry Farrell Racette, and many others have defined Métis identity and actively continue to do so in their works and lectures.

To understand some of the particularities of the ensuing mystery surrounding Riel, it is of interest to note some of the major political and historical occurrences of those decades. In 1885, his trial and execution sparked contradictory responses in the media. On the international scene, 1885 was an eventful year—perhaps too eventful, for that matter. In Germany, within the scope of the Berlin Conference, Africa was divided among the colonial powers; in Indochina, the French were involved in local conflicts in South Vietnam and Cambodia; in Sudan, General Gordon's garrison in Khartoum was under attack by the Mahdists; in the United States, Josiah Strong published his work *Our Country*, which stated that it was the "God-given duty of America to go forth and dominate the world" (Read and Webb 171–72); and in Canada, the newly created dominion from 1867 was expanding, and newly arriving settlers were encroaching on the lands of the Métis people in the North-West (and on lands of all Indigenous peoples, generally). The Canadian North-West thus became the site of two rebellions, which were led by the same person—Louis Riel. The first was the Red River Resistance against the Canadian authorities in 1869–70, while the second uprising, the North-West Resistance, was a protest that took place in 1885 against the "denial of their property rights and the Canadian government's contempt for their complaints" (Read and Webb 172).

Generally speaking, on the basis of most analyses, both the resistance and Riel as a person have come to be considered as part of the narrative of Canadian nation-building. However, this assumption generates a contradiction—since Riel is also identified as an anti-colonial resistor—which suggests that Riel and the Métis cause have been somewhat ambiguous or misunderstood from the beginning. Riel's case certainly created quite a "sensation abroad"; however, his "contemporaries understood him within an imperial rather than a strictly Canadian framework" (172). Riel's trial, death sentence, and execution sparked considerable controversy, which went well beyond Canadian borders. This was evident from the foreign printed media in English and French, in which "European and North American journalists debated each other about Riel's career and about the justice of his death penalty" (173). According to Read and Webb, this process "shaped the narrative of the resistance to suit local circumstances and personal agendas. The Métis leader became something of a blank canvas upon which commentators and readers could paint what they wished" (173). In all the controversy surrounding Riel and the resistance, their voices were hardly heard, although Riel "did speak occasionally in the Canadian press" (174). Nevertheless, this deference seems to have been based on the belief (a view shared by both supporters and detractors) that "as an Indigenous people, they were racially inferior and so incapable of articulating their own grievances, wants and desires" (174).

As critical as this may seem, Riel was viewed as an obstructer of British imperial expansions, but, depending on which side was commenting, he was viewed variously as a "defender of French, Métis, Native and Catholic rights, as the founder of Manitoba, and ... a father of Canadian Confederation, as a traitor, as a murderer, as a millennial prophet, as a heretic suffering from delusions of grandeur, and as an obstacle to Canadian expansion" (194).

Commentators from abroad, however, looked upon Riel not as a figure wholly Canadian, but rather as a

> victim of British oppression and imperialism, as a doomed opponent of the march of British civilization, as a defender of communal property rights, as an inspirational anti-imperial resistor, as a tool of the Fenian movement, as a defender of French and Catholic interests within Canada and beyond, and as a romantic figure of many colours—a kind of noble savage with a French accent—worthy of their sympathy. (194)

Riel, ultimately, became a public figure, which different sides could claim to represent their political agendas or other interpretation of their own causes—and these may not have had anything to do with the Métis matter, or with Riel as an individual.

John A. Macdonald added to this litany of perspectives; he made a reference to Riel as a "'sort of half-breed Mahdi' in the Canadian House of Commons on 26 March 1885" (190). Behind this striking comparison lies the figure of another anti-imperial resistor, Muhammad Ahmad of Sudan, who "declared himself 'the Mahdi' prophesied in Islamic doctrine to be the 'guided one' who would redeem the Islamic faith and purify the community of the faithful in preparation for Judgement Day" (177–78). Macdonald had reasons for making this comparison: Riel also considered himself to be divinely inspired and even called himself "the Prophet of the New World" (Coulter, Riel 69), signing his name as "Louis David Riel." He added "exovede"[3] after his name, thereby clearly identifying himself as the "guided one" (Coulter, Riel 92). Riel, then, was also deemed "the Catholic Mahdi of the North West" by the international press (195). These noticeable points of comparison were picked up by the press and used in both its positive and negative meanings.

The narratives into which Riel has been placed and by which he has been reimagined in relation to political and religious denominations fuelled heated discussions that went beyond the image of Riel as a person. This particular image is enforced in John Coulter's works on Riel, which in fact rediscovers Riel as a notable historical figure. Here, Riel is a silent participator within his own trial and destiny, and only allowed to speak and express his views at the very end, before the jury retires to decide their final verdict. Coulter approaches the somewhat sensitive portrayal of Riel through his focus as a documentary, which turned out to be so politically safe that, in fact, starting from 1967, his play, *The Trial of Louis Riel,* was sponsored annually by the Regina Chamber of Commerce and produced every summer in Regina, where Riel was hanged (Osachoff 65). The documentary form enabled Coulter objectivity and sufficient distance from his main protagonist to ensure total success. Here, Riel is forced into isolation and silence, as he becomes not only the accused, but also the onlooker of his own trial. Coulter's intention was to focus throughout this play—and also in his other Riel plays—on raising him to the status of the tragic hero.

Coulter's other play, *Riel, a Play in Two Parts,* is less documentary, as I have previously discussed; however, it immediately opens up new perspectives by stating in the beginning that the play is to be performed in the "Elizabethan manner." The reader and audience are given no choice but to expect a modern variant of a Shakespearean play. The directions provided for the play clearly state what is meant by the "Elizabethan manner": this is, as the text states, "a continuous flow of scenes on a bare stage with the aid of no more than indicative settings and properties and modern lighting" (Coulter front, n.p. marking). This particular dramatic design also follows the traditional concept of the Shakespearean stage practice. The whole layout and setting of the play further highlight Coulter's intention to present Riel as a Shakespearean tragic hero in its traditional understanding and terminology. Why? We need to understand that, for Coulter, a great hero—and, more specifically, a tragic hero—can only be given due depth and psychological dimensions by going beyond the physical attributes of Riel as an individual and constructing an entity: an enigma and a would-be hero who serves Métis interests beyond everything else. This outstanding hero, therefore, has no personality other than to serve his people.

The classical definition of the tragic hero includes his (or, rarely, her) sense of integrity. The firm insistence that man had a definite choice to make about good and evil, God's grace and the Devil, meant that he had to become master of his own salvation. Certainly, man would suffer, and the only explanation he could find for the cause of suffering lay in the exploration of sin as a force and his own responsibility for it. For Shakespeare, the tragic hero was a man of status, a person of high birth. He usually had a tragic flaw, like Macbeth's "vaulting ambition," because such is the essence of tragedy. The hero is often seen as one extreme side of the spectrum—black or white. If he is too "black" (or evil), he is disparaged. Sometimes both qualities appear in one character, but then the halves are usually kept distinct. By the end, he is isolated and loses everything. Death is a human experience that he must face alone. The

Shakespearean hero knows himself better through his experiences and under-goes a journey of self-knowledge. At the end, he still retains his integrity, since nobody can rob him of it, unless he willingly forfeits it. The hero is often sur-rounded by minor characters, which carries a dramatic purpose, that is, to emphasize the isolation of the hero. This dramatic device is well recognized on the Elizabethan and Jacobean stage.

Coulter creates a tragic hero from Louis Riel, the historical figure. This he is able to do with success because of the ambiguity and mystery that sur-rounds Riel as a man. He is no aristocrat, but a Métis from a financially prosperous family; his father was a businessman and a political leader in the Métis community. He stood out early as a student and, as a result, was given a scholarship to study at a Sulpician school in Montreal. He excelled at this junior seminary, where he soon neared the top of his class. Apparently, his intention was to become a Catholic priest, but, as a result of his father's early death, he decided to care for his mother and stay in Manitoba. He also acquired a passion for poetry, which he nurtured for the rest of his life. Riel, therefore, was not an average, poorly educated Métis. He was an exceptional man—perhaps even a visionary.

But what then may be considered his "tragic flaw"? He was certainly an ambitious, charismatic personality, who is elected first as secretary, then later president of the Métis National Committee. He was a person the Métis trusted and obviously saw as their leader. He was deeply religious like the Métis people in general. Riel thus had a dual character: first, as the charis-matic, proud, and self-assured leader of the Métis people; second, as a man of religion, a humble servant of God, and the divinely inspired "prophet of the New World" (Coulter, Riel 69). Which of these features leads to his ultimate fall? From the records of the trial, it seems that the aim of the defence was to prove that he was insane, and this they did by focusing on the testimony of witnesses, who had first-hand evidence relating to his extraordinary religious views and statements. His religious belief suffuses his whole existence to such an extent that the Catholic priests and the Métis, too, gradually distance themselves, which ultimately leads to his isolation. In the play, Riel's figure as a tragic hero is highlighted through this isolation. The tragic aspect is fur-ther enhanced during his trial, at which time even his defence seems to work against him in their attempt to destroy his integrity.

Riel's other flaw or mistake was the execution of Thomas Scott, which branded him not only a murderer and villain, but a Roman Catholic French Métis, who executed without remorse, and in cold blood, a Protestant anglophone. Or did he really? The circumstances that relate the incident in J.E. Collins' publication present an extremely negative view of him and the Métis in general; the work, therefore, cannot be considered valid in its presentation. Collins' rather frightening contemporary illustration, however, does show that the Métis were marginalized and looked down upon, and not merely because they were Métis, but also because they were French and Catholic. These controversial religious views further entrenched the animosity between the francophone Catholics and anglophone Protestants.

The Catholic and Protestant religious divide was not unknown to Coulter, especially in view of Irish history. The Catholic and Protestant religious conflict has been the cause of considerable suffering and murders on both sides in Ireland. And Belfast, Northern Ireland, which was Coulter's hometown, saw many upheavals that Coulter himself experienced as a child growing up in this milieu. The Métis issue spoke to Irish concerns in several ways, which Coulter imported from Ireland. These obvious parallels were the religious division (the Catholic–Protestant question) and resistance to colonialism (notably, the British monarchy, in both cases). The Riel figure in Coulter's plays, therefore, speaks for the Métis, but also for the Irish. Coulter, in certain instances, merges with his Riel character and speaks through him. Thus, Riel's—and ultimately Coulter's—cause becomes a larger one that is about striving for identity and self-recognition.

For Riel's figure to be elevated to such heights, Coulter must present Riel as an admirable tragic hero, whose features are important to stress in the stage directions, in which he describes Riel as "an intense young man in his mid-twenties. He has some Indian blood ... He bows deeply to the priest" (*Riel* 4). Coulter emphasizes Riel's youth, intensity, honourable behaviour, and respect for the churchmen. By contrast, Thomas Scott is introduced as "a surly, aggressive, fanatical-looking man" (*Riel* 11). This description clearly indicates that whatever circumstances may have ensued, Riel, according to Coulter, was not responsible for the death of Thomas Scott.

Another interesting feature that highlights Riel's symbolic and tragic image is the trial scenes in both plays, in which no Métis are present or even, it seems, allowed into the courtroom. Riel's total isolation in the courtroom and throughout the whole trial is heavily emphasized in both works. We see outsiders, journalists, who bet on whether or not Riel will be found guilty, further heightening Riel's increasing loneliness. When the verdict is read, Riel's simple answer is the tragic hero's cry of pain and anguish in *Riel, a Play in Two Parts*:

[For an intense, silent moment Riel stands motionless. Then, incredulous.] St. Joseph! [Then a cry of anguish.] St. Joseph! (122)

In *The Trial of Louis Riel*, his silent acknowledgment is even more dramatic:

(For a moment Riel stands stricken, motionless. Then he takes the little St. Joseph, looks at it, clasps it to him.)
    Riel (In a low, pleading voice): St. Joseph! (The Constable takes Riel's arm and leads him out.) (66)

We feel Riel's pain and utter hopelessness. The Métis cause is lost and Coulter highlights this dramatic moment to show that the whole trial is based on fraud and deception, instigated by the Canadian government and its representatives, the court, judges, lawyers, and others. The Métis are simply innocent participants from afar, unable to save their leader or themselves. The tragic hero must fall, but, as the playwright suggests, salvation may and will come to the Métis people, with or after Riel's death.

The tension is further increased with an interesting scene that reminds us again of Shakespearean drama, namely *Richard III*, in which Riel is alone in his cell in the police barracks and is visited by ghosts (or, as Coulter calls them, "phantoms"). In *Richard III*, these ghosts were people whom Richard had murdered, and they appear at the very end of the play with the intention to damn him before the final battle the next day. In Coulter's play, however, these phantom voices are those of the judge, André, the Métis, his mother, and a voice echo—that is, voices of living people. One voice, however, does come from the past—namely the phantom voice of Thomas Scott, who cries out, "Riel! You'll hang for this!" (*Riel* 125). In its dramatization, this has the same effect as in *Richard III*, in which all in all eleven ghosts appear, each damming Richard with a final cry of "despair and die!" (Shakespeare Act 5, scene 3). Richard awakes terrified, only to realize that he is alone. This is followed by one of his great soliloquies, in which he questions himself and resolves that he is a villain and murderer. Thomas Scott's cry has the same effect on Riel, and may imply a bad omen, as Riel is thereafter terrified and breaks down. But the other phantom voices are those of the living, such as Riel's mother and the Métis in general, who offer their support and love. The positive presence that Riel perceives through the voices certainly seems to influence his remark to André, the priest, on the day of his execution, when he exclaims:

I had a vision, father. Three persons stood before me. My brother, and a priest.

And one I did not know, a divine being. He pointed to me and said: "God will be with him. They will destroy his body but God will raise him up on the third day." (*Riel* 135)

Although this embarrasses the priest, Riel exclaims, "I shall not die a coward!" (135). And this is, in fact, how Coulter presents Riel in the very last moments before his execution: on the one hand, as someone who is strong and confident, a great hero whose sacrifice serves a great cause, namely the salvation of the Métis people, but also, on the other hand, as someone who represents heroic action in more general terms, that is, someone who fights for the oppressed, whether Métis or Irish, against an oppressor. Both plays showcase Riel as the tragic hero, whose fall is inevitable, but whose integrity remains intact. The Métis cause may have been silenced, the rebellion lost, and the Métis leader executed, and yet both plays end on a sad but nevertheless slightly optimistic note, which implies a forward movement, a development and something better as a future. Riel's sacrifice had been necessary for, as Macdonald says—"he goes down to history as one of the mortal instruments that shaped our destiny" (131).

And where is Louis Riel, the individual human being, the man? Have we come any closer to the true story of Riel? Has Coulter managed to unveil the man behind the mask? Hardly. Instead, Coulter has created yet another layer to the mysterious symbolic image. But this heroic figure ultimately becomes an enigmatic global figure, who is elevated to greater heights. The Shakespearean tragic hero was an appropriate tool with which Coulter was able to create a Canadian national hero, whose individual sacrifice went beyond that of any ordinary man. Riel, the solitary individual, has been lost in the course of historical events; instead, a legendary figure emerges, one who transcends any national (Métis and Irish) boundary and remains an all-encompassing enigma. Riel himself, therefore, still remains an untold story.

NOTES

1 This quotation appears on the dust cover of the book.
2 See Kelleher and Kenneally's *Ireland and Quebec*.
3 As quoted from Coulter's play: "He told me he invented it from the Latin words, *ex*, from, and *ovile*, flock. From the flock. He said he used it to show he was assuming no authority except as one of the flock, an ordinary member of society" (*Riel* 92–93).

CHAPTER SIXTEEN

Supra Legem Interruptio: *Losing Louis Riel* (and His Interruptive Return)

Gregory Betts

When was Louis Riel lost? More to the point, when was the story of Louis Riel lost? Riel, the Canadian politician twice turned rebel leader in 1869 and 1885, the posthumously named Father of Confederation for the province of Manitoba, and the political leader of the Métis people, has not been forgotten as a historical figure. By lost, I ask not when was the story of Riel and source of his fame forgotten or destroyed in an accident of the archives, but in that Derridean sense of when did it become self-contradictory and unfamiliar? It is a question of interiority and the relation of the self to the exterior world, the perils of navigating essence through a public language that "is never owned" (Derrida, "Language" 101). Derrida admits that "even for me my idiom is other" (102), as the self struggles to identify what it is through the features of a system it can never claim or possess or maintain control over. If the self remains elusive even to oneself because of this public schism, then the story of a historical figure, accessible only through traces left behind, becomes even more ambivalent and elusive. Furthermore, the fact that Riel is an Indigenous leader celebrated and even heroized by a colonial government that rushed his execution adds a critical complication to all re-narrativization efforts.

Glen Coulthard offers a useful caution about the politics of the recognition of Indigenous subjects by settler governments that too easily "reproduce the very configurations of colonialist, racist, patriarchal state power that Indigenous peoples' demands for recognition have historically sought to transcend" (3)—including demands made by Riel in his uprisings and political work. Indeed, one of the dominant tropes of scholarship on Riel, the rebel, the poet, the martyr, the madman, and now posthumously the national hero—May 12 is now acknowledged as Louis Riel Day in Manitoba—is the overabundance of contradictory narrative frames competing to claim his story. He is our "false traitor," in Albert Braz's expressive double negative,[1] our postmodern hero, or, if you believe Marshall McLuhan, an apt symbol of our status as the world's first postmodern nation. His diffuse survival—that is *survival*, a life that evokes death, a life that stands above life itself, a spectre, an afterlife in narrative—remains intertwined with the very vitality of the nation itself. Indeed, his biographer Maggie Siggins positions Riel as a great mediator between Indigenous and European civilizations (as he himself claims in his self-defence at the trial) and claims that the very hope of the nation is to become what "remains [of] Louis Riel's legacy" (448).

Riel is further distinguished in Canadian history for the way that the competition over national symbolism overwhelmed his life—the trial itself, as Margery Fee and Jennifer Reid[2] have argued, was overwhelmingly determined by this symbolic conflagration. His story was never originary, never authentic, was always already overdetermined by competing narratives. His trial, in fact, began with a day-long debate about the jurisdiction of the court, and whether the Canadian Confederation of 1867 (and subsequent acts of Canadian parliament governing the territories and province of Manitoba) supersedes the *Magna Carta Liberatum* of 1215 and the Imperial British government—in effect, whether post-Confederation Canada was real enough to claim its own authority despite its ongoing colonial status. The defence lost the objection, and the court maintained its authority, while acknowledging the competing frames of reference for the case. Similarly, the second day involved various appeals to the public debates especially happening in the province of Quebec, wherein it was argued that the public would have "no satisfaction" ("Queen vs. Riel" 40) if various conditions were not met and certain witnesses permitted to testify (including Riel's general Gabriel Dumont, then in exile in the United States as he was also wanted for treason). Many of the petitions were lost, although the trial was delayed for a week to allow certain doctors from Quebec to arrive.

If you were to pin down the moment when Riel realized that he had lost control of his story, and realized the defeat of his self-historicization, it would almost certainly be that moment on the second day of his trial for treason in 1885 when he twice interrupted the proceedings to protest the terms of his own defence. With the Crown prosecutors arguing that although he had been "living within the Dominion of Canada and under the protection of our Sovereign Lady the Queen, not regarding the duty of his allegiance nor having the fear of God in his heart," he had been "moved and seduced by the instigation of the devil as a false traitor against our said Lady the Queen"

("Queen vs. Riel" 15). The defence, led by Francois-Xavier Lemieux, pled his innocence by reason of insanity, which meant, at the time, having been moved and possessed by the devil. The devil was in all the details to the point that, during the trial, Riel had an argument in court with his council about the disastrous implications of this reasoning, should it come to be accepted by the court. He knew it threatened more than his life: the entire Métis uprising would be discredited as a fantastic delusion of a maniacal fiend. The first interruption, on July 29, 1885, went as follows:

> Prisoner [Louis Riel]: If you will allow me, your Honor, this case comes to be extraordinary, and while the Crown, with the great talents they have at its service, are trying to show I am guilty—of course it is their duty, my counselors are trying—my good friends and lawyers, who have been sent here by friends whom I respect—are trying to show that I am insane—

> Mr. Justice Hugh Richardson: Now you must stop.

> Prisoner: I will stop and obey your court. (131)

Fitzpatrick complained to Justice Richardson that Riel was obstructing their line of defence by these protestations, asking Richardson to disallow Riel's intervention into their handling of the case, objecting in particular to his desire to cross-examine witnesses further to their own questions (133). Richardson, however, explained that Riel could take on his own counsel, and do his own cross-examinations if he wanted, but that, if he rejected his council's help, he would lose the privilege of any legal representation (132). Riel accepted that determination and ultimately sat down, but not before protesting a second time:

> Prisoner: Here I have to defend myself against the accusation of high treason, or I have to consent to the animal life of an asylum. I don't care much about animal life if I am not allowed to carry with it the moral existence of an intellectual being.

> Mr. Justice Richardson: Now stop.

> Prisoner: Yes, your Honour, I will. (134)

He did stop, and he did not interrupt the court again. That acquiescence is the moment of climax in his narrative, when the rebel accepts the rules of the system that he claims is illegitimate.

His two long and very famous speeches after this moment, both permitted by the court, are pleas for a *deus ex machina* intervention to avert the impending catastrophe, but, in doing so, they implicitly acknowledge the inevitability of his loss. Thus, he begins his first discourse with a prayer, and, during the course of that talk, admits to a message from "the spirit who guides and assists me" that "to-morrow somebody will come *t'aider*, five English words and one French"—the same composition of the six-man jury (196). It was truly only divine intervention (signalled by the omen of linguistic synchronicity) that could have spared him. With reason and sanity defined at the time in relation to God and pure reason, his crime and his innocence both put him in league with the devil. Against this intolerable conundrum, Riel objected, "I have acted reasonably and in self-defense, while the Government, my accuser, being irresponsible, and consequently insane, cannot but have acted wrong, and if high treason there is it must be on its side and not on my part" (193). A system cannot logically determine itself irrational nor treasonous against itself, without some sort of *supra legem* intervention from above the law. Magistrate Richardson was forced to conclude within the structure that authorized his own power, "For what you did, the remarks you have made form no excuse whatever. For what you have done the law requires you to answer" (225). Those speeches, then, sought to interrupt competing narratives and address something or someone outside of that legalistic, moralistic narrative frame, something, in Derridian terms, outside the structure that defines its epistémé. After his verdict, but before his sentencing, Riel exclaimed, "If I am guilty of high treason I say that I am a prophet of the new world" (224). He had already excised himself, by the authority of his own saying, from the hermeneutics of colonial governance that would imminently condemn him to death.

Considerable attention has been paid to the competition over the meaning and symbolic function of Riel's life and his subsequent execution on the 16th of November 1885. He has since been positioned as a nationalist hero for the Métis, for the First Nations, for Manitoba, for western Canadian separatists, for French-Canadian separatists, for Catholics, and for Canada—he is now recognized as a Father of Confederation. Indeed, the federal government's Bill C-302 (the Louis Riel Act) was introduced in 2013 to pardon and fully exonerate Riel of all crimes and to declare the 15th of July officially as

Louis Riel Day (the Bill, however, did not pass, as the session expired before it was ever voted upon). Against these oxymoronic deployments of the Riel brand, I want to think about Riel's function as an *interruption* of nationalist narratives, as himself, in his martyrdom, as a kind *supra legem* intervention existing outside of the freeplay of the structure of Canada, especially colonial Canada. In particular, I want to revisit Terry Goldie's notion of indigeniza-tion, which he uses to identify the process by which settlers in Canada claim the rootedness of Indigene for themselves, effectively by erasing Indigenous peoples and claiming their cultures (13–18). If we connect indigenization with Gerald Vizenor's work on survivance and Glen Coulthard's rejection of the politics of recognition, we know that settler indigenization was bound to fail precisely because of the ongoing survival of Indigenous peoples and their culture despite the attempted cultural genocide. This is different but related to Adam Gaudry's concerns with the appropriation of Métis identity by set-tler and "New Métis" societies that undermine the Métis cultural continuity and *wahkohtowin*, a Métis term to describe the culture that emerges around the responsibility of being a good relative (168). Appropriations of Riel con-sistently erase his belonging to Indigenous community that has continued to exist since his death. The loss of Riel's life, ending just two years after the establishment of the residential school system in Canada,[3] demonstrates the efforts by the Canadian government to make the nation more internally coherent, through violence if necessary.

With this problem and interruption in mind, I want to turn now to two mid-twentieth-century literary engagements with the increasingly remote life and story of Louis Riel and think about his function as an interruption of their indigenization. Fractures in the narrative of Canadian coherence emerge quickly and insistently, led by a range of mid-century poets attuned to the question of problem of history. John Newlove and bpNichol both use poetry to write about the problem of accessibility and contradiction that now overwhelms the story of Riel. Newlove's imagination fills with "the noise of the men you admire. / And cannot understand. / Knowing little enough about them. The knowledge waxing. / The wax that paves hell's road" ("Crazy Riel" 429). The past becomes an echo mysteriously, precariously heard by subsequent generations. Nichol casts a darker eye askance on those "damn white boys" seeking to "make a myth out of [Riel]" to appease the guilty consciences of their racist inheritance and privilege ("The Long Weekend of Louis Riel" 183).

Scholars such as Margery Fee, Diana Brydon, and Frank Davey have long recognized the problem of colonial logic in Newlove's poetry, although many, especially poets, have risen to his defence. The most contested poems are "The Pride" and "Crazy Riel," which attend to the Indigenous history of the prairies directly. In his research related to the reinvention of Canadian history in poetry, Jeff Weingarten argues that Newlove's representation of Riel and other aspects of prairie history must be recognized as acts of recovery of a history that had been previously and overwhelmingly understood as negative or lacking. Weingarten claims of Newlove that "his personas often articulate both his temporal *and* cultural distance from such pasts, positioning the lyric 'I' as an outsider to Indigenous knowledge who accumulates fragments of the past and gestures to the narrative potential of stories excluded from or inadequately portrayed in conventional history" (82–83). This distance from Indigeneity can, in fact, be recognized in poems like "Ride Off Any Horizon," in which Newlove distinguishes between "men," "women," and "Indians" (43), or "The Double-Headed Snake," in which he distinguishes himself, a "civilized man, / white" (48), from Indians and their Gothic myths. It is not the use of anachronistic, racialized stereotypes and racist rhetoric that is the most significant problem in these particular examples, however, but rather the insistent indigenization with its displacement and replacement of Indigenous people by settlers that runs across Newlove's work. Consistent with the *terra nullius* justification of European colonialism, the loss of history is the mark of possibility for the emergence of a settler culture ready and able to inherit the Indigenous legacy. A similar thematic enters into other poems, such as "East from the Mountains," in which the landscape is erased, "everything is gone" (28–29), or "The Big Bend: By-Passed Highway," in which the "wild woman / of the wood / leaves" and is replaced by new "masters" of the land (65). Such lines echo Charles G.D. Roberts' call for white settlers to become the genuine "autochthons" of the land (15), and to reinscribe D.C. Scott's sense of the "weird and waning race" of Indians and their eventual, necessary assimilation or disappearance ("Onondaga Madonna" 150). Newlove utilizes the habitual romance of the lost civilization, and its self-empowering narrative of Euronormative supplementation, during a peak moment of the government-orchestrated cultural genocide of those groups depicted as already lost. As we have since learned from the *Final Report of the Truth and Reconciliation Commission*, the residential school program remained active and aggressive throughout the 1960s, and was even supplemented by other instruments of state cultural genocide, such as the so-called Sixties Scoop, when approximately 20,000 Indigenous children were aggressively taken from Indigenous homes and forcibly adopted by white, settler families. According to the *Final Report of the Truth and Reconciliation*

Commission, 4.6 percent of all First Nations children were placed in care in mid-century Canada (147). Thus, lamenting, probing, debating, thematizing, or celebrating the narrative of Indigenous disappearance naturalizes the destructive efforts of the federal and provincial governments happening at that exact moment, and sacrifices those people suffering the cultural genocide to a predetermined narrative of their erasure *in media res*.

Newlove's poem "The Pride" begins with a grim portrait of "a desolate country" (68) that has been wiped clear of its previous inhabitants: "This western country crammed / with the ghosts of Indians" (68). The resonance of those lost people yet contain value to the settlers: "they are all ready / to be found, the legends / and the people, or / all the ghosts and memories, whatever is strong enough / to be remembered" (69). Those last notes appeal to the logic of survival of the fittest, as if the erasure of Indigenous peoples from the prairies was natural, permissible, and the use of their cultural legacy by settlers the only sign of their inherent value. In contrast, Gaudry notes the constant presence and continuity of the Métis people and their cultural practices over many centuries despite settler appropriations. It is an identity, he argues, that cannot just be claimed without both historical connection to the Métis community and acceptance by the contemporary Métis nation (167). The "distance" that Weingarten highlights is better registered in "Crazy Riel," also published in 1968, in which Newlove wrestles with an atmosphere of "contempt" surrounding his prairie home and wants "[t]o make things feel better" (39). In admitting that he will never understand Riel or Poundmaker or Big Bear or Wandering Spirit, he confesses discomfiture at the thin line between "saint" and "destroyer" (40). Through this ambivalence, Newlove depicts Riel as both saint and destroyer and his persistence as an uncatchable, interruptive force. Still, Newlove claims the Métis warrior as an unsolved, perhaps uncanny aspect of his own history, setting aside the colonialist privilege that grants him the right to claim that history, and the freedom to ignore the ongoing displacement of Indigenous people on the prairies as exactly the deliberate manoeuvre by a colonial government that Riel rebelled against in the first place.

Whereas Newlove wanted to claim Indigenous cultural legacy as part of his prairie inheritance, bpNichol's response to the prairie pride that swept into Canada in the 1960s was less ambivalent: although he, too, was born on the Canadian prairies, and made use of Indigenous myths in his early work, Nichol came to condemn those who sought to mythologize the Indigenous past as a form of displacement of its Indigenous inhabitants. In particular, his short story "The Long Weekend of Louis Riel" stages Riel's persistence within the contemporary world of mid-twentieth-century Canada. It begins with the Métis hero's travails in a diner, with a waitress ignoring him. Nichol follows this up with perhaps the most acerbic barb in his oeuvre: ignoring Indigenous people in restaurants is "as Canadian as genocide" (192). For Stephen Scobie, "The Long Weekend of Louis Riel" is a minor echo text of "The True Eventual Story of Billy the Kid," the more acclaimed long poem for which Nichol won the Governor General's Literary Award in 1970 (94). The "Billy the Kid" text focuses on the absurdity and persistence of myths, especially myths of hypermasculinity. Nichol retells the story through a paragram: "kid" backwards is "dik," a penis that is missing a letter, hence Billy the Kid spends his life trying to compensate for his small penis, his small d-i-k that you cannot "c." The ur-text of that work is violence, masculinity, and American imperialistic geopolitics, and its expression in popular culture. "The Long Weekend of Louis Riel" follows a similar structure, and also highlights the absurdity of myth, but relies upon a very different referent: instead of American supremacy, he debunks the sublimated Canadian erasure of Indigenous people. The white male characters are wracked with guilt for all the history of racialized violence in Canada's history. Their guilt, however, is another form of myopia, and another means by which to avoid Riel: "they can write down all they want he said they'll never find me" (194). They mourn his death, in fact, before he dies. Furthermore, after Riel dies in this poem, he crawls out of the grave and is resurrected at the end of the three-day weekend. He comes back, not as a messiah, not to redeem nor to be remembered, but rather to escape the perils of master narratives: "theyre crazy these white boys said louis riel." His escape is an interruption of the nationalist myth of indigenization; the mythmaking white boys' cultural inheritance is hollow.

Instead of limiting Riel to a past, especially to a lost past, Nichol's poem explicitly responds to the many poets who began reinvestigating the story of Riel as an essential touchstone in Canadian history. Nichol's contemporaries, poets like Newlove, but also Al Purdy, Dorothy Livesay, and Milton Acorn, as well as novelists like Rudy Wiebe and Robert Kroetsch, investigated the symbolic resonance of Riel's story, especially the grim finality of his death at the hands of the Canadian government. In these depictions, Riel is most often a tragic figure, whose death heralds the turn in Canadian history away from its Indigenous past. But I believe that Nichol was responding more specifically to Newlove, and that it was not his only time doing so. In "Crazy Riel," Newlove writes, "Green frog / Boys catch them for bait or sale" (39). There is a derogatory pun on catching frogs, and catching Frenchmen like Riel in the West. Nichol, I believe in response, wrote a two-line poem called "Catching

Frogs" that capitalized on this pun in Newlove's poem. Nichol's poem reads in its entirety as "jar din"—a two-word bilingual poem of surprising complexity: it contains a locus (the garden, or *jardin*), an action (catching frogs), and a consequence (the frog's protestation in the jar). It distills the pun in Newlove's poem by shifting the allegorical subtext away from claiming Louis Riel to claiming moments of French and English paragrams. I note that Riel is erased in Nichol's poem, but that the slur remains.

"Catching Frogs" was first published posthumously in 1990 in *Art Facts: A Book of Contexts*, but editor Stephen Voyce notes that it was written in October 1975, the same period in which Nichol wrote "The Long Weekend of Louis Riel." Newlove's efforts at indigenization, at prairie indigenization especially, were felt keenly by Nichol, who was born in Winnipeg, the site of Riel's 1869 rebellion: "its not enough they take your life away with a gun they have to take it away with their pens" (194). If there were any doubt about the allusion, Nichol published another poem in *Art Facts* worth mentioning, "The Frog Variations," which he dedicated to "Louise Prael," a friend of his from California who had recently relocated to Vancouver, though the choice of dedicating this poem to her seems to be a play on the name of Louis Riel. While these poems allude to Basho's famous frog pond haiku (Nichol calls himself "one of the Basho Street Kids" [281]), the nine variations include bilingual paragrams, like his definition of a lily-pad: "fragile / frog île" (280). From this perspective, his elaborate and absurd mapping of prairie geography in "probable systems 18," usually interpreted as playful biography (antibiography?), might be taken as a more pointed parody of Newlove's serious and flawed historical work (267–78). Memory poses a significant problem in both Nichol's and Newlove's works, as the recognition of historical, colonial trauma entered into the collective Canadian consciousness.

In 2009, Holocaust scholar Michael Rothberg asked what it means to remember trauma in the age of decolonization, in particular how historical memory is a product of labour in the present, a "making present" of the past that is a perpetual and ongoing form of work (3). His notion of multidirectional memory is instructive for attempting to bridge history and representation, "the individual, embodied, and lived side *and* the collective, social, and constructed side of our relations to the past" (4). Instead of the model of historical memory and identity that is inherently competitive, such as the one that shapes the debates and claims on the story of Louis Riel, Rothberg seeks to recognize a form of solidarity between groups that can foster "new visions of justice" (5)—for instance, how the discourse of the Holocaust has helped provide a vocabulary to African Americans in the United

States and Indigenous groups around the world, among many others, to understand their experience of systemic persecution and collective trauma.

Memories are instrumental to collective identities; they are not owned, but rather participate in a "continual reconstruction" of the terms by which we understand and recognize the world. Thinking of this process, multi-directionality highlights the intentional labour involved in constituting historical memory, and the impact of other memories, especially other people's memories, on our own self-understanding. The white boys in the diner in Nichol's story are thinking multidirectionally when they wrestle with their discomfiture: "man it's the blacks said / billie it what weve done to the blacks   hell said George / what about the Japanese   but johnny said naw its what / weve done to the indians" (193). They are thinking multidirectionally, but they have not bridged history with representation: they do not see Riel, or the other oppressed groups, but only the constructed memory and the affect of the presence of trauma in themselves. In 1976, Nichol published *The Martyrology Book 3*, which surveys Canada from a cultural-historical perspective, critiques our knee-jerk anti-Americanism, and acknowledges the fleeting connection between Canadians and their land. He explicitly rejects any sense of continuity between Indigenous and Canadian cultures: "this city is / no legend but a lie i walk thru / convenient myth of neighbourhood" (n.p.). In a similar way, Nichol's Riel embodies the interruption of our convenient myths. Métis scholar Chris Andersen articulates a shared sense of frustration at the use of Métis history to advance the cause of the Canadian nation through "nationalist narrativization" ("More than the Sum" 621), calling explicitly for complex methods of strategic interruption to that "hegemonic" process (629–30).

What with a comic book biography, an opera, and a play appearing in the past couple of years, Louis Riel continues to haunt contemporary Canada in a manner that is similar to the way Karl Marx haunts Europe: as a spectre that invokes justice in the face of injustice, the spectral moment in the face of the concrete real, and the way forward in the face of inevitable loss. For, as Derrida said, the one "that stands in front of it must also precede it like its origins" (*Spectres* xix). The last image in Nichol's short story is of Riel and Gabriel Dumont pulling themselves from their graves and dusting themselves off "& the two of them walked off into the sunset like a kodachrome postcard from the hudson bay" ("Long" 194). He is a "symbol," we are told, "the perfect image the perfect metaphor," perhaps because he has always been lost, a signifier without a signified: "i'm getting sick of being dished up again & again like so many slabs of back bacon [...] they can write down all they want now he said they'll never find me" (194). If, as Vine Deloria asserts, "the whiteman knows he is alien" (xvi), this final image speaks to the ultimate alienation in the indigenization project: Nichol's narrator sputters out a kitschy simile, a postcard from the Bay, already capitalizing on the loss of Louis Riel. If Riel is the spectral image of Canada's future, that future is, Nichol implies, dissipated. The text anticipates the hollowness of forced commemoration events like Canada 150 celebrations that attempt to foreground continuity rather than overlapping fragmentations.

There is another crucial absence in both Nichol's and Newlove's work: Riel himself. The absence of Riel from representations of his life and career, his impact, his story, tends to diminish his role as an interruptive force of colonial narratives. Indeed, as poets and artists (and politicians and activists) constantly recruit Riel into the service of various national-formation myths, it is striking how rarely his own voice appears in the mix. Riel's interruption of such attempted narrativizations takes many forms, but none more obvious than the fact of the persistence of those traces he did leave behind. Despite the inevitable loss of history, his writings allow his voice to return and recalibrate—*interrupt*—the myths that accrue around him. Although his focus had always been "practical" and inherently political, he did yet also produce a significant body of writings, including over 500 pages of poetry, that constitute a historical trace of his ambitions and his literary talents. These traces, though often deployed, contain an elusive ambivalence for the frames in which they are regularly deployed. I won't explore the full, obvious, and deeply problematic contradictions between Riel and the communities who claim him—his racism against Indigenous people, his comfort with colonial logic, his antipathy to the Catholic Pope (and many of his representatives in Canada), and more—although each of his stated opinions in his writings clearly and directly contradicts many of the claims made upon his name. His writing does the work that Nichol imagined by hollowing out the various Riels that proliferate in Canada (although Nichol, too, disregards Riel's own writing in his poem).

Riel, then, becomes a third poet interested in the loss of Louis Riel. In fact, Riel mentioned his writings and his hopes for them during his trial, already attuned to his demise:

> During my life I have aimed at practical results. I have writings, and after my death I hope that my spirit will bring practical results … I have written not books but many things. All my papers were taken. I destined them to be published, if they were worth publishing, after my death. (192–93)

Accordingly, a small selection of these poems was collected and published in a thin volume called *Poésies Religieuses et Politiques* (under the name Louis "David" Riel) by an imprint series of François-Xavier-Anselme Trudel's newspaper *L'Étendard* in February 1886, less than three months after his execution. The fervour surrounding Riel's state-sponsored murder remained high, and his celebrity status in Quebec remained long after the fact. These poems position Riel as a Catholic conservative, with all the appropriate religious views for that community, and as a French Canadian (including a long epistolary poem attacking Sir John A. MacDonald as "un homme vulgaire" [37]) writing in advance of his martyrdom. Indeed, the fifty-two-page, staple-bound book contains seven poems that conform to the ultramontane Catholicism and general political worldview of its publisher.[4] Strikingly, the book also contains three "certificates" signed by family members Veuve Julie Riel, Veuve Marguerite Riel, Joseph Riel, Octavie Lavallée, Alexandre Riel, and Henriette Poitras, and one by the artist John Lee, guaranteeing the veracity of the documents in the book. The poems were included in the enormous 2,822 pages of *The Collected Writings of Louis Riel* (University of Alberta Press, 1985, as edited by George Stanley, Thomas Flanagan, et al.), but not in the more elegant and literary selections by Paul Savoie and Glen Campbell in *Selected Poetry of Louis Riel* published by Exile Editions in 1993.

I want to conclude this chapter by looking at Savoie's translation of Riel's poetry, highlighting his deployment of Riel, and letting Riel's own words interrupt Savoie's national mythmaking in a poignant moment in Canadian history. The poem "O Québec" is a telling example, with a first stanza that reads as follows:

Québec, our motherland,
You were the precious love of our forebears.
I will cherish all my days
Your lovely name, pronouncing it always.
Québec, beloved home,
Never forget your many Métis sons
By Manitoba shunned.
Their support for you remains as ever strong. (47)

While it seems a simple, nationalistic poem of identification, Savoie has, however, inserted Quebec nationalism more aggressively into Riel's writing than appears in the original: Savoie's "our motherland," for instance, decolonizes Riel's "Mère Colonie!" (Mother Colony); Savoie's "beloved home" denationalizes Riel's "Province chérie!" (Dear Province); Savoie's "your many Métis sons" also de-Canadianizes Riel's "tes Métis-Canadiens!"; and Savoie's "By Manitoba shunned. / Their support for you remains as ever strong" reorients the political appeal of Riel's "De Manitoba trahie / Tes enfants, O Québec, sont pourtant les soutiens!" (By Manitoba betrayed, your children, O Québec, are your support!). The politics of the appeal to Quebec are clarified in the next stanza, in which Riel reminds the Québécois of their pain when France abandoned them. Thus, the appeal in the first stanza is for Quebec to stand with and support French Canadians outside the province ("we in Manitoba will make you stronger"), not a flat, desperate declaration of fealty to the motherland.

Erasing the Canadian context, changing "tes hommes d'ottawa" (your men in Ottawa) to "those who serve you in Parliament," which may be provincial or federal, ignores the national frame of reference and re-maps the boundaries of Riel's political imagination. I am not quibbling with Savoie's right to poetic licence, nor am I suggesting that he has not fashioned a better-sounding and more rhythmically interesting poem—I would argue, however, that Riel's original poem presents a better narrative with a more cogent antagonist force in Ontario Protestantism *contra* Québécois Catholicism, which Savoie effaces for lyrical consistency. By drawing attention to the politics of his adaptation, however, we can extend Braz's observations that we should beware of "Canada's Riel," as an invention of a member of a vanquished group by those who defeated them, to beware even of "French-Canada's Riel."

Paul Savoie's translations appeared in 1993, in the interregnum between the two-pronged referenda on Quebec's place in the Confederation. The English translation, obviously intended for English readers, foregrounds Riel's antagonism to the Canadian national project ("I want the fiercest war waged / To set your empire crumbling" and "You are like the Trembling Seed" 101), his religious devotion (although not his mania), and his literary sensibility as derived from his Québécois education. Riel's writing, presented here in English, interrupts a monolinguistic vision of Canada. The editor of the volume, Glen Campbell, notes that the original French version of the poems appears opposite to each of Savoie's translations in order to facilitate comparison between the two (10). If the English versions of his poems highlight his positive experiences with "French-Canadian nationalism" (11), the French versions of these poems, obviously intended for French readers, specifically foreground Riel's identity as a Franco-Manitoban, an outsider to Quebec politics at the time of the selection's publication. He positions himself as part of "Les Métis-canadiens-français" community and embraces that identity as his ideal: "If a hyphen is placed / Between Canadien and Métis / then be assured that the one and the other race / will be better suited for the Good" ("The French-Canadiens-Métis" 114; my translation[5]). I have shown a few occasions when Savoie's translations minimize that affiliation, but the inclusion of his original French poems allows Riel's writing to assume his ultimate role as a *supra legem interruptio*, an interruptive force from beyond the legal quagmire, disrupting the more than 150 years of Canada's various colonial narratives.[6]

NOTES

1 In *The False Traitor: Louis Riel in Canadian Culture*, Albert Braz discovers that "the reason Riel changes so markedly over time, and across space, is that most of the purported representations of the politician-mystic are less about him than about their authors and their specific social reality" (3).

2 Reid writes of the "dynamic of concealment" (6) in Canadian history that conceals the cultural meaning of hybridity and multiplicity, wherein structural dichotomies functionally obscure third or other modalities. It was this concealment that actually allowed Riel to have any legal representation at all, as he was destitute by the end of the rebellion. When French Canada recognized him as one of their own, and integrated his story in Quebec politics, the province sent out a delegation of legal representatives led by François Lemieux (28). Fee notes that he struggled to make himself comprehensible, but he was deemed incoherent "because his vision did not fit with the dominant views of land ownership, governance, race, or religion" (90).

3 Residential schools pre-existed the Canadian Confederation in 1867, but the system changed dramatically after the implementation of the Indian Act in 1876. The government developed the British industrial school system into a vehicle for their assimilationist program, opening the first three residential schools in 1883.

4 The L'Étendard imprint series of books are more widely known for publishing the first French translation of William Kirby's *The Golden Dog* earlier in 1885 in a series of 138 printed installments, which was registered as a great patriotic account of New France (Hayne 56).

5 Original reads: "Si le trait d'union se place / Entre *Métis* et *Canadien*; / Assuré, l'une et l'autre race / n'en sera que plus apte au bien."

6 In thinking about Riel's writing in the context of the Quebec referenda, and drawing attention to his position as a Franco-Manitoban Indigenous man interrupting both Canadian and Québécois national mythmaking, I feel I need to acknowledge the importance of Elijah Harper as a similarly interruptive force in Canada–Quebec relations. Harper served as an elected MPP for the riding of Rupertsland (poignantly, the name of the territory that Riel was born into, which later became

Manitoba by his rebellion; the riding, itself, has since been renamed Kewatinook). He gained national prominence for disrupting the ratification of the Meech Lake Accord, which sought to end the division between Canada and Quebec, as the province had never ratified the Constitution Act, 1982. Harper protested the exclusion of Indigenous people from an accord that served only to further enshrine the colonial aspirations of the French and English Canadian populations. As he said, "we weren't included in the Constitution. We were to recognize Quebec as a distinct society, whereas we as aboriginal people were completely left out ... our relationship with Canada is a national disgrace, we are fighting for our rightful place in Canadian society" (Coyle, "Canada 150" n.p.).

CHAPTER SEVENTEEN

Thomas D'Arcy McGee and Louis Riel: Minority Nationalists, Extreme Moderates

Margery Fee

Louis Riel (1844–85) is undoubtedly Canada's most famous rebel; Thomas D'Arcy McGee (1825–68) is said to be its most fervent nationalist (Besner). McGee, a member of Parliament, was assassinated for denouncing the violence of Fenianism the year after the Confederation he helped to broker; Riel was hanged in 1885 for leading the Métis resistance against Canada. Riel is better known than McGee today because the Métis cause and any justification for its violence remains contested; McGee's goal, Canadian Confederation, was achieved peacefully. Nonetheless, McGee and Riel have strikingly similar histories and similar ideas about literature, religion, and politics. Both, as ethnic minority Roman Catholic leaders, had to negotiate the tumultuous waters of colonial domination and insurgent reaction. Violent threats from American annexationists, Irish Fenians, and the anti-Catholic Orange Order both produced and hampered the success of their gradualist and multinational approach to an emergent Canada: their "extreme moderation."[1] Despite their violent deaths, both managed to transform Canada, McGee in his lifetime, and Riel only much later, after a long period during which the Métis came to be described as "the forgotten people" (Lischke and McNab). Both men's stance was forged in the crucible of a violent era of nationalist bigotry. Both concluded that democratic British parliamentary traditions best protected the minorities they represented. Their thinking remains salient today, when exclusionary forms of nationalism are on the rise in many democratic countries.

Multinational Experience

They were contemporaries, although McGee was twenty years older; they lived within similar historical and political horizons. McGee came from an Ireland colonized since the sixteenth century; Riel from the Red River Valley in Rupert's Land, which was "owned" and ruled by the Hudson's Bay Company from 1670 until it was sold to Canada in July 1870. They both lived in Montreal between 1858 and 1866, when McGee was at the height of his political power and Riel a young seminarian and law clerk.[2] Both learned about republicanism from direct experience in the United States during the years around the Civil War (1861–65).[3] Perhaps it indicates an equivalent fervour that both were declared traitors by their respective state governments at the height of desperate famines in their homelands: the potato famine that reached its peak in 1847 and the starvation that assailed the Plains peoples in the North-West once the buffalo had been hunted almost to extinction by the late 1870s (see Daschuk).

Extreme Moderates

What was true of McGee by the time he arrived in Canada in 1857 was also true of Riel, even, I would argue, during the resistance of 1885: both were extreme moderates who believed in monarchy and British parliamentary democracy as more balanced than republicanism. They both saw violence as a dangerous way to achieve ethnic minority political goals. Although intent on protecting their own communities, they both saw Canada as offering the hope of accommodation for new national configurations. After all, the Royal Proclamation of 1763 attempted to reconcile Indigenous people to British rule by acknowledging their land rights, and the Quebec Act of 1774 was accommodating toward religion, language, and civil law in francophone Quebec. Both men moved in ultamontane circles in Quebec and promoted alliances between French Canada and their own people as a counterweight to a dominant Protestant Ontario.[4]

Riel's vision was the result of his understanding of two different epistemologies: that of his homeland and that of the urban East where he was educated as a youth. M. Max Hamon writes that in the conflict over the North-West,

[t]he logic of Indigenous peoplehood and kinship was challenged by ideas of sovereignty invested in a universal public will. Riel's ability to navigate between the "opinion" making that had currency in the settler colonial world and the Indigenous worldviews of Red River was essential to the success of the Métis resistance. To create the Red River "Provisional Government" Riel

merged ideas about relationships between people and the land with settler reasoning about citizenship and political representation. ("Many Worlds" 187)

Despite Riel's reputation as a radical, the Resistance was, Darren O'Toole
argues, a conservative movement: "In this regard, [Thomas] Flanagan ... was
not far off the mark when he stated that '[c]ircumstances may have made Riel
a rebel, but his true colour was blue, not red'" (224). He points out that in
its formation, the Métis provisional government "did not innovate so much
as draw upon the traditions of the Métis, including the bison hunt, territorial representation based on the parishes, not to mention the blessing and
support of the lower Catholic clergy" (221). McGee moved from the violent
activism of his youth to a more measured outlook. Although he had once
advocated the annexation of Canada by the United States, "[h]is opinions
began to shift after a series of visits to Canada, where, he concluded, minority
communities enjoyed 'far more liberty and toleration ... than in the United
States,'" at least in the predominantly francophone East (Burns and Block).

Both men envisioned a gradual emergence of a harmonious Canadian
society. McGee in 1858 predicted the establishment of Canadian patriotism
would mean that "distinct Irishism, like every other *ism* founded on race, will
gradually dissolve in it as drift ice does in the gulf stream" (qtd. in Gillespie).
Riel said at his trial that "even if it takes 200 years" he did not "wish these evils
which exist in Europe to continue" and hoped for a time when "my children's
children will shake hands with the Protestants of the new world in a friendly
manner" ("Address to the Jury" 34).

Nationalist Violence, Multicultural Solutions

The moderation of both men accords with the conclusion of many recent
thinkers about the inherent potential for violence in nationalism. Political philosopher Nenad Miscevic sums it up, "The only solution seems to
be extreme moderation. The dialectics of moderating nationalist claims in
the context of pluralistic societies might thus lead to a stance respectful of
cultural differences, but liberal and potentially cosmopolitan in its ultimate goals." He continues, "The idea of moderate nation-building points to an
open multi-culturalism, in which every group receives its share of remedial
rights but, instead of walling itself off from others, participates in a common, overlapping civic culture and in open communication with other
sub-communities." McGee and Riel left their mark on Canada by finding
cosmopolitan compromises designed to forestall ethnic or religious conflicts.
In 1864, at a conference planning Confederation, McGee "introduced the

resolution which called for a guarantee of the educational rights of religious minorities in the two Canadas" (Burns). Similarly, the terms of settlement reached by Riel during the negotiations to bring Manitoba into Confederation attempted to ensure that the French-speaking peoples of Manitoba, the Métis prominent among them, would be granted language rights and denominational schooling (Thomas).[5]

European Theories of the Homogeneous Nation

Nineteenth-century theorists of nationhood, mostly German, argued that the justification for national boundaries was similarity: a proper nation was constituted by a people that shared the same language, religion, history, and culture. This argument made some sense for Germany, which consisted of hundreds of small German-speaking principalities before it was unified in 1871. But even in Europe, a perfectly homogeneous nation does not exist and some of world history's most depressing events have been genocides aimed at producing a hallucinated national ethnic/religious purity. Canada has somehow managed—barely, at times—to accommodate the two acknowledged "founding nations" that Lord Durham described as "warring in the bosom of a single state" (Durham). Durham, dispatched by Britain in 1838 to deal with the French–English conflict, enacted a classical nationalist solution by merging Upper and Lower Canada into the Province of Canada (1841–67). The hope that the Roman Catholic francophone population would thereby be assimilated by Protestant English speakers was unfulfilled, however. And in fact, one impetus toward Confederation was the idea that Quebec's difference would be made less threatening when dominated by the anglophone majority in the rest of what would become Canada. McGee, in his famous "Shield of Achilles" speech in 1865, said, "I see in the not remote distance, one great nationality bound, like the shield of Achilles, by the blue rim of ocean—I see it quartered into many communities—each disposing of its internal affairs—but all bound together by free institutions, free intercourse, and free commerce" (McGee). Riel's vision for Manitoba included immigrants from many nations and religions, as well as territories for the Indigenous peoples and the Métis: "we will invite the Italians of the States, the Irish of the States, the Bavarians of the States, the Poles of the States, the Belgians of the States" and "to show ... that we have a consideration for those who are not Catholics" he added Danes, Swedes, and Norwegians ("Address to the Court" 51). Both believed that multi-ethnic communities would temper violent nationalism.

Violent Pressures from Outside Canada

After the American Civil War, many emigrant Irish veterans joined the Fenian cause. They planned to invade and conquer Canada in order to exchange it for Irish freedom from British rule. This threat, combined with a broader American expansionism, became an impetus for Confederation. Riel was pressured by both American expansionists and Fenians to join his cause to theirs (Hamon, "Many Worlds" 285). Riel was, however, as opposed to them as was McGee, fearing that Fenian interventions would become a Trojan horse for the American annexation of Canada. In fact, at the request of Manitoba's lieutenant governor in 1871, Riel led his armed followers to apprehend some Fenians attempting to invade the province. The fake news that both Riel resistances were somehow orchestrated by Fenians, despite denials from both sides, filled newspapers in Canada and abroad (see Read and Webb).

Both men walked a tightrope to avoid entanglement in these extremist forces, which would have either discredited them politically or swamped their own people in an even larger collective than Canada. What was "extreme" in their positions, then, was their determination to protect the most important cultural, linguistic, and religious practices of their group; what was moderate was their realization that to achieve this protection, they would need to allow other groups the same rights. In other words, they conceived of a multinational state, rather than promoting the classical nationalist ideal of a state that produced cultural homogeneity through the exclusion or assimilation of minorities (the "melting pot"). McGee captured this vision when he said: "So long as we respect in Canada the rights of minorities, told either by tongue or creed, we are safe. For so long it will be possible for us to be united. But when we cease to respect these rights, we will be in the full tide towards that madness which the ancients considered the gods sent to those whom they wished to destroy" (qtd. in Wilson, *McGee* 258). During his trial for high treason, Riel might well have felt that this madness had been projected on to him. In one of his speeches to the court, he said that the Canadian government "by its greatness ... had no greater rights than the rights of the small, because the rights is the same for everyone, and when they began to treat the leaders of the small community as bandits, as outlaws, leaving them without protection, they disorganized that community" ("Address to the Court" 56).

Both came to their extreme moderate position through hard experience. McGee participated in Young Ireland's failed 1848 resistance and, granted bail, fled to North America, "where he proudly proclaimed himself a republican revolutionary and traitor to the British Crown" (Wilson, "McGee").

After immersion in the politics of the United States, however, he lost this revolutionary zeal. Riel was the spiritual leader of both the 1870 and the 1885 resistances, but he did not fight, leaving that to his general, Gabriel Dumont, and his men. Riel hoped that the threat of violence, backed up by a viable fighting force—which led to success in the first resistance—would work in the second (J. Reid 198–99). Riel had not foreseen violence when he arrived back in Canada in 1884 (Hamon, "Your Thesis"). His skills were not those of a military leader, but of a compelling speaker and legal mind. There is no space here to outline the many ways in which he attempted to forestall violence before and during the second Resistance, including petitioning the Canadian government to no avail. Significantly, once fighting broke out, Gabriel Dumont took on the role of "war chief" in Cree terms. However, his hope to mount a "well-conducted guerrilla campaign [that] would force the government to negotiate" was overruled by Riel, who ordered the massing of troops at Batoche (Thomas).

Civic Nationalism

Thus, McGee and Riel rejected a radical ethno-nationalism in favour of what is sometimes called civic nationalism or cosmopolitanism (Miscevic)—a move that was supported by their practicality and their minority position. Their belief in civic nationalism explains why both ran for public office.[6] Riel was elected to the House of Commons three times, although he was never able to take his seat; McGee was elected to the Legislative Assembly for Canada East in 1858 and then to the first Parliament of Canada as the member for Montreal West. Neil Besner argues that McGee was, ironically, the most nationalist of the Fathers of Confederation because his "longstanding use of Irish cultural distinctiveness to combat English oppression provided a model that countered the idea that to be colonial was to be inferior." Riel certainly would have agreed, even though he represented a tiny ethnic minority that the mainstream viewed as barely civilized. As historian M. Max Hamon remarks, "Riel speaks as an Indigenous person who has mastered the Western canon. He used the paradigm of cultural superiority not because he was some pawn of Western civilization but, rather, because it was a historical condition of his own agency" ("Defence" 83). Hamon notes the tendency to downplay Riel's educational accomplishments: "Interpretations of Riel's student experience have favoured a tragic story of failure, stasis, and timeless essentialism (illustrating the incompatibility between schooling and Métis identity)" ("Defence" 63). Hamon demonstrates, however, that the seminary was an elite school that produced confident leaders and that Riel excelled there.

He concludes that Riel's decision to become a politician rather than a priest should not be described as a failure; many of his classmates became leading politicians in Quebec.

Culture as a Moderating Force

For both, politics and artistic production were inextricably connected, a connection derived from the Romantic nationalism that drove the multiple movements for liberation from aristocratic regimes in Europe and the Americas. This ideology required a national culture to justify claims to national sovereignty. McGee wrote in *The New Era* (Montreal, 1857–58) that "every country, every nationality, every people, must create and foster a National Literature, if it is their wish to preserve a distinct individuality from other nations" (McGee, "Protection" 1). As critic Michelle Holmgren notes, the Young Ireland movement, in which McGee spent his early revolutionary years, "was greatly influenced by the work of German nationalist philosophers, including Karl Friedrich Schlegel. When McGee paraphrases Schlegel's dictum, 'no national literature, no national life' (*The New Era*, June 17, 1857), he anticipates Yeats' phrase, 'there is no nationality without literature, no literature without nationality' by nearly forty years" (62). In the same speech he proclaims, "Come! Let us construct a national literature for Canada, neither British nor French, nor Yankeeish, but the offspring and heir of the soil, borrowing lessons from all lands, but asserting its own title throughout all" (quoted in Gillespie).

This dominant belief in the importance of culture to national sovereignty meant that one could contribute as much to one's nation by creative or intellectual work as by engaging in politics or war. Daniel A. Wilson, McGee's biographer, writes that "McGee saw his own future lying more in literature than politics, although he would never view them as entirely separate entities ..." (*McGee* 336). Riel is famous for saying "My people will sleep for one hundred years, but when they awake, it will be the artists who give them their spirit back."[7] Like other Romantic poets, he wrote lyrics for songs intended to inspire his followers to act for the good of their community. McGee's literary criticism was some of the earliest to represent the potential for a viable Canadian literature. Indeed, shortly before his death, he had resolved to abandon politics for literature, writing to a friend "I hope to issue a volume of ballads at New York. What do you say to this title: 'Celtic Ballads and Funeral Songs'" (qtd. in Wilson, *McGee* 336). Riel won prizes for poetry in both Latin and English at the Sulpician seminary in Montreal (Hamon, "Defence" 66) and wrote poetry, both serious and satirical, mostly in French, throughout his life. Although cultural nationalism might well be seen as a support for nationalist violence, its link with civilization was intended to promote peaceful alternatives.

Violence Within: The Orange Order

However, events truncated both men's hopes to serve through intellectual or creative work. The dominant political group threatening their communities' continued existence as a people was the Protestant Orange Order, founded in Northern Ireland in 1795. The Order emerged from a long history of violence between Protestants and Roman Catholics in Great Britain dating to Henry VIII's conquest of Ireland in 1541 and his later abrogation of papal authority. These conflicts were exported with the Irish diaspora. McGee outed prominent members of the Montreal Irish community as Fenians; the man who was hanged for assassinating him was almost certainly a Fenian. And although even John A. Macdonald reluctantly agreed that the provisional government established in the North-West in 1869 was legitimate,[8] this Métis government's execution of an Orangeman, Thomas Scott, was seen as murder by Protestant Ontario. The Métis, however, had strong support in Quebec. Macdonald, who would lose votes in one or the other province by making a clear decision, stalled on granting Riel his promised amnesty, which meant Riel could not take his seat in Parliament without fear of arrest. After the second Resistance in 1885, continuing outrage about Scott's execution made it easier for Macdonald to justify hanging Riel.

Literary and Rhetorical Connections

Would McGee have supported Riel? David Bentley argues that many early Irish writers in Canada were "less amnesiac in regard to the history of the land and the Indians" than their English counterparts because of their own experiences of colonial oppression. Graeme Morton and Daniel Wilson state that

> [i]t was a commonplace among Irish nationalists in Canada, for example, to complain that the Irish people were the only white race without responsible government. Others, however, were more likely to view Indigenous peoples as fellow victims of British imperialism, even though such nationalists often had difficulty shedding their own conscious or unconscious racism. (7)

Popular historian Ken McGoogan argues that had McGee lived, he might have intervened to save Riel from the gallows (115). I am skeptical that a man so devoted to Confederation as McGee would intervene in the execution of a man who was seen as just as much a danger to Canada as were the Fenians McGee so vehemently opposed. Although there is compelling evidence to the contrary (see Stonechild and Waiser), mainstream Canada was convinced that the 1885 resistance was, in fact, a savage "Indian war," and that Riel had fomented it (see Read and Webb). Anglo-Canadians have long consolidated their nationalism by situating themselves as good colonizers of Indigenous people when compared to the bad American colonizers (Fee 47). McGee, for example, remarked that "[b]ut by far the least defensible series of republican aggressions were those committed on the aboriginal nation" (*Speeches* 17). Much virtue-signalling nationalism, which Daniel Coleman calls "white civility," often did little in practice to forward Indigenous aspirations (or those of other minorities) and ignored francophone issues wherever possible. In fact, Donald Harman Akenson argues that the migration between 1815 and 1914—"the Great European Migration," when "55 to 60 million Europeans" moved to North America—was "the greatest single example of land theft, cultural pillage, and casual genocide in world history" (25). Morton and Wilson sum up his argument: "the Irish and Scottish were imperialist to the core" (5). Akenson concludes that all incomers were part of a systemic imperialism that included the African slave trade.

However, Bentley's idea nonetheless may well be true at one level: Irish and Scottish immigrants were more likely than the English to see their own desperation during the famine and the clearances as analogous to the plight of Indigenous peoples under British colonization. Michael Newton says of some Scottish authors who did draw this analogy that their goal was not to support Indigenous aspirations, but to achieve "the rhetorical aims of the author"—that is, to emphasize the oppression of their own immigrant group, and to support its claims for equality in the new land (237). Indeed, Riel, despite his acknowledgment of Indigenous ancestry, also made this rhetorical move on behalf of the Métis. He did draw attention to the starvation of the Plains peoples who were suffering along with the "half-breeds," and "eating the rotten pork of the Hudson's Bay Company" because there were no buffalo left to hunt (Riel, "Address to the Jury" 26). Nonetheless, he saw them as in need of civilized Métis guidance (Stonechild and Waiser 77), just as white settler Canadians saw the Métis as in need of a superior people's firm governing hand. Hamon argues that "[p]rotecting civilization against barbarism became central to the platform of legitimacy of his new government, the Métis Resistance and to Riel's nationalism" ("Defence" 81).

Civilization and Barbarism

Romantic nationalism was grounded on ideas of civilization, which brought along with it the notion that the "older" European nations provided the model for everywhere else. Discussing Riel's seven years of schooling at the Sulpician seminary in Montreal, Hamon outlines how deep this linkage was. He uncovered an undated composition topic on the "Advantages of the Arts and Sciences"; the rubric reads: "Nothing brings greater honour to a nation than arts and sciences; that is their principal merit ... a barbarous people may equal [such a nation] in strength and riches, but are also inferior to an educated people ..." (Hamon, "Defence" 75). Riel revised theories that categorized him and his people as barbaric to demonstrate that their culture and beliefs were worthy of the sovereignty granted to Canadians in other provinces. Indeed, Riel used the rhetorical tactics he learned as a successful debater at the college to make clear that in many cases, he saw the Métis as more civilized than the Canadians who illegally invaded the North-West before the transfer of the territory from Hudson's Bay Company. His view was that Indigenous people were in need of protection from the "demoralization" that British rule had brought them (Riel, "Address to the Jury" 33). In fact, Riel himself embodied the civilization that supposedly justified white settler domination. Richard Gwyn says that Riel was "better educated than Macdonald—if in a narrowly classical way" (103).

Both Riel and McGee had to walk the line that would allow them to preserve the distinctive cultures and rights of their people while avoiding a virulent and violent majority backlash. Toronto was once called the "Belfast of Canada" for a reason; Orangemen often consolidated their power in street riots (see McGowan; Smyth). Realizing where such partisan politics could lead based on his experiences in Ireland and the United States, McGee argued for Confederation, because it would "provide for the survival of French Canada." He also "urged Canadian colonization of the Hudson's Bay Company territory, but, at the same time ... his plan included the establishment of a separate province for the native people and extensive Canadian economic assistance" (Wilson "McGee"). Certainly this temperate approach matches Riel's plan for diverse ethnic and religious settlement of the North-West. He too proposed "a sort of self-governing reserve" for the Métis (Gwyn 438). However, by the time Riel was able to describe it to a wider public in his speech to the court, it was too late for moderation in the North-West.[9]

Although Irish Catholics were certainly racialized by Protestant Anglo-Canadians at the time and often relegated to the economic margins, the Irish did not face internal colonization, as did the Plains peoples. The

Métis were also divided by ethnic and religious attachments, as their cat-
egorization as "half-breeds" (English-speaking, Protestant) and "Métis"
(francophone, Roman Catholic) revealed.[10] Riel argued for responsible government as an umbrella under which all the people of the North-West could
be governed: "I have directed my attention to help the Indians, to help the
half-breeds and to help the whites to the best of my ability." He continues,
"We have taken time, we have tried to unite all classes, even, if I may speak,
all parties" ("Address to the Jury" 27). The ways in which Canada moved in to
make treaties after 1870, however, explicitly divided the Indigenous peoples,
the Métis, and the whites into different groups with different rights.

Macdonald's government was driven by the fear of invasion from the
south, either by Americans or Fenians or both, and the need to "clear the
plains" of apparently warring Indigenous people so that "orderly" settlement
could take place. In 1885, the newly completed railway made military intervention much easier than the negotiations of 1870. In refusing to consider
Métis petitions and instigating violence, Canada failed the test that Riel
posed.[11] Kevin Bruyneel writes that

> Louis Riel's life, death and legacy have come to embody the nexus of colonial
> and liberal–democratic dynamics defining Canadian political life, where he is
> now constructed as both the victim of Canadian colonial practices and a founder
> of the Canadian liberal state. At this nexus, Riel's political figure is variously
> employed to reveal and mask the colonial history and present of Canadian pol-
> itics and society. As a result, Riel is perpetually exiled, executed and exalted in
> ways that serve to mark out the boundaries of Canadian sovereignty and people-
> hood but which also exposes the violent essence of these boundaries. (712)

Riel cannot rest until a new politic emerges. McGee's reputation is much
more settled. He has come to symbolize someone who relinquished ethnic
violence in a new country where he was accepted not just as a citizen, but
as someone who could participate freely at the highest level (see Geddes).
Nonetheless, when he denounced Fenianism in Montreal, he lost much of
his Irish Catholic support and, ultimately, his life. Although this chapter may
seem to be about the past, it is, in fact, about what Robert Young calls "postcolonial remains," that is, unresolved issues that linger beyond what some
have declared to be the end of any need for critical postcolonial theoretical
approaches.

Bruyneel's representation of Riel as *homo sacer* fits with Young's notion:
Riel continues to haunt the nation because he stands for a historical injustice

that has not yet been remedied. Since 1982, however, when the Métis were included as "aboriginal peoples" in section 35 of the Constitution Act, his ghost is being laid through the workings of the politics he stood for: nonviolent and democratic.[12] As with other Indigenous claims in Canada, court cases have resolved some central questions, particularly the question of who counts as Métis (see Teillet; Voth). The Supreme Court decision *R. v. Powley* (2003) laid out legal requirements for Métis identity: personal identification as Métis along with ties to both a modern and a historical Métis community that "emerged in an area prior to the Crown effecting control over a non-colonized region." Such a community was constituted by a group of people of mixed ancestry descended from "Indian-European" or "Inuit-European" people who "formed a 'distinctive' collective social identity; lived together in the same geographic area; and, shared a common way of life." Importantly, this definition does not "encompass all individuals with mixed Indian and European heritage" (Indigenous and Northern Affairs Canada). Nonetheless, eager to claim Indigenous links to Canada, many have used evidence—including DNA evidence—of a distant Indigenous ancestor to identify as Métis in the loose sense of "mixed-race" (see Leroux). The energies of a new generation of Métis scholars have been spent on countering this white settler indigenization by emphasizing historical ties and articulating cultural values. Central to these is the Cree notion of *wahkohtowin*, often translated as "kinship," a broad conception that includes the land and all living beings, as well as one's human relatives and neighbours. They argue that a claim to Métis identity cannot be made solely by demonstrating a genealogical relationship. Even if one's ancestry connects one to a historical Métis community, a further requirement is the responsibility to form a living contemporary relationship with that community, one that is affirmed by that community (see Adese; Andersen, *Métis*; Gaudry; Reder, "Awina Maga Kiya").

The Irish-Canadian immigrant community has for the most part merged into a mainstream Canadian society that may not even remember their earlier history of discrimination (see McGowan). The Métis, however, are actively articulating and adapting their longstanding principles, even from within the context of elite institutions that never expected to include them, such as the academy (see Gaudry and Lorenz). Inclusion is not their goal; their focus is on sovereignty, a sovereignty based on the formation of their Indigenous peoplehood "prior to the Crown effecting control." As June Scudeler writes, "eurowestern ideas of nationhood and governance" are "too limited for Métis conceptions of self-determination."

NOTES

I thank the Musqueam Indian Band, as always, for their hospitality to me on their unceded territory. I thank M. Max Hamon for answering my email questions about Riel's time in the seminary. I thank June Scudeler for allowing me to quote from her unpublished essay. I also thank the anonymous readers for their helpful comments.

1 "Extreme Moderate" is the subtitle of volume two of Daniel Wilson's 2011 biography of McGee.

2 McGee attended at least one event at the Sulpician seminary when Riel was a student, but there is no evidence that they ever met (Hamon, "Your thesis").

3 McGee lived there between 1842 and 1845 and again between 1848 and 1857; Riel was there for about two years after 1865. Later, in 1883, during his exile after the first Resistance, he became a US citizen.

4 Ultramontanism supported the authority of the church over civil society. See Choquette. McGee moved toward this conservative Catholicism later in life, while Riel broke with Roman Catholic authorities at a few points in his life when he saw it as a negative influence on his cause. See Gillespie for more on McGee's promotion of Irish–French alliance. Riel consistently worked his political networks in Quebec (Hamon, "Many Worlds"). M. Max Hamon's thesis is now a book: see his *The Audacity of His Enterprise: Louis Riel and the Métis Nation that Canada Never Was, 1840–1875*, McGill Queen's UP, 2020.

5 In fact, these rights were not fully recognized in practice as the controversy over the Manitoba Schools Act of 1890 and the Supreme Court of Canada decision on language rights in Manitoba (1985) makes clear. The latter declared that the laws in Manitoba, published in English only after 1890, were invalid unless translated into French.

6 Both founded newspapers, McGee *The New Era* (1857–58) and Riel *The New Nation* (1870).

7 Although this saying is much repeated, so far I have been unable to find it in an original source.

8 The Hudson's Bay Company failed to maintain order there, and Canada hesitated to conclude the purchase that would secure its authority because of the violence. In the interim, the Métis established a representative government that maintained law and order. Thus, Canada negotiated the Manitoba Act (1870) with this government, making Riel a father of Confederation.

9 The Manitoba Métis received new consideration for their land claim in 2013, when the Supreme Court ruled that the honour of the Crown had not been upheld in the provision of land to the Métis as required by the Manitoba Act, 1870 (Canada). Negotiations with the federal government are under way.

10 Jennifer Adese comments on the history and meaning of "half-breed" as a term of identification (77–78).

11 Conflicting versions exist of how the Battle of Duck Lake began, but the federal government's refusal to consider the many Métis petitions certainly contributed. See Virtual Museum of Canada.

12 Several Métis writers made major interventions in the 1970s, notably Maria Campbell with her life story, *Halfbreed* (1973); Howard Adams, with *Prison of Grass: Canada from a Native Point of View* (1975); and Harry W. Daniels, with *We Are the New Nation: The Metis and National Native Policy* (1979). The founding of the Métis National Council (1983) and its provincial affiliates was central to a renewed Métis–federal conversation.

CHAPTER EIGHTEEN

Before Secret Path: *Residential School Memoirs from the 1970s*

Linda Warley

In 2016, Gord Downie, the late lead singer of the Canadian rock band The Tragically Hip, used his celebrity status to bring attention to Indigenous rights generally and, in particular, to the shameful history and the continuing legacy of Indian residential schools, which still have devastating effects not just on survivors themselves but also on their families, even entire communities. At his final concert in Kingston, Ontario, he gave a shout out to Prime Minister Justin Trudeau (who was in the audience), remarking that Trudeau is the federal leader to end the ongoing colonization of Indigenous peoples in the settler colony known as Canada. Downie's faith in a decolonizing future under Prime Minister Trudeau's leadership was moving, if rather naive, given the plethora of issues that Indigenous people face to this day, including theft of their land and its resources; extreme poverty and lack of basic rights, such as access to clean drinking water and health care; the thousands of missing and murdered Indigenous women and girls; youth suicide; and much more. Downie's attention, though, appears to have been mainly on residential schools. Indeed, shortly after that concert, he released an album called *Secret Path*, and an accompanying video and graphic novel (drawn by Jeff Lemire) of the same title. *Secret Path* tells the story of Chanie Wenjack, a twelve-year-old boy from Ogoki Post, in northwestern Ontario, who escaped from the Cecilia Jeffrey Indian residential school in Kenora, Ontario, and died while trying to walk home, which was 600 kilometres away, in the midst of winter. Downie had heard about Chanie through his brother Mike Downie and later met the Wenjack extended family. Clearly, he was deeply affected by this one boy's story.

But before Downie heard about Chanie Wenjack and began his *Secret Path* project, many Indigenous people had written memoirs about their lives, including, for some, their time at residential schools. In this chapter, I focus on the 1970s because in that decade alone, a substantial number of memoirs were published in Canada by Indigenous authors, some of them focusing on residential school experiences or referring to school as part of a larger life narrative. Given that the deliberate government policy of forced assimilation of Indigenous children through their removal from family and culture and placement in residential schools ran through the twentieth century, authors publishing memoirs in the 1970s would inevitably have been personally affected in some way. Memoirs from this period offer nuanced, sometimes ambivalent, accounts of residential school experiences that do not necessarily provoke the anger, sadness, and outrage that more recent texts such as *Secret Path* tend to provoke. Nevertheless, those stories were told and those voices need to be heard.

For example, Augusta Tappage Evans in her 1973 "as told to" life narrative, *The Days of Augusta*, includes two stories about her time at what she called "mission school." She says that "[it] was fun once you got used to it" (18) but also notes that the students only spent part of the day studying and the other part working. She blames herself for not learning enough—"Should have looked after my book instead of closing it when it got hot" (18)—but in the next breath she reveals that she was punished ("They made me kneel down in a corner" [18]) for not reading her book. Maria Campbell was sent for one year to the residential school at Beauval when she was seven years old. She writes in *Halbreed* (1973): "I can recall little from that part of my life besides feeling lonely and frightened when I was left with the Sister at the school" (44). But she then goes on to recall that "[t]he place smelled unpleasantly of soup and old women … [and that she] cannot recall ever doing much reading or school-work." "Most vividly" she recalls being locked in a closet as punishment for speaking her language (44). Mini Aodla Freeman's *Life Among the Qallunaat*, first published in 1977, also includes a few sections about her time at Bishop Horden School in Moose Factory. She writes that "[b]y Christmas, I had found my own playmates, and I had gotten used to some of the routines, no longer being afraid" (104). In time, she even got used to the strange food that white people eat and comes to like peanut butter and jam sandwiches (105). Nonetheless, she yearns to leave the school and return to her family. When her father and grandfather do come one day, they leave the next day but without her after meeting with school authorities. Freeman writes a story heading that reads "I Think I Was Kidnapped" (105), and after telling of her father and grandfather disappearing again, writes: "I am pretty sure that they came to get me out and bring me home, but I guess they had no ransom"

(107). Even the same boy who died while trying to escape residential school and walk home and whose story captured Gord Downie's attention was remembered by Indigenous people in the 1970s. Singer Willie Dunn, of mixed Mi'kmaq and Scottish/Irish background, had written a song about Chanie (who was also called Charlie, as is the title of Dunn's song) in 1978.

In one view, Gord Downie can be commended for using his celebrity status, acutely focused through the lens of his impending death from terminal brain cancer, to draw Canadians' attention to the brutal legacy of residential schools. He went about his work in a respectful manner. He met the family and developed a relationship with them, particularly Chanie's sister, Pearl. He asked permission to write about Chanie. And he established the Gord Downie & Chanie Wenjack Fund to solicit donations to pay for education about residential schools and healing initiatives to support those who continue to be impacted by them. As stated on the website, "The goal of the fund is to continue the conversation that began with Chanie Wenjack's residential school story, and to support the reconciliation process through awareness, education, and action."[1] Reconciliation—or ReconciliACTION as on the website—is Downie's aim.

In another view, Downie's *Secret Path* is not unproblematic. Laudable as his aim is, it is entangled in and complicated by the very resilient structure of settler colonialism. Without action that would lead to the dismantling of settler-colonial power structures—institutions, legal frameworks, policies, and more—as well as the restitution of land to Indigenous people, many well-intentioned attempts at reconciliation remain merely discursive. This is what Eve Tuck and K. Wayne Yang mean when they warn that "decolonization is not a metaphor."

> The too-easy adoption of decolonizing discourse (making decolonization a metaphor) is just one part of that history [settler colonialism] and it taps into pre-existing tropes that get in the way of more meaningful potential alliances. We think of the enactment of these tropes as a series of *moves to innocence* (Malwhinney, 1998), which problematically attempt to reconcile settler guilt and complicity, and rescue settler futurity. (3)

"Settler moves to innocence" come in many forms, but according to Tuck and Yang they have in common a strategic aim: "[They] are those strategies or positionings that attempt to relieve the settler of feelings of guilt or responsibility without giving up land or power or privilege, without having to change much at all" (10). Downie's *Secret Path* project can be critiqued as one such "settler move to innocence." As Sean Carleton notes, *Secret Path* offers "a narrow vision of reconciliation that favours martyrdom over restitution." In his view, and it is one that I share, *Secret Path* "promote[s] a settler-controlled vision of reconciliation that is entirely compatible with assimilation, continued colonialism, and renewed Canadian nation-building."

The timing of Downie's *Secret Path* is significant, not just because of his personal commitment to complete the project before his death, but also because it can be placed within the context of the ninety-four Calls to Action outlined by the Truth and Reconciliation Commission (TRC) Report (2015). The TRC Report is the product of several years of investigation and interviews conducted by the Commissioners, who were charged with hearing the testimonies of residential school survivors, their family members, and those who were involved in running the schools and teaching in them. Not only did the Commissioners report on what happened, they also drew attention to how Indigenous people are still living with the consequences of the residential school system, both the trauma of the survivors and the intergenerational trauma experienced by their families and communities.

Since the release of the TRC Report and the Commissioners' justified characterization of the Indian residential school system as a deliberate policy of "cultural genocide," more non-Indigenous Canadians are paying attention to this particular history. Many Canadians now seem to get the point that residential schools played a formidable role in colonizing Indigenous people by removing children from their homes and families and by breaking both personal and cultural ties. They might also finally realize that their own ignorance about the systemic colonization of Indigenous people on Turtle Island since contact is a failure of mainstream educational systems and other institutions, though to characterize this absence of knowledge as a "failure" implies that it was an oversight, not a deliberate policy of maintaining white dominance.

Today, largely in response to the TRC Report, Canadian educational institutions, from primary schools to universities, are all trying to find ways to "Indigenize." Although this might also be characterized as a "settler move to innocence," to do nothing is no longer an option, especially now that so much information about the residential school system and its insidious outcomes is so readily available. The TRC archives are online and searchable. One entire volume of the TRC Report is dedicated to the (excerpted) testimonies of survivors and is available for download or purchase. Excerpts of survivor testimonies have also been taken from three volumes of the Aboriginal Healing Foundation series and published as an anthology titled *Speaking My Truth*. Numerous websites focus on particular residential schools. The internet is awash with photographs of school buildings, Indigenous children in classrooms, or working—in kitchens, laundries, gardens, carpentry shops, sewing rooms, and so on. There are even photographs of the graves of some of the estimated 6,000 children who died at the schools—died from diseases, accidents, beatings, or suicide. So much information. So much testimony. So much attention. Now.

But before the release of the TRC Report or Downie's multimedia *Secret Path* project, survivors had been telling their stories for years. They told their stories to academics such as historian Celia Haig-Brown, who interviewed survivors of the Kamloops Indian Residential School, to give just one example of academic case studies. They told their stories to the Commissioners of the Royal Commission on Aboriginal Peoples—twenty-five years ago. They told their stories in public venues, as former Chief of the Assembly of First Nations Phil Fontaine did—in 1990. The Assembly of First Nations commissioned its own report on residential schools and published it in 1994 under the title *Breaking the Silence*. And before all of that, and ongoing today, survivors have been telling their stories in works of art, including written memoirs. As Ojibwe critic Jesse Wente points out, "Secret Path is not the first work of art to approach the legacy of residential schools on Turtle Island—but it is the one likely to reach the most people." Downie's privileged social and cultural status ensures that. In fact, following the concert and the subsequent release of *Secret Path*, Downie became a face of Indigenous rights. Candy Palmater writes that in the media coverage of Gord Downie's receipt of the Order of Canada she "was shocked at the number of articles that referred to him as a leader in Indigenous activism." Commenting in an interview, Palmater denies being angry at Downie as an individual, but says in frustration, "No, I'm angry that I live in a country where, still, no one listens until a white man says it." Exactly. Residential school survivors told, wrote, painted, sang, danced their stories; but they went largely unheard.

I turn my attention now to three memoirs published in the 1970s that bear witness to their authors' residential school experiences: Jane Willis' *Geniesh: An Indian Girlhood*, Alice French's *My Name Is Masak,* and Anthony Apakark Thrasher's *Thrasher: Skid Row Eskimo.* But before I discuss these texts in detail, I want to think about why these memoirs were published in that decade. The political climate in the 1970s opened a space for Indigenous activism generally. The civil rights movement, anti–Vietnam War activism, the work of second-wave feminists, the growing awareness of environmental issues all coalesced in this period and the general climate of protest and resistance also led to the formation of Indigenous activist groups like the American Indian

Movement and Red Power. It was the time of the occupation of Wounded Knee. It was the time when Marlon Brando refused to accept an Academy Award in protest over the stereotypical and negative portrayal of Native Americans in Hollywood films. It was also a moment when Indigenous people used the written word to argue for their rights. As Cheryl Suzack comments in her essay in *The History of the Book in Canada*, the infamous "White Paper" of 1969, which sought to eradicate the Indian Act and assimilate Indigenous people into Canadian society, spurred a flurry of publications. Suzack notes that Harold Cardinal, Howard Adams, and Wilfried Pelltiers all published widely read and influential nonfiction books at this time. In 1973, Maria Campbell published her memoir *Halfbreed*, a book that many credit with opening the door to the production of many other works of literature by Indigenous authors. In 1975, Lee Maracle published *Bobbi Lee: Indian Rebel*, which recounts her early life and her involvement with Red Power. The 1970s were, to say the least, heady times for political activism on Turtle Island, and Indigenous writing was making an impact.

The 1970s was also, of course, the decade that followed Canada celebrating its centennial anniversary and, in that euphoric time of nationalist pride, there was a boom in both Canadian writing and Canadian publishing. It was in this period that small presses were influential. These presses were independent operations largely run by part-timers and volunteers. They published established and up-and-coming writers, as well as first-time authors. Coach House Press and House of Anansi Press had been founded in 1965 and 1967 respectively, and many others followed across the country: Breakwater Books, Pottersfield Press, Brick Books, Talonbooks, Borealis, Quarry, Turnstone—and many more. According to George L. Parker, it was during this period that "writers and audiences developed a curiosity about their own part of the world, which inspired a host of memoirs, local histories and literary works that had limited national appeal but enthusiastic local sales. Small presses in every part of the country catered to these needs." David McKnight further notes that small presses were interested in "identity-based narratives" (310), such as memoirs. Lesser-known and now mostly defunct publishers also flourished during the 1970s, and it is these presses that were most likely to publish Indigenous authors, including memoirs that focused on the experiences of those who attended residential schools.

New Press in Toronto published Jane Willis' *Geniesh: An Indian Girlhood* in 1973; Griffin House, also in Toronto, published Anthony Apakark Thrasher's *Thrasher: Skid Row Eskimo* in 1976. Also in 1976, Peguis in Winnipeg published Alice French's *My Name Is Masak*. But who read these books?

And what was their reception? What happened to these books, as well as to their authors? One wonders if they suffered the same fate as Inuit author Mini Aodla Freeman's 1978 memoir *Life Among the Qallunaat*. In the afterword to the republished edition (2015), the editors reveal that "half of the print run was somehow acquired by the Department of Indian and Northern Affairs and kept in storage for up to eight months" (273). Little wonder that people could not read Freeman's memoir; they could not find it in bookstores or libraries. In an interview with the editors published in the same new edition, Freeman speculates that the Department of Indian and Northern Affairs "were afraid [she] might talk badly about residential schools. And remember: at that time, Northern Affairs kept denying, denying about residential schools" (xvi). Memoirs by Indigenous people can make the government look bad. Memoirs about residential school experiences often do.

In the early 1990s, when I was doing my doctoral research at the University of Alberta, I happened upon Jane Willis' memoir *Geniesh: An Indian Girlhood* in the Rutherford Library. This was the book that first opened my eyes to the residential school system and its impact on the Indigenous children who were forced to study, work, and live there. Willis was born on the small island the Cree people of the eastern shores of James Bay in northern Quebec call "jisah-seebee" (Great River). What she calls "the system" (i.e., the government) required her to attend residential school. There were two on the island: one Catholic and one Anglican. As Willis writes, in her typically ironic tone, "Our parents were too terrified by the constant threats of eternal hell and damnation to send their children to the Catholic school" (26). But when the time came, the local Anglican school was full. Although she was told that she could still attend as a day student, Willis—somewhat surprisingly—really wanted to live at a school.

> By Christmas I had already been attending classes for five months at the Anglican school as a day student—a "privilege" whose significance held no meaning for me at the time. I wanted to live at the school and could not understand my family's reaction whenever the subject was brought up. (26)

The following August she registered to live at the St. Philip's Indian and Eskimo Residential School of Fort George, Quebec. Later she did her high school grades and lived at the Shingwuak Indian Residential School in Sault Ste. Marie, Ontario. Why would Willis want to live at a residential school? As a young child, she had romanticized ideas about school; she was excited by the promise of newness; she was keen to learn. She associated the school with privilege, privilege that she felt she deserved. But these ideas were quickly overturned by her actual experiences, which Willis writes about with considerable irony, at times sarcasm, in her memoir.[2]

I wrote a chapter about the book in my doctoral dissertation and later turned that chapter into an article that was published in 1998 in the journal *Canadian Literature*. It was a proud moment for me as a young scholar to have my work appear in that prestigious journal, and I was also proud that I had brought some scholarly attention to a work of Indigenous memoir that was (to put it mildly) somewhat obscure. I recall writing a note to the then-editor hoping that someone, someday would republish *Geniesh*, which had been out of print for years. My work joined a scattered handful of commentaries and analyses.

Willis' memoir is mentioned in some surveys of Indigenous literature, such as Penny Petrone's *Native Literature in Canada: From the Oral Tradition to the Present*. There were also a handful of reviews published in periodicals— well, not quite a handful; I have only found three. Sam McKegney comments on *Geniesh* in the first chapter of his important study of residential school texts as literature—*Magic Weapons*—but does not discuss it at length. As far as I know, only three other critics—Deena Ryhms, Renate Eigenbrod, and Toni Culjak—have written articles solely or in part about this particular memoir. Ryhms and Culjak are concerned with the ambivalence of Willis' mixed white and Cree identity and the tensions exposed in the text between Willis and her maternal Cree relations. Eigenbrod also comments on Willis' rejection of her Indigenous family and her apparent willingness to "embrace assimilation" ("For the Child Taken" 280). *Geniesh* might be the "earliest published residential school memoir" (280) according to Eigenbrod, but its ambivalence about Indigenous land-based identity did not deliver what a reading audience in the 1970s might have expected. Ryhms worries about "[Willis'] combined adherence to and subversion of the dominant values of her institutional context" (120), and Eigenbrod speculates that Willis' *not* supplying "an unambiguous condemnation of colonial authority and a clear distancing from the colonial discourse, may explain the book's lack of success" (281).

Not all memoirs written by Indigenous people about their residential school experience are overtly critical or focused on the neglect, punishment, and abuse that we now know was common. Perhaps this is another reason why memoirs from the 1970s did not and do not receive much attention from critics. Alice French finds many things about the All Saints Anglican residential school at Aklavik to be strange, but she often depicts events and routines in a neutral or even positive light. Food was plain and offerings at mealtimes were repetitive but she does not report feeling hungry or that the food was spoiled. She states matter-of-factly that all students had to work to keep the school running. She even writes about experiences where the children were given treats and when she and her little brother (who was also at the school but kept separate in the boys' wing) felt happy. At Christmastime, for instance, they received special food and gifts. While she was understandably sad that she was not able to go home during the summer—because her father could not come to Aklavik to get them—she comments that the teachers who also remained behind "tried to make our summer pass as pleasantly as possible by taking us on camping trips and picnics during those lonely weeks" (51–52). Much of the memoir is devoted to her life on the land, elements of which she can still access even while at the school, such as taking long walks "in the bush" (42), snaring rabbits on those walks to sell to the school "for 25 cents each" (42), enjoying the return of songbirds in the spring, and berry picking. Nevertheless, the memoir ends with her jubilation at being able to go home for good after seven (of her fourteen) years at the residential school: "It was sad to say goodbye to my friends but at the same time I felt a great sense of relief, like a prisoner whose sentence was finally over. When the door closed behind me and my father I felt like a bird flying home to the vast open tundra" (105). Nothing can replace home and family.

Of course, we cannot know for sure if French is downplaying or even omitting the more negative aspects of her own residential school experiences. Indeed, if we put *My Name Is Masak* beside *Fatty Legs*, a narrative aimed at young adult readers and based on a "true story" about the Catholic residential school at Aklavik, questions emerge. In *Fatty Legs*, Christy Jordan-Fenton and Margaret Pokiak-Fenton narrate Margaret's school years. Like Jane Willis, Margaret initially begged her parents to let her attend the school. But she quickly encounters many of the events that recur in these memoirs and that speak to the harsh treatment the children routinely received. Long hair is cut short, which the children experience as humiliation; she is made to wear ill-fitting, uncomfortable, and inadequate (given the cold in the North) clothing; she is assigned a Christian name and not permitted to speak her language; she is persecuted by a mean nun she names "the Raven" (though there is also a kind nun). The only good thing to come out of her school experience is that she learned how to read. The narrator describes the children being taken away as small birds who are "plucked" from their homes. She is held "prisoner" at the school by the Brothers and Sisters who "were not family; they were like owls and ravens raising wrens" (26). *Fatty Legs* was published recently (2010); those authors who published in the 1970s were perhaps more guarded in their writing for fear that their work would not be well received or that they themselves would get into trouble of some sort. After all, when children told damning stories about what was going on at these schools they were punished or not believed. I doubt, however, that these authors expected their books would so quickly disappear or attract so little public or scholarly attention.

I can offer two other possible explanations as to why residential school memoirs written and published in the 1970s went more or less unnoticed, both by the general public and by academics. One is that the very notion of an Indigenous author was, to some, incredible. Indians did not write. They might *tell* stories; those stories might be recorded, transcribed, and published, but as myths and legends and only through the involvement of (usually white) co-authors or editors. Reflecting on her early years touring with her memoir *Bobbi Lee: Indian Rebel* (first published in 1975), Lee Maracle remarks that one question she was often asked after a reading was "Who wrote it for you?" (*My Conversations* 14). Given Maracle's current stature as an author, educator, performer, orator, and activist, this question seems absurd;[3] however, it speaks to the general assumption during that period that Indigenous people were not capable of writing books.

A second possible explanation is the general undervaluing of memoir as a genre. This bias is evident in Petrone's 1990 survey, when she implies that Indigenous writers may begin with memoir or autobiography but then mature into authors who go on to write more sophisticated works, i.e. novels. Memoirs and other written works by Indigenous authors were usually shelved in the anthropology section, not the literature section, of libraries, as was (and is) *Geniesh*. That is, these books were assumed to have historical and sociological interest but were not considered to be works of art. Those of us who situate our scholarship in life writing studies are all too familiar with that particular prejudice.

It is gratifying to see that in this century (Culjak 2001; Ryhms 2003; Eigenbrod 2012) Jane Willis' residential school memoir has received some critical attention. *Geniesh* remains, however, out of print. Access to works of Indigenous literature, including autobiographical works, is an ongoing problem—even works published later than the period under discussion here. How do we bring these important works of life writing into the corpus of Indigenous literature? How can we teach these books if students cannot buy them?

The situation is changing. New works by both established and emerging Indigenous authors are published at an unprecedented rate, and these contemporary works are reaching wide audiences, winning awards, becoming book club picks, and appearing on school and university curricula. The current flood of new literary works by Indigenous authors partly explains why memoirs are also proliferating. Yet there is still a need to bring back earlier texts in new editions and with appropriate editing and contextualization. Through the work of both settler and Indigenous scholars, early to mid-century works of fiction and nonfiction that have long been out of print are now being rereleased. The University of Manitoba's First Voices, First Texts series is exemplary in this respect.[4] Under the general editorship of Warren Cariou, the series republishes early works of Indigenous literature that have been out of print for years. Crucially, the texts are "presented with particular sensitivity toward Indigenous ethics, traditions, and contemporary realities. The editors strive to indigenize the editing process by involving communities, by respecting traditional protocols, and by providing critical introductions that give readers new insights into the cultural contexts of these unjustly neglected classics."[5] To date the series has republished four early works of Indigenous literature. All four are works that are entirely or substantially based on their authors' personal experiences: *Devil in Deerskins: My Life with Grey Owl*, by Anahareo; *Indians Don't Cry: Gaawiin Mawisiiwag Anishinaabeg*, by George Kenny; *Life Among the Qallunaat*, by Mini Aodla Freeman; and *From the Tundra to the Trenches*, by Eddy Weetaltuk.

George Kenny's *Indians Don't Cry: Gaawiin Mawisiiwag Anishinaabeg* is a collection of stories and poems, first collected and published in 1977 and later republished in an expanded edition in 1982. In her afterword to the new edition, Renate Eigenbrod draws attention to the title story, "Indians Don't Cry," as a residential school story. In that narrative, the father looks at the small dot in the sky that is the airplane transporting his children to Pelican Lake Indian Residential School. Kenny himself attended that school but, according to Eigenbrod, did not speak or write of that time until 2012 when "he went through the Individual Assessment Process as part of the Indian Residential Schools Settlement Agreement." She refers to an "unpublished memoir," which one hopes will join the present and expanding corpus of residential school memoirs.

The story of another Inuit autobiography, first published in 1976, again marks this change in editorial protocols but also reveals the challenges of bringing classic works of Indigenous memoir back into print. Anthony Apakark Thrasher's *Thrasher: Skid Row Eskimo* is being re-edited by Keavy Martin and Sam McKegney for eventual republication in the First Voices, First Texts series. However, the project is currently on hold. Martin and

McKegney were working with Thrasher's brother, Tommy Thrasher, in Tuk-toyaktuk and they had "a very effective editing arrangement worked out, based on our discussions of the work, its intended audiences, and its com-plexities." But then Tommy died, and although "other family members were happy for the project to proceed under Tommy's guidance, given his esteem within the family, there were more questions raised after his passing" (per-sonal email correspondence with McKegney). So the editors have, at least for the moment, stopped their work.

Thrasher wrote his life story while in prison at the urging of his law-yer. What was "literally thousands of scraps of paper" (viii) was eventually transcribed, edited, and published. The editors of the first edition, Gerard Deagle and Alan Mettrick, were both journalists who admitted, "As repor-ters, and as whites, we were skeptical often" (ix). Whatever other editorial decisions they made are not revealed in the text itself. McKegney and Mar-tin are working from the original typescript, which McKegney obtained from Thrasher's lawyer. If the project proceeds, and always in collaboration with Thrasher's family, they plan to reinsert "[Thrasher's] extensive critical and artistic commentary on the socio-cultural circumstances that accounted for [the] events" ("Inuvialuit" 65) that Deagle and Mettrick focused on, which tend to be the usual harrowing stories of addiction, poverty, homelessness, cultural alienation, and violence. McKegney and Martin remark in an arti-cle about their process that "Deagle and Mettrick were constrained in their editing choices during a period when there was scarcely a market for Inuit autobiography at all" ("Inuvialuit" 65). In his book *Magic Weapons*, in which he devotes a lengthy chapter to Thrasher's work, McKegney warns that *Skid Row Eskimo*'s "political effects must be weighed in relation to its] poor pub-lication record—having been out of print since the 1970s—and its mediocre distribution among northern peoples" (62). When there is attention at all, it comes from a small group of academics who are primarily interested in such memoirs as ethnographic accounts and who actually prefer stories that focus solely on northern experience (76).

Only a small portion of Thrasher's autobiography is devoted to his time at residential school, but it is a significant feature of the life narrative because it provides crucial context as to how Thrasher ended up on skid row. As with all residential schools, the dominant ideology was "to kill the Indian to save the man"; however, in the Arctic, there was also an assumption that Inuit— an Indigenous group that, because of their isolation, were among the last to feel the force of government-imposed policies of assimilation—were going to have to change and adapt to southern ways very quickly. This meant forced relocations of entire communities, the deliberate attempt to destroy a subsistence economy based on harvesting and hunting (by, for example, the RCMP slaughtering hundreds of sled dogs), and the rapid imposition of Christianity, in which the church-run residential schools played a huge role. Thrasher was six when he was first sent to school; in terms of his culture, he was almost old enough to go on his first hunt. But he becomes, instead, "a Grade 1 captive" (12) put in the "baby class." All he wants to do is become a good hunter— which is what it means to be a man in traditional Inuit culture—but instead he is made to feel dumb: "I was closer to wildlife than I was to the three R's," he writes (30). And although he goes on to write a book, he never succeeds in academic terms, let alone socio-economic ones. Nevertheless, I concur with McKegney here: "*Skid Row Eskimo* remains an enormously important (albeit sadly neglected) text because it both argues against colonial imposition and embodies the effects of such imposition with the texture of the narrative" (*Magic* 98).

Old books can get new lives, and through re-editing and re-publication can become a vital part of the thriving corpus of Indigenous literature in Canada. A large federally funded research project called *The People and the Text: Indigenous Writing in Northern North America to 1992* is currently doing such work. A collaboration of scholars and graduate students led by Cree-Métis scholar Deanna Reder, *The People and the Text* aims to bring back into view authors and texts that have been obscured. Researchers are "collecting and studying one of the most neglected literary archives in English Canada, an archive neglected because settlers used literature to consolidate a narrative of Canada starring the British-descended resulting in university curricula that featured the British canon."[6] Moreover, the archiving, editing, and republishing processes are informed by Indigenous protocols and follow Indigenous methods of knowledge production. Crucially, this new way of doing literary scholarship is responsible to the communities from which the literature emerges and to whom it belongs. As noted on their website, the researchers are aware that literary criticism and Indigenous research methods have not and do not necessarily inform one another. Their work will "bridge that gap" by consulting with communities and being accountable to them. Not only will forgotten texts see new light; new readers and scholars will learn Indigenous ways of reading and understanding them. I anticipate with enthusiasm that some of these texts will be memoirs.

The residential school memoirs that were published in the 1970s are complicated texts, often edited by non-Indigenous editors and displaying ambivalent subjects whose identities are shaped both by their early lives with their families in their communities and by colonial oppression. Sometimes their very tone is difficult to understand, especially given what we know now about what went on at residential schools. And yet the genre of the memoir does something that excerpted testimonies or broad case studies cannot; it provides the author with a space for telling his or her story in his or her own words. Authors (not just editors) make choices. The writing strategies and narrative tones of these works are not general; they are specific. Each text has a particular narrative quality, which an informed reader, a careful reader can interpret. More than ethnographic accounts, memoirs convey what Deborah Britzman (in another context) terms "difficult knowledge" (qtd. in Kadar 223). Here they convey "difficult knowledge" about residential schools— what they were like as institutions, but more importantly what it was like to be confined in them. As Marlene Kadar astutely remarks, "Memory registers what it felt like, not exactly what it was like" (223). While there is ample historical evidence that tells the story of residential schools, memoirs—or *life telling* in whatever genre—provide an emotional context that shapes our responses to and interpretation of the experiences of Indigenous people whose lives and worlds were marked by them.

While it might seem that more non-Indigenous Canadians are now aware of and learning more about the Indian residential school system and its continuing legacies of survivor and intergenerational trauma, we cannot be complacent. The TRC did enormously important work. The TRC Report is available for anyone to read. New memoirs about residential school experiences are being published today, as is the case with Augie Merasty's "national bestseller" *The Education of Augie Merasty* and Chief Bev Sellars' *They Called Me Number One*, which has won several awards. Anthologies of survivor testimonies such as *Speaking My Truth* have been published recently. Graphic novels and children's books have dealt with the topic: David Alexander Robertson's *Sugar Falls* is one such graphic book aimed at high school children, as is *Fatty Legs*, a young adult illustrated work previously mentioned. One hopes that through careful reading of such books, present and subsequent generations of Canadians will no longer be able to say that they did not know what was going on in those schools and how a colonial ideology shaped them. And yet it is still possible today for a prominent white Canadian—in this case a senator and a (now former) member of the Senate Committee on Aboriginal Peoples—to ignore the truth willfully about residential schools and the damage they did and continue to do to Indigenous people. When Conservative Senator Lynn Beyak says publicly, "I speak partly for the record, but mostly in memory of the kindly and well-intentioned men and women and their descendants—perhaps some of us here in this chamber—whose remarkable works, good deeds and historical tales in the residential schools go unacknowledged for the most part and are overshadowed by negative reports" (qtd. in Kirkup), then we know that our work as Canadians and as critics is not yet done. And this is true despite Gord Downie's confidence in Prime Minister Trudeau's government. Personal accounts of residential schools—whether published yesterday or forty or fifty years ago—matter. They mattered then. They matter now.

NOTES

1 See http://secretpath.ca/#Donate.
2 See Warley for a detailed analysis of Willis' use of irony and sarcasm in her memoir.
3 In 2017, Maracle received the Order of Canada for her work.
4 See https://uofmpress.ca/books/category/first-voices-first-texts.
5 This information about the First Voices, First Texts series is presented on the page following the title page of each book.
6 See https://thepeopleandthetext.ca/about.

Still Here

Kim Anderson (Metis) and Rene Meshake (Anishinaabe)

When it comes to Native men, the stories Canada likes to tell are based in negative stereotypes that link us to violence and crime. But where are the stories we know of fathers, uncles, grandpas, sons or nephews; where is the humour, the respect, the kinship, the ingenuity?

—Robert Alexander Innes[1]

★ ★ ★

Morning News (Kim)

"Canada is a shithole racist country." It's February 10, 2018, and I have just woken up to this comment on Facebook along with a flood of other posts related to the acquittal of Gerald Stanley, a white prairie farmer who shot and killed a young Cree man on August 9, 2016. The youth, Colten Boushie, had pulled into Stanley's farm with a few friends after having lost a tire on their SUV, and Stanley, so the story goes, "accidentally" shot the sleeping Boushie in the back of the head. Boushie died immediately, and now, eighteen months later, an all-white jury has set Stanley free.

As I write, a family is deeply grieving, and Indian country is, once again, raging. Many of us are wondering if this story will ever change.

★ ★ ★

Overtold Stories of Canada (Kim)

What are the stories of Native men in Canada, and how can we re-story to make change?

As Robert Innes has indicated, Canada doesn't "know" much more about Native men than what was re-storied in the Boushie tragedy. Innes, an Indigenous studies professor and member of Cowessess First Nation, has written about how Native men are stereotyped as dangerous and violent, and how this increases the likelihood that they will be subject to violence themselves. Within this racist and gendered story logic, Stanley acted out of fear for his property and his wife. Much of the social media around the homicide recycled a well-worn narrative of white victimry in the face of the savage (MacDougall), going so far as to engage in rhetoric around immunity for those (white subjects) who shoot to "protect their property," akin to a white knight protecting his "castle" (Starblanket and Hunt).

Settler nationalism is built on such recurring narratives, with one of the most ubiquitous pertaining to the "savage Indian"—the masculine racialized menace on the frontier that is met with violent colonial heroicism.[2] The story of Canada as a "shithole racist country" for Native men has a much smaller audience. Canada knows even fewer stories about—and from—the theorists, philosophers, storytellers, and artists among our men; men like my friend and teacher Rene Meshake. We need to tell these stories, not only because they offer a different vision of who Native men are, but because they offer a different vision of the type of society we might become in this project called Canada.

Perhaps today is a day to share one such story.

* * *

Not Guilty (Rene)

One time the court workers needed a translator, and so they came to find me in the bar. There was a visitor on trial; lots of times there were these old guys from outside our community and they would get charged with hunting out of season.

My grandmother had always taught me to treat outsiders with respect and think of them as Biwide. Biwide is a visitor, and there's a VIP treatment that goes with that. Biwide is just passing through. You give him food, lodgings, respect. But they were bringing me to court to ask if he was "guilty" or "not guilty."

As I was walking along, I started thinking about how I didn't know if he did it or not, so how was I going to ask the question? I was also really uncomfortable because he was Biwide from the north, and my grandmother had taught me that many of these northern elders had powerful medicines.

At the time, we had this habit in our community where a phrase would go around for a while. So, there was this expression going around: "Andjiidana gitodem," which means, "Did you do it as a prank?" And that's what went through my head when the court workers came, because I didn't know how to translate, "Do you plead guilty or not guilty?"

I kept thinking about this thing, "Andjiidana gitodem." It also implies "did you fake your dodem?" It was funny but it wasn't funny, because I knew about dodem, or clans, and their responsibilities. It has to do with whether you did it on purpose—but it's not that. "Did you do it as a prank" is the closest. And there's that word *dodem*: "Did you dishonour your dodem?" Because, whatever you do in our culture in terms of your behaviour, you're honouring your dodem. It's self-governing. It gives you a conscience.

So, the teachings, to me, have a way of influencing your behaviour. And how you behave is your dodem. When people ask you "What do you do"?— dodem is what do you do. Anish endodamaan is "What are you doing?" You're asking what is your dodem. And if it's me, I'll tell you I'm from the Ming clan. I teach.

So, then there's the judge; if he says yes to this white man, then he's guilty. But that's another worldview. So, this guilty thing—we don't know how to say that.

I soon realized that by asking my question (Did you do it as a prank?), the person couldn't win. If he said "Yes," it meant that it was just a prank to him. But the court would take it as "Yes, I am guilty." But if he answered "No," the court would understand it as "No, not guilty." But, in my mind, the "No" would mean that he wasn't joking; that he knew he was dishonouring his dodem and doing wrong.

So, I didn't go. In any case, I was still drunk when I got there. I walked away. I had to respect this old guy, who was Biwide to me. I had enough Grandmother in me to say "No, don't do it."

* * *

Still Here. (Kim)

If Canada were to listen to Native men's stories, what might it learn? That, whether it is the tragic loss of a young Native man who made the mistake of going onto a white man's property—or the prosecution of an old Native man for hunting "out of season"—Canada, with all her "property," fear, hostility, and entitlement offers little space for Native men in their own homelands. That a "drunken Indian" summoned from a bar in Thunder Bay has more sense of responsibility and ethics than an all-white jury in a settler court of law. That Indigenous systems of justice, honour, self-regulation, and conscience live on through our languages, clan systems, grandmothers' teachings, and practices of basic decency about how to treat a stranger when they arrive in your territory. That these culture-based practices are what make up our men.

For today, I am keenly aware that people are mourning, fed up with talk of reconciliation. We worry about the violence. But one thing is for sure: in spite of all the threats and the losses, we are still here, Canada. And we will keep telling—until, one day, our stories will shape the narrative.

★ ★ ★

Still Here (Rene)

Nidjaaniss
Dangerous!

It's alright if we make
arts and crafts.
It's not alright if we partake
when songend da mowin staffs
self-determination.

The power of spirit,
Manidoo wisi win.
Steep in the gift,
too deep to keep in
a reservation.

Nidjaaniss
Dangerous!

Mother our blood and bone.
Gather to light
the sober wiing gashk koon.
Sweet grass bright
with transformation.

Reconciliation then
will see the first glint
of bon nend da mowin,
fire and flint.

Life is sincere
on the Ojibwe camp, and oh!
We are still here!
Awa'si aginz zo!

NOTES

1 Robert Alexander Innes, public lecture on "Indigenous Men and Masculinities,"
 Linnaeus University, Växjö, Sweden, Feb. 27, 2017.

2 See Berkhofer; Francis; McKegney, "Warriors"; Starblanket and Hunt.

Works Cited

Abbott, Brett. *Engaged Observers: Documentary Photography Since the Sixties*. Getty Publications, 2010.

Aboriginal Healing Foundation. 2017, http://www.ahf.ca/. Accessed 30 July 2019.

———. *Speaking My Truth: Reflections on Reconciliation and Residential School*. Selected by Shelagh Rogers, Mike DeGangé, Jonathan Dewar, and Glen Lowry, AHF, 2012.

Adese, Jennifer. "The New People: Reading for Peoplehood in Métis Literature." *Studies in American Indian Literature*, vol. 28, no. 4, 2016, pp. 53–79.

Adorno, Theodor W. *Aesthetic Theory*. Translated by C. Lenhardt, Routledge and Kegan Paul, 1984.

Aguila-Way, Tania. "Seed Activism, Global Environmental Justice, and Avant-Garde Aesthetics in Annabel Soutar's Seeds." *Studies in Canadian Literature / Études en littérature canadienne*, vol. 43, no. 1, Nov. 2018, pp. 5–25.

Ahenakew, Edward. *Black Hawk*. Unpublished manuscript, to be released by the Ahenakew family and specifically grandniece Heather Hodgson.

———. *Voices of the Plains Cree*. Edited by Ruth M. Buck, Canadian Plains Research Centre, 1973.

Ahmed, Sara. "A Phenomenology of Whiteness." *Feminist Theory*, vol. 8, no. 2, 2007, pp. 149–68.

———. *The Promise of Happiness*. Duke UP, 2010.

Akenson, Donald Harmon. "Great European Migration and Indigenous Populations." *Irish and Scottish Encounters with Indigenous Peoples: Canada, the United States, New Zealand and Australia*, edited by Graeme Morton and David A. Wilson, McGill-Queen's UP, 2013, pp. 22–48.

Alfoldy, Sandra. *Theory and Craft: A Case Study of the Kootenay Christmas Faire.* Concordia U, 1997.

———. Correspondence. 2 Jan. 2018.

———. Correspondence with Mary Ann Steggles. 18 Mar. 2007.

———. *Crafting Identity: The Development of Professional Fine Craft in Canada.* McGill-Queen's UP, 2005.

Andersen, Chris. *"Métis": Race, Recognition and the Struggle for Indigenous Peoplehood.* UBC P, 2015.

———. "More Than the Sum of Our Rebellions: Métis Histories Beyond Batoche." *Ethnohistory,* vol. 61, no. 4, Fall 2014, pp. 619–33.

Anderson, Benedict. *National Imagined Communities: Reflections on the Origin and Spread of Nationalism.* Verso, 1993.

Andrew-Gee, Eric. "The Making of Joseph Boyden." *The Globe and Mail,* 4 Aug. 2017, https://www.theglobeandmail.com/arts/books-and-media/joseph-boyden/article35881215/. Accessed 17 June 2020.

Andrews, Jennifer. "Taking Stock of Atlantic Canada's Role in World War I: An Interview with American Novelist P.S. Duffy." *Canadian Review of American Studies,* vol. 48, no. 1, 2018, pp. 144–61.

Ann Savage Fonds. Library and Archives Canada, Ottawa.

Anthony, Geraldine. *John Coulter.* Twayne, 1976.

Antkowiak, Thomas M. "Remedial Approaches to Human Rights Violations: The Inter-American Court of Human Rights and Beyond." *Columbia Journal of Transnational Law,* vol. 46, 2007–8, pp. 351–419.

Armstrong, Jeannette. *Slash.* 1985. Theytus, 2007.

Art Gallery of Ontario. *Group of Seven.* Art Gallery of Toronto, 1920.

Assembly of First Nations. *Breaking the Silence: An Interpretive Study of Residential School Impact and Healing as Illustrated by the Stories of First Nation Individuals.* Assembly of First Nations, 1994.

Atwood, Margaret. "The Writers' Union of Canada." *The Canadian Encyclopedia Online,* 2 July 2006, http://www.thecanadianencyclopedia.ca/en/article/writers-union-of-canada/. Accessed 9 Dec. 2015.

Audley, Paul. Letter to Anna Porter and copy to Glenn Witmer and Don Roper. 31 Aug. 1973. McClelland and Stewart Ltd. Fonds, William Ready Division of Archives and Research Collections, McMaster University Library, box 2CA84.

———. Letter to Anna Porter. 28 Sept. 1973. McClelland and Stewart Ltd. Fonds, William Ready Division of Archives and Research Collections, McMaster University Library, box 2CA84.

Austin, J.L. *How to Do Things with Words: The William James Lectures.* Edited by J.O. Urmson and Marina Sbisà, Clarendon P, 1962.

Authers, Benjamin, Maïté Snauwaert, and Danile Laforest. *Inhabiting Memory in Canadian Literature / Habiter la mémoire dans la littérature canadienne*. U of Alberta P, 2017.

Avon, Susan. "The Beaver Hall Group and Its Place in the Montreal Art Milieu and the Nationalist Network." 1994. Concordia U, MA thesis, Art History.

A.Y. Jackson Fonds. National Gallery of Canada, Ottawa.

Banks, Catherine. *It Is Solved by Walking*. Playwrights Canada, 2012.

Banks, R.A., and P. Marson. *Drama and Theatre Arts*. Hodder & Stoughton, 2004.

Barad, Karen. "On Touching—the Inhuman That Therefore I Am." *Differences*, vol. 23, no. 3, 2012, pp. 206–23.

Barerra, Jorge. "Author Joseph Boyden's Shape-Shifting Indigenous Identity." *APTN*, 23 Dec. 2016, http://aptnnews.ca/2016/12/23/author-joseph-boydens-shape -shifting-indigenous-identity/. Accessed 17 June 2020.

Barthes, Roland. *Camera Lucida: Reflections on Photography*. Translated by Richard Howard, Hill and Wang, 1981.

Batachayra, Sheila. "Racism, 'Girl Violence' and the Murder of Reena Virk." *Girls' Violence: Myths and Realities*, edited by Carolyn Alder and Anne Worrall, SUNY P, 2004.

Batchen, Geoffrey. "Beyond Recognition? Writing Photography's National Histories." Global Photography and Its Histories, symposium organized by Rutgers, State U of New Jersey, New Brunswick, 8 Feb. 2011. In "Summaries of Scholarly Symposia." *Trans Asia Photography Review*, vol. 1, no. 2, Spring 2011, https://quod .lib.umich.edu/t/tap/7977573.0001.215/--summaries-of-scholarly-symposia -12?trgt=div1_02;view=fulltext. Accessed 8 Dec. 2017.

———. *Forget Me Not: Photography and Remembrance*. Van Gogh Museum and Princeton Architectural P, 2004.

Benson, E., and William Toye, editors. *Oxford Companion to Canadian Literature*. Oxford UP, 1997.

Bentley, D.M.R. Introduction. *The Huron Chief*, by Adam Kidd, www.canadianpoetry .ca/longpoems/huron/introduction.htm. Accessed 12 Feb. 2018.

Berkhofer, Robert F. *The White Man's Indian: Images of the American Indian from Columbus to the Present*. Vantage Books, 2011.

Berlant, Lauren. *The Anatomy of National Fantasy: Hawthorne, Utopia, and Everyday Life*. U of Chicago P, 1991.

———. *Cruel Optimism*. Duke UP, 2011.

———. *The Queen of America Goes to Washington City: Essays on Sex and Citizenship*. Duke UP, 1997.

Berry, David. Letter to Jack McClelland. 23 Nov. 1972. McClelland and Stewart Ltd. Fonds, William Ready Division of Archives and Research Collections, McMaster University Library, box 2CA84.

———. Letter to June Stifle. 15 Jan. 1972. McClelland and Stewart Ltd. Fonds, William Ready Division of Archives and Research Collections, McMaster University Library, box 2CA84.

———. Letter to June Stifle. 12 Jan. 1973. McClelland and Stewart Ltd. Fonds, William Ready Division of Archives and Research Collections, McMaster University Library, box 2CA84.

Besner, Neil. "Thomas D'Arcy McGee." *Canadian Writers Before 1890*, edited by William H. New, *Dictionary of Literary Biography*, vol. 99, Gale, 1990, pp. 234–40, http://www.gale.com. Accessed 20 Apr. 2018.

Blackman, Margaret B. "Studio Indians: Cartes de visite of Native People in British Columbia, 1862–1872." *Archivaria*, vol. 21, Winter 1985–86, pp. 68–86.

Blauvelt, Andrew. *Hippie Modernism: The Struggle for Utopia*. Walker Art Center, 2016.

Bodnar, John. *Remaking America: Public Memory, Commemoration, and Patriotism in the Twentieth Century*. Princeton UP, 1993.

Bonspiel, Steve. "Canada's 150-Year Celebration Doesn't Fly Here." *CBC News*, 25 Feb. 2017, https://www.cbc.ca/news/indigenous/canada-s-150-year-celebration-doesn-t-fly-here-1.3992457. Accessed 1 Sept. 2018.

Boyden, Joseph. *Louis Riel and Gabriel Dumont*. Penguin Canada, 2010.

Braidotti, Rosi. "The Ethics of Becoming Imperceptible." *Deleuze and Philosophy*, edited by Constantin Boundas, Edinburgh UP, 2006, pp. 133–59.

Braunstein, Peter, and Michael Doyle, editors. *Imagine Nation: The American Counterculture of the 1960s and 1970s*. Routledge, 2002.

Braz, Albert. *The False Traitor: Louis Riel in Canadian Culture*. U of Toronto P, 2003.

Briesmaster, Allan, and Steven Michael Berzensky, editors. *Crossing the Line: Poets Who Came to Canada in the Vietnam Era*. Seraphim Editions, 2008.

Brockes, Emma. "Me Too founder Tarana Burke: 'You have to use your privilege to serve other people.'" *The Guardian*, 15 Jan. 2018, https://www.theguardian.com/world/2018/jan/15/me-too-founder-tarana-burke-women-sexual-assault. Accessed 17 June 2020.

Bruyneel, Kevin. "Exiled, Executed, Exalted: Louis Riel, *Homo Sacer* and the Production of Canadian Sovereignty." *Canadian Journal of Political Science*, vol. 43, no. 3, 2010, pp. 711–32.

Burke, Peter. *Eyewitnessing: The Uses of Images as Historical Evidence*. Cornell UP, 2002.

Burns, Robin B. "Thomas D'Arcy McGee." *Dictionary of Canadian Biography*, 1976, www.biographi.ca/en/bio/mcgee_thomas_d_arcy_9E.html. Accessed 20 Apr. 2018.

Burns, Robin, and Niko Block. "Thomas D'Arcy McGee." *Canadian Encyclopedia*, 22 Apr. 2013, www.thecanadianencyclopedia.ca/en/article/thomas-darcy-mcgee. Accessed 23 Sept. 2018.

Buss, Helen M. Introduction. *Working in Women's Archives: Researching Women's Private Literature and Archival Documents.* Wilfrid Laurier UP, 2001, pp. 1–6.

Butler, Judith. *Undoing Gender.* Routledge, 2004.

Caldwell, Lynn, and Darryl Leroux. "The Settler-Colonial Imagination: Comparing Commemoration in Saskatchewan and in Quebec." *Memory Studies,* vol. 12, no. 4, 2019, pp. 451–64.

Cameron, Silver Donald. *The Prophet at Tantramar.* Playwrights Atlantic Resources Centre Script Library, http://www.playwrightsatlantic.ca/library/the-prophet-of-tantramar.

———. "Trotsky in Amherst (Canadian Geographic, 1988)." https://www.silver donaldcameron.ca/articles/trotsky-in-amherst-canadian-geographic-1988/.

Campbell, Glen. Introduction. *Selected Poetry of Louis Riel,* Exile Editions, 1983, pp. 9–12.

Campbell, Maria. *Halfbreed.* McClelland & Stewart, 1973.

———. "Halfbreed Woman." Circa 1972. McClelland and Stewart Ltd. Fonds, William Ready Division of Archives and Research Collections, McMaster University Library, Series X, Manuscript Inventory.

———. "Re: Research after Dublin." Received by Deanna Reder and Alix Shield, 20 Feb. 2018.

Campbell, Wanda. "Strange Plantings: Robert Kroetsch's *Seed Catalogue.*" *Studies in Canadian Literature,* vol. 21, no. 1, 1996, pp. 17–36.

Canada. *House of Commons Debates.* Queen's Printer, 1988.

"Canada 150." *Government of Canada,* 22 Feb. 2018, https://www.canada.ca/en/canadian-heritage/services/anniversaries-significance/canada-150.html. Accessed 17 June 2020.

Cardinelli, Wayne. Personal interview. 21 Sept. 2017.

Carleton, Sean. "Confronting the Secret Path and the Legacy of Residential Schools." *Active History,* 26 Oct. 2016, http://activehistory.ca/2016/10/confronting-the-secret-path-and-the-legacy-of-residential-schools/. Accessed 5 Apr. 2018.

Carr, Diane. Personal interview. 7 Aug. 2015.

Caruth, Cathy. *Unclaimed Experience: Trauma, Narrative, History.* Johns Hopkins UP, 2016.

Cassils. *Cuts: A Traditional Sculpture.* 2011, https://www.cassils.net/cassils-artwork-cuts. Accessed 19 Oct. 2020.

———. *The Powers That Be.* Los Angeles, 2015, http://cassils.net/portfolio/powers-that-be/. Accessed 2 Feb. 2018.

———. *Tiresias.* 2010–13, https://www.cassils.net/cassils-artwork-tiresias. Accessed 19 Oct. 2020.

Chakraborty, Chandrima, Amber Dean, and Angela Failler *Remembering Air India: The Art of Public Mourning.* U of Alberta P, 2017.

Chare, Nicholas, and Ika Willis. "Introduction: Trans-: Across/Beyond." *Parallax*, vol. 22, no. 3, 2016, pp. 267–89.

Chinn, Sarah, and Anna Mae Duane, editors. *Child. Women's Studies Quarterly*, no. 43, 2015, pp. 1–2.

Choquette, Robert. *Canada's Religions: An Historical Introduction.* U of Ottawa P, 2004.

Chrisjohn, Roland, Andrea Bear Nicholas, Karen Stote, James Craven (Omahkokiaayo i'poyi), Tanya Wasacase, Pierre Loiselle, and Andrea O. Smith. "An Historic Non-Apology, Completely and Utterly Not Accepted." *Marxmail.org*, 2008, http://www.marxmail.org/ApologyNotAccepted.htm. Accessed 17 June 2020.

Ciarlo, David. *Advertising Empire: Race and Visual Culture in Imperial Germany.* Harvard UP, 2011.

Clarence Gagnon Fonds. McCord Museum, Montreal.

Clarke, George Elliott. *Beatrice Chancy.* Polestar, 1999.

———. "*Beatrice Chancy*: A Libretto in Four Acts." *Canadian Theatre Review*, no. 96, 1998, pp. 62–77.

———. "Embracing Beatrice Chancy." *Performing Adaptations: Essays and Conversations on the Theory and Practice*, edited by Michelle MacArthur, Lydia Wilkinson, and Keren Zaiontz, Cambridge Scholars, 2009, pp. 223–26.

Clarke, Margaret. "Gertrude and Ophelia: A Play." 1987. *Canadian Adaptations of Shakespeare Project*, edited by Daniel Fischlin, U of Guelph, 2004.

Coates, Colin M. *Canadian Countercultures and the Environment. Canadian History and Environment Series*, no. 4. U of Calgary P, 2016.

Cobb, Jasmine Nichole. *Picturing Freedom: Remaking Black Visuality in the Early Nineteenth Century.* New York UP, 2015.

Cole, Douglas. "Artists, Patrons and Public: An Enquiry into the Success of the Group of Seven." *Journal of Canadian Studies*, vol. 13, no. 2, Summer 1978, pp. 69–78.

Coleman, Daniel. *White Civility: The Literary Project of English Canada.* U of Toronto P, 2008.

Collins, J.E. *The Story of Louis Riel: The Rebel Chief.* Rose, 1885.

———. *Thomas Scott's Execution.* Edited by David Long. Kindle edition, 2015.

"Company History." *McKenzie Seeds*, 10 July 2009, http://mckenzieseeds.com/company-history/. Accessed 17 June 2020.

Compton, Anne. "Standing Your Ground: George Elliott Clarke in Conversation." *Studies in Canadian Literature*, vol. 23. no. 2, 1998, pp. 134–64.

"A Conversation with Ruth Ozeki." 8 March 2018, http://www.penguinrandom houseaudio.com/discussion-guide/312488/a-tale-for-the-time-being/. Accessed 17 June 2020.

Coulson, Ray. Transcript of a public lecture about the Amherst internment camp given to the Amherst Rotary Club, undated, pp. 1–5.

Coulthard, Glen. *Red Skin, White Masks: Rejecting the Colonial Politics of Recognition.* U of Minnesota P, 2014.

Coulter, John. *Riel, a Play in Two Parts.* Ryerson P, 1962.

———. *The Crime of Louis Riel.* Theatre Communications Group, Toronto, 1977.

———. *The Trial of Louis Riel.* Oberon, 1968.

Coyle, Jim. "Canada 150: When a Man with an Eagle Feather Thwarted the High and the Mighty." *Toronto Star,* 27 May 2017, https://www.thestar.com/news/insight/2017/05/27/canada-150-when-a-man-with-an-eagle-feather-thwarted-the-high-and-mighty.html. Accessed 17 June 2020.

Coyote, Ivan. *Tomboy Survival Guide.* Arsenal Pulp Press, 2016.

Coyote, Ivan, and Rae Spoon. *You Are Here.* Washboard Records, 2007.

Craig, Layne. *When Sex Changed: Birth Control Politics and Literature between the World Wars.* Rutgers UP, 2013.

"The Craig Dobbin Chair in Canadian Studies and the UCD Centre for Canadian Studies Present: Untold Stories of the Past 150 Years. 28–30 April 2017." *UCD College of Arts and Humanities,* https://www.ucd.ie/artshumanities/newsand events/events/untoldstories/. Accessed 17 June 2020.

Culjak, Toni. "Searching for a Place in Between: The Autobiographies of Three Canadian Métis Women." *The American Review of Canadian Studies,* vol. 3, no. 1, 2001, pp. 137–57.

Cumberland County Museum. "The Amherst Prisoner of War Internment Camp, 1915–1919."

Cumming, Ed. "This Much I Know: Emma Donoghue." *The Guardian,* 7 May 2016, http://www.theguardian.com/lifeandstyle/2016/may/07/emma-donoghue -this-much-i-know. Accessed 17 June 2020.

Cupido, Robert. "Public Commemoration and Ethnocultural Assertion: Winnipeg Celebrates the Diamond Jubilee of Confederation." *Urban History Review,* vol. 38, no. 2, Spring 2010, pp. 64–74.

Cuthand, Stan. "On Nelson's Text." *Orders of the Dreamed: George Nelson on Cree and Northern Ojibwa Religion and Myth,* 1823, edited by Jennifer S.H. Brown and Robert Brightman, Minnesota Historical Society P, 1988, pp. 189–98.

Cvetkovich, Ann. "9-1-1 Every Day." *Signs: A Journal of Women in Culture and Society,* vol. 28, no. 1, 2002, http://www.journals.uchicago.edu/doi/pdfplus/10.1086/ 341104. Accessed 17 June 2020.

———. "In the Archive of Lesbian Feelings." *An Archive of Lesbian Feelings: Trauma, Sexuality, and Lesbian Public Cultures.* Duke UP, 2003, pp. 239–71.

Da Costa, Beatriz, and Kavita Philip, editors. *Tactical Biopolitics: Art, Activism, and Technoscience*. MIT P, 2010.

Daschuk, Peter. *Clearing the Plains: Disease, Politics of Starvation and the Loss of Aboriginal Life*. U of Regina P, 2013.

David, Emmanuel. "The Art of Trans Politics." *Contexts*, vol. 17, no. 1, Feb. 2018, pp. 82–85.

Dean, Tim. "The Antisocial Homosexual." PMLA, no. 121, 2006, pp. 826–28.

"Delivery Required by September 26th," Re-print Purchase Order for "Half Breed," Alger Press Limited. August/September 1973? McClelland and Stewart Ltd. Fonds, William Ready Division of Archives and Research Collections, McMaster University Library, box 2CA84.

Deloria Jr., Vine. "American Fantasy." *The Pretend Indians: Images of Native Americans in the Movies*. Iowa State UP, 1980, pp. ix–xvi.

Denison, Merrill. *Marsh Hay*. Simon and Pierre, 1973.

Derrida, Jacques. *Archive Fever: A Freudian Impression*. Translated by Eric Prenowitz, U of Chicago P, 1996.

———. "Language Is Never Owned: An Interview." *Sovereignties in Question: The Poetics of Paul Celan*, Fordham UP, 2005, pp. 97–107.

———. *Spectres of Marx*. Stanford UP, 1993.

Des Rochers, Jacques and Brian Foss, *1920s Modernism in Montreal: The Beaver Hall Group*. Montreal Museum of Fine Arts / Black Dog, 2015

De Szegheo-Lang, Naomi. "Disruptive Desires: Reframing Sexual Space at the Feminist Porn Awards." *Disrupting Queer Inclusion: Canadian Homonationalisms and the Politics of Belonging*, edited by OmiSoore H. Dryden and Suzanne Lenon, UBC P, 2015, pp. 66–81.

Dickerson, James. *North to Canada: Men and Women Against the Vietnam War*. Praeger, 1999.

Dillon, Grace. "Imagining Indigenous Futurisms." *Walking the Clouds: An Anthology of Indigenous Science Fiction*, edited by Grace Dillon, U of Arizona P, 2012, pp. 1–12.

———. "*Miindiwag* and Indigenous Diaspora: Eden Robinson's and Celu Amberstone's Forays into 'Postcolonial' Science Fiction and Fantasy." *Extrapolation*, vol. 48, no. 2, 2007, pp. 219–43.

Dolphijn, Rick, and Iris van der Tuin. "'Matter Feels, Converses, Suffers, Desires, Yearns and Remembers': Interview with Karen Barad." *New Materialism: Interviews & Cartographies*, Open Humanities P, 2012, pp. 48–70.

Dominello, Francesca. "Political Apologies and Their Challenges in Achieving Justice for Indigenous Peoples in Australia and Canada." *Oñati Socio-legal Series*, vol. 7, no. 2, 2017, pp. 277–303.

Donato, Al. "Author Joshua Whitehead 'It's Time to Infect CanLit with Queer, Indigenous Voices.'" *Huffington Post*, 7 July 2018, https://www.huffingtonpost.ca/ 2018/07/04/joshua-whitehead-indigenous-two-spirit-author_a_23473957/. Accessed 17 June 2020.

Donoghue, Emma. *The Wonder*. Picador, 2016.

———. "The Wonder." www.emmadonoghue.com/books/novels/the-wonder.html. Accessed 2 Feb. 2018.

Douglas, Jim. Letter to Jack McClelland. 17 Nov. 1971. McClelland and Stewart Ltd. Fonds, William Ready Division of Archives and Research Collections, McMaster University Library, box 2CA84.

Downie, Gord. *Secret Path*. http://secretpath.ca/. Accessed 17 June 2020.

———. *Secret Path*. Illustrated by Jeff Lemire, Simon & Schuster, 2016.

Dryden, OmiSoore H., and Suzanne Lenon, editors. *Disturbing Queer Inclusion: Canadian Homonationalisms and the Politics of Belonging*. UBC P, 2015.

Duffy, P.S. *The Cartographer of No Man's Land: A Novel*. Penguin, 2013.

Duggan, Lisa. "The New Homonormativity: The Sexual Politics of Neoliberalism." *Materializing Democracy: Toward a Revitalized Cultural Politics*, edited by Russ Castronova and Dana D. Nelson, Duke UP, 2002, pp. 175–94.

Dummitt, Christopher. "After Inclusiveness: The Future of Canadian History." *Contesting Clio's Craft*, edited by Chrisopher Dummitt and Michael Dawson, Institute for the Study of the Americas, University of London, 2009, pp. 98–122.

Dummitt, Christopher, and Michael Dawson, editors. *Contesting Clio's Craft: New Directions and Debates in Canadian History*. Institute for the Study of the Americas, University of London, 2009.

Dunn, Willie. "Charlie Wenjack." *Akwasasne Notes*, Trikont, 1978. Song.

Durham, Earl of [John George Lambton]. "Lower Canada." *Report on the Affairs of British North America*, London, 1839, www.en.wikisource.org. Accessed 15 Mar. 2018.

Dzodan, Flavia. "My Feminism Will Be Intersectional or It Will Be Bullshit!" *Tiger Beatdown*, 10 October 2011, http://tigerbeatdown.com/2011/10/10/my-feminism -will-be-intersectional-or-it-will-be-bullshit/. Accessed 17 June 2020.

Edelman, Lee. *No Future: Queer Theory and the Death Drive*. Duke UP, 2004.

Editorial. "Why Exactly Are We Spending $500-Million on an Anniversary?" *The Globe and Mail*, 6 Jan. 2017, https://www.theglobeandmail.com/opinion/ editorials/why-exactly-are-we-spending-500-million-on-an-anniversary/ article33528594/. Accessed 17 June 2020.

Edwards, Brendan Frederick R. "Maria Campbell's Halfbreed: 'Biography with a Purpose.'" *Historical Perspectives on Canadian Publishing*, McMaster University

Library Digital Collections, http://pw2oc.mcmaster.ca/hpcanpub/case-study/ maria-campbells-halfbreed-biography-purpose. Accessed 18 Oct. 2017.

Edwards, Elizabeth. "Photography and the Sound of History." *Visual Anthropology Review*, vol. 21, no. 1–2, March 2005, pp. 27–46.

Eigenbrod, Renate. "Afterword: George Kenny—Anishinaabe, Son, and Writer." *Indians Don't Cry: Gaawiin Masisiiwag Anishinaageg*, by George Kenny, edited by Eigenbrod, translated by Patricia M. Ningewance, First Voices, First Texts series, U of Manitoba P, 2014.

———. "'For the child taken, for the parent left behind': Residential School Narratives as Acts of 'Survivance.'" ESC *(English Studies in Canada)*, https://journals .library.ualberta.ca/esc/index.php/ESC/article/view/22311/16600. Accessed 30 July 2017.

———. *Travelling Knowledges: Repositioning the Im/Migrant Reader of Aboriginal Literatures in Canada*. U of Manitoba P, 2005.

Elliott, Alicia. "CanLit Is a Raging Dumpster Fire." *Open Book*, 7 Sept. 2017, http:// open-book.ca/Columnists/CanLit-is-a-Raging-Dumpster-Fire. Accessed 17 June 2020.

———. "The Cultural Appropriation Debate Isn't about Free Speech—It's about Context." CBC *Arts Online*, 16 May 2017, www.cbc.ca/arts/the-cultural -appropriation-debate-isn-t-about-free-speech-it-s-about-context-1.4117142. Accessed 17 June 2020.

Epp, Frank H. *Mennonites in Canada, 1786–1920: The History of a Separate People*. Macmillan, 1974.

E.P. Taylor Library and Archives, Art Gallery of Ontario, Toronto.

Evans, Augusta Tappage, and Jean E. Speare. *The Days of Augusta*. Douglas & McIntyre, 1973, 1992.

Favorini, Attilio, editor. *Voicings: Ten Plays from the Documentary Theater*. Ecco P, 1994.

Fee, Margery. *Literary Land Claims: The "Indian Land Question" from Pontiac's War to Attawapiskat*. Wilfrid Laurier UP, 2015.

Fee, Margery, and Deanna Reder. *The People and the Text: Collecting an Inclusive Library*. 2016. In the possession of the authors.

Findley, Len. "Redress Rehearsals: Legal Warrior, COSMOSQAW, and the National Aboriginal Achievement Awards." *Reconciling Canada: Critical Perspectives on the Culture of Redress*, edited by Jennifer Henderson and Pauline Wakeham, U of Toronto P, 2013, pp. 218–35.

Fishbane, Joel. "Seeds of Prophecy: Annabel Soutar's *Seeds*." *Canadian Theatre Review*, vol. 154, 2013, pp. 82–83, *Project Muse*, https://muse.jhu.edu/article/ 504673. Accessed 17 June 2020.

Fisher, Mark. "No Future Together." *Frieze*, no. 109, 2 Sept. 2007, https://frieze.com/article/no-future-together. Accessed 17 June 2020.

Fitterman, Rob, and Vanessa Place. *Notes on Conceptualisms*. Ugly Duckling Presse, 2009.

Flanagan, Thomas, editor. *From the Diary of Louis Riel*. Hurtig, 1976.

Foucault, Michel. "Friendship as a Way of Life." *Michel Foucault: Ethics Subjectivity and Truth*, edited by Paul Rabinow, translated by John Johnston, The New Press, 1997.

———. "Of Other Spaces: Utopias and Heterotopias." *Diacritics*, vol. 16, no. 1, Spring 1986, pp. 22–27.

Francis, Daniel. *The Imaginary Indian: The Image of the Indian in Canadian Culture*. Arsenal Pulp Press, 1992.

Freeman, Elizabeth. *Time Binds: Queer Temporalities, Queer Histories*. Duke UP, 2010.

Freeman, Mini Aodla. *Life Among the Qallunaat*. Edited and afterword by Keavy Martin, Julie Rak, and Norma Dunning, First Voices, First Texts series, U of Manitoba P, 2015.

French, Alice. *My Name Is Masak*. Peguis, 1976.

French, William. "Archives Want Bills if Writers Don't." *The Globe and Mail*, 29 May 1979, p. 16.

———. "Calgary Leads CanLit Paper Chase." *The Globe and Mail*, 24 May 1984, p. E1.

———. "Union Rejuvenated, Writers Demand Publishing Probe." *The Globe and Mail*, 12 May 1980, p. 18.

———. "Writers' Dramatics Exceed Hamlet's." *The Globe and Mail*, 7 May 1979, p. 18.

Friesen, Joe. "Shooting Death of Colten Boushie a 'Freak Accident,' Stanley Defence Argues in Laying Out Its Case." *The Globe and Mail*, 5 Feb. 2018, https://www.theglobeandmail.com/news/national/shooting-death-of-colten-boushie-a-freak-accident-stanley-defence-argues-in-laying-out-its-case/article37853099/. Accessed 1 Sept. 2018.

Fuller, Linda K. *National Days, National Ways: Historical, Political and Religious Celebrations Around the World*. ABC-Clio, 2004.

Furlong, Pauline. *Historic Amherst*. Nimbus, 2001.

Gagnon, François-Marc. "La peinture des années trente au Québec." *Journal of Canadian Art History*, vol. 3, no. 1 & 2, Autumn 1976, pp. 2–20.

Gagnon, Monika Kin. *Other Conundrums: Race, Culture and Canadian Art*. Arsenal Pulp Press, 2000.

García Zarranz, Libe. "Carving, Cutting, Fasting: Cassils and Emma Donoghue's Bodily Wonders." *Beyond Canada 150: Untold Stories*. UCD, Dublin, Ireland, 30 April 2017.

———. *TransCanadian Feminist Fictions: New Cross-Border Ethics.* McGill-Queen's UP, 2017.

Gardner, David. "John Coulter." *The Literary Encyclopedia,* 2 Sept. 2004, http://www .litencyc.com/php/speople.true&UID=1036. Accessed 10 Oct. 2008.

Gaudry, Adam. "Communing with the Dead: The 'New Métis,' Métis Identity Appropriation, and the Displacement of Living Métis Culture." *The American Indian Quarterly,* vol. 42, no. 2, Spring 2018, pp. 162–91.

Gaudry, Adam, and Danielle Lorenz. "Indigenization as Inclusion, Reconciliation, and Decolonization: Navigating the Different Visions for Indigenizing the Canadian Academy." *AlterNative,* vol. 14, no. 3, 2018, pp. 218–27.

Geddes, John. "Jagmeet Singh Should Ask 'What Would Thomas D'Arcy McGee Do?'" *Maclean's Magazine,* 19 Mar. 2018, www.mcleans.ca. Accessed 20 Apr. 2018.

Gepts, Paul. "Who Owns Biodiversity and How Should the Owners Be Compensated?" *Plant Physiology,* vol. 134, no. 4, 2004, pp. 1295–1307.

Gerson, Carole. "Locating Female Subjects in the Archives." *Working in Women's Archives: Researching Women's Private Literature and Archival Documents,* Wilfrid Laurier UP, 2001, pp. 7–22.

Giannacopoulos, Maria. "The Nomos of Apologia." *Griffith Law Review,* vol. 18, no. 2, 2009, pp. 331–49.

Gibson, Graeme. *Eleven Canadian Novelists.* Anansi, 1973.

———. "Letter—October 25, 1971." Timothy Findley and William Whitehead Fonds, Library and Archives Canada, Ottawa, Ontario, box 98, file 20, Correspondence, Gibson, Graeme, 1971–1984. 15 May 2015.

Gillespie, Alastair C.F. "Thomas D'Arcy McGee: The Idealist." Macdonald Laurier Institute, June 2017, www.macdonaldlaurier.ca/files/pdf/MIConfederation SeriesMcGeeF_Web.pdf. Accessed 23 Sept. 2018.

Gillis, John, editor. *Commemorations: The Politics of National Identity.* Princeton UP, 1996.

Godfrey, Rebecca. *Under the Bridge.* Simon and Schuster, 2005.

Goldie, Terry. *Fear and Temptation: The Image of the Indigene in Canadian, Australian, and New Zealand Literatures.* McGill-Queen's UP, 1989.

Goldman, Marlene. "A Dangerous Circuit: Loss and the Boundaries of Racialized Subjectivity in Joy Kogawa's *Obasan* and Kerri Sakamoto's *The Electrical Field.*" *Modern Fiction Studies,* vol. 48, no. 2, 2002, pp. 362–88.

Gordon, Colin, editor. *Power/Knowledge: Selected Interviews and Other Writings 1972–1977 by Michel Foucault.* Pantheon Books, 1981.

Government of Canada. "About #IndigenousReads." *Indigenous and Northern Affairs Canada,* 3 Dec. 2017, https://www.aadnc-aandc.gc.ca/eng/1472736453262/14727 36477408. Accessed 17 June 2020.

————. "Bill C-16: An Act to amend the Canadian Human Rights Act and the Criminal Code." Statutes of Canada 2017, 19 June 2017, http://www.parl.ca/DocumentViewer/en/42-1/bill/C-16/royal-assent. Accessed 17 June 2020.

————. "Indian Residential Schools." *Indigenous and Northern Affairs Canada*, 24 Aug. 2016, https://www.aadnc-aandc.gc.ca/eng/1100100015576/1100100015577. Accessed 17 June 2020.

————. "Indian Residential Schools Resolution Health Support Program." *Government of Canada*, Health Canada, 27 May 2015, https://www.canada.ca/en/health-canada/services/first-nations-inuit-health/health-care-services/indian-residential-schools-health-supports/indian-residential-schools-resolution-health-support-program.html. Accessed 17 June 2020.

————. "Newfoundland and Labrador Residential Schools Healing and Commemoration." *Indigenous and Northern Affairs Canada*, 3 Apr. 2018, https://www.aadnc-aandc.gc.ca/eng/1511531626107/1511531669002. Accessed 17 June 2020.

Government of Canada and the National Association of Japanese Canadians. "Terms of Agreement between the Government of Canada and the National Association of Japanese Canadians." *Reconciling Canada: Critical Perspectives on the Culture of Redress*, edited by Jennifer Henderson and Pauline Wakeham, U of Toronto P, 2013, pp. 439–40.

Gower, John Gordon. *The Impact of Alternative Ideology on Landscape: The Back-to-the-Land Movement in the Slocan Valley*. Carleton U, 1986.

Grace, Sherrill. *On the Art of Being Canadian*. UBC P, 2009.

Grafftey, Heward. *Portraits from a Life*. Véhicule Press, 1996.

Gray, Charlotte. "Canada 150, Doomed from the Start, Now Ends with a Whimper." *The Globe and Mail*, 30 Dec. 2017, https://www.theglobeandmail.com/opinion/why-canada-150-was-doomed-from-the-start/article37441978/. Accessed 17 June 2020.

Grimké, Angelina. "The Closing Door." *Selected Works of Angelina Grimké*, edited by Carolivia Herron, Oxford UP, 1991, pp. 252–81.

————. "'Rachel' the Play of the Month: The Reason and Synopsis by the Author." *Selected Works of Angelina Grimké*, edited by Carolivia Herron, Oxford UP, 1991, p. 413.

Gunn, Julian. "A Portable Frontier: Two Gender-Divergent Navigations of Western Canada." *Canadian Literature*, vol. 224, 2015, pp. 150–56.

Gwyn, Richard. *Nation Maker: Sir John A. Macdonald: His Life, Our Times*. Vol. 2, 1867–1891, Random House, 2011.

Hagan, John. *Northern Passage: American Vietnam War Resisters in Canada*. Harvard UP, 2001.

Haig-Brown, Alan. *Hell No, We Won't Go: Vietnam Draft Resisters in Canada*. Raincoast, 1996.

Haig-Brown, Celia. *Survival and Renewal: Surviving the Indian Residential School.* Arsenal Pulp Press, 1988.

Halberstam, Jack. *In a Queer Time and Place: Transgender Bodies, Subcultural Lives.* NYU P, 2005.

Halberstam, Judith. *The Queer Art of Failure.* Duke UP, 2011.

Hamm, Peter M. *Continuity and Change among Canadian Mennonite Brethren.* Wilfrid Laurier UP, 1987.

Hamon, M. Max. "Louis Riel's Defence of Culture at the Collège de Montréal." *Canadian Historical Review,* vol. 97, no. 1, 2014, pp. 59–87.

———. "The Many Worlds of Louis Riel: A Political Odyssey from Red River to Montreal and Back 1840–1875." 2017. McGill U, PhD diss.

———. "Your thesis." Email correspondence with Margery Fee, 30 Aug. 2018.

Haraway, Donna. "Awash in Urine: DES and Premarin® in Multispecies Response-ability." *WSQ: Women's Studies Quarterly,* vol. 40, no. 1 & 2, Spring/ Summer 2012, pp. 301–16.

———. "Situated Knowledges: The Science Question in Feminism and the Privilege of Partial Perspective." *Feminist Studies,* vol. 14, no. 3, Autumn 1988, pp. 575–99.

———. *Staying with the Trouble: Making Kin in the Chthulucene.* Duke UP, 2016.

Hardwick, Susan. "Canadian and American Cross-Border Migration, Settlement, and Belonging." *Transnational Borders. Transnational Lives. Academic Mobility at the Borderland,* edited by Remy Trembly and Susan Hardwick, Presses de l'Université du Québec, 2014, pp. 7–23.

Harkin, Keelan. "Symptoms, Care, and Power." *The Great Irish Famine: Global Contexts,* special issue of *Breac: A Digital Journal of Irish Studies,* 11 Jan. 2018, https://breac.nd.edu/articles/symptoms-care-and-power/. Accessed 20 Oct. 2020.

Harper, J. Russell. *Painting in Canada: A History.* U of Toronto P, 1966.

Harper, Stephen. "House of Commons Apology to Inuit, Métis, and First Nations Peoples for Residential Schools, 2008." *Reconciling Canada: Critical Perspectives on the Culture of Redress,* edited by Jennifer Henderson and Pauline Wakeham, U of Toronto P, 2013, pp. 335–37.

Haskins, Ekaterina V. Introduction. *Popular Memories: Commemoration, Participatory Culture, and Democratic Citizenship,* U of South Carolina P, 2015, pp. 1–20.

Hayday, Matthew. "Fireworks, Folk-Dancing, and Fostering a National Identity: The Politics of Canada Day." *Canadian Historical Review,* vol. 91, no. 2, 2010, pp. 287–314.

Hayday, Matthew, and Raymond B. Blake, editors. *Celebrating Canada: Commemorations, Anniversaries, and National Symbols.* U of Toronto P, 2018.

Hayne, David M. "*The Golden Dog* and *Le Chiend'or*: Le May's French Translation of Kirby's Novel." *Papers of the Bibliographic Society of Canada*, vol. 20, 1981, pp. 50–62.

Heiland, Donna. "George Elliott Clarke's *Beatrice Chancy*: Sublimity, Pain, Possibility." *Postfeminist Gothic: Critical Interventions in Contemporary Culture*, edited by Benjamin A. Brabon and Stéphanie Genz, Palgrave Macmillan, 2007, pp. 126–39.

Henderson, James (Sa'ke'j) Youngblood. "Incomprehensible Canada." *Reconciling Canada: Critical Perspectives on the Culture of Redress*, edited by Jennifer Henderson and Pauline Wakeham, U of Toronto P, 2013, pp. 115–25.

Henderson, Jennifer. "The Camp, the School, and the Child: Discursive Exchanges and (Neo)liberal Axioms in the Culture of Redress." *Reconciling Canada: Critical Perspectives on the Culture of Redress*, edited by Jennifer Henderson and Pauline Wakeham, U of Toronto P, 2013, pp. 63–83.

Henderson, Jennifer, and Pauline Wakeham. Introduction. *Reconciling Canada: Critical Perspectives on the Culture of Redress*, edited by Henderson and Wakeham, U of Toronto P, 2013, pp. 3–27.

———, editors. *Reconciling Canada: Critical Perspectives of the Culture of Redress*. U of Toronto P, 2013.

———. *Settler Feminism and Race Making in Canada*. U of Toronto P, 2003.

"Henry II." BBC *History*, last updated 2014, http://www.bbc.co.uk/history/historic_figures/henry_ii_king.shtml. Accessed 14 Jan. 2018.

Highway, Tomson. "Dry Lips Oughta Move to Kapuskasing." *Modern Canadian Plays*, edited by Jerry Wasserman, vol. 2, Talonbooks, 2001, pp. 187–224.

Hill, Charles C. *The Group of Seven: Art for a Nation*. National Gallery of Canada / McClelland & Stewart, 1995.

Hill, Lawrence. *The Book of Negroes*. HarperCollins, 2007.

Holmgren, Michele. "Ossian Abroad: James Macpherson and Canadian Literary Nationalism, 1830–1994." *Canadian Poetry*, vol. 50, Spring/Summer 2002, pp. 52–81.

Hopper, Robin. E-mail correspondence with Mary Ann Steggles. 7 June 2016.

Horvat, Ana. "Tranimacies and Affective Trans Embodiment in Nina Arsenault's *Silicone Diaries* and Cassils's Becoming an Image." *a/b: Auto/Biography Studies*, vol. 33, no. 2, 2018, pp. 395–415.

Housser, F.B. *A Canadian Art Movement: The Story of the Group of Seven*. Macmillan, 1926.

Huebener, Paul. *Timing Canada: The Shifting Politics of Time in Canadian Literary Culture*. McGill-Queen's UP, 2015.

Hull, Gloria. *Color, Sex and Poetry: Three Women Writers of the Harlem Renaissance*. Indiana UP, 1987.

Huneault, Kristina. "'As Well as Men': The Gendering of Beaver Hall." *1920s Modernism in Montreal: The Beaver Hall Group*, edited by Jacques Des Rochers and Brian Foss, Montreal Museum of Fine Arts / Black Dog, 2015, p. 263–92.

Hutcheon, Linda. *A Theory of Adaptation*. Routledge, 2006.

Iannacci, Elio. "The Art That Comes from Bodybuilding and Death-Defying Stunts." *Maclean's*, 4 July 2016, https://www.macleans.ca/culture/arts/cassils-mixes-bodybuilding-and-death-defying-stunts-to-create-art/. Accessed 25 Sept. 2018.

Idle No More. "#CancelCanadaDay." https://idlenomore.ca/cancelcanadaday/. Accessed 8 July 2020.

Indigenous and Northern Affairs Canada. "Metis Rights." www.aadnc-aandc.ce.ca/eng. Accessed 25 July 2019.

Innes, Robert Alexander. "Moose on the Loose: Indigenous Men, Violence and the Colonial Excuse." *Aboriginal Policy Studies*, vol. 4, no. 1, 2015, pp. 46–56.

International Covenant on Civil and Political Rights. Adopted and opened for signature, ratification and accession by General Assembly resolution 2200A (XXI) of 16 December 1966.

Jackson, A.Y. "Prudence Heward." *Prudence Heward, 1896–1947*, National Gallery of Canada, 1948, p. 10.

Jacobus, Lee. *The Bedford Introduction to Drama*. St. Martin's Press, 1989.

Jacobs, Beverley. "House of Commons Apology to Inuit, Métis, and First Nations Peoples for Residential Schools, 2008." *Reconciling Canada: Critical Perspectives on the Culture of Redress*, edited by Jennifer Henderson and Pauline Wakeham, U of Toronto P, 2013, pp. 338–39.

Janovicek, Nancy. "Rural Countercultures." *Back to the Land: Ceramics from Vancouver Island and the Gulf Islands, 1970–1985*, edited by Diane Carr and Nancy Janovicek, Art Gallery of Greater Victoria, 2013, pp. 9–19.

Jessup, Lynda. "Bushwhackers in the Gallery: Antimodernism and the Group of Seven." *Antimodernism and Artistic Experience: Policing the Boundaries of Modernity*, edited by Jessup, U of Toronto P, 2001, pp. 130–52.

Johns, Fleur. "The Temporal Rivalries of Human Rights." *Indiana Journal of Global Legal Studies*, vol. 23, no. 1, 2016, pp. 39–60.

Johnson, E. Pauline. "The Cattle Thief." *Flint and Feather: The Complete Poems of E. Pauline Johnson*, Musson, 1912.

Jones, Joseph. *Contending Statistics: The Numbers for U.S. Vietnam War Resisters in Canada*. Quarter Sheaf, 2005.

Jordan-Fenton, Christy, and Margaret Pokiak-Fenton. *Fatty Legs*. Illustrated by Liz Amini-Holms, Annick Press, 2010.

Justice, Daniel Heath. "Significant Spaces Between: Making Room for Silence." *Or Words to That Effect: Orality and the Writing of Literary History*, edited by Daniel F. Chamberlain and J. Edward Chamberlin, John Benjamins, 2016, pp. 115–25.

———. *Why Indigenous Literatures Matter*. Wilfrid Laurier UP, 2018.

Kadar, Marlene. "The Devouring: Traces of Roma in the Holocaust: No Tattoo, Sterilized Body, Gypsy Girl." *Tracing the Autobiographical*, edited by Marlene Kadar, Linda Warley, Jeanne Perreault, and Susanna Egan, Life Writing series, Wilfrid Laurier UP, 2005, pp. 223–46.

Kafer, Alison. *Feminist, Queer, Crip*. Indiana UP, 2013.

Kamboureli, Smaro. Preface. *Trans.Can.Lit: Resituating the Study of Canadian Literature*, edited by Smaro Kamboureli and Roy Miki, Wilfrid Laurier UP, 2007, pp. vii–xv.

Kamboureli, Smaro, and Roy Miki, editors. *Trans.Can.Lit: Resituating the Study of Canadian Literature*. Wilfrid Laurier UP, 2007.

Kamboureli, Smaro, and Christl Verduyn. *Critical Collaborations: Indigeneity, Diaspora, and Ecology in Canadian Literary Studies*. Wilfrid Laurier UP, 2014.

Kammen, Michael. "Commemoration and Contestation in American Culture: Historical Perspectives." *Amerikastudien / American Studies*, vol. 48, no. 2, 2003, pp. 185–205.

Keen, Suzanne. *Empathy and the Novel*. Oxford UP, 2007.

Kelleher, Margaret, and Michael Kenneally. *Ireland and Quebec: Multidisciplinary Perspectives on History, Culture and Society*. Four Courts P, 2016.

Kenny, George. *Indians Don't Cry: Gaawiin Masisiiwag Anishinaageg*. Edited and afterword by Renate Eigenbrod, translated by Patricia M. Ningewance, First Voices, First Texts series, U of Manitoba P, 2014.

King, Moynan. "Canada's Dandy Duet: The Performance Collaboration of Ivan Coyote and Rae Spoon." *Canadian Theatre Review*, vol. 149, 2012, pp. 46–51.

Kinsman, Gary, and Patrizia Gentile. *The Canadian War on Queers: National Security as Sexual Regulation*. UBC P, 2010.

Kirkup, Kristy. "Lynn Beyak Removed from Senate Committee over Residential School Comments." *The Globe and Mail*, 5 Apr. 2017, http://www.theglobe andmail.com/news/politics/beyak-removed-from-senate-committee-over -residential-school-comments/article34610016/. Accessed 30 July 2017.

Knowles, Ric. "*Othello* in Three Times." *Shakespeare in Canada: A World Elsewhere?*, edited by Diana Brydon and Irena R. Makaryk, U of Toronto P, 2002, pp. 371–95.

Kogawa, Joy. *Emily Kato*. Penguin, 2005.

———. *Itsuka*. Penguin, 1993.

Kollar, Kathryn L. *Women Painters of the Beaver Hall Group.* Sir George Williams Art Galleries, Concordia U, 1982.

Kraybill, Donald B. "Photography." *Concise Encyclopedia of Amish, Brethren, Hutterites, and Mennonites,* edited by Kraybill, Johns Hopkins UP, 2010, pp. 186–87.

Kroetsch, Robert. "On Being an Alberta Writer." *Open Letter,* 1983, pp. 69–80.

———. *Seed Catalogue.* Turnstone P, 1977.

L'Abbé, Sonnet. "Painful Sympathies." Review of *Tell* by Soraya Peerbaye, *The Walrus,* 1 June 2016, http://thewalrus.ca/painful-sympathies/. Accessed 17 June 2020.

Laberge, Albert. "Au fil de l'heure: Le Groupe Beaver Hall." *La Presse,* 20 Jan. 1921, p. 2.

Lai, Larissa. "Community Action, Global Spillage: Writing the Race of Capital." *Slanting I, Imagining We: Asian Canadian Literary Production in the 1980s and 1990s.* Wilfrid Laurier UP, 2014, pp. 211–27.

———. "How to Do 'You': Methods of Asian / Indigenous Relation." *RANAM: Recherches anglaises et nord-américaines,* vol. 46, 2013, pp. 11–27.

———. "Other Democracies: Writing Thru Race at the 20 Year Crossroad." *Smaro Kamboureli,* 2015, http://smarokamboureli.ca/wp-content/uploads/2015/01/Lai_Essay.pdf. Accessed 17 June 2020.

Langford, Martha. "Hitching a Ride: American Know-How in the Engineering of Canadian Photographic Institutions." *Narratives Unfolding: National Art Histories in an Unfinished World,* edited by Langford, McGill-Queens UP, 2017, pp. 209–30.

———. Introduction. *Narratives Unfolding: National Art Histories in an Unfinished World,* edited by Langford, McGill-Queen's UP, 2017, pp. 3–41.

———. *Suspended Conversations: The Afterlife of Memory in Photographic Albums.* McGill-Queen's UP, 2001.

Langford, Martha, Karla McManus, Elizabeth Anne Cavaliere, Aurèle Parisien, Sharon Murray, and Philippe Guillaume. "Imaged Communities: Putting Canadian Photographic History in Its Place." *Meeting Places / Lieux de rencontres,* special issue of *Journal of Canadian Studies / Revue d'études canadiennes,* edited by Renée Hulan and Christl Verduyn, vol. 2, no. 49, Spring 2015, pp. 296–354.

Larson, Katherine. "Resistance from the Margins in George Elliott Clarke's *Beatrice Chancy.*" *Canadian Literature,* vol. 189, 2006, pp. 103–18.

Latimer, Heather. *Reproductive Acts: Sexual Politics in North American Fiction and Film.* McGill-Queen's UP, 2013.

Lee, Jen Sookfong. "On Margaret Atwood and the New CanLit." *Open Book,* 17 Jan. 2018, http://open-book.ca/Columnists/On-Margaret-Atwood-and-the-new-Canlit. Accessed June 2020.

Lee, Rachel C. *The Exquisite Corpse of Asian America: Biopolitics, Biosociality, and Posthuman Ecologies.* New York UP, 2014.

Lepage, Robert, and Éric Bernier. *The Seven Streams of the River Ota*. Methuen Drama, 1996.

Leroux, Darryl. "'We've been here for 2000 years': White Settlers, Native American DNA and the Phenomenon of Indigenization." *Social Studies of Society*, vol. 48, no. 1, 2018, pp. 80–100.

Lindsay, James. "An Interview with Canisia Lubrin." *Open Book*, 21 Nov. 2017, http://open-book.ca/Columnists/An-Interview-with-Canisia-Lubrin. Accessed 17 June 2020.

Lischke, Ute, and David T. McNab, editors. *The Long Journey of a Forgotten People: Métis Identities and Family Histories*. Wilfrid Laurier UP, 2007.

Lord, Barry. *The History of Painting in Canada: Toward a People's Art*. NC Press, 1974.

Lorimer, Rowland. *Ultra Libris: Policy, Technology, and the Creative Economy of Book Publishing in Canada*. ECW Press, 2012.

Luciuk, Lobomyr. *In Fear of the Barbed Wire Fence: Canada's First National Internment Operations and the Ukrainian Canadians, 1914–1920*. Kashtan, 2001.

Luckyj, Natalie. *Expressions of Will: The Art of Prudence Heward*. Agnes Etherington Art Centre, Queen's U, 1986.

Lutz, Hartmut. *Contemporary Challenges: Conversations with Canadian Native Authors*. Fifth House, 1991.

Mac, Carrie. *The Beckoners*. Orca, 2004.

Macdougall, Brenda. "After Boushie, It's Time for Honest Talk about Racism in Saskatchewan." *The Globe and Mail*, 24 Aug. 2016, updated 24 Mar. 2017.

Mackey, Eva. "The Apologizers' Apology." *Reconciling Canada: Critical Perspectives on the Culture of Redress*, edited by Jennifer Henderson and Pauline Wakeham, U of Toronto P, 2013, pp. 47–62.

———. *The House of Difference: Cultural Politics and National Identity in Canada*. U of Toronto P, 2001.

MacLeod, Joan. *The Shape of a Girl/Jewel*. Talonbooks, 2002.

MacPherson, Myra. *Long Time Passing: Vietnam and the Haunted Generation*. Double Day, 1984.

MacSkimming, Roy. *The Perilous Trade: Book Publishing in Canada, 1946–2006*. McClelland & Stewart, 2007.

Manuel, Vera. *Honouring the Strength of Indian Women: Plays, Stories, Poetry*, edited by Michelle Coupal, Deanna Reder, Joanne Arnott, and Emalene Manuel, U of Manitoba P, 2019.

———. Interview by Peter Morin. "Letting Go of Trauma On and Off Stage." *Redwiremag.com*, vol. 7, no. 1, Redwire Media, 2004. Accessed 9 April 2017.

Maracle, Lee. *Bobbi Lee: Indian Rebel*. 1975. Women's Press, 2017.

—————. *Memory Serves: Oratories*. NeWest P, 2016.

—————. *My Conversations with Canadians*. Book Thug, 2017.

Mathur, Ashok. "Transubracination: How Writers of Colour Became CanLit." *Trans. Can.Lit: Resituating the Study of Canadian Literature*, edited by Smaro Kamboureli and Roy Miki, Wilfrid Laurier UP, 2007, 141–51.

Matthews, Kim, and Vic Satzewich. "The Invisible Transnationals? Americans in Canada." *Transnational Identities and Practices in Canada*, edited by Vic Satzewich and Lloyd Wong, UBC P, 2006, pp. 164–79.

Maynard, Robyn. *Policing Black Lives: State Violence in Canada from Slavery to the Present*. Fernwood, 2017.

Mbembe, Achille. "Necropolitics." Translated by Libby Meintjes, *Public Culture*, no. 15, vol. 1, 2003, pp. 11–40.

McCall, Sophie, Christine Kim, and Melina Baum Singer. *Cultural Grammars of Nation, Diaspora, and Indigeneity*. Wilfrid Laurier UP, 2012.

McClelland, Jack. Letter to Mr. James Douglas. 30 Nov. 1971. McClelland and Stewart Ltd. Fonds, William Ready Division of Archives and Research Collections, McMaster University Library, box 2CA84.

McClelland, J.G. Letter to Mr. Robert I. Martin. 27 Nov. 1972. McClelland and Stewart Ltd. Fonds, William Ready Division of Archives and Research Collections, McMaster University Library, box 2CA84.

McClelland and Stewart Ltd. Fonds, William Ready Division of Archives and Research Collections, McMaster University Library, Hamilton.

McCullough, Norah. *The Beaver Hall Hill Group / Le Groupe de Beaver Hall Hill*. National Gallery of Canada, 1966.

McCrone, David, and Gayle McPherson. *National Days: Constructing and Mobilising National Identity*. Palgrave, 2009.

McGee, Thomas D'Arcy. "Constitutional Difficulties between Upper and Lower Canada" ("The Shield of Achilles"). 2 May 1860, www.macdonaldlaurier.ca/ speech-by-thomas-darcy-mcgee-constitutional-difficulties-between -upper-and-lower-canada-the-shield-of-achilles-may-2-1860/. Accessed 20 Apr. 2018.

—————. "Protection for Canadian Literature." *The New Era*, 24 Apr. 1858, p. 1.

—————. *Speeches and Addresses Chiefly on the Subject of British-American Union*. Chapman and Hall, 1865.

McGill, Robert. *War Is Here: The Vietnam War and Canadian Literature*. McGill-Queen's UP, 2017.

McGoogan, Ken. *Celtic Lightning: How the Scots and the Irish Created a Canadian Nation*. Patrick Crean / HarperCollins, 2015.

McGowan, Mark G. *The Waning of the Green: Catholics, the Irish, and Identity in Toronto, 1887–1922.* McGill-Queen's UP, 1999.

McGregor, Hannah. Review of "Untold Stories of the Past 150 Years: Canada 150." *U.S. Studies Online: A Forum for New Writing,* 2 June 2017, https://usso.uk/untold-stories. Accessed 20 Oct. 2020.

McGregor, Hannah, Julie Rak, and Erin Wunker. *Refuse: CanLit in Ruins.* Book*hug, 2018.

McKegney, Sam. *Magic Weapons: Aboriginal Writers Remaking Community after Residential School.* U of Manitoba P, 2017.

———. Personal email correspondence. 4 Apr. 2018.

———. "Warriors, Healers, Lovers, and Leaders: Colonial Impositions on Indigenous Male Roles and Responsibilities." *Canadian Perspectives on Men and Masculinities: An Interdisciplinary Reader,* edited by Jason A. Laker, Oxford UP, 2011, pp. 241–68.

———. "Writer–Reader Reciprocity and the Pursuit of Alliance through Indigenous Poetry." *Indigenous Poetics in Canada,* edited by Neal McLeod, Wilfrid Laurier UP, 2014, pp. 43–60.

McKegney, Sam, and Keavy Martin. "Inuvialuit Critical Autobiography and the Carceral Writing of Anthony Apakark Thrasher." *Canadian Literature,* vol. 208, Spring 2011, pp. 65–83.

McKinley, Donald. Personal interview. July 1976.

McKnight, David. "Small Press Publishing." *History of the Book in Canada,* vol. 3, 1918–1980, edited by Carole Gerson and Jacques Michon, U of Toronto P, 2007, pp. 308–18.

mclennan, rob. "12 or 20 questions: With Rita Wong." *12 or 20 questions,* 5 Jan. 2008, http://12or20questions.blogspot.ca/2008/01/12-or-20-questions-with-rita-wong.html. Accessed 17 June 2020.

Meadowcroft, Barbara. *Painting Friends: The Beaver Hall Women Painters.* Véhicule Press, 1999.

Medina, José. "Toward a Foucaultian Epistemology of Resistance: Counter-Memory, Epistemic Friction, and *Guerrilla* Pluralism." *Foucault Studies,* vol. 12, Oct. 2011, pp. 9–35.

Menkel-Meadow, Carrie. "Unsettling the Lawyers: Other Forms of Justice in Indigenous Claims of Expropriation, Abuse, and Injustice." *University of Toronto Law Journal,* vol. 64, 2014, pp. 620–39.

Mennonite Heritage Centre Archives. "Cornelius Krause fonds." http://www.mennonitechurch.ca/programs/archives/holdings/papers/Krause,%20Cornelius%20fonds.htm. Accessed 29 Jan. 2018.

———. "William Janzen collection." http://www.mennonitechurch.ca/programs/ archives/holdings/papers/Janzen,%20William%20collection.htm. Accessed 29 Jan. 2018.

Merasty, Joseph Auguste, with David Carpenter. *The Education of Augie Merasty: A Residential School Memoir*. U of Regina P, 2015.

Michener, Sally. Email correspondence. 3 Mar. 2017.

Miki, Roy. *Redress: Inside the Japanese Canadian Call for Justice*. Raincoast, 2005.

Miller, Ericka M. *The Other Reconstruction: Where Violence and Womanhood Meet in the Writings of Wells-Barnett, Grimké, and Larsen*. Garland, 2000.

Miscevic, Nenad. "Nationalism." *The Stanford Encyclopedia of Philosophy*, edited by Edward N. Zalta, Summer 2018, plato.stanford.edu/archives/sum2018/entries/ nationalism/. Accessed 20 Aug. 2018.

Mitchell, Timothy. "The Stage of Modernity." *Questions of Modernity*, edited by Timothy Mitchell. U of Minnesota P, 2000, pp. 1–34.

Moore, Christopher. "The Writers' Union of Canada 1973–2007." *The Writers' Union of Canada*, www.writersunion.ca/content/history. Accessed 15 Dec. 2017.

Moore, Henrietta L. *Still Life: Hopes, Desires, and Satisfactions*. Polity, 2011.

Morgan, Cecilia. *Commemorating Canada: History, Heritage, and Memory, 1850s–1990s*. U of Toronto P, 2016.

———. "Making Heroes, Selling Heritage: Commemoration and History-Making in 19th and 20th Century Canada." Review Essays, *Acadiensis: Journal of the History of the Atlantic Region*, vol. 34, no. 2, Autumn 2010, pp. 1–17.

Morra, Linda M. *Unarrested Archives: Case Studies in Twentieth-Century Canadian Women's Authorship*. U of Toronto P, 2014.

Morrison, Toni. *Beloved*. Vintage Books, 2004.

Morton, Erin. *For Folk's Sake: Art and Economy in Twentieth-Century Nova Scotia*. McGill-Queen's UP, 2016.

Morton, Graeme, and David A. Wilson. Introduction. *Irish and Scottish Encounters with Indigenous Peoples*, edited by Morton and Wilson, McGill-Queen's UP, 2013, pp. 3–21.

Morton, W.L. "The North in Canadian Historiography." *Contexts of Canada's Past: Selected Essays of W.L. Morton*, edited and with an introduction by A.B. McKillop, McGill-Queen's UP, 1980.

Mosby, Ian. "Administering Colonial Science: Nutrition Research and Human Biomedical Experimentation in Aboriginal Communities and Residential Schools, 1942–1952." *Histoire sociale / Social History*, vol. 46, no. 1, 2013, pp. 145–72.

———. "Of History and Headlines: Reflections of an Accidental Public Historian." 29 Apr. 2014, http://www.ianmosby.ca/of-history-and-headlines-reflections -of-an-accidental-public- historian/. Accessed 8 May 2017.

Moynagh, Maureen. "'This history's only good for anger': Gender and Cultural Memory in *Beatrice Chancy*." *Signs: A Journal of Women in Culture and Society*, vol. 28, no. 1, 2002, pp. 97–124.

Muñoz, José Esteban. *Cruising Utopia: The Then and There of Queer Futurity*. New York UP, 2009.

———. "Thinking Beyond Antirelationality and Antiutopianism in Queer Critique." *PMLA*, no. 121 2006, pp. 825–26.

Murphy, Colleen, Jennifer K Robbennolt, and Lesley Wexler. "State Amends for Lawful Harm Doing." *Oñati Socio-legal Series*, vol. 7 no. 3, 2017, pp. 547–68.

Murphy, Michael. "Apology, Recognition, and Reconciliation." *Human Rights Review*, vol. 12, 2011, pp. 47–69.

Myrsiades, Linda S. *Splitting the Baby: The Culture of Abortion in Literature and Law, Rhetoric and Cartoons*. Peter Lang, 2002.

National Inquiry into Missing and Murdered Indigenous Women and Girls. *Reclaiming Power and Place: The Final Report*. 3 June 2019, https://www.mmiwg-ffada.ca/final-report/. Accessed 8 Dec. 2019.

Nelson, Maggie. *The Argonauts*. Graywolf, 2015.

Neufeld, David. "The Commemoration of Northern Aboriginal Peoples by the Canadian Government." *Oral History and Public Memories*, edited by Paula Hamilton and Linda Shopes, Temple UP, 2008, pp. 7–29.

Newlove, John. "The Big Bend: By-Passed Highway." *The Fatman: Selected Poems 1962–1972*, McClelland & Stewart, 1977, pp. 64–66.

———. "Crazy Riel." *An Anthology of Canadian Literature in English*, vol. 2, Oxford UP, 1983, pp. 428–29.

———. "The Double-Headed Snake." *The Fatman: Selected Poems 1962–1972*, McClelland & Stewart, 1977, pp. 48–49.

———. "East from the Mountains." *The Fatman: Selected Poems 1962–1972*, McClelland & Stewart, 1977, pp. 28–29.

———. "The Pride." *The Fatman: Selected Poems 1962–1972*, McClelland & Stewart, 1977, pp. 67–74.

———. "Ride Off Any Horizon." *The Fatman: Selected Poems 1962–1972*, McClelland & Stewart, 1977, pp. 41–45.

Newton, Michael. "'Going to the Land of the Yellow Men': The Representation of Indigenous Americans in Scottish Gaelic Literature." *Irish and Scottish Encounters with Indigenous Peoples: Canada, the United States, New Zealand and Australia*, edited by Graeme Morton and David. A. Wilson, McGill-Queen's UP, 2013, pp. 236–52.

Nichol, bp. "Catching Frogs." 1990. *a book of variations: love—zygal—art facts*, Coach House Books, 2013, p. 334.

———. "The Frog Variations." 1990. *a book of variations: love—zygal—art facts*, Coach House Books, 2013, pp. 280–81.

———. "The Long Weekend of Louis Riel." *The Alphabet Game: A bpNichol Reader*, Coach House Books, 2007, pp. 191–93.

———. *The Martyrology Book 3 & 4*. Coach House Books, 1976.

———. "probable systems 18." 1990. *a book of variations: love—zygal—art facts*, Coach House Books, 2013, pp. 267–78.

Nickel, Cira. "An Interview with Soraya Peerbaye, Author of *Tell: Poems for a Girlhood*." *Canthius*, 13 Dec. 2016, http://www.canthius.com/blogcontent/2016/12/11. Accessed 17 June 2020.

Niedzviecki, Hal. "Winning the Appropriation Prize." *Write Magazine*, The Writers' Union of Canada, Spring 2017, p. 8.

Nobbs-Thiessen, Benjamin. "Mennonites in Unexpected Places: An Authentic Tradition and a Burdensome Past." 2009. UBC, MA thesis.

Nochlin, Linda. "Why Have There Been No Great Women Artists?" *Women in Sexist Society: Studies in Power and Powerlessness*, edited by Vivian Gornick and Barbara Moran, Basic Books, 1971.

Nuttall-Smith, Chris. "The Seeds of a Play: The Monsanto Story on Stage." *The Globe and Mail*, 21 Feb. 2012, https://www.theglobeandmail.com/life/food-and-wine/food-trends/seeds-of-a-play-the-monsanto-story-on-stage/article547813/. Accessed 17 June 2020.

O'Brian, John, and Peter White. *Beyond Wilderness: The Group of Seven, Canadian Identity, and Contemporary Art*. McGill-Queen's UP, 2007.

O'Connor, Joseph. *The Irish Male, His Greatest Hits*. New Island, Dublin, 2009.

Osachoff, Margaret Gail. "Louis Riel in Canadian Literature: Myth and Reality." *Canadian Story and History 1885–1985*, edited by Colin Nicholson and Peter Easingwood, Edinburgh University Centre of Canadian Studies, 1985.

Ostrom, Walter. Email correspondence. 5 Mar. 2017.

O'Toole, Darren. "The Red River Resistance: The Machiavellian Moment of the Red River Métis of Manitoba." 2010. U of Ottawa, Phd diss.

Palmater, Candy. "Gord Downie Was Celebrated for Championing Indigenous Rights. Now That He's Gone, Do People Still Care?" *Chatelaine*, 4 Dec. 2017, http://www.chatelaine.com/opinion/gord-downie-indigenous-activism/. Accessed 28 Dec. 2017.

Palmater, Pamela. "Why Canada Should Stand Trial for Tina Fontaine's Murder." *NOW*, 25 Feb. 2018, https://nowtoronto.com/news/why-canada-should-stand-trial-for-tina-fontaine-murder/. Accessed 1 Sept. 2018.

Parker, George L. "Small Presses." *Canadian Encyclopedia*, http://www.thecanadian encyclopedia.ca/en/article/small-presses/. Accessed 30 July 2017.

Parsons, Sarah, editor. *Emergence: Contemporary Photography in Canada.* Gallery 44, 2009.

Parvalescu, Anca. "Reproduction and Queer Theory: Between Lee Edelman's *No Future* and J.M. Coetzee's *Slow Man.*" PMLA, vol. 132, no. 1, 2017, pp. 86–100.

Payne, Carol. *The Official Picture: The National Film Board of Canada's Still Photography Division and the Image of Canada, 1941–1971.* McGill-Queen's UP, 2013.

Peerbaye, Soraya. *Tell: poems for a girlhood.* Pedlar Press, 2015.

Pelletier, Yves Yvon J. "The Politics of Selection: The Historic Sites and Monuments Board of Canada and the Imperial Commemoration of Canadian History, 1919–1950." *Journal of the Canadian Historical Association*, vol. 17, no. 1, 2006, pp. 124–50.

Penner, Tom, and Abe Warkentin. "Featured Review: Larry Towell's *The Mennonites: A Biographical Sketch.*" *Journal of Mennonite Studies*, vol. 22, Jan. 2004, pp. 259–63.

The People and the Text: Indigenous Writing to 1992. http://www.thepeopleandthetext .ca/about. Accessed 2 Jan. 2018.

"Percy Schmeiser." *Monsanto*, 11 Apr. 2017, https://monsanto.com/company/media/ statements/percy-schmeiser/. Accessed 17 June 2020.

Peritz, Ingrid. "Aboriginal Women 'Feel Anger' No Charges Laid against Val-d'Or Officers." *The Globe and Mail*, 18 Nov. 2016, updated 7 Apr. 2017, https://www .theglobeandmail.com/news/national/two-retired-quebec-police-officers -charged-after-val-dor-assault-investigations/article32928990/. Accessed 1 Sept. 2018.

———. "Montreal's Sir John A. Macdonald Statue Vandalized with a Vengeance." *The Globe and Mail*, 17 Aug. 2018, https://www.theglobeandmail.com/canada/ article-montreals-sir-john-a-macdonald-statue-vandalized-with-a-vengeance/. Accessed 17 June 2020.

Petrone, Penny. *Native Literature in Canada: From the Oral Tradition to the Present.* Oxford UP, 1990.

Phelan, Peggy. *Unmarked: The Politics of Performance.* Routledge, 1990.

Philip, NourbeSe. "Race-Baiting and The Writers' Union of Canada." *Antipode Foundation*, 12 June 2017, http://www.antipodefoundation.org/2017/06/12/ race-baiting-and-the-writers-union-of-canada/. Accessed 15 Dec. 2017.

———. "Why Multiculturalism Can't End Racism." *Toronto Star*, 6 Mar. 1990, A21.

Phung, Malissa. "Asian-Indigenous Relationalities: Literary Gestures of Respect and Gratitude." *Canadian Literature*, vol. 227, 2015, pp. 56–72.

Pitts-Taylor, Victoria, and Talia Schaffer. "Editors' Note." WSQ: *Women's Studies Quarterly*, vol. 36, no. 3 & 4, Fall/Winter 2008, pp. 9–10.

Porter, Anna. Letter to Dave McGuill and copy to Paul Audley. 17 Oct. 1973. McClelland and Stewart Ltd. Fonds, William Ready Division of Archives and Research Collections, McMaster University Library, box 2CA84.

———. Letter to Glenn Witmer. 27 Nov. 1972. McClelland and Stewart Ltd. Fonds, William Ready Division of Archives and Research Collections, McMaster University Library, box 2CA84.

———. Letter to Jack McClelland. 9 Feb. 1972. McClelland and Stewart Ltd. Fonds, William Ready Division of Archives and Research Collections, McMaster University Library, box 2CA84.

"Preliminary Publishing Plan," circa 1972. McClelland and Stewart Ltd. Fonds, William Ready Division of Archives and Research Collections, McMaster University Library, box 2CA84.

Puar, Jasbir K. *Terrorist Assemblages: Homonationalism in Queer Times.* Duke UP, 2007.

"Public Profession of Artistic Faith: Nineteen Painters Represented in Beaver Hall Group's Exhibition Are Not Secessionists." Montreal *Gazette*, 18 Jan. 1921, p. 5.

"The Queen vs. Louis Riel." *Epitome of Parliamentary Documents in Connection with the North-West Rebellion, 1885.* Printed by Order of Parliament, 1886, pp. 14–225.

Queyras, Sina. "Lyric Conceptualism: A Manifesto in Progress." *Barking & Biting: The Poetry of Sina Queyras*, edited by Erin Wunker, Wilfrid Laurier UP, 2016.

Quiring, David M. "Intervention and Resistance: Two Mennonite Visions Conflict in Mexico." *Journal of Mennonite Studies*, vol. 22, Jan. 2004, pp. 83–101.

———. *The Mennonite Old Colony Vision: Under Siege in Mexico and the Canadian Connection.* Crossway, 2003.

Randolph S. Hewton Fonds. National Gallery of Canada Library and Archives, Ottawa.

Read, Geoff, and Todd Webb. "The Catholic Mahdi of the North West: Louis Riel and the Métis Resistance in Transatlantic and Imperial Context." *The Canadian Historical Review*, vol. 93, no. 2, June 2012, pp. 171–95.

Reczynska, Anna. "Louis Riel the Rediscovered Hero." *Place and Memory in Canada: Global Perspectives*, Polska Akademia Umiejetnasci, 2005, pp. 409–18.

Redekop, Calvin Wall. *Mennonite Society.* Johns Hopkins UP, 1989.

———. *The Old Colony Mennonites: Dilemmas of Ethnic Minority Life.* Johns Hopkins UP, 1969.

Reder, Deanna. "'Awina Maga Kiya' (Who is it that you really are)? Cree and Métis Autobiographical Writing." *Canadian Literature*, no. 204, Spring 2010, pp. 131–34.

———. "Writing Autobiographically: A Neglected Indigenous Intellectual Tradition." *Across Borders / Across Cultures: Canadian Aboriginal and Native American Cultures*, edited by Emma LaRocque, Paul DePasquale, and Renate Eigenbrod, Broadview, 2009, pp. 153–69.

Reese, Renford. "Canada: The Promised Land for U.S. Slaves." *Western Journal of Black Studies*, vol. 35, no. 3, 2011, pp. 208–17.

Regan, Paulette. *Unsettling the Settler Within: Indian Residential Schools, Truth Telling, and Reconciliation in Canada.* UBC P, 2011.

Reid, Dennis. *A Concise History of Canadian Painting.* Oxford UP, 1973.

Reid, Jennifer. *Louis Riel and the Creation of Modern Canada: Mythic Discourse and the Postcolonial State.* U of New Mexico P, 2008.

"Re-print Purchase Order for 'Half Breed Woman.'" Alger Press Limited, 23 Apr. 1973. McClelland and Stewart Ltd. Fonds, William Ready Division of Archives and Research Collections, McMaster University Library, box 2CA84.

Riel, Louis. *The Collected Writings of Louis Riel.* Edited by George Stanley, Thomas Flanagan, et al., U of Alberta P, 1985.

———. "Louis Riel's Address to the Court, 1 August 1881." *Riel's Defence: Perspectives on His Speeches,* edited by Hans V. Hanson, McGill-Queen's UP, 2014, pp. 45–89.

———. "Louis Riel's Address to the Jury, 31 July 1885." *Riel's Defence: Perspectives on His Speeches,* edited by Hans V. Hanson, McGill-Queen's UP, 2014, pp. 25–44.

———. *Poesies: Religieuses et Politiques.* L'Étendard, 1886.

———. *Selected Poetry of Louis Riel.* Edited by Glen Campbell, translated by Paul Savoie, Exile Editions, 1983.

Rifkin, Mark. *Beyond Settler Time: Temporal Sovereignty and Indigenous Self-Determination.* Duke UP, 2017.

Ringwood, Gwen Pharis. *Still Stands the House: A Drama in One Act.* French, 1955.

Roberts, Charles G.D. "Autochthons." *Poems,* L.C. Page, 1907, p. 15.

Roberts, Dorothy. *Killing the Black Body: Race, Reproduction and the Meaning of Liberty.* 2nd ed., Vintage Books, 2017.

Robertson, David Alexander. *Sugar Falls.* Illustrated by Scott B. Henderson, Highwater P / Portage and Main, 2011.

Rodgers, Kathleen. "American Immigration, the Canadian Counterculture, and the Prefigurative Environmental Politics of the West Kootenay Region, 1969–1989." *Canadian Countercultures and the Environment,* edited by Colin M. Coates, U of Calgary P, 2016.

———. *Welcome to Resisterville: American Dissidents in British Columbia.* UBC P, 2014.

Rosler, Martha. *3 Works: 1. The Restoration of High Culture in Chili; 2. The Bowery in Two Inadequate Descriptive Systems; 3. In, Around, and Afterthoughts (on Documentary Photography).* Press of the Nova Scotia College of Art and Design, 1981.

Ross, Sinclair. *As for Me and My House.* Reynal & Hitchcock, 1941.

Roszak, Theodore. *The Making of a Counter Culture: Reflections on the Technocratic Society and Its Youthful.* U of California P, 1995.

Rothberg, Michael. *Remembering the Holocaust in the Age of Decolonization.* Stanford UP, 2009.

Royal Commission on Aboriginal Peoples. Indian and Northern Affairs Canada, Government of Canada, http://www.aadnc-aandc.gc.ca/eng/1100100014597/110 0100014637. Accessed 17 June 2020.

Ruti, Mari. "Why There Is Always a Future in the Future." *Angelaki*, vol. 13, no. 1, 2008, p. 113.

Rymhs, Deena. *From the Iron House: Imprisonment in First Nations Writing*. Indigenous Studies series, Wilfrid Laurier UP, 2008.

Sabatini, Sandra. *Making Babies: Infants in Canadian Fiction*. Wilfrid Laurier UP, 2003.

Saito, Hiro. "From Collective Memory to Commemoration." *The Handbook of Cultural Sociology*, edited by John R. Hall, Laura Grindstaff, and Ming-Cheng Lo, Routledge, 2010, pp. 629–38.

Saito, Natsu Taylor. "At the Heart of the Law: Remedies for Massive Wrongs." *The Review of Litigation*, vol. 27, no. 2, 2008, pp. 281–305.

Sakamoto, Kerri. *The Electrical Field*. Vintage Canada, 1998.

Sandywell, Barry, and Ian Heywood. *The Handbook of Visual Studies*. Berg, 2012.

Satin, Mark. *Manual for Draft-Age Immigrants to Canada*. House of Anansi, 1968.

Saussy, Haun. "Sustainability." *Impasses of the Post-Global: Theory in the Era of Climate Change*, vol. 2, edited by Henry Sussman, Open Humanities P, 2012, pp. 212–15.

Savoie, Donald. *Visiting Grandchildren: Economic Development in the Maritimes*. U of Toronto P, 2006.

Schwartz, Barry. "The Social Context of Commemoration: A Study in Collective Memory." *Social Forces*, vol. 16, no. 2, Dec. 1982, pp. 374–402.

Schwartz, Joan M., and Terry Cook. "Archives, Records, and Power: The Making of Modern Memory." *Archival Science*, vol. 2, no. 1, 2002, pp. 1–19.

Scobie, Stephen. *bpNichol: What History Teaches*. Talonbooks, 1984.

Scofield, Gregory. *Witness, I Am*. Harbour, 2016.

Scollard, David. Letter to Peter Scaggs, David Berry, Pat McLoughlin. 15 Feb. 1973. McClelland and Stewart Ltd. Fonds, William Ready Division of Archives and Research Collections, McMaster University Library, box 2CA84.

Scott, D.C. "Onondaga Madonna." *Canadian Anthology*, edited by Carl F. Klink and Reginald Watters, Gage, 1974, pp. 149–50.

Scudeler, June. "'We're still here and Métis': Rewriting the 1885 Resistance in Marilyn Dumont's *The Pemmican Eaters*." *New Directions in Contemporary Métis Studies*, edited by Jennifer Adese, Chris Andersen, and Adam Gaudry, UBC P, forthcoming.

Sears, Djanet. "Harlem Duet." *Modern Canadian Plays*, edited by Jerry Wasserman, vol. 2, Talonbooks, 2001, pp. 337–69.

———. Personal interview. 21 Oct. 2011.

Sedgwick, Eve Kosofsky. "A Poem Is Being Written." *The Cultural Display of the Body*, special issue of *Representations*, vol. 17, Winter 1987, pp. 110–43.

Sekula, Allan. *Geography Lesson: Canadian Notes*. Vancouver Art Gallery and MIT Press, 1997.

———. "Photography between Labour and Capital." *Mining Photographs and Other Pictures: A Selection from the Negative Archives of Shedden Studio, Glace Bay, Cape Breton 1948–1968*. Photographs by Leslie Shedden, edited by Benjamin Buchloh and Robert Wilkie, Press of the Nova Scotia College of Art and Design, 1983, pp. 193–268.

Sellars, Bev. *They Called Me Number One: Secrets and Survival at an Indian Residential School*. Talonbooks, 2013.

Shakespeare, William. *Richard III*. The Folger Shakespeare Library, 1996.

Shildrick, Margrit. "Living On; Not Getting Better." *Feminist Review*, vol. 111, Nov. 2015, pp. 10–24.

Shotwell, Alexis. *Against Purity: Living Ethically in Compromised Times*. Minnesota UP, 2016.

Shraya, Vivek. *even this page is white*. Arsenal Pulp Press, 2016.

Siggins, Maggie. *Riel: A Life of Revolution*. HarperCollins, 1994.

Simpson, Audra. "On Ethnographic Refusal: Indigeneity, 'Voice,' and Colonial Citizenship." *Junctures*, no. 9, Dec. 2007, pp. 67–80.

Sinclair, Niigaanwewidam James. "Kanata 150+, Not Canada 150." *UM Today*, 30 June 2017, http://news.umanitoba.ca/kanata-150-not-canada-150/. Accessed 1 Sept. 2018.

"Sir John A. Macdonald Statue in Regina Vandalized with Paint for Second Time This Year." *The Globe and Mail*, 21 Aug. 2018, https://www.theglobeandmail.com/canada/article-sir-john-a-macdonald-statue-in-regina-vandalized-with-paint-for/. Accessed 17 June 2020.

Skelton, Robin. *Authors and Archives: A Short Guide*. Writers' Union of Canada, 1979.

Smith, Charlie. "Jailed Pipeline Protester and Poet Rita Wong Calls for More Prison Programs for Fellow Inmates." *The Georgia Straight*, 29 Aug. 2019, https://www.straight.com/news/1293131/jailed-pipeline-protester-and-poet-rita-wong-calls-more-prison-programs-fellow-inmates. Accessed 17 June 2020.

Smyth, William J. *Toronto, the Belfast of Canada: The Orange Order and the Shaping of Municipal Culture*. U of Toronto P, 2015.

Sorkin, Jenni. *Live Form: Women, Ceramics and Community*. U of Chicago P, 2016.

Soutar, Annabel. *Seeds*. Talonbooks, 2012.

Spears, Heather. *Required Reading*. Wolsak and Wynn, 2000.

Spears, Tom. "The Little Blue Pill: Researchers Are Convinced of the Health Benefits of the Common, Delicious Blueberry." *National Post*, 24 Aug. 2004, p. A7.

Spillers, Hortense. *Black, White, and in Color: Essays on American Literature and Culture*. U of Chicago P, 2003.

Spoon, Rae, and Ivan Coyote. *Gender Failure*. Arsenal Pulp Press, 2014.

———. "Gender Failure." *vimeo.com*, 11 Oct. 2013.

Squires, Jessica. *Building Sanctuary: The Movement to Support Vietnam War Resisters in Canada, 1965–73*. UBC P, 2013.

Starblanket, Gina, and Dallas Hunt. "How the Death of Colten Boushie Became Recast as the Story of the Knight Protecting His Castle." *Globe and Mail*, 13 Feb. 2018, updated 15 Feb. 2018.

Steggles, Mary Ann. "Just Across the Border: Vietnam Era Resisters Change the Landscape of Canadian Ceramics." *Studio Potter*, vol. 45, no. 2, Summer 2017, pp. 55–59.

Stevenson, Garth. *Building Nations from Diversity: Canadian and American Experience Compared*. McGill-Queens UP, 2014.

Stevenson, Winona. "Calling Badger and the Symbols of the Spirit Language: The Cree Origins of the Syllabic System." *Oral History Forum d'histoire orale*, vol. 19, 2000, pp. 19–24.

Stewart, Jane. "Notes for an Address by the Honourable Jane Stewart, Minister of Indian Affairs and Northern Development, on the Occasion of the Unveiling of Gathering Strength—Canada's Aboriginal Action Plan, 1998." *Reconciling Canada: Critical Perspectives on the Culture of Redress*, edited by Jennifer Henderson and Pauline Wakeham, U of Toronto P, 2013, pp. 323–32.

St. Germain, Jill. "Book Review: *The False Traitor: Louis Riel in Canadian Culture*." *Great Plains Quarterly*, no. 298, 2004, pp. 49–50, http://digitalcommons.unl.edu/greatplainsquarterly/298. Accessed 17 June 2020.

Stonechild, Blair, and Bill Waiser. *Loyal till Death: Indians and the North-West Rebellion*. Fifth House, 1997.

Strong-Boag, Veronica. "Experts on Our Own Lives: Commemorating Canada at the Beginning of the 21st Century." *The Public Historian*, vol. 31, no. 1, Winter 2009, pp. 46–68.

Stryker, Susan. "Biopolitics." *TSQ: Transgender Studies Quarterly*, vol. 1, no. 1–2, May 2014, pp. 38–42.

Sugars, Cynthia, and Eleanor Ty. *Canadian Literature and Cultural Memory*. Oxford UP, 2014.

Supreme Court of Canada. *Monsanto Canada Inc. v. Schmeiser*, [2004] 1 S.C.R. 902, 2004 SCC 34. 21 21 May 2004. *Lexum*, https://scc-csc.lexum.com/scc-csc/scc-csc/en/item/2147/index.do?r=AAAAAQAJc2NobWVpc2VyAAAAAAE. Accessed 17 June 2020.

———. *R. v.* Powley, [2003] 2 S.C.R. 207, 2003 SCC 43. *Lexum*, http://scc.lexum.org/en/2003/2003scc43/2003scc43.html. Accessed 17 June 2020.

Suzack, Cheryl. "Publishing and Aboriginal Communities." *History of the Book in Canada*, vol. 3, 1918–1980, edited by Carole Gerson and Jacques Michon, U of Toronto P, 2007, pp. 293–97.

Teillet, Jean. *Metis Law in Canada*. Pape, Salter, Teillet, 2013.

Tener, Jean. "Problems of Literary Archives: A Commentary." *Archivaria*, no. 18, Summer 1984, pp. 228–31.

Thom, Kai Cheng. "Sometimes Women Have to Make Hard Choices to Be Writers." *GUTS Magazine*, 15 Feb. 2017, http://gutsmagazine.ca/sometimes-women-have-to-make-hard-choices-to-be-writers/. Accessed 17 June 2020.

Thomas, Lewis H. "Louis Riel." *Dictionary of Canadian Biography*, 1982, rev. 2016, http://www.biographi.ca/en/bio/riel_louis_1844_85_11E.html. Accessed 17 June 2020.

Thrasher, Anthony Apakark. *Thrasher: Skid Row Eskimo*. Griffin Press, 1976.

Thrasher, Steven W. "Claudia Rankine: Why I Am Spending $625,000 to Study Whiteness." *The Guardian*, 16 Oct. 2016, https://www.theguardian.com/books/2016/oct/19/claudia-rankine-macarthur-genius-grant-exploring-whiteness. Accessed 17 June 2020.

Towell, Larry. *The Mennonites: A Biographical Sketch*. Phaidon, 2000.

———. *The World from My Front Porch*. Chris Boot LTD, in association with the Archive of Modern Conflict, 2008.

Tremblay, Michel. "Les Belles-Soeurs." *Modern Canadian Plays*, edited by Jerry Wasserman, translated by John Van Burek and Bill Glassco, vol. 1, Talonbooks, 2001, pp. 101–30.

Trotsky, Leon. *My Life: An Attempt at an Autobiography*. Dover, 2007.

Trudeau, Justin. "Remarks by Prime Minister Justin Trudeau to Apologize to LGBTQ2 Canadians." *Justin Trudeau, Prime Minister of Canada*, 28 Nov. 2017, https://pm.gc.ca/en/news/speeches/2017/11/28/remarks-prime-minister-justin-trudeau-apologize-lgbtq2-canadians. Accessed 17 June 2020.

Truth and Reconciliation Commission of Canada. http://www.trc.ca/websites/trcinstitution/index.php?p=3. Accessed 1 Aug. 2017.

———. "Truth and Reconciliation Commission of Canada: Calls to Action." *National Centre for Truth and Reconciliation*, Truth and Reconciliation Commission of Canada, 2015, http://nctr.ca/assets/reports/Calls_to_Action_English2.pdf. Accessed 17 June 2020.

———. *Final Report of the Truth and Reconciliation Commission of Canada. Volume One: Summary. Honouring the Truth, Reconciling for the Future*. Truth and Reconciliation Commission and James Lorimer & Company, 2015.

Tsaconas, E. Hella. "Bad Math: Calculating Bodily Capacity in Cassils's *Cuts: A Traditional Sculpture.*" *Women & Performance: A Journal of Feminist Theory,* vol. 26, no. 2–3, 2016, pp. 197–207.

Tuck, Eve. "Suspending Damage: A Letter to Communities." *Harvard Educational Review,* vol. 79, no. 3, Fall 2009, pp. 409–27.

Tuck, Eve, and K. Wayne Yang. "Decolonization Is Not a Metaphor." *Decolonization: Indigeneity, Education & Society,* vol. 1, no. 1, 2012, pp. 1–40.

Turnbull, Jay. "Organizer Apologizes after Ad for Montreal's 375th Features Only White People." CBC *News,* 22 Nov. 2016, https://www.cbc.ca/news/canada/montreal/montreal-375th-anniversary-ad-commercial-white-diversity-1.3861843. Accessed 1 Sept. 2018.

TVO. *Transcript: Whose CanLit Is It Anyway? Nick Mount, Canisia Lubrin, Jael Richardson, and Antanas Sileika.* 10 Oct. 2017, https://tvo.org/transcript/2461578/video/programs/the-agenda-with-steve-paikin/whose-canlit-is-it-anyway. Accessed 17 June 2020.

UBC *Accountable: Archived Documents.* 14 Nov. 2016, http://www.ubcaccountable.com. Accessed 30 Aug. 2018.

Vaccaro, Jeanne. "Embodied Risk: Cassils." QED: *A Journal in* GLBTQ *Worldmaking,* vol. 5, no. 1, 2018, pp. 112–16.

Vaillant, Nora. *Bernard Leach and British Columbia Pottery: An Historical Ethnography of a Taste Culture.* UBC P, 2002.

Van Styvendale, Nancy. "The Trans/historicity of Trauma in Jeanette Armstrong's *Slash* and Sherman Alexie's *Indian Killer.*" *Studies in the Novel,* vol. 40, nos. 1 & 2, 2008, pp. 203–23.

Vernon, Karina. "Invisibility Exhibit: The Limits of Library and Archives Canada's 'Multicultural Mandate.'" *Basements and Attics, Closets and Cyberspace: Explorations in the Materiality and Ethics of Canadian Women's Archives,* edited by Linda M. Morra and Jessica Schagerl, Wilfrid Laurier UP, 2011, pp. 193–204.

Vipond, Mary. "The Nationalist Network: English Canada's Intellectuals and Artists in the 1920s." *Canadian Review of Studies in Nationalism,* vol. 7, no. 1, Spring 1980, pp. 32–52.

Virk, Manjit. *Reena: A Father's Story.* Heritage House, 2008.

Virtual Museum of Canada. "The Battle of Duck Lake, March 26, 1885." www.virtualmuseum.ca. Accessed 29 July 1885.

Visvis, Vikki. "Trauma Remembered and Forgotten: The Figure of the Hysteric in Kerri Sakamoto's *The Electrical Field.*" *Mosaic,* vol. 40, no. 3, 2007, pp. 67–83.

Vizenor, Gerald. *Survivance: Narratives of Native Presence.* U of Nebraska P, 2008.

Vosters, Helene. *Unbecoming Nationalism: From Commemoration to Redress in Canada.* U of Manitoba P, 2019.

Voth, Daniel. "Her Majesty's Justice Be Done: Métis Legal Mobilization and the Pitfalls to Indigenous Political Movement Building." *Canadian Journal of Political Science*, vol. 49, no. 2, 2016, pp. 243–66.

Wagley, Catherine. "Heather Cassils Gets Ripped for LACE Performance Art Show." *Weekly*, no. 29, Sept. 2011, www.laweekly.com/arts/heather-cassils-gets-ripped -for-lace-performance-art-show-2172171. Accessed 22 Oct. 2017.

Wakeham, Pauline. "Reconciling 'Terror': Managing Indigenous Resistance in the Age of Apology." *American Indian Quarterly*, vol. 36, no. 1, 2012, pp. 1–33.

Walcott, Rinaldo. "Foreword: The Homosexuals Have Arrived!" *Disrupting Queer Inclusion: Canadian Homonationalisms and the Politics of Belonging*, edited by OmiSoore H. Dryden and Suzanne Lenon, UBC P, 2015, pp. vii–ix.

Walters, Evelyn. *The Women of Beaver Hall: Canadian Modernist Painters*. Dundurn Press, 2005.

Wang, Phoebe. "Rusty Talk with Soraya Peerbaye." *The Rusty Toque*, vol. 11, no. 6, January 2016, http://www.therustytoque.com/rusty-talk/-soraya-peerbaye-poet.

Warkentin, Abe, editor. *Reflections on Our Heritage: A History of Steinbach and the R.M. of Hanover from 1874*. Derksen Printers, 1971, http://manitobia.ca/ resources/books/local_histories/096.pdf. Accessed 23 Jan. 2018.

Warley, Linda. "Unbecoming a 'dirty savage': Jane Willis's *Geniesh: An Indian Girlhood*." *Canadian Literature*, vol. 156, 1998, pp. 83–103.

Weaver, Sharon. *First Encounters: 1970s Back-to-the-Land, Cape Breton, NS and Denman, Hornby and Lasqueti Islands, BC*. University of Guelph, 2010.

———. *Making Place on the Canadian Periphery: Back-to-the-Land on the Gulf Islands and Cape Breton*. University of Guelph, 2013.

Weheliye, Alexander G. *Habeas Viscus: Racializing Assemblage, Biopolitics, and Black Feminist Theories of the Human*. Duke UP, 2014.

Weingarten, Jeffrey. *Sharing the Past: The Reinvention of History in Canadian Poetry since 1960*. Manuscript, 2018.

Weingarten, Karen. *Abortion in the American Imagination: Before Life and Choice, 1880–1940*. Rutgers UP, 2014.

Wente, Jesse. "With Secret Path Gord Downie Is Illuminating a Way Forward for Indigenous Artists." http://www.cbc.ca/arts/with-secret-path-gord-downie-is -illuminating-a-way-forward-to-indigenous-artists-1.3810699. Accessed 30 July 2017.

Werner, Michael, and Bénédicte Zimmermann. "Beyond Comparison: *Histoire Croisée* and the Challenge of Reflexivity." *History and Theory*, vol. 45, no. 1, Feb. 2006, pp. 30–50.

Whitfield, Harvey Amani. "African and New World African Immigration to Mainland Nova Scotia, 1749–1816." *Journal of the Royal Nova Scotia Historical Society*, vol. 7, 2004, pp. 102–11.

————. *North to Bondage: Loyalist Slavery in the Maritimes.* UBC P, 2016.

Whitehead, Joshua. "Writing as a Rupture: A Breakup Note to Canlit." *Refuse: CanLit in Ruins,* Book*hug, 2018, pp. 191–98.

Whittall, Zoe. "CanLit Has a Sexual-Harassment Problem." *The Walrus,* 9 Feb. 2018, https://thewalrus.ca/canlit-has-a-sexual-harassment-problem/. Accessed 17 June 2020.

Wigmore, Gregory. "Before the Railroad: From Slavery to Freedom in the Canadian-American Borderland." *The Journal of American History,* vol. 98, vol. 2, 2011, pp. 437–54.

Williams, Carol Jane. *Framing the West: Race, Gender and the Photographic "Frontier" on the Northwest Coast, 1858–1912.* State U of New Jersey P, 1999.

Willis, Jane. *Geniesh: An Indian Girlhood.* New Press, 1973.

Wilson, David A. "McGee, Thomas D'Arcy." *Oxford Companion to Canadian History,* edited by Gerry Hallowell, Oxford UP, 2004.

————. *Thomas Darcy McGee: The Extreme Moderate, 1857–1868.* Vol. 2, McGill-Queen's UP, 2011.

Wilson, Sheri-D. *Open Letter: Woman Against Violence Against Women.* Frontenac House, 2014.

Wong, Rita. "Decolonizasian: Reading Asian and First Nations Relations in Literature." *Canadian Literature,* vol. 199, 2008, pp. 158–80.

————. *Forage.* Nightwood, 2007.

Woo, Andrea. "Victoria to Remove Statue of Sir John A. Macdonald." *The Globe and Mail,* 8 Aug. 2018, https://www.theglobeandmail.com/canada/british-columbia/article-victoria-to-remove-statue-of-sir-john-a-macdonald/. Accessed 17 June 2020.

Woods, Brenda. "A Halfbreed Finds Her Way." *Sunday News,* 4 Nov. 1973. McClelland and Stewart Ltd. Fonds, William Ready Division of Archives and Research Collections, McMaster University Library, box 2CA84.

Wright, Kailin. "Failed Futurity: Performing Abortion in Merrill Denison's *Marsh Hay.*" *Canadian Literature,* vol. 232, 2017, pp. 100–16.

Writers' Union of Canada. "Archives Committee Files." Writers' Union of Canada Fonds, William Ready Division of Archives and Research Collections, McMaster University Library, first accrual, box 64, files 1–3; second accrual, box 104, files 5–8, 3 Dec. 2015.

————. *Canada Writes! The Writers' Union of Canada Members' Book.* Edited by K.A. Hamilton, Writers' Union of Canada, 1977.

————. "Press Release—November 4, 1973." Austin Clarke Fonds, William Ready Division of Archives and Special Collections, McMaster University Library, first accrual, box 44, file 1, 17 May 2017.

Wunker, Erin. *Notes from a Feminist Killjoy: Essays from Everyday Life.* Book*hug, 2016.

Wyile, Herb. *Anne of Tim Hortons: Globalization and the Reshaping of Atlantic-Canadian Literature.* Wilfred Laurier UP, 2011.

Young, Marilyn. Introduction. *Imagine Nation: The American Counterculture of the 1960s and 1970s,* edited by Peter Braunstein and Michael William Doyle, Routledge, 2002.

Young, Robert J.C. "Postcolonial Remains." *New Literary History,* vol. 43 no. 1, Winter 2012, pp. 19–42.

Zangwill, Israeli. *The Melting-Pot.* Macmillan, 1909.

Index

Keeshig-Tobias, Lenore, 161
Kennedy, Bobby, 170
Kennedy, John, 170
Kenny, George, 295
Kim, Christine, 14
King, Martin Luther, Jr., 169, 170
King, Moynan, 102
King, Thomas, 13
Kinsman, Gary, 98
Klaus, Fritz, 233
Kodó, Krisztina, 6, 21
Kogawa, Joy, 54, 62
Kootenay Barter Bank, 173
Kootenay Christmas Faire, 174
Krause, Cornelius, 194–95, 195
Kraybill, Donald B., 188, 191
Kroetsch, Robert, 17, 69–70, 79, 263;
    Seed Catalogue, 68, 69

Lacan, Jacques, 143
landscape, 93–94, 95–96
Lange, Dorothea, 188
Langford, Martha, 20, 180
Lantz clays and majolica, 176
Larson, Katherine, 150n8
Latimer, Heather, 99, 150n7
Lavallée, Octavie, 267
Leach, Bernard, 168
Lee, John, 267
Lee, Rachel C., 108
Lemieux, François-Xavier, 258, 269n2
Lepage, Robert, 140
Leroux, Darryl, 11
Lesbian Herstory Archives, 164n10
Levine, Marilyn, 175
LGBTQ(2S+) community, 91, 107n1;
    AIDS crisis and, 97; archives of,
    164n10; official apology to, 97–98;
    past persecution of, 18

Life Among the Qallunaat (Freeman),
    286, 291, 295
Lismer, Arthur, 207
literacy: and civilization, 27
literature: on environmental issues,
    67–68; immigrant, 83–86; redress
    culture and, 52–53, 54, 61–66
Livesay, Dorothy, 263
Lockerby, Mabel, 205, 210, 215, 216; por-
    trait of, 211–12, 213
Lord, Barry, 216
Louis Riel Day, 256, 260
love: racialization of, 145
Lowenthal, David: In the Province of
    History, 24
Luciuk, Lubomyr: In Fear of the Barbed
    Wire Fence, 232
Lunenburg, NS, 228
Lutz, Hartmut, 45, 49
lyric conceptualism, 130

MacDonald, J.E.H., 207
Macdonald, John A., 2, 250, 267, 278, 281
Machado, Ana Rodriguez, 84
MacPherson, Myra, 168, 169
McGill, Robert, 180
McGoogan, Ken, 278
McGregor, Hannah, 121
McKay, Ian, 238
McKegney, Sam, 5, 292, 295–96, 297
McKenzie, Albert Edward: career, 71
McKenzie Seed Catalogue, 69, 70, 71
McKenzie Seeds Co. Ltd., 71
McKnight, David, 290
McLuhan, Marshall, 257
Magic Weapons (McKegney), 296
Manitoba Act (1870), 283n8, 283n9
Manitoba Craft Council, 178
Manitoba Schools Act (1890), 283n5